KNOWLEDGE PRODUCTION IN COLD WAR ASIA

KNOWLEDGE PRODUCTION IN COLD WAR ASIA

US Hegemony and Local Agency

EDITED BY
**YUKA TSUCHIYA MORIGUCHI,
SHIN KAWASHIMA, AND
SOMEI KOBAYASHI**

INDIANA UNIVERSITY PRESS

This book is a publication of

Indiana University Press
Herman B Wells Library 350
1320 East 10th Street
Bloomington, Indiana 47405 USA

iupress.org
Originally published in Japanese as 文化冷戦と知の展開—アメリカの戦略・東アジアの論理
(Bunka reisen to chi no tenkai: Amerika no senryaku, higashi-ajia no ronri)
© 2022 Kyoto University Press
English translation © 2025 by Indiana University Press

All rights reserved
No part of this book may be reproduced or utilized in any form or by any means, electronic or
mechanical, including photocopying and recording, or by any information storage and retrieval system,
without permission in writing from the publisher.

Manufactured in the United States of America

First printing 2025

Cataloging information is available from the Library of Congress.

ISBN 978-0-253-07205-4 (hardback)
ISBN 978-0-253-07206-1 (paperback)
ISBN 978-0-253-07207-8 (ebook)

CONTENTS

Acknowledgments *vii*

Introduction / Yuka Tsuchiya Moriguchi, Shin Kawashima, and Somei Kobayashi *1*

PART I: Area Studies

1. The United States and Taiwanese Sinology during the Cold War: The Ford Foundation and the Institute of Modern History, Academia Sinica / Shin Kawashima *21*

2. Cold War Collaborations: Japanese Studies in the United States, 1945–60 / Miriam Kingsberg Kadia *47*

3. Debates on Modernization Theory at the Hakone Conference: Discrepancies in Value Systems and Perspectives on History / Masaki Fujioka *79*

4. The Dawn of Korean Studies and Knowledge Production on Korea during and after the Pacific War / Somei Kobayashi *108*

PART II: Scientific Knowledge

5. The Emergence of China's Nuclear Research: Between the Civil War and the Cold War / Yuko Sato *139*

6. The Michigan Memorial Phoenix Project and Taiwan: Nuclear Technological Aid by a US Public University / Yuka Tsuchiya Moriguchi *167*

7. Rediscovery of a Cold War Space: The Politics of Science in the DMZ Ecological Survey / Manyong Moon *197*

PART III: Practicing Knowledge

8. US Aid, Journalism Education in Taiwan, and a Transnational Network of Chinese-Speaking Journalists / Mike Shichi Lan *225*

9. The Cold War, US International Educational Exchange, and the Development of Hong Kong's Journalism and Communication Education / Yang Zhang   255

10. US Educational Exchange Programs for Foreign Journalists and Changes in South Korean Journalism / Jae Young Cha   281

11. Civic Action as Counterinsurgency in South Korea: Cold War at the Grassroots within and beyond the National Borders / Eun Heo   308

Index   331

ACKNOWLEDGMENTS

THIS VOLUME WOULD NOT HAVE been possible without the generous support of Kyoto University's Grant-in-Aid in 2019–20 and the Japan Society for the Promotion of Science Grant-in-Aid (JSPS KAKEN, no. 17H02238) in 2017–20. The editors would also like to thank Professor Nick Cullather of Indiana University for his precious advice in the early stage of this international collaborative project. We are extremely grateful for the hard work and collegiality of all the contributors to and translators of the volume, to two anonymous referees, and to the indefatigable Dr. Daniel Pearce, who painstakingly proofread the manuscript written by nonnative speakers of English. Our thanks also go to two office assistants at Kyoto University, Ms. Mayuko Morita and Mr. Toshiaki Kato, who assisted with checking and double-checking the manuscript's stylistic issues. There are many other people and organizations to whom contributors would like to express deep appreciation, and these individual acknowledgments are included in each chapter.

August 31, 2023

Yuka Tsuchiya Moriguchi
Shin Kawashima
Somei Kobayashi

KNOWLEDGE PRODUCTION IN COLD WAR ASIA

INTRODUCTION

YUKA TSUCHIYA MORIGUCHI, SHIN KAWASHIMA, AND SOMEI KOBAYASHI

THE CULTURAL COLD WAR AND KNOWLEDGE CONSTRUCTION

Studies on the Cold War have constantly diversified over the past few decades, integrating formerly underexplored geographical regions, actors, issues, and topics. As Odd Arne Westad has demonstrated, the Cold War is no longer portrayed as a simple East-West confrontation but is understood as a multifaceted phenomenon involving decolonization and nation building in the Third World. The Cold War encompassed not only ideological rivalry and the nuclear arms race but also a competition of lifestyles and cultures and a battle to win the hearts and minds of the peoples of the Third World. Francis Saunders has popularized the term Cultural Cold War, and Kenneth Osgood has introduced the notion of Total Cold War, both aptly capturing new interpretations of this period in history. Even the chronological perception of the Cold War has been modified. For example, Nick Cullather has demonstrated that modernization and development concepts, frequently linked to the Cold War, could be traced back to the 1930s or even earlier. Concurrently, scholars have begun to question the simple binary understanding of provider versus receiver in cultural diplomacy. Penny Von Eschen, for example, has illuminated the fluid and elusive character of music, which transcended policymakers' intentions across national and cultural boundaries. Also, in the recent scholarship, greater attention has been paid to local agencies and local conflicts. For example, Hajimu Masuda argued that the attempts to restore tranquility in domestic societies created a collective fantasy, or a mindset of the Cold War.[1] Scholars in Japan, Korea, China, and Taiwan have also begun to turn their attention to the diverse cultural elements of the Cold War, including music, films, radio, television, art, and literature, with special attention to local memories, experiences, and problems.[2]

Academic and professional knowledge, however, has been a relatively under-explored field in this genealogy of studies on the Cultural Cold War. Although there are some scholarly works dealing with the relationships of universities with the Cold War, very little work has been done on postwar knowledge pro-duction in East Asia—the central theme of this volume.[3] "Academic and pro-fessional knowledge" is a rather broad concept, and particular attention in this book is given to area studies, nuclear science, biology, and journalism. These were some of the most contested fields in which scholars, students, and pro-fessionals were entangled in local, regional, and international struggles over the legitimacy and ownership of knowledge. It was also in these fields that governments and private organizations—both US and East Asian—attempted to assert control through funding aids and training programs. Their attempts to do so were sometimes in vain, but at other times, they witnessed a certain degree of success. Area studies not only explain the cultural and historical char-acteristics of a country or a region but also occasionally define the meaning of international and regional conflicts, and therefore, various governmental and nongovernmental actors attempted to exert influence over the establishment of the discipline. The leaders of developing nations enthusiastically sought to import Western scientific knowledge and build their own research and edu-cational institutions because they thought doing so could improve national prestige and economic prosperity. The US, in turn, found stakes in offering fi-nancial or educational aid in science and technology, both to win the allegiance of the recipients and to bring them under US scientific hegemony. Professional knowledge, whether in journalism or in the military, was also important in that it could be employed in establishing certain theoretical and methodologi-cal frameworks and developing them into universal standards. Once these theories and methodologies were established, professionals across national boundaries would follow them, thereby further endowing them with certain authority. Academic and professional knowledge established in the early Cold War era remained influential in East Asia for many years, as such knowledge provided the discursive framework of various intellectual and professional communications, ultimately influencing people's worldviews or value systems. Political scientist Susan Strange has pointed out the importance of "structural power" derived from "knowledge structure." She defines structural power as the power "to decide how things shall be done, the power to shape frameworks within which states relate to each other, relate to people, or relate to corporate enterprises."[4] According to Strange, structural power based on knowledge structure is often overlooked and underestimated because it tends to be elusive and intangible. Examples in this book illuminate the process of knowledge structure formation, from which governmental and nongovernmental actors expected to draw power. The cases in this book focus not only on US influences in knowledge production but also on the agency of the East Asian nations and regions, through which US influence was sometimes creatively adapted, counteracted, diluted, or even neutralized.

Postwar knowledge production in East Asia occurred under the specter of the hegemonic influences of either the US or the Soviet Union, albeit to differing degrees depending on the country or region. In the "Western bloc," for example, Korea (the Republic of Korea, or ROK) and Taiwan (the Republic of China, or ROC) were almost entirely dependent on US aid for the reconstruction of academic institutions and the training of educators. Korea and Taiwan were both liberated from Japanese colonial rule at the end of the Second World War. The ROK government was established in August 1948, and the Democratic People's Republic of Korea (DPRK) government in September 1948. However, Korea was divided by the thirty-eighth parallel into the North and the South, which were administered by the Soviet Red Army and the US Army, respectively. Subsequently, the peninsula was devastated by the Korean War (1950–53). Taiwan, on the other hand, came under the rule of the Kuomintang (KMT), as Mao Zedong's Chinese Communist Party (CCP) established the People's Republic of China (PRC) in Beijing, and KMT leader Chiang Kai-shek retreated to Taiwan in 1949. The US saw ideological and strategic value in investing in, and building anew, the academic and scientific institutions of both the ROK and ROC; the envisioned modern, industrialized nations of "free Korea" and "free China" would illuminate the righteousness of capitalist ideology and prove the effectiveness of US aid. Japan, by contrast, maintained its prewar academic institutions and human resources to some degree, despite the devastation of its land resulting from the war. However, the US occupation forces stationed in Japan from August 1945 to April 1952 worked to reform the Japanese academic and educational institutions according to the US model. As a result, the postoccupation Japanese intellectual landscape became a curious mosaic of imperial Japanese knowledge (much of which was of European, especially German, origin) and newly instilled US knowledge.

With these complicated situations in mind, one of the overarching concerns of this volume is exploring how, and to what degree, each East Asian country accepted, appropriated, resisted, or simply disregarded US-produced knowledge. The influx of US knowledge was often accompanied by monetary aid provided by either government agencies or philanthropic organizations—aid that developing countries desperately needed to reconstruct their academic and scientific institutions. Therefore, another common interest of the authors lies in the relationship between aid and the penetration of knowledge. In each chapter, various providers and receivers of knowledge and monetary aid will be introduced, and their relationships explored. Each case will demonstrate how different degrees of cooperation between provider and receiver resulted in various forms of penetration of knowledge, skills, or technologies in the subject society. Furthermore, the relationships between the providers and receivers of knowledge and aid were never static but changed over time, and both providers and receivers demonstrated internal conflicts and differences of opinions.

Still another important theme of this book is how East Asian countries influenced—or tried to influence—the US or other Asian nations through their own commitment to academic or professional knowledge production. In the US, the Second World War had fundamentally changed the way in which knowledge was produced and applied for strategic purposes. The federal budget for academic research increased dramatically, especially for the applied sciences but also for social sciences. Area studies, originating in wartime research coordinated by the Office of Strategic Services (OSS) and the Office of Scientific Research and Development (OSRD), developed into a full-fledged academic field in the immediate postwar years. Sociologists and economists developed modernization theory, which was applied to foreign policy decisions toward developing countries. These academic fields deeply influenced East Asian intellectual communities. However, as some chapters in this book reveal, East Asian scholars and experts also contributed to the formation or alteration of this US-produced knowledge. These findings disrupt the dichotomy of the provider versus receiver of knowledge and demand a renewed perspective in considerations of the intellectual landscape of East Asia in the Cold War era.

Moreover, such findings challenge the concept of "national" knowledge, because while governments can fund knowledge production, they cannot attach national flags to the knowledge itself. For instance, consider Chinese journalists trained in the ROC who worked for newspapers sympathetic to Communism, US-trained Chinese scientists acting as "American" consultants to Asia, or Japanese anthropologists helping to construct Japanese studies in the US—these examples serve to demonstrate how knowledge traverses national borders through individuals, regardless of the intentions of those in power or those who provide research funds. The governments of the US, Japan, Korea, the PRC, and the ROC all sought to rein in knowledge, bringing it under their control, and sometimes their attempts succeeded. At other times, scholars,

INTRODUCTION

scientists, and intellectuals were uncontrollable. Since they acted for their own convenience—whether it was for economic, social, or any other reason—governments or quasi-governmental agencies gained little reward for the resources they devoted. Cold War knowledge in East Asia was built on the ideological divide between East and West, glaring disparities between North and South, and the material and cultural dominance of the US. However, such Cold War knowledge also contained seeds of dissent, the leeway of freedom, and transnational (or even postnational) possibilities.

THE COLD WAR IN EAST ASIA

During the past few decades, thanks in part to newly declassified archival sources, historians have begun to examine the Cold War within the specific contexts of each geographical area. Such an approach has enabled us to see the Cold War not as a simple clash between superpowers but as an intersection of locally unique problems within the East-West rivalry. Especially in East Asia, where military confrontations and national security issues persisted even after the official "end" of the Cold War, scholarly attention has been focused on the local contexts of the Cold War. One conspicuous feature of the Cold War in East Asia was the legacy of Japanese colonial rule and the vacuum left by its departure, a vacuum that drew in US and Soviet influences. Consequently, East Asia never returned to the prewar power balance but rather saw the birth of new fault lines and confrontations, with postwar reconstruction and nation building developed under US or Soviet influence.

Until 1945, Japan colonized Taiwan and Korea, leased a territory on the tip of Liaodong Peninsula (Kwantung Leased Territory), and ruled the mandate islands of Micronesia. From the 1930s on, the Japanese empire expanded into Northeast China and French Indochina, and after the breakout of the Pacific War, it further integrated Hong Kong and much of Southeast Asia. Within this vast geographical space, Japan sought to establish not only a geopolitical but also an intellectual empire. For example, the quasi-private, quasi-governmental South Manchurian Railway Company, in addition to its main business of railway construction in Northeast China, handled diverse matters related to the economy and governance of the region. The research institute established by the company covered various fields such as geography, ethnology, agriculture, biology, geology, and mineralogy. Japan also built the Institute of Humanities in Beijing and the Institute of Natural Science in Shanghai and further established two imperial universities in its colonies: Keijō Imperial University (which would later become Seoul National University) and Taipei Imperial

University (later, National Taiwan University). Japan's defeat and subsequent decolonization wiped out most of the imperial legacies in these academic institutions. Even in Japan itself, some imperial knowledge was excluded quite intentionally, and more was simply forgotten in the postwar deimperialization process, although some of the era's knowledge survived. When Japan was defeated by the Allied powers, a military, political, and intellectual power vacuum emerged in the former Japanese spheres of influence. US government and private foundations filled much of the gap created by the collapse of the Japanese empire and invested considerable human and financial resources in academic and educational institutions in East Asia.

The second characteristic of the Cold War in East Asia lay in the divided nations. In the Korean Peninsula and Vietnam, the Allied requisition of former colonies resulted in geographical and political divisions. In China, by the end of 1949, two different regimes—one Communist and the other Nationalist Party (Kuomintang)—stood face-to-face across the Taiwan Strait, and the Korean War resulted in the consolidation of this division. The spatial division was accompanied by a division in academic communities and individual research and educational institutions. In China, Academia Sinica (the national academy) moved to Taiwan with the Nationalist regime, although some research institutions under its jurisdiction remained in continental China and would eventually establish the Chinese Academy of Sciences. The divided nations also brought about a tug-of-war between the two opposing camps over talented scientists and academicians. As Yuko Sato demonstrates in chapter 5, the Communist and Nationalist regimes competed to recruit Chinese scholars and students affiliated with US and European universities. At the same time, the division inevitably produced borderlands, which could have acted as a zone of contact for different groups and actors.

The divided nations attempted to demonstrate both their legitimacy and their differences from their counterparts. In criticizing each other, the divided nations employed similar rhetoric, and consequently, opposing camps often came to bear a striking resemblance, as if mirror images of each other. For example, if one counterpart tried to develop nuclear weapons, the other rushed to do the same. Also, both sides of the divided nations maintained authoritarian regimes with one-party dictatorships, albeit with one embracing Socialism and the other capitalism. The US government supported authoritarian regimes so long as they were pro-American. While the Nationalist regime called themselves "free China," their interest was focused on "retaking China" and developing nuclear capabilities, not on promoting academic freedom. Although the US did not support the project to retake China, it nevertheless offered economic aid until 1965, as the goal of the US was to establish the "free China" in Taiwan as liberated, modern, and industrialized. However, as the Vietnam War devolved into a quagmire and Taiwan's export economy expanded, US aid gradually shrank, finally ceasing altogether in 1965. It was Japan that thereafter took over the role of aid provider to Taiwan.

The third characteristic of the Cold War in East Asia was that it was never entirely "cold." The Korean War left serious scars on all aspects of Korean society, including social and political structures, academic and cultural institutions, and people's perceptions and emotions. The tension continued after the armistice, with various incidents that could have triggered anew a hot war, from the Pueblo Incident (1968), the failed terrorist attack against the Blue House (1968), to the Axe Murder Incident (1976). In Vietnam, the struggle for independence from French colonial rule developed into a civil war, with one side supported by the US and the other by the Soviet Union and the PRC. When the US sent a regular army to Vietnam, the Civil War expanded into an all-out war. Both in Korea and Vietnam, the PRC played a key role by offering military assistance to the Communist camp, making the "hot" Cold War in East Asia even more complicated. Moreover, low intensity conflicts continued between the PRC and ROC in the southeastern part of China throughout the 1950s and the early 1960s. The so-called first Taiwan Strait Crises occurred in 1954–55, then the second crisis in 1958, with the People's Liberation Army carrying out bombardment of offshore islands under KMT control and thereby eliciting a response from the KMT army. In particular, the second crisis of 1958 became so serious that the US government even considered the use of nuclear weapons against the PRC. In addition to these officially recorded crises, the ROC has repeatedly operated small-scale, clandestine guerrilla attacks. Therefore, the war between Communists and Nationalists practically continued until 1991, when the ROC finally abandoned its policy to "retake China."

All these examples indicate that postwar knowledge in East Asia, unlike in its European counterpart, was constructed under the shadow of armed conflicts.

US CULTURAL HEGEMONY IN EAST ASIA

Although the Cold War in East Asia was characterized by unique complexity, the region still received significant influences from the US and the Soviet Union. Especially, the US influences on non-Communist countries were by no means negligible. US intellectuals dramatically expanded scholarly interest in the Asia-Pacific region during and after the Second World War, and the knowledge they produced on Asia held hegemonic influence not only in US academia but also in Asia itself. There were several routes through which young scholars and students developed interest in Asia.

First, when the Second World War broke out, there were a handful of "missionaries' sons and daughters," born and raised in Asia, who used their language skills, cultural understanding, and human networks with the locals to become area specialists. John W. Hall, who was born in Kyoto to a missionary family and later became a pioneer in Japanese studies, is one such example. The McCunes, whom Somei Kobayashi focuses on in chapter 4, were other examples. George McAfee McCune, born and raised in Pyongyang, Korea, as a son of an American Presbyterian missionary, became a pioneer of Korean studies in the US. His wife, Evelyn Becker McCune, was also born to an American missionary of the Methodist Church in Pyongyang and was educated in Keijō (Seoul). Evelyn McCune became a specialist in Korean art history in the postwar US.

Second, wartime strategic research and intelligence activities were a cradle for fostering postwar area specialists. Notable anthropologists such as Ruth Benedict and John Embree were mobilized for the Office of War Information (OWI) research project on enemy countries. Benedict later published *The Chrysanthemum and the Sword*, a famous ethnography on Japanese culture based on her study for the OWI. In addition, the OWI's deputy director, George Taylor, was an influential China specialist who would later direct the Far Eastern and Russian Institute at the University of Washington. Another wartime intelligence organization, the OSS, compiled the *Civil Affairs Handbook* series—several dozens of booklets containing comprehensive knowledge about countries and regions that US troops might occupy or be stationed in temporarily along the path toward the Allied victory. Asian studies scholars provided information for the handbook volumes on Asia. George M. McCune, mentioned above, served the OSS during the war, as did famous China specialists such as Esson M. Gale and John K. Fairbank. Charles B. Fahs was an OSS Japan specialist who later played a key role in the Rockefeller Foundation's financial aid to Asia. Such an impressive list of names indicates that a wide array of intellectuals became area specialists through their experiences in the wartime intelligence agencies.

The third route that young US scholars took to Asia was through the army and navy language schools established during the Second World War. Herbert Passin, an anthropologist, was inducted into the army and sent to the army's Japanese-language school in Ann Arbor, Michigan. In the immediate postwar years, he became chief of the Public Opinion and Sociological Research Division of the Allied occupation forces, and he later became an influential Japan specialist. Donald Keene, renowned scholar of Japanese literature, studied in the navy's Japanese-language school and served in the Pacific front during the war. Robert E. Ward also attended the navy language school, became a Japanese translator for the occupation forces, and later joined the University of Michigan and directed the Center for Japanese Studies.[5] Many of those who became involved in wartime area studies or language training projects continued their inquiry into Asian cultures in the postwar era, forming the first generation of Asia specialists in the subsequent Cold War years.

In sum, Christian missions, wartime intelligence organizations, and military language schools were three major routes through which young American intellectuals became interested in, and eventually became specialists in, East Asia. From its inception, therefore, the field of East Asian studies in the US was imbued with the cultural and political authority inherent in religious, governmental, and military organizations. However, as several chapters in this book successfully demonstrate, indigenous knowledge and local intellectuals contributed to the formation and transformation of US knowledge of East Asia to a substantial degree, despite its origins being intimately linked to American cultural and political authorities.

Even outside the intellectual community, US interest in the Asia-Pacific region expanded during the early Cold War era, with popular knowledge about Asia coming to be widely shared among middle-class citizens. As Christina Klein's influential book has aptly pointed out, the "middle-brow Americans' imagery" concerning the Asia-Pacific region was formed as the region's strategic importance to the US grew and as the US became more closely tied with "free" nations in Asia. Hollywood films and popular novels were saturated with themes such as overcoming racial prejudice and making friends with Asian people or fulfilling love and marriage across racial and cultural boundaries. Klein described US popular knowledge about Asia as "Cold War Orientalism," in which middle-class Americans imagined Asia as friendly and welcoming yet respectful of Western knowledge and those who bring such knowledge.[6] US citizens participated in the People-to-People international friendship programs, such as pen pal movements and educational and professional exchanges. Although the People-to-People programs appeared on the surface to be grassroots activities, they were in fact proposed by the White House and later supported by the International Cooperation Administration (ICA, later renamed USAID), a US government agency related to the Department of State.

Knowledge of Asia was sustained not only by the US government and individual scholars but also by nongovernmental funding organizations such as the Rockefeller Foundation and the Ford Foundation. From the mid-1940s to the 1950s, the Rockefeller Foundation increased its support to US universities such as University of California, Berkley, and Harvard, which opened new courses and purchased books and collections on East Asia. The Rockefeller Foundation also granted fellowships for scholars and graduate students specializing in East Asia. The Ford Foundation, on the other hand, provided financial aid for establishing research institutions in East Asia, including the Asiatic Research Institute at Korea University and the Center for Southeast Asian Studies at Kyoto University during the 1950s and 1960s. Academia Sinica in Taiwan, discussed by Shin Kawashima in chapter 1, was also supported by the Ford Foundation. The Asia Foundation, which was established in 1951 as a Central Intelligence Agency front organization, hid its CIA connection and acted like a nongovernmental organization. The foundation supported diverse academic and educational activities, including a *zainichi* Korean (Korean residents in Japan) students' organization and the *zainichi* Korean YMCA during the 1950s.[7]

These private (and quasi-private) foundations did not necessarily try to intervene in the activities of the recipient organizations, but they selectively funded projects that were likely to serve US national interest. There has been debate among scholars as to whether support from these foundations actually influenced the academic activities or knowledge produced therein. This same debate took place in a workshop held at Kyoto University in January 2020, in which authors of this volume met to discuss the book project. Some scholars argue that they had little influence because scholars took advantage of the resources provided by the foundations and not vice versa. Others argue that freedom of academic research was threatened by such funding, even if there were no clear strings attached to the money. When the Asia Foundation was publicly identified as a CIA conduit in the late 1960s, a heated debate broke out among US scholars on academic ethics and the possibility of the CIA's influence. Although the Asia Foundation denied any CIA influence, scholars such as David Price have pointed out that information collected by anthropologists concerning the Third World countries was exploited by the CIA and sometimes used for clandestine operations.[8]

The authors of this volume are interested in the degrees of autonomy of the students, scholars, and specialists who were involved in the knowledge production of the early Cold War era. If they received federal or private funds, how much control did the funding organizations exert over them? What degrees of freedom did the recipients enjoy? What were the relationships between the state, private organizations, and academia? Was US hegemony in academic, scientific, or professional knowledge flexible enough to allow resistance or creative

INTRODUCTION   11

appropriations by East Asian intellectuals? Those are some of the questions the authors of this volume share.

WHY KNOWLEDGE CONSTRUCTION IN EAST ASIA?

A focus on knowledge construction provides a useful new perspective for understanding the Cold War in East Asia. First, for the divided nations, academic and scientific knowledge was important for demonstrating their legitimacy and superiority in the eyes of the people in the other halves. In contrast to the European situation in which the defeated nation was divided, Japan remained unified. In East Asia, it was rather the victor, China; the former Japanese colony, Korea; and a former French colony, Vietnam, that were divided. Those divisions were brought about by the Allied occupation at the end of the Second World War, the Korean War, and the war in Indochina. While the divided nations engaged in armed conflicts, they attempted to not only establish military predominance but also demonstrate their legitimacy as authentic successors. Seeking to reunite their respective countries, leaders of the divided nations felt it necessary to win over the *people* living in enemy territory, even while denigrating each other. Academic research into their past and present *had to* demonstrate their authenticity, and scientific research *had to* demonstrate their modernity and economic superiority.

Second, this logic of the divided nations was closely related to the global Cold War in the sense that the confrontation of capitalist versus Socialist blocs was sometimes taken advantage of and at other times simply nullified in the East Asian context. The "free" nations of East Asia concluded mutual security treaties with the US, producing a hub-and-spoke formation with the US in the center, which was distinct from the Western European multilateral security systems such as the North Atlantic Treaty Organization (NATO). However, countries connected with the US by spokes, such as Taiwan and Korea, often cooperated with one another and formed anti-Communist alliances of their own. Socialist countries in East Asia, on the other hand, mutually concluded security treaties and developed a multilateral national security system to some degree. Sometimes, however, the goal of national unification eclipsed all other factors, pushing political and ideological alliances to the background; this is why Taiwan approached the Soviet Union toward the end of the 1960s and China approached the US in the early 1970s. Even if the US and the Soviet Union approached East Asian academic communities in accordance with their Cold War strategies, different motivations, such as traditional values, the legitimacy of revolutions, or the unification of people and nations, sometimes defined the academic and scientific activities in East Asia. The divided nations cultivated academic and scientific knowledge to demonstrate their superiority over their counterparts, with the ultimate goal of reunifying their countries.

Third, diverse actors were involved in knowledge production in East Asia, both in countries with democratic political systems and in those under authoritarian regimes, such as Korea and Taiwan. Actors included not only scholars and technocrats but also political parties, militaries, industrialists, and various other groups and individuals. Those diverse actors, and the relationships between them, greatly influenced state-level relations with the US or with the Soviet Union. The Japanese Liberal Democratic Party, the ROC's KMT, and even the PRC's CCP included diverse factions, who either promoted or disrupted state-to-state relations with the US or with the Soviet Union. The same dynamics applied to the arena of knowledge production.

Fourth, the relationships between the state, academic or scientific communities, and the knowledge they produced were defined by the political background of each East Asian country. Academic and scientific freedom was usually respected in democratic countries, but even authoritarian regimes could not completely eschew such freedom, as scientific research endeavors inevitably required objectivity and autonomy. It was difficult for any government to reflect political influences directly on scientific findings. Even so, state intervention in knowledge production, especially in terms of institutional and financial aspects, was most rampant under the authoritarian regimes. The authoritarian governments strictly controlled academic and scientific institutions and funding because they feared the power of the academic and scientific communities to influence the public.

Out of these analyses of knowledge construction emerge some fresh understandings of the Cold War in East Asia, especially of the relations between the global Cold War and the non–Cold War factors specific to the East Asian context. That is the primary reason the authors of this volume find meaning in exploring the construction of academic, scientific, and professional knowledge in East Asia.

COMPLEXITY OF US–EAST ASIAN RELATIONS

US influences on East Asian academic, scientific, or professional knowledge during the Cold War cannot be overemphasized, regardless of whether they resulted from US government maneuvering or the initiatives of private groups and individuals. However, it is also important to remember that the relations between the US and East Asian academic communities were not unilateral but interactive. There was a constant flow of people, information, and programs from East Asia to the US, in spite of the common image of unidirectional educational or technical aid from US to East Asia. Furthermore, East Asian countries did not show unanimous attitudes in their relations with the US. For example, the Ford Foundation aid invoked entirely different reactions in Korea, Japan, and Taiwan. Such complex relations between the US and East Asia—on the one hand, the US maintained a hub-and-spoke relationship with East Asian countries and viewed each country as part of the overarching East Asian strategy, while on the other hand, each country maintained its own agency in interactive relations with the US—are clearly shown in the field of knowledge construction, much more so than in the conventional research fields of national security or political history.

Some chapters in this book emphasize interactive relations between the US and East Asia. For example, chapter 1 by Shin Kawashima focuses on the US financial aid for Chinese studies in Taiwan during the 1960s, which resulted in growing US academic influence on Chinese studies in Taiwan. Through the same program, however, Chinese studies in Taiwan also influenced US academia through the ROC scholars who studied in the US and the US scholars who researched in Taiwan. Miriam Kingsberg Kadia's chapter 2 deals with the US-Japanese interactive relations and reevaluates the Japanese researchers' contribution to the dawn of postwar Japanese studies in the US. Chapter 3, by Masaki Fujioka, discusses the US-Japanese academic debate over modernization theory in the late 1960s. Chapter 4, by Somei Kobayashi, focuses on the interactive relations between the US and Korea. Although funds and information were overwhelmingly transferred from the US to Korea, the project also provided opportunities for Americans to learn about Korea. Chapter 10, by Jae Young Cha, also demonstrates that even in the presence of the overwhelming influx of US knowledge and information to Korea, some adaptation and appropriation by Korean recipients was observed.

The multilayered and interactive process in which academic, scientific, and professional knowledge was constructed should be paid due attention, which will reveal a new dimension of the "hot" Cold War in East Asia, complicating the conventional image of the US as an overwhelming power that dominated not only political and economic spheres but also the world of knowledge in East Asia.

—∞—

This volume consists of three parts. Part I, "Area Studies," deals with the emergence of postwar Chinese studies, Japanese studies, Korean studies, and modernization theory, in which American and East Asian scholars collaborated, debated, and learned from each other in the construction of new academic knowledge. Chapter 1 by Shin Kawashima focuses on the Ford Foundation's aid to Chinese studies programs in Taiwan. It demonstrates that the large-scale aid for the Institute of Modern History, Academia Sinica, formed the cornerstone of Chinese studies in Taiwan, that conflicts among KMT scholars complicated the flow of US aid, and that the KMT scholars, with their eyes on US-PRC relations, tried to define "China" in their terms for American scholars. Chapter 2 by Miriam Kingsberg Kadia explores the development of Japanese studies in the US by the first postwar generation of scholars. The author revises the conventional genealogies of Japanese studies by highlighting the important contributions of Japanese translators, local experts, and coordinators that enabled the early postwar US field research in Japan. Chapter 3 by Masaki Fujioka focuses on the US-Japanese debate on modernization theory at the Hakone Conference held in Japan in 1960 and points out the important discrepancies in understanding between the US and Japanese scholars, particularly concerning the value of democracy and historical interpretations of prewar Japan. Chapter 4 by Somei Kobayashi deals with the development of Korean studies as an academic field from the mid-1940s to the early 1950s. By focusing on George McAfee McCune, Evelyn Becker McCune, and the Rockefeller Foundation, all significantly involved in the development of Korean studies, this chapter sheds light on the interactions between academia and government agencies and between American and Korean specialists.

Part II, "Scientific Knowledge," illuminates the tension between state control and the autonomy of science and scientists. It covers the geographical areas of the PRC, the ROC, Korea, and the US through the themes of nuclear science and biology. As a whole, part II illuminates science both as an effective tool of Cold War diplomacy and as an inherently uncontrollable entity that is transnational and transideological by nature. Chapter 5 by Yuko Sato focuses on the dawn of the PRC's nuclear science in the late 1940s and early 1950s, when the Chinese Civil War ended and the Cold War began. Scientists trained overseas were a precious source of Western knowledge as well as Western research funds, and thus both the CCP and KMT approached overseas scientists, attempting to have them repatriate either to the PRC or to the ROC, respectively. Chapter 6 by Yuka Tsuchiya Moriguchi explores why the Michigan Memorial Phoenix Project, a university grant-in-aid program for researchers in nuclear science, was involved in a government foreign aid program. It reveals how scientific knowledge became a diplomatic tool, but at the same time, the case of the ROC disrupts the simple dichotomy of the provider versus recipient of scientific knowledge. Chapter 7 by Manyong Moon focuses on the first ecological survey of the Korean demilitarized zone (DMZ) in the mid-1960s, conducted under the cooperation of the Smithsonian Institution and Korean biologists. However, the project ceased at the preliminary stage because of heightened military tension between the two Koreas and an incident called the CIA scandal. This chapter illuminates the multifaceted meaning of the DMZ and scientific surveys by an international research team.

Part III, "Practicing Knowledge," explores how professional knowledge produced in the US was brought to the ROC, Hong Kong, and Korea; how it invoked resistance or conflict; and how it was selectively accepted by each society. More specifically, knowledge in communication and journalism, journalism education, and military civic activities are used as examples. Chapter 8 by Mike Shichi Lan explores the development of journalism education in Taiwan under US influence, particularly in conjunction with the education of overseas Chinese students supported by US aid between 1955 and 1965. He draws special attention to the journalism education program at National Chengchi University (NCCU) and the career path of its alumni. While some alumni who worked in news media helped carry out the anti-Communist ideological agenda, others took a different path, and some even actively worked against the agenda. Chapter 9 by Yang Zhang focuses on the US support for the establishment of journalism and communication professions in Hong Kong and examines politically oriented knowledge-diffusion activities. It reveals Hong Kong's strong local initiative and self-consciousness in light of the huge influence of the US in the field of journalism and communication education. It also points out that Hong Kong scholars had academic flexibility in that they did not reject academic pluralism. Chapter 10 by Jae Young Cha discusses a US educational exchange program that aimed to train South Korean journalists to be pro-American and to Americanize them in accordance with American-style professionalism. The chapter concludes that while the former purpose was fully accomplished, the same was not true of the latter, as South Korean journalists maintained a custom of emphasizing opinion ahead of fact and the authoritarian government and media owners did not allow autonomy of the press. Chapter 11 by Eun Heo analyzes the role of the military in close contact with local communities by examining the Civil Assistance Program of the US Army in South Korea in the late 1950s. The military in underdeveloped East Asian countries emerged as a sponsor or provider of modern knowledge and enlightenment education for "the grass roots" in the Cold War era. This chapter analyzes the role of the US Army as a provider of knowledge and the subsequent Korean reactions.

—⁂—

In this volume, authors' names are written in the Western style—in other words, with the given name first—while in the text of chapters, Chinese and Korean names are written with the family name first, as in "Mao Zedong," except when the person adopts an American name, such as David Wong. All other names, including Japanese names, are written with the given name first.

NOTES

1. Odd Arne Westad, *The Global Cold War: Third World Interventions and the Making of Our Times* (Cambridge: Cambridge University Press, 2005); Westad, *The Cold War: A World History* (New York: Basic Books, 2017); Nick Cullather, *The Hungry World: America's Cold War Battle Against Poverty in Asia* (Cambridge, MA: Harvard University Press, 2010); Frances Stonor Saunders, *Cultural Cold War: The CIA and the World of Arts and Letters* (New York: New Press, 1999); Kenneth Osgood, *Total Cold War: Eisenhower's Secret Propaganda Battle at Home and Abroad* (Lawrence: University Press of Kansas, 2006); Penny Von Eschen, *Satchmo Blows Up the World: Jazz Ambassadors Play the Cold War* (Cambridge, MA: Harvard University Press, 2005); Hajimu Masuda, *Cold War Crucible: The Korean Conflict and the Postwar World* (Cambridge, MA: Harvard University Press, 2015).

2. For publications in Asia, for example, articles included in Toshihiko Kishi and Yuka Tsuchiya, eds., *Decentering the Cultural Cold War: The U.S. and Japan* (Tokyo: Kokusai Shoin, 2009), available in the Japanese, Korean, and Chinese languages; Yuka Tsuchiya and Shun'ya Yoshimi, eds., *Occupying Eyes, Occupying Voices: CIE/USIS Films and VOA Radio* (Tokyo: University of Tokyo Press, 2012); Yang Zhang, *The Cold War and Academics: Chinese Studies in the United States, 1949–1972* (Beijing: China Social Sciences, 2019); Yang Zhang, *Cultural Cold War: The U.S. Young Leaders Program, 1947–1989* (Beijing: China Social Sciences, 2020); Eun Heo, *The U.S. Hegemony and Korean Nationalism* (Seoul: Research Institute of Korean Studies, Korea University, 2008).

3. For works dealing with universities and the Cold War, see, for example, Noam Chomsky, Ira Katznelson, R. C. Lewontin, David Montgomery, Laura Nader, Richard Ohmann, Ray Siever, Immanuel Wallerstein, and Howard Zinn, *The Cold War and the University: Toward an Intellectual History of the Postwar Years* (New York: New Press, 1997); Rebecca S. Lowen, *Creating the Cold War University: The Transformation of Stanford* (Berkeley: University of California

Press, 1997); Natalia Tsvetkova, *The Cold War in Universities: U.S. and Soviet Cultural Diplomacy, 1945–1990* (Leiden: Brill, 2021).

4. Susan Strange, *States and Markets: An Introduction to International Political Economy*, Bloomsbury Revelations version (London: Bloomsbury, 2015), 27.

5. Herbert Passin, *Encounter with Japan* (Tokyo: Kodansha International, 1982); Otis Cary, ed., *War-Wasted Asia: Letters, 1945–46* (New York: Kodansha USA, 1975); Jessica Lemieux, Robert Edward Ward papers (Hoover Institution Library and Archives, 2009, 2019), https://oac.cdlib.org/findaid/ark:/13030/kt6xonf3jz/entire_text/, last accessed on July 29, 2024.

6. Christina Klein, *Cold War Orientalism: Asia in the Middlebrow Imagination, 1945–1961* (Berkeley: University of California Press, 2003).

7. Somei Kobayashi, "CIA, US Philosophy Foundations, and Support to Zainichi Koreans," *Kohro* 7 (July 2020): 142–55.

8. David Price, *Cold War Anthropology: The CIA, the Pentagon, and the Growth of Dual Use Anthropology* (Durham, NC: Duke University Press, 2016).

AUTHOR BIOS

YUKA TSUCHIYA MORIGUCHI is Professor of American History at Kyoto University. She is author of *Science, Technology and the Cultural Cold War in Asia: From Atoms for Peace to Space Flight* (2022) and many other books and articles on US cultural/science diplomacy during the Cold War.

SHIN KAWASHIMA is Professor of International Relations at the University of Tokyo. He authored *China in the 21st Century* (2016) and *Frontier of China* (2017), among others, and edited *Xi Jinping's China* (2022) and many other volumes.

SOMEI KOBAYASHI is Professor at Nihon University College of Law. He is author of *Media Space of Koreans in Japan: Newspapers during the Allied Occupation of Japan* (2007) and many articles on East Asian history in the Cold War era and Korean studies.

PART I

AREA STUDIES

ONE

THE UNITED STATES AND TAIWANESE SINOLOGY DURING THE COLD WAR

The Ford Foundation and the Institute of Modern History, Academia Sinica

SHIN KAWASHIMA

TRANSLATED BY GEORGE REMISOVSKY

INTRODUCTION

This chapter primarily addresses American support for sinology in the 1960s. In doing so, it takes into consideration the significant influence of the US on academic knowledge in postwar East Asia generally and, employing Taiwan as a specific contextual lens, what this influence meant to, and how it was interpreted by, recipients. The US influence (and its reception) in Taiwan is exemplary of how Cold War strategy functioned in a context ostensibly separate from overt military security. In other words, in the academic Cold War, aid offered by the US did not always materialize as intended but was often reinterpreted and reframed within the domestic contexts of each recipient nation or region. Thus, as will be argued in this chapter, understanding US academic aid as a one-sided influence is overly simplistic, as the transfer of knowledge was more often than not bilateral, including outreach movements from Asia to the US. Contributing to the latter movements was the uniquely complex nature of East Asia during the Cold War, including its divided states.

In raising Taiwan as a representative example, this chapter focuses on the Ford Foundation's support for sinology in Taiwan, with specific focus on the difficulties and challenges that the Taiwanese recipients faced domestically as a result of receiving such aid, as well as the influence of the Taiwanese scholars' intellectual outreach to the US through research projects.

In the 1960s, the US increased its support for sinology across East Asia, and in Japan, the support that the Ford Foundation channeled to Tōyō Bunko library became a major controversy. In 1967, marking the fiftieth anniversary of Tōyō Bunko's establishment, Enoki Kazuo, professor of Oriental history at the University of Tokyo and contributor to the library, proclaimed, "With the help of the Rockefeller, Ford, and Asia Foundations in acquiring books related to the modern history of East Asia, Tōyō Bunko has amassed a collection that is without equal."[1] The Ford Foundation also provided support to the Center for Modern Economics at Rikkyo University and research on Southeast Asia at Kyoto University (on Indonesia and Burma).[2] Among Asian studies scholars and historians, it is well known that the Ford Foundation's support for Tōyō Bunko led to a significant wave of criticism, with critiques attacking the political nature of the support, and that accepting such financial assistance made the library complicit in America's Cold War.[3]

Echoing the contemporary criticisms, Maiko Ichikawa, using recently released documents, analyzes different support goals for each country and region by the Asia Foundation and other groups: "The CIA wished to perform a fact-based investigation of Communist China and release the results to the Japanese public. In so doing, they hoped to influence Japanese public opinion toward China. As part of this initiative, the documents state, they sought to promote anti-Communist ideas among Japanese researchers who had been educated in Marxism and had been swayed by Communist thought."[4] Ichihara also argues, "The Asia Foundation thought that Japanese empirical research on modern China was of poor quality. By offering the foundation's support and guaranteeing the objectivity of that research, they hoped to attract Japanese sinologists."[5] She also notes that the support given to Tōyō Bunko was qualitatively different from that offered to Hong Kong, as "it was with the primary aim to collect information on China that the Americans provided funding to the Union Research Institute and the Institute of Modern Asian Studies at the University of Hong Kong."[6] It is precisely because of these other outlays that support for the building of collections and empirical research at Tōyō Bunko was of primary import. With this, there was hope that, at least to some extent, the influence of the Communist Party of China on Japanese academia might be diminished.

Within the complex context of East Asia during the Cold War, this chapter seeks to explore the Ford Foundation's decade-long support started in 1961, for the Institute of Modern History at Academia Sinica, including the forms this support took and the aims behind it.

There has already been a considerable amount of research on the Ford Foundation's support in this context. The most directly relevant is Zhang Pengyuan's

Guo Tingyi, Fei Zhengqing, Wei Muting: Taiwan yu Meiguo Xueshu Jiaoliu ge an Chutan (Triangular partnership: Kuo Ting-yee, John K. Fairbank, C. Martin Wilbur, and their contribution to Taiwan-US academic exchange), which focused on Kuo Tingyi, a researcher at Academia Sinica who accepted the Ford Foundation's support and subsequently became a target of criticism because of that. Zhang, who was an understudy of Kuo, combined the accounts of those involved in the controversy with other historical documents in an objective examination; despite his efforts to remain objective, however, Zhang's work is still clearly aimed at dispelling lingering questions surrounding Kuo Ting-yee, including why he needed to go to the US in the middle of his Ford Foundation–funded research project and why he could never return to Taiwan. Chung Moon Sang's "Cong 'chongji-fanying lun' dao 'shidai huanjing-shiying lun'-meiguo xuewen moshi de chuanbo yu Taiwan zhi zhongguo jindai shi yanjiu" (From "impact-response theory" to "era environment-adaptation theory": Taiwanese studies of modern Chinese history and Cultural Cold War) uses the factual evidence that Zhang uncovered to argue that aid from the Ford Foundation served as an opportunity to spread American thinking such as the "impact-response theory" to Taiwan and the rest of East Asia. However, Chung's work does not devote much attention to the internal dynamics of the Taiwanese organizations that accepted assistance from the Ford Foundation, nor does it make comparisons with other parts of the region.[7]

Related memoirs and the work of Wu Lin-Chun on the Rockefeller Foundation in Taiwan have served to supplement the above research, but none deal directly with the support the Ford Foundation provided for sinology in Taiwan.[8]

In contexts other than Taiwan, Cold War historians have primarily focused on the unilateral aims of the Ford Foundation's support for intellectuals. For instance, Volker R. Berghahn explores the cultural impact of the US, particularly the US East Coast, on Europe as a result of the Ford Foundation's programs.[9] Also, Kathleen D. McCarthy traces the Ford Foundation's global cultural activities in a consideration of the role of US Cold War strategy.[10] While both of these studies are significant in understanding the foundation's strategies, the focus on the aims of the foundation itself essentially limits the historiography. This chapter seeks to address this limitation by focusing primarily on the response of the recipients and considering the influences of the foundation's activities through the lens of the recipient society. To do so, the analyses in this chapter will employ the diplomatic archives of the Republic of China (ROC) and related documents to explain the significance of the Ford Foundation's work in Taiwanese sinology, while also drawing comparisons with Japan and other places in East Asia.[11]

THE FORD FOUNDATION'S SUPPORT FOR THE
INSTITUTE OF MODERN HISTORY, ACADEMIA SINICA

Academia Sinica was established by the ROC while it still maintained a presence on mainland China. At the academy, historical studies were originally included within the purview of the Institute of History and Philology. After the ROC government moved to Taiwan, however, the academy established the separate Institute of Modern History in 1955, with Kuo Ting-yee serving as its first director.[12] Chu Chia-hua, who was director of Academia Sinica at the time, supported the establishment of the Institute of Modern History despite the opposition of the Institute of History and Philology.[13] After Chu resigned in 1957, however, Kuo's position as director became significantly more precarious.[14]

The Ford Foundation's support likely began as a result of the 1960 Sino-American Conference on Intellectual Cooperation, where Kuo met with George Taylor, Franz Michael, and Hsiao Kung-chuan, discussing with them the possibility of applying for American funding. John K. Fairbank and Columbia's C. Martin Wilbur also recommended that Kuo apply.[15] After considering his options, Kuo ultimately decided to make a formal application to the Ford Foundation in 1961, and he received approval in October for support that would begin in January of the next year.[16]

However, all did not go smoothly with the foundation's funding of the Institute of Modern History. A pressing question raised at the outset of the proffered support was whether the institute, or Kuo himself, was qualified to receive such generous funding. Wu Hsiang-hsiang launched an especially severe attack on Kuo in the December 28 issue of the *Central Daily News*; in an article titled "Why Should We Avoid Researching the History of the Republic [of China]?" he lambasted the Institute of Modern History for having achieved little since its founding.[17] Wu also argued that diplomatic history was simply not a major theme of modern historical research. Perhaps because of Wu's article, Hu Shih, who was then president of Academia Sinica, took on management of the advisory committees in charge of research planning and personnel assignments related to the Ford Foundation's funding, rather than allowing the decision-making process to remain within the Institute of Modern History.[18] These committees included a significant number of faculty members from National Taiwan University, including Yang Shuren, Yao Congwu, Li Chi, and Liu Chonghong, ultimately leading Kuo to submit a letter of resignation in light of the increasingly hostile environment he faced.[19] By chance, C. Martin Wilbur happened to be in Taipei when Kuo submitted his resignation. Upon hearing the news, he worked to ensure that Kuo would stay on, in part by sending Hu Shih messages in support of Kuo's retention. Perhaps as a result of Wilbur's efforts, Hu subsequently began actively working to dissuade Kuo's departure.[20] Kuo eventually withdrew his resignation, but because of Hu's sudden death from a heart attack during a late February 1962 meeting at Academia Sinica, his project faced a highly uncertain future.

Despite such turbulent beginnings, the Ford Foundation's sponsorship of the Institute of Modern History continued for ten years, spanning from 1962 to 1971, and it provided around US$420,000 in overall funding (phase 1: US$153,000; phase 2: US$268,000).[21] Details of how the funding was used are included in table 1.1, but of particular note are the facts that the second phase of funding was larger than the first and that most of the funding was spent on research support, including books, other research materials, and fellowships. The institute primarily spent that money on archival organization and research, library construction, book acquisitions, and support for overseas research by department members. Of course, some of the institute's funds were also allocated to covering individual living expenses and wages, with the latter increasing 1.5-fold after the Ford Foundation began its support.[22] Priority for overseas research funding was given to younger faculty members. As will be discussed in more detail below, while this allocation sparked a significant amount of debate, from 1962 to 1973, every two years, twenty individuals were dispatched to the US, Great Britain, France, and Japan. This was precisely the sort of effect that Kuo Ting-yee wanted the program to have.

The Ford Foundation also facilitated visits in the other direction, resulting in an increasing number of American scholars visiting the Institute of Modern History. Zhang Pengyuan contends that "Fairbank wanted the Institute of Modern History to be a research organization of the highest level. That way, Western scholars could visit on their own and experience Chinese society for themselves while conducting research." Knight Biggerstaff, Mary Wright, Albert Feuerwerker, and over twenty scholars and thirty graduate students spent time at the institute, realizing Fairbank's original goals.[23]

The Ford Foundation, however, was not the only organization that worked toward establishing a base for research in Taiwan. For example, the Association for Asian Studies established the Advisory Committee to Chinese Materials and Research Aids Service Center, with Feuerwerker of the University of Michigan Center for Chinese Studies as its head. This committee went on to make appeals to the Embassy of the ROC in Washington and other organizations.[24] The chief representative of the Harvard East Asia Center, John M. H. Lindbeck, was also involved with the committee's work. The committee proposed

26   AREA STUDIES

Table 1.1 Details of Ford Foundation Funding

Financial statement in US dollars	1962–66	1967–June 1972
Receipt		
Appropriations	153,000.00	268,600.00
Interest from the above	1,508.73	7,179.00
Total	154,508.73	275,179.00[1]
Expenditure		
Research support	*39,987.50	89,842.50
Oral history	8,523.80	8,523.81
Fellowships	66,064.81	70,177.60
Books, research materials	6,243.34	48,749.41
Administrative support	**14,035.00	24,908.13
Miscellaneous	692.23	3,774.92
Index making		4,477.50
Publication		22,202.50
Reserve		***781.00
Travel allowance for Lee En-han		647.00
English synopsis		936.27
Total	153,057.88	275,179.00[2]
Balance	1,450.85	158.37[3]

Source: Table based on "Financial Statement, 1962–1966," "Financial Statement, January 1,1967–June 30, 1972" in Zhang, *Guo Tingyi, Fei Zhengqing, Wei Muting*, 169–70. Some of the original figures have been rounded.

*includes project director (1962, 1963);**includes secretary (1962)
***for trips abroad by members of institutes, etc.

[1] 275,779, but follow the original text.
[2] Some of the calculations do not seem to add up, but we will follow the numbers and explanations in the original text.
[3] Some of the calculations do not seem to add up, but we will follow the numbers and explanations in the original text.

an affiliated research center in Taipei that would also play host to educational activities, with the aim of encouraging cooperation between Taiwanese publishers and bookstores and American libraries and research organizations to republish out-of-print books on sinology and to produce new reference works, and the American Embassy in Taipei was generally supportive of their plan.[25] The ROC government saw Fairbank, Wilbur, and Wright as the three academics at the core of this effort.[26] The committee's plan ultimately led to the establishment of the Chinese Materials and Research Aids Service Center.[27]

CRITICISMS OF FAIRBANK AND THEIR IMPACT

The Institute of Modern History was beset by troubles both internal and external in origin during the period it was receiving the auspices of the Ford Foundation. For one thing, Kuo Ting-yee, because of his work with the foundation, gradually became a target of criticism and finally left Taiwan for the US, never to return. For another—and this was the largest internal problem—the institute grappled with the order in which it granted funding for research and study abroad. Kuo wished to prioritize young researchers, a stance that drew the ire of other members of the institute. Externally, the institute's acceptance of Ford Foundation funding came under criticism from scholars such as National Taiwan University professor Wu Hsiang-hsiang, although Zhang Pengyuan considers such criticisms "minor troubles" when compared with the events beginning in 1967, sparked by comments by Fairbank that were perceived as supporting "Two Chinas" and Taiwanese independence.[28]

Zhang points to the Twenty-Seventh Congress of Orientalists held at the University of Michigan in 1967 as the start of the controversy.[29] Previously, Fairbank's comments during an open session of the Senate Foreign Relations Committee in March 1966, which expressed sympathy for the People's Republic of China (PRC), had received a significant amount of attention in Taiwan. His decision to express these views was likely impelled by the US entry into the Vietnam War.[30] Twenty-three scholars from the ROC attended the Michigan conference, with Kuo heading the delegation. While the conference was ongoing, the *Economic Daily News*, part of the United Daily News Group, published an article titled "Kuo Ting-yee Argues Down John K. Fairbank," which recounted Fairbank's speech on how Mao Zedong's regime might be overthrown by the people of mainland China in short order.[31] It was precisely because Fairbank had been in recent contact with Kuo, the article asserted, that he adopted a stance more closely aligned to Kuo's position on the Communist Party of China (perceived as leaning toward more positive support for ROC). However, while the article appeared to be in praise of Kuo, it was in fact published to lay the groundwork for a new round of criticism of his work. Li Dongfang published a response in the conservative *Zhonghua Zazhi* in short order, calling the story of Fairbank's "persuasion" implausible because, as he pointed out, Kuo could neither speak nor write English, and similarly, Fairbank could do neither in Chinese. Li then declared that the whole affair was likely closely related to the Ford Foundation and went on to criticize the Institute of

Modern History's decision to give Fairbank access to its diplomatic archives.[32] Even though these accusations were baseless, Kuo and Wang Shih-chieh subsequently had to defend themselves in the face of repeated questioning by members of the Legislative Yuan (the supreme legislative body of the ROC).

In a file titled "Fei Zhengqing" (John K. Fairbank), the ROC Ministry of Foreign Affairs archive kept Chinese translations of Fairbank's speeches and recorded their concerns regarding his potentially pro-Communist statements. The file also includes materials from a report authored by He Haoruo of the Chinese Culture University titled "Why I Criticized the Appeaser John K. Fairbank," which he presented to the Foreign Affairs Committee of the Legislative Yuan. This purely private report was not entered into the official record. Misunderstandings and distortions of the Chinese situation in the 1940s by US "international appeasers," he said, were the root of current problems. He launched attacks at both the past and the present work of Academia Sinica and criticized the leadership of Fairbank and Owen Lattimore over the Institute of Pacific Relations, claiming that the conference had "sold" mainland China to the Communist Party.[33] Fairbank, he said, not only supported the idea of "Two Chinas" but also backed "Taiwanese independence." The conservative media in the ROC subsequently lobbed a series of criticisms at Fairbank, including a republishing of He's report in the twenty-fourth issue of *Xiandai*.[34]

At the time, however, Fairbank was a frequent visitor to Taiwan and a student at the Taipei Language Institute, and he often extolled Taiwan as ideal for training American students of China.[35] Remaining documents include materials related to a visit Fairbank, with the aid of Jiang Yuntian of the China Democratic Socialist Party, planned to make to Taiwan in 1959, eight years before the 1967 Congress of Orientalists. A March 24, 1959, telegraph from George Yeh, ROC ambassador to the US, to Huang Shao-ku, minister of foreign affairs, stated that Yeh was to meet Fairbank and his wife at a meeting of the Association of Asian Studies (AAS) the following day. Yeh said that he was not going to raise the topic of Fairbank's visit to Taiwan in their conversation but would follow Jiang Yuntian's lead on the matter.[36] Yeh stressed that the Fairbanks believed in the need for America to recognize the "Communist bandits," while at the same time America continuing to offer support for Taiwan. Yeh also remarked, "For the past two years, Fairbank has had a number of dealings with Taiwanese students in the United States who have been in contact with Thomas Liao (Liao Wenyi)," an advocate for Taiwanese independence. He added, "It might be possible to change [Fairbank's] views on Taiwan if he visits, but it would likely be difficult to budge him from his position on the recognition of the Communist bandits."[37] Although Yeh was alarmed at

Fairbank's associations with "Taiwanese individuals who are displeased with us"—namely, advocates of Taiwanese independence—he was not at all against Fairbank's visit. He proposed that, instead of visiting the Government Information Office, Fairbank could give a special lecture at Academia Sinica or National Taiwan University.[38] Fairbank later mentioned that he would not be using any ROC funds to travel to Taiwan, instead having his expenses covered as a John Simon Guggenheim Fellow. The Ministry of Foreign Affairs, initially unaware of precisely what a Guggenheim Fellowship was, opened an investigation into the matter. In the end, however, the ROC government granted Fairbank and his family a two-to-three-month visa for their stay in Taiwan.[39] Yeh recognized Fairbank's wide-reaching influence and pointed out that while Fairbank's views had changed during his previous visit to Taiwan, "he indeed supports recognizing the Communist bandits, but American anti-Communists still believe him to fundamentally be on the same side as themselves." He explained the American anti-Communists' thinking: "Recently, his [Fairbank's] view has been that Taiwan has to be defended, but we have to work to increase his consciousness of the facts related to the bandits." Yeh finally noted, "I cannot be sure whether their attitudes will change for the better during their upcoming visit to Taiwan," but he said that the ROC should make efforts to that effect.[40] Yeh's views were quite different from those held by conservative party officials and intellectuals, though they were shared by a part of the bureaucracy that similarly believed Fairbank was more than simply a supporter of the Communist Party of China and viewed him as an "operational target" for their influence efforts, a target who could be induced to change his views. Their opposition to a black-and-white view of the situation, however, became a target of conservative attacks.

These views also differed from the opinions of Kuo Ting-yee, head of the Institute of Modern History. Kuo was a member of the Kuomintang (KMT), as part of its liberal faction.[41] Because of his liberal views, he welcomed researchers who had been arrested as part of the White Terror back into the institute after their release. But because he was not a conservative, Kuo's association with the Ford Foundation's project left him open to groundless attacks—the project's association with Fairbank being an especially serious issue. According to the logic of the conservatives within the KMT, Kuo was a suitable target because of his friendship with Fairbank, who, according to the conservatives, had a positive assessment of the "Communist bandits." Even if Kuo held views close to George Yeh's, their differing social positions meant that their social standings also differed.

Yu Ying-shih later commented: "In reality, Fairbank did not harbor any secret intentions of using their cooperation to achieve political aims at all. All he wanted was to extend his research methods to Taiwan, rather than hope to make the Institute of Modern History a colony for American historians. He only had direct influence over Harvard University, which he at most used to determine how research funding was allocated. He had absolutely no long-term impact on dictating the broader direction of research on modern Chinese history."[42]

Kuo was nevertheless personally caught up in an environment that made his situation untenable. He traveled to the US in 1969 to write his *Jin dai Zhongguo shi gang* (Survey of modern Chinese history) and would never again set foot in Taipei before his passing in 1975. His decision to relocate permanently to the US was likely in part to avoid the suspicions lobbed at him for his relationship with Fairbank, but Zhang Pengyuan has proposed a different explanation. According to Zhang, the primary reason was that Kuo had been placed on a black list by the Taiwan Garrison Command as part of the White Terror.[43]

The ROC faced a worsening international environment during the mid-1960s, with the PRC successfully testing a nuclear weapon in 1964 and France ending diplomatic relations with the ROC. Once the Cultural Revolution began in 1966, however, the ROC had an opportunity to bolster its project to retake the mainland and improve its international standing. The US launched support for a number of different organizations in Taiwan; while the Ford Foundation's sponsorship of the Institute of Modern History was exceptional in its scale, other funding avenues were also open to Taiwanese institutions. One such avenue was the China Foundation for the Promotion of Education and Culture, which had overseen the Boxer Indemnity of some US$12.5 million from 1917 to 1940. The China Foundation's funds had largely been exhausted by the time the ROC government moved to Taiwan in 1949, but through the determination and efforts of those involved, its activities continued. If we focus on direct organizational support, for instance, the foundation budgeted US$8,000 for the Institute of Economics in 1964 and US$15,000 for research on ancient Chinese history by the Institute for History and Philology in 1965 (culminating in a total of US$60,000 over a period of four years).[44] In contrast, the Institute of Modern History received US$153,000 of phase 1 funding and US$268,000 of phase 2 funding from the Ford Foundation, with each funding period lasting five years; the funding provided to this institute was truly unparalleled. This did not mean that other research institutes were without support from the US. Further work is needed to survey the overall funding that Americans provided for scholarly organizations in the ROC and compare these other projects with the Ford Foundation's collaboration with the Institute of Modern History, and the author plans to continue along this line of research in the future.

Given the analysis in this section, one might say that both parties to the Ford Foundation's support for the Institute of Modern History essentially met their original goals. The US was, to some extent, successful in creating a base for sinology in Taiwan. Academia Sinica, on the other hand, was able to establish a global hub for research on China by training young scholars, constructing a new library building, and undertaking large-scale projects. However, American support was exposed to all sorts of strife within Taiwan's internal context; part of the issue was which people and institutions received that support. Furthermore, American researchers with ties to the recipients—such as Fairbank—had their views on Chinese political questions scrutinized.

THE US AS A TARGET

In contrast to issues related to military security, when one examines culture—especially academic culture—one presumes that America's relationship with its "allies" was interactive rather than merely unidirectional. This is especially the case when it comes to research on Asia, where one cannot adequately explain events merely in terms of unilateral US support. In other words, one must consider not only the influence the US had on East Asia but also the work East Asian countries devoted to influencing the US. This is particularly pertinent when it comes to the ROC, which, because of the lingering issue of the recognition of the PRC, viewed American understanding of "China" as a top priority. It does not stretch the imagination to assume that the more important the US cultural activities became, the more intensely East Asian countries expended effort in offering proposals and seeking funding to shape such activities in accordance with their own interests.

The ROC had a number of frameworks and opportunities for exchange with the United States. First, the ROC had a number of cultural exchange organizations from before the war, and second, the ROC was a permanent member of the United Nations Security Council. The ROC uses these frameworks and opportunities to approach and involve the US in competition with the PRC as part of the wider Cold War.[45] Meetings between the leaderships of both countries were common, and in May 1961, the same year the Ford Foundation's project began, US president Dwight Eisenhower visited Taiwan, and Vice President Chen Cheng and his wife reciprocated with a visit to the US at the end of July. In August 1965, Soong Mei-ling traveled to the US, subsequently staying for a total of fourteen months. That same month, US vice president Richard Nixon made a visit to Taiwan, and in September, Minister of Defense Chiang Ching-kuo spent ten days in the US.

In the autumn of 1966, before she returned to Taiwan, Soong visited several American research organizations to speak about the issue of recognition and appeal for the destruction of Chinese nuclear capabilities.[46] Aside from this short-term influence project, a number of government organs also worked to put pressure on the US government. Overall policies related to the US were largely decided by the Combined Propaganda and Foreign Relations Research Group, located within the Office of the President. During the group's 128th meeting, it established a Research Group on International Scholarly and Cultural Activities, which held its first meeting at the Taipei Guest House on May 19, 1966. The group was considered part of the government's "Official Diplomacy and International Propaganda" work, and its membership included Wang Shih-chieh, Cheng Tien-fong, Chang Chi-yun, and Huang Shao-ku.[47] When it came to influence activities directed at the US, they specifically mentioned actions such as deciding who would attend large international conferences and forge bonds with foreign researchers and students who visited Taiwan and distributing Chinese-language textbooks to all American universities.[48] For example, the group targeted the August 1967 International Congress of Orientalists, writing, "Committee Member Milton Shieh will investigate the particulars of the conference and those in attendance, giving a report at the next meeting." As mentioned earlier, Kuo Ting-yee came under attack for having headed the group attending the conference. The Ministry of Education was tasked with working to influence researchers and students who visited Taiwan when it came to the question of Chinese-language textbooks, they pointed to the spread of the use of Pinyin (as employed by Communist China but not by the ROC) across American universities as a major problem.[49] The consulates general of the ROC in the US worked to confirm whether Chinese-language instructors at each university were using Pinyin-based textbooks.

On August 3, 1966, the Research Group on International Scholarly and Cultural Activities convened its second meeting, during which a member gave a report on the Fourth American Consular Conference.[50] The consulate staff members primarily met to discuss planning work for the 1967 Strength Project. The Strength Project was aimed at improving American understanding of China; resolving issues related to overseas Chinese residents, students, and scholars in the US; and seeking ways to inculcate in them a sense of loyalty to the government. Specifically, they planned to open bookstores in New York and other large cities to spread knowledge about China and hold conferences to discuss issues related to China in the eastern, central, and western US.[51] The ROC government would decide who could attend, ensuring that individuals from the PRC did not join the proceedings. Meanwhile, they chose five major conferences held by Beijing, to each of which they would send two individuals to offer refutations. The group

Table 1.2 Resolutions of the First Meeting of the Research Group on International Scholarly and Cultural Activities and Their Implementation

Resolution	Implemented by	Current progress
1. Publish a joint letter by ROC scholars in the *New York Times*	Government Information Office	Preparations complete
2. Encourage Chinese and foreign individuals to refute arguments for appeasement	Intermediary Group 4; Government Information Office	Complete
3. Urge American labor unions etc. to pay attention to correcting viewpoints on arguments for appeasement	Ministry of Foreign Affairs; Government Information Office	Complete
4. Compile and edit anti-American statements made by the Communist Bandits and their reactions to American hearings	Ministry of Foreign Affairs; Government Information Office	In progress
5. Promote understanding of and support for our steadfast opposition to there being "Two Chinas"	Ministry of Foreign Affairs	Continuing to strengthen implementation
6. Supplement investigations into international academic conferences	Academia Sinica; Ministry of Education	Awaiting survey report
7. Investigate particulars of the Congress of Orientalists	Committee Member Milton Hsieh	Complete
8. Survey and contact foreign researchers and students visiting Taiwan	Ministry of Education	To be reported on this meeting
9. Publish and distribute Chinese language textbooks	Ministry of Education	To be reported on this meeting

Source: Table compiled using information from "Guoji xueshi wenhua huodong yanjiu xiaozu di yici huiyi jueyi zhixing jindu biao" [Resolutions of the First Meeting of the Research Group on International Scholarly and Cultural Activities and their current progress], in "Guoji xueshu wenhua huodong yanjiu xiaozu," [MFAA] 1966, 11-13-07-02-050,11-INF-00263.

looked into inviting scholars from Hong Kong and Taiwan who were skilled in English to go on lecture tours across the US and even considered having scholars from the mainland engage in counterpropaganda activities. Furthermore, they planned on holding a Symposium on Chinese Issues in San Francisco.[52]

In a report to the Ministry of Foreign Affairs, the ROC Embassy in the US noted that America was "beset by an atmosphere of appeasement that

34   AREA STUDIES

grows heavier by the day."[53] Mentions of "appeasement" or an "atmosphere of
appeasement" referred to the fact that even though US official diplomatic
relations with the ROC were maintained, the US advanced at least some degree of contact with the PRC. Toward such atmospheres, the ROC Embassy
to the US noted that organizing and counseling nongovernmental organizations and taking every opportunity to oppose those US's "compromise"
with the PRC was effective at combating this "atmosphere of appeasement,"
and this task originally would be undertaken by "the Committee of One
Million." But because there were limits to this committee's activities, it
recommended the ROC Embassy to organize new groups and activities
involving overseas Chinese and ROC students and researchers that could
advance activities, like making speeches, publishing articles, and holding
symposia. This was the Strength Project, or "1967 Research Plan to Expand
Propaganda to the United States," which included specific decision points
on implementation, such as those listed in table 1.2.[54] From this, one can
understand precisely what was planned and to what extent it had been implemented. US-facing operations arose from the very same 1967 Michigan
Congress of Orientalists that had exposed Kuo to such severe criticism;
the links between government influence operations and attacks on Kuo are
thus ripe for future research.

   Finally, it should be noted that the ROC and its allies maintained a competi-
tive relationship when it came to influence activities. Somewhat later, in 1974,
the ROC government would come to pay particular attention to Japan's support
of Japanese research at the University of Washington. However, documents related to this Japanese support were part of a government file that also included
a proposal by George Taylor, close friend of Kuo Ting-yee, that called for the
establishment of a fund for Chinese studies at the University of Washington. In
short, the ROC saw Japan as a rival in influence operations in the US, while the
US was engaged in influence operations involving both Japan and the ROC.[55]

                                    CONCLUSION

The aim of this chapter has been to investigate American support for sinology
in Taiwan in the 1960s. It began by considering the support's significance for
Taiwan and the historical context in which it was interpreted in Taiwan. It then
argued that this sort of activity undertaken during the Cultural Cold War was
not merely a one-way influence operation by the US in Asia but was instead
part of a bilateral set of influence activities, with Taiwan seeking to influence
American sinology and shift Americans' understanding of China. From this
research, we can draw a few conclusions.

First, American support for Taiwanese sinology was the result of the work of a diverse set of actors and was directed at a number of different targets. The Ford Foundation's support for the Institute of Modern History was a massive undertaking and undoubtedly did much to lay the foundation for Taiwanese sinology. This can clearly be seen in scholarly development, the establishment of libraries and construction of library buildings, and the infrastructure established for archival organization and publication. One cannot deny the possibility that this also led to the spread of American conceptual research frameworks to Taiwan—an area worthy of further investigation. Until the 1970s, the Nankang School's approach to empiricism was still dominant, with its argument regarding modernization coming to the fore somewhat later, in the 1980s.[56] In addition, since organizations like the Institute of History of Philology received support for research on ancient history from the China Foundation for the Promotion of Education and Culture, one cannot overlook the fact that the Institute of Modern History was not the only organization to have received American support. Future research will analyze these issues from a comparative perspective.

Second, the support that the Ford Foundation and the Association for Asian Studies provided to Taiwan was also in part meant to help establish a base for American scholars to study the Chinese language and Chinese history in Taiwan. This was, at the very least, *one* of the main aims of the funding they provided. According to previous research, support for sinology in Hong Kong was aimed at information gathering, while in Japan it was aimed at supporting empirical research and stemming the spread of leftist interpretations of China's past and present. In Taiwan, by contrast, while information gathering and empirical research were not entirely absent from the list of goals, funding was primarily meant to help establish a base for American sinologists. This was especially the case for John K. Fairbank and his students.

In addition, the launch of the Ford Foundation's funding project shook the very foundations of the Institute of Modern History. This was not only because of disputes over the order in which researchers would be sent overseas but also because there was an internal struggle within the KMT—namely, over the differences that existed between the liberal and conservative factions of the party. From the perspective of the conservative faction, American scholars in favor of funding the Institute of Modern History, such as Harvard's Fairbank, appeared to be "Communist-leaning." Kuo Ting-yee, a liberal member of the KMT, was already at risk of being attacked by the conservatives. However, the conservatives also held serious doubts about Fairbank, who appeared to support both the normalization of US relations with the PRC and Taiwanese independence. In short, "America" was not at all monolithic, and thus, from the perspective of the ROC or the KMT, there existed multiple Americas. To the conservative faction of the KMT, there was a dangerous America that was developing a closer relationship with Beijing as well as a benign America that was not making any sort of rapprochement. In that regard, although the ROC at that time was under an authoritarian regime, there was still a certain diversity within the Kuomintang and the government, and this diversity created a complex relationship with the diversity within democratic America. Kuo, a liberal within the KMT, was suspected by the KMT conservatives of having a relationship with Fairbank, who was thought to be sympathetic to the CCP in the US. It was precisely because of this diversity that issues arose throughout the Ford Foundation's implementation of its support project, and it remained controversial until its conclusion. In the end, the diversity of "America" was reflected in fields related to learning and scholarship. From the perspective of those within a divided country between the ROC and the PRC, precisely who was involved had a major impact on how the project was evaluated, both by the government and by the foundation itself. Ties with the "enemies" were points of particular sensitivity—to the ROC, the Communist Party and the Taiwanese independence movements were enemies on two different fronts, and both "enemies" and "supporters" alike existed in "America." This chapter has shown that such a view was not imposed by the US as part of the Cultural Cold War but was instead constructed by those looking into the US from outside. Once the diversity of views within the Taiwanese side became entangled, the situation became even more complex. Within the Cultural Cold War, and especially in relation to learning, this complexity stood out. It was perhaps precisely because of this fact that there were certain circumstances under which the US was not able to easily achieve its own goals.

Furthermore, one cannot overlook the fact that this issue is not merely one of perspective—the ROC also actively worked to influence the US. This influence work was largely limited to lectures and other means of shaping public discourse, undertaken on a somewhat ad hoc basis, rather than long-term, systematic projects. Such activities were not solely undertaken for the sake of restraining or opposing the Communist Party of China and the Taiwan independence faction; the ROC also saw Japan and other allies as having become their competitors. Of course, when compared with the support that the US had offered Taiwan, the efficacy of Taiwan's influence operations, especially in relation to academia, was limited. However, it is assumed that such operations had a major impact on Chinese American researchers and on Chinese researchers engaged in activities such as giving lectures and presenting reports in the US.

It is possible that the critiques launched against Kuo Ting-yee in 1967 emerged as part of the ROC's influence operations on the US.

The Cultural Cold War was not a simple competition between countries or solely a strategy directed from the US to the rest of the world. One cannot see the same degree of complexity and diversity in either security agreements or economic arrangements as in the activities that this chapter has explored—a key feature of the "Cultural" Cold War.

NOTES

1. Kazuo Enoki, "Nihon no Tōyōgaku: Tōyō Bunko Gojū Shūnen ten ni yosete" [Oriental studies in Japan: On the occasion of the Fiftieth Anniversary Exhibition at Tōyō Bunko], *Yomiuri Shimbun*, evening edition, October 25, 1967.

2. "Ridai Kindai Keizaigaku Kenkyūjō nado ni 20 man doru: Bei Fōdo Zaidan" [$200,000 for the Center for Modern Economics at Rikkyo University et al.: The American Ford Foundation], *Mainichi Shimbun*, evening edition, February 9, 1967; "Kyōdai nado ni 3 oku en zōyo: Beikoku no Fōdo Zaidan" [300 million yen granted to Kyoto University and others: The American Ford Foundation], *Mainichi Shimbun*, evening edition, November 6, 1967. In addition, in 1964, support was also given to the Asian Productivity Organization.

3. See, for instance, Ono, "Chūgoku Gendai Kenkyū ni okeru anpo Taisei," 12–20; Kamachi, "Historical Consciousness and Identity," 981–94.

4. Ichihara, "Ajia zaidan o tsūjita nichibei tokushū kankei no keisei?," 308.

5. Ichihara, 313.

6. Ichihara, 309.

7. Eclipsing the "impact-response" paradigm, the rise of the "regional modernization" thesis at the Institute of Modern History in the 1980s was of much greater significance. It was only because of this rise that trends in American historiography gained a following at the institute. For more information, see Kawashima, "Chūgoku no Chūka Minkokushi Kenkyū." Chen Zhijie's article on the International Relations Research Institute at National Chengchi University, predecessor to the current Institute of International Relations, focuses on similar topics to the above article. Chen also draws comparisons with the Institute of Modern History, but his work is highly theoretical. See Chen, "Jiangou Xianghu Zhuguan de Xiangxiangti: Pouxi Lengzhan Qiyuan Shiqi de Guoji Guanxi Yanjiusuo ji qi Zhongguo Yanjiu (1953–1975)."

8. Wu, "Sengō Taiwan ni okeru Rokkuferā zaidan no enjō jigyō," 119–40.

9. Berghahn, *America and the Intellectual Cold Wars in Europe.*

10. McCarthy, "From Cold War to Cultural Development," 93–117.

11. Lin Ming-teh compared debates over the funding the Ford Foundation provided to Japan and Taiwan in his memoir detailing these events. The difference, he noted, was that opposition forces in Japan stopped the second round of funding from taking place, while they had been unable to do so in Taiwan. See "Records from the Interview with Mr. Lin Ming-the," in *Guo Tingyi Xiansheng Mensheng Gujiu Yiwang Lu* [Reminiscences of Mr. Kuo Ting-yee by his disciples and friends], Chen Yishen and Wang Jingling et al. (Taipei: Zhongyang Yanjiyuan Jindaishi Yanjiusuo, 2004), 285–86.

12. Regarding Kuo Ting-yee's standing in modern Chinese history and Chinese diplomatic history, see Kawashima, "Higashi Ajia Kokusai Seijishi: Chūgoku wo meguru Kokusai Seijishi to Chūgoku Gaikōshi," 75–95.

13. Chu Chia-hua (1893–1963) was a politician and a geologist in the ROC. He participated in the first meeting of UNESCO in 1945 as the first representative of Chinese delegation.

14. Zhang, *Guo Tingyi, Fei Zhengqing, Wei Muting*, 3.

15. Hsiao Kung-chuan (1897–1981) was a historian and scholar of political science and the "academician" of Academia Sinica. In late 1949, he moved to the University of Washington in Seattle.

16. As he was drawing up the application, Kuo Ting-yee sought the advice of George Taylor, C. Martin Wilbur, and John Fairbank. Fairbank thought that the reorganized archives should include Sino-Japanese relations in addition to Sino-Russian and Sino-American relations. Wilbur thought that the country's internal affairs should also be included, rather than being constrained to diplomatic history. (See Zhang, *Guo Tingyi Fei Zhengqing, Wei Muting*, 5.) John Everton, who was head of the Overseas Training and Research Center at the Ford Foundation, and vice-director A. Doak Barnett traveled to Taipei and visited Academia Sinica as part of the evaluation process. They also asked Taylor, Wilbur, and Fairbank for their opinions, and Albert Feuerwerker of the University of Michigan provided an additional recommendation. (See Zhang, 6). Although the foundation approved the application, Fairbank thought the amount initially proposed to be too little, and he sought an increase that was ultimately granted, boosting the Phase 1 funding from US$100,000 to just over US$150,000. (See Zhang, 7.)

17. Wu Hsiang-hsiang (1912–2007) was a historian and professor at National Taiwan University. In 1962, he was stripped of his Kuomintang (KMT) party membership because some articles in a volume he edited were criticized as anti-KMT. He moved to the US in 1975. The KMT revoked Wu's party membership in November 1962, and he subsequently left Taiwan. The *History of the Kuomintang*, published by the Western Hills Group, attacked Chiang Kai-shek for having been a member of the Communist Party. In his preface to this book, Wu defended the accuracy of the materials it used, but he was forced to leave the country, likely

because this information was considered humiliating to the national leadership. See Lee, *Bashi Yiwang*, 97.

18. Hu Shih (1891–1962) was an essayist, literary scholar, philosopher, and Chinese ambassador to the US from 1938 to 1942. Hu was a professor at Peking University and its president from 1945 to 1948. He moved to the US in 1949 and then to Taiwan in 1957. His political stance was considered liberal under KMT's authoritarian rules, but he did not have a real political power against the KMT.

19. Zhang, 19. Yao had grown up in the same town and was an old acquaintance of Kuo's. His attack on Kuo is thought to have happened because *he* was not the one entrusted with distributing Ford Foundation funds. See "Records of Interviews with Ms. Wang Ping," in Chen and Wang et al., *Guo Tingyi Xiansheng Mensheng Gujiu Yiwang Lu*, 119.

20. "Wang Ermin Xiansheng Fangwen Jilu" [Records of interviews with Wang Erh-min], in Zhongyang Yanjiuyuan Jindaishi Yanjiusuo, *Jindaishisuo Yi Jiazi: Tongren Yiwang Lu*, 170–71. Hu's efforts to convince Kuo to stay at the beginning of January 1962 are recalled in his long-form chronological biography. A passage from January 7, 1962, notes, "After ten, Yang Shuren visited, and we talked about Kuo Ting-yee's resignation, Hu Shih decided to send Yang in his stead to persuade Kuo. Yang suggested that Hu forget about the whole affair and said that he would take full responsibility for handling it." One can see how this event had a large impact on those surrounding Hu Shih at the time. See Hu, *Hu Shizhi Xiansheng Nianpu Changbian Chugao Bubian*, 613. Regarding Wilbur's activities, see "Jia Tingshi Xiansheng Fangwen Jilu" [Records of an interview with Chia Ting-shih], in Chen and Wang et al., *Guo Tingyi Xiansheng*, 335–36.

21. Zhang, 3–4.

22. Zhang, 11.

23. Zhang, 15–16.

24. Fairbank was president of the Association for Asian Studies from 1958 to 1959. In 1959, Fairbank, Wilbur, and Arthur Steiner of the University of Southern California held the Gould House Conference under the AAS banner. There they stressed the importance of sinology and called for a shared set of institutions for the study of China across the US. The Joint Committee on Contemporary China was one of the groups formed as a result. The Ford Foundation served as the sponsor for the Gould House Conference. See Zhang, *Guo Tingyi, Fei Zhengqing, Wei Muting*, 57–60.

25. Republic of China Embassy in the United States to the Ministry of Foreign Affairs, "*Meiguo Yazhou Yanjiuhui ni zai Tai sheli Hanxue ziliao yu yanjiu gongju fuwu zhongxin*" [The American Association for Asian Studies plans to establish Chinese studies materials and Research Aids Service Center in Taiwan], received April 14, 1964, Republic of China Ministry of Foreign Affairs

Archives, Institute of Modern History, Academia Sinica (hereafter MFAA), 11–07-02-17-09-017, 11-NAA-08020.

26. Ibid.

27. The Committee on American Library Resources on the Far East (CALRFE) may have been behind the AAS's proposal. See Eugene Wu, *Meiguo Dongya Tushuguan Fazhanshi ji qita* [A history of the development of East Asian libraries in the United States, among other things] (Taipei: Lianjing chuban shiye gongsi, 2016), 110.

28. Zhang, 25.

29. Zhang, 25.

30. The records of these hearings have also been published in Japanese. See Nozue, *Chūgoku hondo ni kansuru Beikoku no seisaku*. However, criticism of Fairbank first began in Taiwan. For more on Xu Gaoruan of the Institute of History and Philology, see Yeh, "Xu Gaoruan yu 1960 Niandai Taiwan de Maiguo Kongsu." Fairbank's "New Thinking about China," *Atlantic Monthly*, March 10, 1966, also caused a stir in Taiwan. Fairbank argued for the acceptance of the ROC's sovereignty over Taiwan but posited that Taiwan should become an independent country on its own based on the principle of national self-determination. This was taken as a slight to the existence of the ROC. Investigating the connections between Fairbank's approach toward China and Taiwan and Henry Kissinger's policies toward both is an important topic for future research.

31. "Kuo Ting-yee Persuades John K. Fairbank," *Economic Daily News*, August 22, 1967.

32. Li Dongfang, "The Whole Truth about the Chinese Representative Group to the 27th Congress of Orientalists." In fact, Kuo had made no such agreement to exchange diplomatic archives for funding. This was likely a misunderstanding—or intentional misrepresentation—of the real question as to whether microfilm copies of archival documents should be sent to individuals who make requests. Zhang Pengyuan argues that Wilbur had planned for the acquisition of microfilm documents as part of the budget, while Fairbank was focused on making Taipei a base for American researchers. Thus, Fairbank thought that individuals should read documents in Taipei rather than rely on microfilm. On this issue, see "Suowei an" [microfilm problem] in Zhang, 35–43.

33. Wei Tao-ming to Zhou Shujie, "Fei Zhengqing" [John K. Fairbank], May 17, 1968, MFAA, 11–07-02-06-02-167, 11-NAA-02098.

34. Ibid. The file includes a special series of articles on Fairbank apart from the twenty-fourth issue of the magazine, including parts of the twenty-fifth issue.

35. The Taipei Language Institute had an agreement with the US State Department to provide its officials in Taiwan with language training. The American Embassy in China, American Military Assistance Advisory Group,

United States Taiwan Defense Command, and family members were also included. See the organization's website at http://www.tli.com.tw/tw/about/golden_ages.aspx.

36. Interestingly, the Fairbanks had known Yeh since their time in Beiping (Beijing) twenty years prior. Six years before the controversy began, Fairbank had made inquiries about visiting Taiwan and received help in obtaining a visa. Fairbank's primary aim in visiting Taiwan at that time was to meet with his old friends, such as Li Jizhi and Dong Zuobin. After he arrived, he went on to have a lengthy conversation with Yeh. George Yeh to Huang Shao-ku, "Renwu juan" [Individual portrait], received by the Ministry of Foreign Affairs March 24, 1959, MFAA, 11–07-02-06-02-020, 11-NAA-01934.

37. Thomas Liao (1910–1986) was the leader of the Taiwanese independence movement that established the Provisional Government of the Republic of Taiwan in 1955. He later adopted an anti-Communist stance and renounced his independence movement, thereby receiving a full pardon from Chiang Kai-shek.

38. George Yeh to Huang Shao-ku, "Renwu juan."

39. Fairbank served as a fellow twice in the 1950s. See the fellowship's website at https://www.gf.org/fellows/all-fellows/john-king-fairbank/.

40. George Yeh to Huang Shao-ku, "Renwu juan."

41. "Zhang Pengyuan Xiansheng Fangwen Jilu" [Records of interviews with Mr. Zhang Pengyuan], in Chen and Wang et al., *Guo Tingyi Xiansheng*, 267.

42. Ying-shih Yu, "Yu Xu" [Yu's preface], in Zhang P., *Guo Tingyi, Fei Zhengqing, Wei Muting*, vi.

43. Zhang Pengyuan bases this on the account of Liu Zhen, who was the head of National Taiwan Normal University. See "Fang Liu Zhen xiansheng tan Guo Tingyi suo zhang," in S. Chen, *Zou Guo Youhuan de Sui Yue*, 154. See also Zhang P., *Guo Tingyi, Fei Zhengqing, Wei Muting*, 31–33; "Zhang Pengyuan Xiansheng Fangwen Jilu," 267. However, Wang Ping expressed doubts about Zhang's explanation. Even if a researcher was suppressed during the White Terror, she argues, the situation would have been dealt with in a careful manner. Though his name may have been added to a block list, he would not have suddenly faced a higher degree of personal risk. See "Wang Ping nüshi fangwen jilu" [Records of conversations with Ms. Wang Ping], in Chen and Wang et al., *Guo Tingyi Xiansheng*, 128.

44. "Report of the Director," Thirty-Fourth Annual Meeting, September 24, 1965, in "Zhonghua jiaoyu wenhua jijin dongshihui" [China Foundation for the Promotion of Education and Culture], MFAA, 11–07-02-17-05-010, 11-NAA-07627.

45. One important group that included members of both houses of Congress was the Committee of One Million. See Bachrack, *Committee of One Million*.

46. Regarding the content of these speeches, see the transcripts in "Jiang furen zai Mei yanlun" [Madame Chiang's speeches in the US], MFAA, 11–13-01-02-019, 11-INF-00005.

47. Wang had experience as the minister of foreign affairs and Huang as the minister of education. All four were minister-level members.

48. "Guoji xueshu wenhua huodong yanjiu xiaozu di yici huiyi yicheng" [Agenda for the First Meeting of the Research Group on International Scholarly and Cultural Activities], June 1966, in "Guoji xueshu wenhua huodong yanjiu xiaozu" [Research Group on International Scholarly and Cultural Activities], Ministry of Foreign Affairs Archives, Academia Historica (hereafter MFAH), 11-13-07-02-050, 11-INF-00263. A meeting was held on influence activities directed at foreigners who visited Taiwan. They broadcast targeted television programs and special exhibitions, in addition to creating a system of foreign student advisers for exchange students. The advisers were charged with working with and giving guidance to exchange students, and they organized exchange opportunities and farm homestays with Taiwanese students. See "Cujin zhu Tai geguo lingshi renyuan, jizhe, jiaoshou ji xuesheng zhi youhao guanxi yantao huiyi jilu" [Proceedings of the Workshop on Promoting Friendship with Diplomats, Journalists, Professors, and Students from Abroad], July 8, 1966, in "Guoji xueshu wenhua huodong yanjiu xiaozu," 1977, MFAA, 11–33-02-07-014, 11-INF-00263.

49. "Xuanchuan waijiao zonghe yanjiu zu guoji xueshu wenhua huodong yanjiu xiaozu di yici huiyi jilu" [Proceedings of the First Meeting of the Research Group on International Scholarly and Cultural Activities, Combined Propaganda and Foreign Relations Research Group], May 19, 1966, in "Guoji xueshu wenhua huodong yanjiu xiaozu," 1977, MFAA, 11–33-02-07-014, 11-INF-00263. Regarding the issue of Chinese-language textbooks, see "Zhu Meilijian hezhongguo dashiguan zhi benbu" [From the ROC Embassy in the United States to the Ministry of Foreign Affairs], March 2, 1966, in the same file.

50. "Di si ci zhu mei lingshi huiyi zonghe baogao" [Comprehensive report of the Fourth American Consular Conference], June 1966, in "Guoji xueshu wenhua huodong yanjiu xiaozu," MFAA, 11–13-07-02-050, 11-INF-00263.

51. "56 nian du qiang an gongzuo jihua" [Planning work for the 1967 Strength Project], June 1966, in "Guoji xueshu wenhua huodong yanjiu xiaozu," MFAA, 11–13-07-02-050, 11-INF-00263.

52. "Juban Jinshan 'Zhongguo Wenti Taolunhui' jihua gangyao" [Outline of the plan to hold a Symposium on Chinese Issues in San Francisco], June 1966, in "Guoji xueshu wenhua huodong yanjiu xiaozu," MFAA, 11–13-07-02-050, 11-INF-00263.

53. "Zhonghua Minguo zhu Meilijian hezhongguo dashiguan zhi waijiaobu cizhang" [From the ROC Embassy in the US to the vice minister of foreign

affairs], July 16, 1966, in "Guoji xueshu wenhua huodong yanjiu xiaozu," MFAH, 11–13-07-02-050, 11-INF-00263.

54. "Di si ci zhu mei lingshi huiyi zonghe baogao" [Comprehensive report of the Fourth American Consular Conference], June 1966, in "Guoji xueshu wenhua huodong yanjiu xiaozu," MFAA, 11–13-07-02-050, 11-INF-00263.

55. Kenneth B. Pyle of the University of Washington also began publishing the *Journal of Japanese Studies* in 1974. For the ROC response to this, see "Zhong Mei wenjiao jiaoliu" [Sino-American cultural and educational exchanges], 1974, MFAA, 11–13-07-02-050, 020–050207.

56. Nankang School is a name based on the location of Academia Sinica—an eastern area of Taipei city. This school called for maintaining a certain amount of distance from the official history of the KMT, strongly rejecting historical interpretation, and spending a significant amount of effort on reading historical materials and understanding the relationships between them. This was different from the "empiricism" the Ford Foundation was looking for when it provided support to Tōyō Bunko, but it bears a resemblance in terms of how it sought to separate itself from political ideology.

REFERENCES

Bachrack, Stanley D. *The Committee of One Million: "China Lobby" Politics, 1953–1971.* New York: Columbia University Press, 1976.

Berghahn, Volker R. *America and the Intellectual Cold Wars in Europe: Shepard Stone between Philanthropy, Academy, and Diplomacy.* Princeton, NJ: Princeton University Press, 2002.

Chen, Sanjing, ed. *Zou Guo Youhuan de Sui Yue* [Walking through the years of the storms]. Taipei: Zhongyang Yanjiuyuan Jindaishi Yanjiusuo, 1995.

Chen, Yishen, and Jingling Wang et al., eds. *Guo Tingyi Xiansheng Mensheng Gujiu Yiwang Lu* [Reminiscences of Mr. Kuo Ting-yee by his disciples and friends], Taipei: Zhongyang Yanjiyuan Jindaishi Yanjiusuo, 2004.

Chen, Zhijie. "Jiangou Xianghu Zhuguan de Xiangxiangti: Pouxi Lengzhan Qiyuan Shiqi de Guoji Guanxi Yanjiusuo ji qi Zhongguo Yanjiu (1953–1975)" [Constructing an intersubjective imaginality: Analyzing Taiwan's Institute of International Relations and its China studies during the early Cold War (1953–1975)]. *Renwen ji Shehui Kexue Jikan* [Journal of social sciences and philosophy] 28, no. 1 (2016): 61–104.

Chung, Moon Sang. "Cong 'chongji-fanying lun' dao 'shidai huanjing-shiying lun': meiguo xuewen moshi de chuanbo yu Taiwan zhi zhongguo jindai shi yanjiu" [From "impact-response theory" to "era environment-adaptation approach": Taiwanese studies of modern Chinese history and Cultural Cold War]. *Chung*

Kuk Hak Po [Korean Society for Chinese Studies, *Journal of Chinese Studies*] 87 (March 2019): 199–217.

Evans, Paul M. *John Fairbank and the American Understanding of Modern China.* Oxford: Blackwell, 1988.

Fairbank, John K. *Chinabound: A Fifty-Year Memoir.* New York: Harper Colophon Books, 1982.

Hu, Songping, ed. *Hu Shizhi Xiansheng Nianpu Changbian Chugao Bubian* [Supplemental edit to the full-length chronology of Mr. Hu Shih]. Taipei: Lianjing Chubanshe, 2015.

Ichihara, Maiko. "Ajia zaidan o tsūjita nichibei tokushū kankei no keisei? Nihon no gendai Chūgoku kenkyū ni taisuru CIA no sofutopawā kōshi" [Japan-US special relations through the Asia Foundation? CIA's exercise of soft power over contemporary China studies in Japan]. *Nagoya Daigaku Hōsei Ronshū* [Nagoya journal of law and politics] 260 (2015): 299–318.

Kamachi, Noriko. "Historical Consciousness and Identity." *Journal of Asian Studies* 34, no. 4 (August 1975): 981–94.

Kawashima, Shin. "Higashi Ajia Kokusai Seijishi: Chūgoku wo meguru Kokusai Seijishi to Chūgoku Gaikoshi" [The History of International Relations in East Asia: The History of International Relations in China and Chinese Diplomatic History]. In *Nihon no Kokusai Sijigaku* [The Academic Trend of International Politics in Japan], edited by JAIR (Japan Association of International Relations), Kyoto:Yūhikaku, 2009, 75–95.

Kawashima, Shin. "Chūgoku no Chūka Minkokushi Kenkyū: *Chūka Minkoku Sentai Shi* no ichi tsuke ni tsuite kangaeru" [Chinese research on the history of the Republic of China: Thinking about the positioning of *Chūka Minkoku Sentai Shi* (Special topics in the history of the Republic of China)]. In *Chūka Minkoku Kenkyū no Dōkō: Chūgoku to Nihon to Chūgoku Kindai Shi Rikai* [Trends in research on the Republic of China: Chinese and Japanese understandings of modern Chinese history], edited by Shin Kawashima and Motoya Nakamura. Kyoto: Kōyō Shobō, 2019, 37–54.

Kawashima, Shin, and Motoya Nakamura. *Chūka Minkoku Kenkyū no Dōkō: Chūgoku to Nihon to Chūgoku Kindai Shi Rikai* [Trends in research on the Republic of China: Chinese and Japanese understandings of modern Chinese history]. Kyoto: Kōyō Shobō, 2019.

Lee, En-han. *Bashi Yiwang: Guojia yu Jindai Waijiao Shixue* [Autobiography of Dr. Lee En-han]. Taipei: Xiucheng Chuban, 2011.

Li, Dongfang, "The Whole Truth about the Chinese Representative Group to the 27th Congress of Orientalists," *Zhonghua Zazhi* 5, no. 5, 1967, 8–13.

Lin, Ming-the. "Records from the Interview with Mr. Lin Ming-the." In Yishen Chen and Jingling Wang et al., eds. *Guo Tingyi Xiansheng Mensheng Gujiu*

Yiwang Lu [Reminiscences of Mr. Kuo Ting-yee by his disciples and friends]. Taipei: Zhongyang Yanjiyuan Jindaishi Yanjiusuo, 2004, 285–86.

Lu, Baoqian, ed. *Kuo Tingyi Xiansheng Shuxin xuan* [Selected correspondence by Mr. Kuo Ting-yee]. Taipei: Zhongyang Yanjiuyuan Jindaishi Yanjiusuo Tekan (3), Zhongyang Yanjiyuan Jindaishi Yanjiusuo, 1995.

Lü, Shiqiang. "Guo Suozhang Bilulanlü Chuangsuo yu Cizhi Fengbo" [Director Kuo's tribulations in establishing the institute and the tempest over his resignation]. In *Guo Tingyi Xiansheng Mensheng Gujiu Yiwang Lu* [Reminiscences of Mr. Kuo Ting-yee by his disciples and friends], by Yishen Chen and Jingling Wang et al., 511–42. Taipei: Zhongyang Yanjiu Yuan Jindai Shi Yanjiusuo, 2004.

McCarthy, Kathleen D. "From Cold War to Cultural Development: The International Cultural Activities of the Ford Foundation, 1950–1980." *Daedalus*, Winter 1987, 116, no.1, Philanthropy, Patronage, Politics, 93–117.

Nozue, Kenzō, trans. *Chūgoku hondo ni kansuru Beikoku no seisaku (jō): Beikoku Jōin Gaikō Iinkai Kōchōkai kiroku* [US policy with respect to mainland China, records of hearings by the Senate Foreign Relations Committee, vol. 1]. *Kokusai mondai shirīzu* vol. 52. Tokyo: Nihon kokusai mondai kenkyūjō, 1966.

Ono, Shinji. "Chūgoku Gendai Kenkyū ni okeru anpo Taisei" [Security arrangements in research on modern China]. In Atarashi rekishigakuno tameni [For new historical science], vol. 77. Kyoto: Minka (April 9, 1961): 12–20.

Wu, Lin-Chun. "Sengō Taiwan ni okeru Rokkuferā zaidan no enjō jigyō" [Aid work undertaken by the Rockefeller Foundation in postwar Taiwan]. In *Bunka Reisen no Jidai: Amerika to Ajia* [Decentering the Cultural Cold War: The US and Asia], edited by Toshihiko Kishi and Yuka Tsuchiya, 119–40. Tokyo: Kokusai Shoin, 2009.

Yeh, Nai Chih. "Xu Gaoruan yu 1960 Niandai Taiwan de Maiguo Kongsu" [Xu Gaoruan and the 1960s: Taiwan's treason trial]. *Shi Yun* 15 (June 2011), 99–131.

Zhang, Pengyuan. *Guo Tingyi, Fei Zhengqing, Wei Muting: Taiwan yu Meiguo Xueshu Jiaoliu ge an Chutan* [Preliminary exploring of triangular partnership: Kuo Ting-yee, John K. Fairbank, C. Martin Wilbur, and their contribution to Taiwan-US academic exchange]. Taipei: Zhongyang Yanjiyuan Jindaishi Yanjiusuo, 1997.

Zhang, Yang. *Lengzhan yu xueshu: Meiguo de zhongguoxue 1949–1972* [The Cold War and academics: Chinese studies in the United States, 1949–1972]. Beijing: Zhongguo Shehui Kexue Chubanshe, 2019.

Zhongyang Yanjiuyuan Jindaishi Yanjiusuo [Institute of Modern History, Academia Sinica]. *Jindaishisuo Yi Jiazi: Tongren Yiwang Lu* [Sixty years of the Institute of Modern History: The reminiscences of colleagues and friends]. Taipei: Zhongyang Yanjiuyuan Jindaishi Yanjiusuo, 2015.

———. *Zhongyang Yanjiuyuan Jindaishi Yanjiusuo Sanshi nian Shigao* [A draft history of the past thirty years of the Institute of Modern History, Academia Sinica]. Taipei: Zhongyang Yanjiuyuan, 1985.

AUTHOR BIOS

SHIN KAWASHIMA is Professor of International Relations at the University of Tokyo. He authored *China in the 21st Century* (2016) and *Frontier of China* (2017), among others, and edited *Xi Jinping's China* (2022) and many other volumes.

GEORGE REMISOVSKY is a PhD candidate in the Department of History at Yale University. His research currently focuses on the interactions between civil law and state-society relations in nineteenth- and twentieth-century China and Japan.

TWO

—ɯ—

COLD WAR COLLABORATIONS

Japanese Studies in the United States, 1945–60

MIRIAM KINGSBERG KADIA

INTRODUCTION: THE FIRST GENERATION
OF JAPANESE STUDIES

The study of Japan in the United States largely took shape during the initial phase of the Cold War (ca. 1945–60). As the traditional field genealogy narrates, a small cadre of American men were trained to read and speak Japanese during World War II (1941–45) to serve as intelligence officers and interpreters in the enemy language. After working for the US occupation of Japan between 1945 and 1952, they returned to the academy with the interest, background, and connections needed to develop Japanese studies as a discipline. Today, some of the best-remembered individuals who followed this trajectory include sociologist Marion J. Levy Jr. (1918–2002); economists Leon Hollerman (1916–2006) and Raymond Vernon (1913–99); anthropologists Richard K. Beardsley (1918–78) and Robert J. Smith (1927–2016); political scientists Robert Scalapino (1919–2011) and Robert E. Ward (1916–2009); literary scholars William Theodore de Bary (1919–2017), Donald Keene (1922–2019), and Edward Seidensticker (1921–2007); and historians F. Hilary Conroy (1919–2015), Marius B. Jansen (1922–2000), and Thomas C. Smith (1916–2004).

In one of the first attempts to narrate the history of Japanese studies, Jansen emphasized, "The contribution of the Japanese academy to American Japan Studies cannot be omitted from any discussion of the development of Japanology in the United States."[1] However, for students of Jansen and his contemporaries, admiration for their teachers tended to overwhelm remembrance of this legacy. Today early Cold War US scholars are generally regarded as intrepid explorers of an intellectual terra incognita, and their veneration as lone heroes obscures their reliance on knowledge produced by Japanese experts and their collaboration with Japan's early postwar academic establishment. Shifting the focus from the personalities to the process of research, this article uses the archival materials of American scholars of Japan to draw attention to the importance of Japanese contributions to the initial phase of the development of Japanese studies in the United States. In the years after 1945, the American understanding of Japan stood atop a foundation assembled by Japanese experts and supported by Japanese translators, interpreters, and field coordinators.

Cooperation between American academics, representing a victorious power, and their Japanese counterparts, shamed by defeat and dogged by their complicity in the prewar order, did not take place on equal terms. US scholars did not generally venture to Japan, as they so often did among Native Americans and colonized peoples, to study "primitivity." Nonetheless, World War II represented the culmination of decades of explicit racism and virulent hate on both sides. While Japan's surrender blunted the most visceral aversions, bitterness lingered. Postwar American sentiments often reflected a sense of superiority and paternalism toward the former enemy, famously compared to a boy of twelve by occupation chief General Douglas A. MacArthur (1880–1964).[2]

Equally significantly, binational intellectual collaboration was both nourished and constrained by the project of perpetuating US global hegemony in the opening phases of the Cold War. To be sure, many American scholars actively resisted or simply denied the intrusion of state power into their work. Yet whether they acknowledged it or not, their research was enabled and deeply informed by, first, the formal condition of US authority over Japan and, then, the lasting impact of that control after the occupation had ended. Even more insidious, perhaps, was the "soft power" of the ideals that American academics brought to Japan and demanded that their Japanese colleagues uphold as a condition of recognition. Under the banner of the purported US values of democracy, capitalism, and peace, early postwar scholars constructed an intellectual network that allowed Japanese studies to flourish on both sides of the Pacific.

CREATING A CORPS OF AMERICAN SCHOLARS OF JAPAN

Japan, unlike most of the non-West, did not become a colony or semi-colony during the nineteenth century. As a result, none of the great powers had an instrumental reason (or opportunity) to study its culture or history, and the development of Japanese studies in most of Europe and the United States lagged behind the consolidation of knowledge of other non-Western societies. Even in the first half of the twentieth century, courses on Japan remained almost unheard of in American secondary schools. At the university level, faculty born and educated in Japan spearheaded the study of their nation at a handful of institutions. These included Yoshio Kuno (1865–1941) at Berkeley, Kan'ichi Asakawa (1873–1948) at Yale, Masaharu Anesaki (1873–1949) at Harvard, Ryūsaku Tsunoda (1877–1964) at Columbia, Daisetsu Teitarō Suzuki (D. T. Suzuki, 1870–1966) at Chicago, and Tasaku Harada (1863–1940) at the University of Hawai'i.[3] By the time of the Great Depression of the 1930s, however, "new subjects of study which meant new burdens on the budget were not welcomed."[4] As a result, on the eve of Pearl Harbor, "few universities offered instruction in the Japanese language, and fewer still offered more than a handful of courses on Japanese history, society, or culture. The available courses were frequently taught by non-specialists unable to read Japanese."[5] Aside from a certain antiquarian interest on the part of individuals and organizations such as the American Oriental Society, "American education of course bred educated Americans who saw no reason to pay attention to Eastern Asia."[6]

As a result of this situation, before World War II only a handful of Americans had experience in studying Japan. Many were missionaries who traveled to the archipelago in pursuit of converts. They, and their Japan-reared children, were responsible for the relatively large number of dissertations on Japanese religions written at US universities in the late nineteenth and early twentieth centuries.[7] Edwin O. Reischauer (1910–90), the son of Presbyterian missionaries, produced a study and translation of a travelogue of Tang-era China by the ninth-century itinerant Japanese Buddhist monk Ennin. Reischauer's brother, Robert K. Reischauer (1907–37), also worked on early Japanese history. John Whitney Hall (1916–97), Roger F. Hackett (1922–2017), and Donald H. Shively (1921–2005) grew up in missionary families in Japan and subsequently pursued careers in Japanese history and literary studies at American universities.

Quakers were among the most active seekers of Christian converts in early twentieth-century Japan. Hugh Borton (1903–95) traveled to the country to spread the faith in 1928. He later earned a doctoral degree at the University of Leiden with a dissertation on peasant rebellion in early modern Japan. A junior colleague observed that the study remained "the only substantial work on the subject for the better part of the next fifty years."[8] During the early 1940s, Borton gave lectures on Japanese history and culture to army officers stationed in Charlottesville, Virginia, to prepare them to serve the forthcoming occupation. He later worked on a draft of the San Francisco Treaty, which was signed in 1951 and set the terms of peace between Japan and the United States after

World War II. In the postwar period, Borton continued developing Japanese studies as a faculty member at Columbia. He ended his career as the president of Haverford College, a Quaker institution of higher learning.[9]

Gordon Bowles (1904–91), another Quaker missionary who was to assist in the wartime and postwar development of Japanese studies, was born into a Friends family that had settled in Japan four years before his birth. Educated through high school in Japan, Bowles attended a Quaker college, followed by graduate school at the University of Pennsylvania and at Harvard. With no Japanese studies programs then available, he specialized in Chinese anthropology, carrying out fieldwork in mainland China. A conscientious objector, Bowles eschewed combat duty during World War II but put his knowledge of Asia to use on the Board of Economic Warfare in Washington, DC. During the occupation, he returned to Japan to work on the reform of the national education system. Afterward, he became a professor of anthropology at Syracuse University.[10]

A handful of exceptional women also spearheaded the early development of Japanese studies in the United States. Eleanor Hadley (1916–2007) took advantage of an unusual opportunity to visit Japan during her junior year of college in 1936 and subsequently spent eighteen months there learning the language. Upon her return to the United States, she enrolled in graduate school in economics at the University of Washington at Seattle and at Harvard. After the imperial attack on Pearl Harbor, she was recruited by the Research and Analysis Branch of the US Office of Strategic Services. During the occupation, she developed economic plans for Japan, focusing on antitrust and antimonopoly legislation. Hadley ultimately became a professor of economics at Smith College and at George Washington University.[11]

Like Hadley, John Maki (1909–2006) had the unusual credential of prewar training in Japan. Maki was born to Japanese parents in the United States but was adopted in infancy by an American couple of Scottish ancestry. He learned Japanese in graduate school and studied Japanese literature on a Japanese government fellowship at Tokyo Imperial University (the leading institution of higher education in Japan) in the late 1930s. Upon repatriation, Maki worked as a lecturer in Oriental studies at the University of Washington at Seattle (where he briefly taught Hadley).[12] In 1942, he and his wife were dispatched to a relocation center to await internment as "enemy aliens" under the infamous Executive Order 9066. He gained release to translate Japanese propaganda for the Federal Communications Commission in Washington, DC. After the war, Maki worked for the Supreme Commander of the Allied Powers, or SCAP (an acronym applied to the entire occupation bureaucracy) before enrolling in a

PhD program in government at Harvard. He later became a noted scholar of Japanese politics and constitutionalism.[13]

Japanese ancestry like Maki's was not uncommon among early Cold War pioneers of Japanese studies in the United States. Key Kobayashi (1922–92) was born in California to immigrant parents and spent his early years in Japan before returning to his birthplace for school. He grew up speaking both Japanese and English. Kobayashi matriculated at Berkeley in 1940 but was forced to withdraw due to the internment of Japanese and Japanese American citizens. Drafted in 1944, he trained as a translator; subsequently, he served in the occupation. Upon returning to the US, he studied political science at Berkeley and Columbia, eventually becoming assistant director of the Japanese collection at the Library of Congress.[14]

A few remarkable individuals followed more idiosyncratic paths to the study of Japan. After dropping out of Columbia, Oklahoma-born Faubion Bowers (1917–99) whimsically boarded a steamship across the Pacific and enrolled in a Japanese-language school alongside a handful of American missionaries. He later remembered, "My year alone in Japan with the Japanese, when there were still rickshaws and still geishas and . . . the Sumida-gawa [river] was not a roadway, is what changed my life."[15] Bowers repatriated and was drafted just before the bombing of Pearl Harbor. When the military learned of his Japanese-language proficiency, he was sent to Australia to work in intelligence. After the war, he served as secretary to General MacArthur. An expert in Japanese theater and music, Bowers is today remembered as "the man who saved kabuki" for having defended the art when SCAP considered banning it for its alleged militarist overtones.[16]

Emerging from the diversity of midcentury pioneers of Japanese studies was a common denominator: the revolutionary impact of the outbreak of war between Japan and the United States. World War II both exposed American ignorance of Japan and created an unprecedented demand for information about the country. The *Far Eastern Quarterly*, an academic journal founded in 1941, produced a stream of articles with background information for policymakers, under titles such as "The Role of the Shan States in the Japanese Conquest of Burma" and "Origin of Japanese Interests in Manchuria."[17] The US government also became involved in knowledge production. The Office of War Information (OWI) was established in June 1942 to take on the tasks of analyzing foreign news reports and generating international and domestic propaganda. Among its most renowned employees were John F. Embree (1908–50), author of the only prewar ethnographic field study of Japan, and Columbia anthropologist

Ruth Benedict (1887–1948), who wrote the famed analysis *The Chrysanthemum and the Sword: Patterns of Japanese Culture* (1946).[18]

Meanwhile, the US military assembled a network of language academies to supplement the slender ranks of Japanese speakers. During the early 1940s, nearly eight thousand elite recruits undertook an intensive twelve-month language program at the University of Michigan at Ann Arbor, the University of Colorado Boulder, or elsewhere in preparation for service as intelligence officers, interpreters, and occupation attachés. Although the majority of trainees were male, sixty-eight women also completed the course, while others assisted in various capacities.[19] Eleanor Jorden (1920–2009) was a graduate student in linguistics at Yale when she was asked to supervise a Japanese-language program for army officers. Those who used her textbook included Robert J. Smith, who subsequently became an anthropologist and her colleague at Cornell.[20] In the late 1940s, Jorden began a dissertation on syntax in modern colloquial Japanese. She became the first woman to secure permission from SCAP to carry out fieldwork in occupied Japan. Jorden eventually went on to a long and distinguished career in Japanese linguistics and language pedagogy.[21]

By the end of the war, the United States had built up a substantial cadre of Japanese speakers eager to learn about the defeated nation. Together with Japanese colleagues, this generation would shape the development of Japanese studies in the United States in its formative stage.

THE IMPORTANCE OF JAPANESE KNOWLEDGE

The foundation of early postwar American knowledge of Japan was laid in Japan, which had a long tradition of self-study dating back to the first written texts. During the early modern period (1600–1868), the long-standing emphasis on philology, or the close reading of classic works, came to be supplemented by a focus on empirical knowledge.[22] This methodological shift established the groundwork for the reception of Western-style social science and humanities disciplines in the late nineteenth century. At this time, Japanese scholars embraced the procedural, theoretical, and stylistic conventions of their European and American counterparts. They built universities, museums, scientific institutions, and professional societies to conduct research and founded journals, monograph series, and academic publishing houses to disseminate the output.[23]

Japanese scholars' growing fluency in the international norms of credible knowledge formation enabled them to publicize their work beyond Japan. Prewar Japanese academics participated in foreign conferences, including those hosted by the Institute of Pacific Relations (IPR, an international forum engaging the nations of the Pacific Rim, founded in 1925). US journals such as the *Far Eastern Quarterly* reviewed select Japanese history and social science monographs. However, most American scholars encountered the vast reserves of Japanese research during or after the occupation. "I was astounded upon coming here to discover how much good work has been done by Japanese anthropologists that few of us know about and even fewer of us can read," marveled one social scientist.[24] Another anticipated, "When thoroughly disseminated ... [imperial scholarship] will give Westerners nearly as satisfactory an understanding of the cultures of the Japanese islands ... as we have for any other region."[25]

US leaders hungered for this potentially strategic knowledge, or at least wished to prevent its acquisition by America's Cold War rival: the Soviet Union. Interest in their scholarship proved an important consideration in the decision to absolve most Japanese academics of their active or tacit support for militarism, fascism, and war.[26] As articulated by the International Military Tribunal for the Far East, convened by the Allies in 1946 to pursue justice for the victims of Japanese war crimes and crimes against humanity, punishable offenses included "laying down an ideological basis for the policies for the Greater East Asia" and "advocating the supremacy of the Japanese nation to be a leader of other nations"—the very mission of imperial scholarship.[27] However, after scrutinizing the records of nearly twenty-five thousand academics, commissions dismissed fewer than one hundred. (Furthermore, by the end of the occupation nearly all those affected by purges had received permission to return to their posts.)[28] Many US scholars defended their Japanese counterparts as "no more than normally patriotic for a period of nationalism."[29] One attendee at the 1947 meeting of the American Anthropological Association (AAA) explained, "At first glance we considered blackballing those who had used their positions for propaganda, but we soon realized that a great number of our own anthropologists had done the same thing and if we had supported that course of action we would have had to condemn some of our own colleagues."[30]

Moved by the demand for strategic information as well as by intellectual curiosity, American scholars worked to access Japanese imperial knowledge. For the most part, their colleagues across the Pacific readily made research results available. Exculpation from war responsibility helped to assuage some lingering hostility toward former enemy Americans. In a few cases, preexisting relationships smoothed the transmission of information: for example, Oka Masao (1898–1982) and Clyde Kluckhohn (1905–60), leaders of Japanese and American anthropology, respectively, had studied together at the University of Vienna in the 1930s. Perhaps the most decisive motivation was the need for pay. Japanese academics of the early postwar years faced a "terrible fight to keep themselves alive." Advisers to SCAP wrote, "Totally inadequate university salaries do not give the individual scholars even a minimum living wage, with the result that time which would otherwise be devoted to research is instead devoted to supplementing the family income through repeating lectures in other universities and schools, through hack writing, and through other activities even further removed from research and the scholarly life."[31]

Given the paucity of Japanese speakers in the midcentury United States, the relatively large numbers of Japanese scholars proficient in English were an asset to the diffusion of knowledge. Although Japanese citizens were generally not permitted to leave the archipelago during the occupation, SCAP extended travel privileges to researchers presenting at certain international conferences; for instance, in 1949, two physical anthropologists ventured to Christchurch, New Zealand, to speak at the Pacific Science Congress.[32] American scholars also learned from Japanese colleagues who affiliated with academic institutions in the United States. Japanese university students had studied in the West in large numbers since the mid-nineteenth century. Openings plummeted in the years leading up to World War II, with the result that many Japanese scholars enjoyed their first opportunity to travel to the United States only after 1945; already mature researchers, they were able to teach as well as learn.[33]

Study abroad solidified binational connections in the development of Japanese studies. In 1956, Seiichi Izumi (1915–70), a cultural anthropology professor at the University of Tokyo (formerly Tokyo Imperial University), began a fourteen-month period of study at Harvard and the University of Chicago. Supporting him were the Rockefeller Foundation and the Asia Foundation, two private, nongovernmental organizations closely identified with the promotion of US geopolitical interests. During his time in the United States, Izumi liaised with fellow social scientists at dozens of universities, research bodies, and museums. He attended and presented at conferences hosted by the AAA, Far Eastern Association, and International Congress of Anthropological and Ethnological Sciences.[34] His account of fieldwork among Japanese settlers in Brazil—a population of which few US scholars were even aware—inspired a group of anthropologists led by Robert J. Smith to undertake similar research in the 1960s.[35]

American academics also devoted considerable resources to translating and cataloging prewar studies of Japan. One bibliography of Japanese literature ran to seventy-four pages, encompassing publications in archaeology, ethnology, physical anthropology, and other disciplines.[36] Another work, edited by Japanese social scientists under SCAP direction, selected and annotated twenty significant writings in each of fifty subfields pertaining to Japanese culture and society.[37] The Rockefeller Foundation provided a 2.5 million yen grant for compiling a guide to Japanese reference materials; this work was subsequently translated into English and remains a fundamental bibliography for Japanese studies in the United States to this day.[38]

Some ambitious projects failed to launch owing to lack of financial support. In 1956, the AAA worked with a Japanese team to prepare a volume of some 350 pages composed of abstracts of "the most important Japanese anthropological research." The collection faltered when editors were unable to raise the 726,000 yen (over US$2,000) needed to cover the cost of selecting and revising materials, drafting translations, and preparing an introduction, bibliography, and glossary.[39] Also in 1956, anthropologist Richard Beardsley suggested translating a recently published encyclopedia of Japanese folklore: "It has some absolutely priceless stuff in it. It is very broad in concept, very competently done, concisely written.... And I don't know but that Japan is the most interesting area of all to anthropologists, sociologists, psychologists, and others, currently." This idea, too, was scuttled after the AAA, Wenner-Gren Foundation, and Asia Foundation all declined to offer funding.[40]

Perhaps the most ambitious attempt to access Japanese knowledge was the Human Relations Area Files (HRAF), supervised by anthropologist George P. Murdock (1897–1985) of Yale University. The groundwork for HRAF was laid during World War II, when the US Navy assigned Murdock to an intelligence unit in preparation for the invasion of Japanese-occupied Micronesia and Okinawa. Few Americans had ever been granted permission even to travel to these island chains, so Murdock was forced to rely on published Japanese data for his sources. Using Japanese American translators drawn from internment camps, he supervised the preparation of strategic bulletins and civil affairs handbooks on population and geography. After the war, these texts facilitated the US administration of former Japanese possessions in the Pacific.[41]

In the late 1940s, Murdock adapted the classification system he had designed for the navy to develop HRAF as a comprehensive database of empirical information indexed not only by region and population but also by cultural traits, structures, and phenomena. He imagined that subscribers might use the database to identify knowledge gaps suitable for research, to test hypotheses about human behavior, and to extrapolate fundamental social laws.[42] The resulting scholarship, Murdock believed, would have practical as well as academic significance: "It was obvious that ... the world had not settled all of its problems, and that an understanding of the world's peoples was even more urgently needed now to maintain peace than it had been to end the war."[43]

56   AREA STUDIES

In recognition of the potential for the project to contribute to US geopolitical dominance, the government, military, CIA, National Institutes of Health,
and various foundations all contributed funding.[44] In exchange, HRAF's architects prioritized the creation of a multilingual bibliography on strategic
areas. Japan's indigenous Ainu population was an early focus of information
gathering, both for reasons of anthropological interest and because of its sensitive zone of inhabitation on Japan's border with the Soviet Union. HRAF included translations of several works by Japanese scholars on the Ainu. Perhaps
the most important was *Ainu seisaku shi* (*Ainu of Northern Japan: A Study in
Conquest and Acculturation*) (orig. 1942), based on twenty years of research by
Shin'ichirō Takakura (1902–90). Although historians today deplore Takakura's
chauvinism, he was one of only a handful of scholars to study the Ainu before 1945. His American translator called attention to the unique value of the
work, declaring, "as a contribution to the history of Japan this is a pioneer[ing]
study."[45]

In addition to cataloging the backlog of Japanese intellectual resources, US
scholars also sought access to ongoing Japanese research. "In the present postwar inflationary period, scholars in static salaries often suffer hardships, but
they appear to have kept up and even increased the rate of growth of Japanese
anthropological resources," Beardsley adjudged in 1950.[46] With the encouragement of SCAP, *Minzokugaku Kenkyū* (Japanese journal of ethnology), Japan's
premier cultural anthropology journal, began publishing English-language
abstracts of articles. Its editors, Beardsley remarked, "were very cordial to the
proposal to abbreviate, select, or alter—anything to get them into print in
English."[47] The *Far Eastern Quarterly* resumed its reviews of Japanese-language
monographs and began publishing research articles by Japanese scholars. Such
work also appeared in US academic publications that did not specifically focus
on Asia; for example, "The Concepts behind the Ainu Bear Festival (Kumamat-
suri)," by Kyōsuke Kindaichi (1882–1971), was published in the *Southwestern
Journal of Anthropology* in 1949. Through these means, American pioneers of
Japanese studies absorbed major developments from across the Pacific into
their own store of knowledge.

BUILDING A TRADITION OF
COLLABORATIVE FIELDWORK

In addition to sharing their past work with US colleagues, Japanese experts
acted as vital partners in undertaking new research. Historians have often
characterized American scholarship on Japan produced in the 1940s and 1950s

as area studies, the primary means of gathering information about world regions considered strategically important to the United States during the Cold War. Area studies constituted a multidisciplinary attempt to advance both theoretical and empirical knowledge of diverse societies through intensive language preparation, on-the-ground investigation, and the incorporation of the voices of local informants. It relied heavily on funding from private foundations and government sources—a fact that gave these institutions outsize power in promoting the ideology of modernization as the animus of research.[48] Modernization offered a putatively scientific framing of history as a succession of universal stages defined by certain fixed characteristics, culminating in the end point of civilization embodied by the (singular, superior) United States. In the words of one historian, modernization "took the American exception and made it the world's rule."[49] Denying the coevalness of a diverse humanity, it envisaged a chronologically asynchronous world. As the Cold War intensified, modernization whitewashed the consolidation of a bloc of US-aligned nations, including Japan, as progress along an irresistible telos.[50]

In practical terms, modernization operated as a shorthand for the US mission to spread its "signature values" of democracy, capitalism, and peace throughout the world.[51] At its most basic, democracy encompassed an expectation of just, representative government freely chosen by informed and empowered citizens. Capitalism suggested a free market economy with few state-imposed barriers to participation or profit. Peace meant secure borders, domestic stability, and (paradoxically) armed forces capable of defending the nation's interests abroad. Collectively, these values functioned less as on-the-ground realities than as the moral core of American identity and the alleged antithesis of the beliefs of the Soviet enemy.

In Japan, SCAP's challenge was to instill democracy—including academic freedom and freedom of speech—while simultaneously suppressing damaging Communist influences. By 1948, the intensification of the Cold War had led the occupation to perform what has been dubbed a "reverse course" on its initial liberalism. Leftist American scholars faced persecution and exclusion from the academic profession at home, while those who ventured to Japan were carefully screened for unorthodox political views. SCAP created organs of censorship, confining discussion of Japan's past, present, and future to approved visions of modernization. The construction of Japanese studies thus took place in the context of a robust suppression of alternatives to national development as an ally and analogue of the United States.[52]

Believing that the stability of the nation depended on aligning political, social, and economic institutions with cultural values, American scholars designed studies to test interventions cultivating a prosperous, pacific, empowered citizenry. Fieldwork flourished as the signal methodology of area studies. In the late 1940s and 1950s, the field sciences, especially anthropology, archaeology, political science, and sociology, dominated the production of knowledge about Japan. Meanwhile, disciplines that had engaged earlier American students of the country, such as demography, religious studies, and statistics, languished. The humanities (with the exceptions of history and literary translation) also contributed little to Japanese studies until well into the 1960s.[53]

Much early postwar fieldwork in Japan took the form of interdisciplinary team ventures. During the occupation, group studies mobilizing scholars of multifarious disciplines were understood to enact democracy through the open exchange of ideas, discussion, and debate. (By contrast, individual disciplines were suspected of susceptibility to both noxious Fascist and Communist influences.)[54] As the American study of Japan did not boast a robust prewar tradition, the methodological fashion of the day exercised a particularly decisive influence over its development. Group fieldwork also dovetailed with the traditions of Japanese scholars, many of whom had participated in interdisciplinary team ventures in the empire during World War II.[55]

Spearheading field research in occupied Japan was an institution often overlooked by genealogies of Japanese studies: SCAP's Public Opinion and Sociological Research Division (hereafter referred to as PO&SR). PO&SR was created in early 1946 to supply SCAP with data on Japan's "national mood." In the United States, public opinion surveys had formed a conduit for popular influence on government since the interwar period.[56] In the hands of the division, such research assessed the convergence of Japanese political culture with the ideals of modernization.

The first director of PO&SR was John C. Pelzel (1914–99), a cultural anthropologist then pursuing a PhD at Harvard. Pelzel had enlisted in the US Marines in 1941 and spent three and a half years in the Pacific theater and in Japan.[57] Assisting him as deputy director was his close friend Herbert Passin (1916–2003), a doctoral candidate in sociology from the University of Chicago. Passin was an experienced survey researcher who became interested in Japan while working with former inmates of US internment camps for Japanese and Japanese American citizens. He was fluent in written and spoken Japanese, having studied at the US Army language school in Ann Arbor during World War II. "In my wildest dreams, I could never have concocted a better job for myself at that particular stage of my life," he later recalled.[58]

Both Passin and Pelzel wished to undertake field as well as public opinion research—an ambition authorized by SCAP only after Pelzel had decommissioned and returned to the US to accept a position at Harvard in early 1949.[59] To replace the director, Passin recommended a former classmate, John W. Bennett (1915–2005). As Bennett himself admitted, he "didn't know much of the language, and . . . did not intend to make Japan a lifelong preoccupation"—a fact that may help explain why the significance of PO&SR to the early development of Japanese studies is seldom remembered today.[60] Bennett had recently finished his PhD at the University of Chicago and was working as an assistant professor of anthropology at Ohio State. Joining PO&SR at the same time were two Japanese American researchers: Tamie Tsuchiyama (1915–84) and Iwao Ishino (1921–2012). Raised in modest circumstances in Hawai'i, Tsuchiyama received a BA in anthropology from Berkeley in 1938 and stayed on in the department as a graduate student. When she was forced to withdraw amid the executive order to intern Japanese and Japanese American citizens, her mentors recommended her to a research team conducting fieldwork in a camp. After the war, Tsuchiyama became the first Asian American to earn a PhD in anthropology from Berkeley.[61] Ishino, some years younger, also served as a surveyor in an internment camp, which furthered his interest in social science. After working at the OWI in Washington, DC, he enrolled in a PhD program at Harvard. Ishino joined PO&SR with the intention of carrying out field research for his dissertation.[62]

Rounding out PO&SR's US staff were Cynthia Mazo (dates unknown), the wife of a SCAP official, and David L. Sills (1920–2015), a Yale graduate student in sociology. Supporting them were over thirty Japanese temporary and secretarial staff: advisers, clerks, drafters, secretaries, analysts, and typists. Seven interpreters withstood several months of interviews and translation tests to demonstrate "a command of English extend[ing] into special technical vocabularies and into the sensitive range of colloquial speech."[63] Sills's interpreter had spent a year at Yale before enlisting in the Japanese army in Southeast Asia.[64] Bennett's interpreter, Masako Inugai (dates unknown), quickly became indispensable to him for her professional acumen and remained a lifelong friend.[65]

Given Bennett's unfamiliarity with the Japanese academic landscape, he solicited recommendations for Japanese social scientists from Kunio Yanagita (1875–1962). Yanagita, typically characterized as a folklorist or "native ethnologist," was among the earliest and most active fieldworkers of imperial Japan. His interest in diverse local traditions, coupled with his search for a primordial and unifying "Japanese essence," inspired the generation of Japanese social scientists who came of age in the 1930s and 1940s. Yanagita was not only intellectually but also personally influential. Through marriage or other familial ties, he was connected to leading social scientists such as Masao Oka and Eiichirō

60   AREA STUDIES

Ishida (1903–68). During one visit, Bennett described him as a "great ideologist of the conservative movement in Japan—a kind of folk-soul-interpreter role, since his life work has been in language, folklore, religion, and historical anthropology. He is conservative to the core—a courtly old guy who wears Japanese-style clothes only, and sits in the center of his enormous library-study, with his students and followers working at tables quietly, and with you, as his guests, sitting in chairs around a couple of hibachi (braziers), trying to keep warm."[66] Despite their ideological differences, the context of the occupation necessitated, perhaps even forced, a collaboration between Japan's most renowned prewar fieldworker and the director of its first postwar field research agency.

Each prospective employee recommended to PO&SR submitted to a language exam and an interview of up to ninety minutes with three American officers. Sociologist Takeshi Koyama (1899–1983) later recalled his nervousness during the ordeal: not only did he find the questions challenging but he also feared that the division might discover his service in an imperial ethnological research institute.[67] Conversely, Eiichirō Ishida was scrutinized for his youthful activism in Japan's prewar Marxist movement, for which he served a six-year prison sentence under the imperial government. His application to PO&SR occasioned much hand-wringing: the division was both eager to hire the "competent, retiring, and gentlemanly scholar" and loath to discharge him for fear of appearing ideologically biased. In the end, SCAP adjudged that Ishida's wartime research supporting militarism, Fascism, and empire offered positive evidence that he had abandoned his early Socialist inclinations. Ironically, Ishida's most compromising writings vouchsafed him in an era in which American anxieties about Communism dominated all other concerns.[68]

Ultimately, PO&SR brought on board about twenty-five Japanese social scientists, including some of the most prominent voices within prewar scholarship, such as Masao Oka, Yuzuru Okada (1911–81), and husband-and-wife sociologists Kunio Odaka (1908–93) and Kyōko Odaka (1914–2013). In contrast to their relatively junior American colleagues, the Japanese social scientists were largely well-published midcareer scholars. Defeat had seemingly relegated them to a supporting role, but their experience and expertise would prove critical to carrying out PO&SR's research agenda.

After a year of preparation and desk research, PO&SR undertook the first major field study of occupied Japan: an assessment of the impact of land reform. In 1946, SCAP had mandated the breakup and redistribution of large landholdings, seeking to "replace traditional agrarian feudalism with a democratic way of life" by creating a class of independent yeoman farmers.[69] To analyze the resulting social and economic changes, MacArthur invited Arthur F. Raper (1899–1979), a respected sociologist at the US Department of Agriculture, to work with PO&SR. Raper led a team of four American and fifteen Japanese social scientists, representing multiple disciplines, over the course of three stints of fieldwork totaling nearly seven months between 1947 and 1949. "I had the choice of the Japanese scholars in rural sociology," he later recalled. His selections included Takeshi Koyama, Seiichi Kitano (1900–1982), and Eitarō Suzuki (1894–1966). He also engaged numerous interpreters and translators.[70]

After Raper's study, PO&SR undertook interdisciplinary group field research on traditional fishery rights, neighborhood associations, family and household composition, labor management, problems of urban workers and consumers, the changing status of women, the reform of big business, literacy and language education, and other topics.[71] For American researchers, collaboration offered a means of circumventing the formidable barrier of language. Bennett described the procedure for one survey: "The [Japanese] sociologists would arrange to have village officials distribute a batch of questionnaires to fill out, and then go out and do intensive interviews on their own. Masako [Bennett's personal interpreter] and I would go out in the nearby burakus [villages] and make interviews—rather rambling and general, since I was getting educated."[72]

Teamwork gave Japanese scholars an opportunity to participate in field research at a moment when they were almost completely unable to fund their own projects. In cases where using an interpreter proved too inefficient or formal, they worked independently on behalf of their American colleagues. Ultimately, they collected up to 95 percent of PO&SR's data.[73] Sills, who did not speak Japanese, recalled spending little time in the field. Instead, he sat at his desk editing reports submitted by Japanese researchers.[74]

Even American scholars who spoke Japanese often found that they lacked the fluency to represent what they encountered in the field. Passin remembered, "When I started on this research I drew upon my recent sociological research in southern Illinois during my graduate student days, my knowledge of black sharecroppers in the American South, my experience with Mexican peasants, and my general reading in the fields of anthropology and rural sociology. But I did not even have a vocabulary to describe the new phenomena that came to my attention. Fortunately, I had as advisors some of Japan's leading rural sociologists, and I also benefited from association with the great folklorist Kunio Yanagita and his disciples and coworkers."[75]

In addition to the language barrier, American fieldworkers also confronted the distrust of their informants. Many early postwar rural communities associated information gathering with the wartime secret police and closely supervised the researchers in their midst. On one excursion, Bennett lamented, "We already have a representative of the Hokkaido prefectural government and a nice old Episcopal minister (Jap[anese]) with us, and at [a certain village] we also had the mayor, 3 other village gov[ernment] officials, our host and a collection of other people whose role I didn't catch clearly. Tomorrow, thank God, we lose the prefectural gov[ernor], but the old minister sticks to the bitter end!"[76] Faced with this retinue, he lamented, "The people wouldn't say a thing worth recording."[77] Under these circumstances, Japanese researchers were indispensable allies in alleviating public suspicion. Passin remembered one occasion on which they successfully groomed the community for a survey: "The previous knowledge of the area of one of the members of the [PO&SR] staff, Prof. [Seiichi] Kitano, resulted in a very pleasant welcome to the researchers by the local people."[78]

PO&SR dissolved in June 1951 after the decision was made to terminate the occupation itself the following year. Its demise, however, marked a new phase in, rather than the end of, collaboration between Japanese and American researchers. The task of approving and funding scholarship passed from SCAP, with its explicit authority over Japan, to American foundations, the military, universities, and other institutions invested in the US geopolitical agenda and ideology. Bennett returned to Ohio State, where, with the support of the academic community, the military, and various grant agencies, he continued to act as a liaison between Japanese and American social scientists. He remained in contact with former associates, built a Japanese studies library, and planned exchange programs. Among the many visiting researchers he hosted was Michio Nagai (1923–2000), a sociologist who later served as Japan's minister of education.[79] He also founded the Research Program in Japanese Social Relations to write up PO&SR's backlog of data. Both Passin and Ishino assisted with this project, the former for a year from 1953 to 1954 and the latter for nearly five years from 1951 to 1956 in the capacity of research associate and assistant professor. Ishino subsequently gained a faculty appointment at Michigan State University and returned to Japan for fieldwork periodically throughout his long career.[80] Tsuchiyama, who had worked alongside him at PO&SR, also pursued an academic position in anthropology but, victimized by racism and sexism, eventually retrained as a librarian.[81]

Meanwhile, Japanese scholars remained essential partners of Americans in the field. Toward the end of the occupation, SCAP granted permission for the establishment of the so-called Okayama Field Station, the interdisciplinary brainchild of University of Michigan faculty Richard Beardsley, John Hall, and

Robert Ward. In addition to its founding anthropologist, historian, and political scientist, Okayama drew economists, sociologists, psychologists, medical doctors, historians, and specialists in the Japanese language and literature. From spring 1950 through summer 1954, a rotating team placed its target village, Niike, under almost continuous observation; follow-up visits took place through spring 1957. A summary of the results of the study, titled *Village Japan*, appeared in 1959. "Through the participation of many Japanese scholars . . . the project became to an unusual extent a deeply satisfying and mentally enriching experience in intercultural and international academic cooperation," recalled Beardsley.[82] He also called attention to the "substantial literature in the field of community studies [that] exists in Japanese. The authors [of *Village Japan*] consulted this extensively . . . and wish to acknowledge their indebtedness to it."[83]

Japanese scholars also assisted American researchers in venturing beyond Okayama. Robert J. Smith sailed to Japan in the summer of 1951 to undertake dissertation research at the field station. However, he found its cloistered conditions inimical to the immersion he regarded as a necessary precondition of anthropological research. Advised to explore possibilities on the largely rural island of Shikoku, he serendipitously encountered the professional interpreter Tetsuo Satō at the Kagawa prefectural office. Satō's professional credentials dazzled the mayor of Smith's target village, securing unprecedented access to and cooperation from the local population.[84] Smith's study was ultimately published in 1978 under the title *Kurusu: The Price of Progress in a Japanese Village, 1951–1975*. In his acknowledgments, he thanked Satō for the "inestimable value" of his assistance. He also described his Japanese-born wife Kazuko Smith, whom he wed in 1955, as an "equal partner" in his study.[85] Smith's career, like that of many men of his generation, was facilitated not only by Japanese scholars but also by the linguistic and intellectual talents of his spouse.

Beginning in the early 1950s, the regeneration of the Japanese economy allowed Japanese professional societies to sponsor their own interdisciplinary group field ventures—some of which welcomed American participants. In the summer of 1950, Beardsley and his graduate student Edward Norbeck (1915–91) joined a Japanese-organized research expedition to the island of Tsushima. Beardsley warmly appreciated the experience, writing to his wife, "I'm beginning to be delighted more each day that I came to Tsushima."[86] The following summer, John B. Cornell (1921–93), a graduate student in anthropology, joined a venture to Hokkaido organized by the Japanese Society of Ethnology (Nihon Minzoku Gakkai). Cornell published his results in the flagship journal *American Anthropologist* in 1964, in what became the first American-authored

64   AREA STUDIES

scholarly article on the Ainu in the postwar period. Within its pages, he expressed particular gratitude for the mentorship of Eiichirō Ishida.[87]

Collaboration in the field built Japanese studies not only through the creation of knowledge but also through the establishment of lasting interpersonal bonds. In accounts of early postwar fieldwork, Japanese scholars often emphasized harmony and cooperation with American colleagues. Many remembered Raper as "an excellent person" who "built up great rapport."[88] Addressing a group of American and Japanese scholars in 1953, Tadao Yanaihara (1893–1961), an economist and the president of the University of Tokyo, captured the mutually respectful mood: "The American professors are our guests and at the same time they are our colleagues. They did not come here to make American propaganda nor did they come to diagnose Japanese feeling toward Americans. We stand on the equal ground of academic learning and are colleagues striving toward the common goal in search of scientific truth.... Thus we shall become, without being aware of it, co-workers in building up the true foundation for world peace."[89]

American scholars expressed similarly positive sentiments regarding collaboration. During his time in Tsushima, Beardsley wrote, "My experience thus far ... is that it is immensely profitable to be around 2 or 3 of these ethnologists, who are only too anxious to explain their findings simply and systematically. On their part ... they realize our language problem handicaps our work and they'd like to help ... [and] they feel concerned about our safety, lest we get lost."[90] Raper too recalled his team favorably, though not without reference to certain national stereotypes: "I was tremendously impressed with the capability of the people. They were very thoroughly regimented. I came back very convinced that if our civilization turned on learning calculus and theirs turned on learning calculus, they would survive and we wouldn't—because if they needed to learn calculus, they'd all learn calculus in one year, because they have it fixed up so they could operate in that kind of fashion."[91]

Within PO&SR, the relative seniority and knowledge of the Japanese scholars compared with the youth and inexperience of the US staff helped to forestall anticipated hierarchies of victor and vanquished. American respect for the expertise and stature of Japanese researchers, coupled with the latter's humility toward the Allies, facilitated generally productive working relationships. The low status of PO&SR within the occupation bureaucracy further liberated the division from the inflexible chain of command that characterized much of SCAP. Bennett captured the difference in attitudes held by his team members and other occupation attachés in his reflections on a group field venture: "The other Americans on the trip—all older, tall, handsome, aggressively American males or women—cannot quite understand our relationship [with our Japanese coworkers], which is one of sympathy and friendship . . . bewildering to the robust and materialistic American males, who take it as a matter of course that the Japanese on the trip are in a basically servant category."[92]

Frustrated with this perspective, many PO&SR employees "avoided overly close contact with other Americans in the Occupation, and with Occupation society in general. . . . [They] mingled chiefly with those Americans who thought about Japan as [they] did, and this meant [they] excluded [themselves] from most social circles of Occupation society." Bennett speculated that his team's relative familiarity with Japanese colleagues may even have compromised its credibility in the eyes of SCAP. "We had no important influence on top policymaking," he stated bluntly.[93]

And yet protestations of equality could not entirely mask a stark power differential in which American academics enjoyed the power to make or break the careers of their colleagues across the Pacific. The occupation favored those scholars who served it, allowing Japanese researchers hand-selected by US authorities to dominate the domestic intellectual landscape well into the 1960s. Experience working with Americans was a nearly universal qualification of Japanese academics who succeeded in obtaining a faculty position in the early postwar years. SCAP also placed its supporters in libraries, museums, newspaper and journal editorial boards, and independent research organizations.[94] It gave them preferential access to valuable study-abroad opportunities: one survey of fifty-one recipients of fellowships to universities in the United States found that no fewer than seventeen had worked for the occupation, while numerous others had been provided with unofficial encouragement and assistance by SCAP.[95] American foundations such as Rockefeller and Carnegie offered grants exclusively to scholars able to portray themselves as allies of the US global agenda. Meanwhile, those who rejected modernization were marginalized both institutionally and professionally.

The pressure to conform intellectually weighed no less heavily on early postwar US scholars of Japan. To be sure, many were liberal for their time and chafed against right-wing elements of SCAP. As McCarthyism took hold of the American government in the 1950s, some came to frown upon direct service to the state.[96] But it was no coincidence that, at the height of the Cold War, grants, publications, prestigious tenure-stream posts, and organizational leadership opportunities attended the most ardent exponents of modernization. In interviews toward the end of their lives, many of these "success stories" denied feeling, in their words, "any particular political pressure," suggesting the extent to which they identified with this ideology.[97] Their experiences stand in direct

66 AREA STUDIES

contrast to those of left-wing dissenters who failed to flourish in the academy. One such scholar was Herbert Passin, who was purged by McCarthyites in the early 1950s for his involvement in the student movement and editorship of a Socialist magazine during his time at the University of Chicago. Partly as a result, Passin never secured a tenured faculty post.[98] However vibrant the discipline of Japanese studies in the early Cold War period, it took place in a context that insisted on allegiance to the ideological dictates of the United States.

EPILOGUE: JAPANESE STUDIES BEYOND THE FIRST GENERATION

By 1960, Japanese studies in the United States had become "a very good-sized organism with a very big backbone and a very firm one," as Edwin Reischauer wrote.[99] Academics who specialized in Japan numbered over five hundred, distributed among close to twenty disciplines at nearly 150 universities. In the absence of a national organization for Japanese studies, the Association for Asian Studies (heir to the Far Eastern Association) served in this role. It published a journal, newsletter, annual bibliography, and monograph series; convened annual meetings and supported regional conferences; offered job placement services; and managed grants and contracts with other foundations and agencies.[100] The American Council of Learned Societies, the Social Science Research Council, and the Fulbright Foundation extended fellowships to graduate students and professors for research on Japan. At the undergraduate level, one observer wrote of "the comparative rush of students into courses about Asia and the Pacific." Nearly two thousand college students studied the Japanese language in 1960; by 1963 numbers had grown to almost three thousand. Education on East Asia even flourished in elementary and secondary schools.[101]

Initially, bonds between Japanese and US academia remained strong. In 1962, President John F. Kennedy and Prime Minister Hayato Ikeda established the US-Japan Conference on Cultural and Educational Interchange (CULCON). With the support of American institutions, Japanese scholars continued to travel to the United States as students and lecturers. They also joined the Association for Asian Studies in record numbers: in 1964 the organization boasted almost sixty members from Japan—nearly twice the number from any other foreign country.[102] Scholars continued to collaborate on their own initiative and through academic institutions. Together with Japanese colleagues, faculty at the Center for Japanese Studies at the University of Michigan began a follow-up observation of village life in Okayama. Other binational group projects focused on the translation of modern and classical texts and addressed topics such as early modern intellectual, social, legal, and demographic history; Japan's resident Korean minority; the political economy of rice; and foreign policy.[103] Beyond the field, additional forms of cooperation included sharing and offering feedback on works in progress, providing introductions and affiliations, and organizing and presenting at joint conferences.[104]

These ties notwithstanding, during the 1960s Japanese studies became more self-sufficient on both sides of the Pacific. Thanks to the regenerating economy, Japanese researchers were able to overcome their reliance on American funding. Meanwhile, in the United States, the generation that had served in the occupation earned tenure, and with it, the privilege of training successors in Japanese studies. Assisting scholars was an expanded array of supporting resources such as museums, libraries, language courses, and publication venues. For the first time, the serious study of Japan at home became possible. The burgeoning corpus of English-language secondary literature and translated materials even allowed the production of academic studies on Japan without mastery of the Japanese language. Nonetheless, one observer declared:

> Today it is expected of PhD candidates that they make full use of Japanese materials in their original form and that they add to these an original contribution which makes the work significant to both the Japanese and American scholarly worlds. . . . In this sense Japanese studies have come of age. . . . No longer is the strictly descriptive or data-gathering approach considered a primary need. Our capacity to get answers of a descriptive sort is taken for granted. It is the more theoretical problems which are of primary concern to the field.[105]

Reinforcing the divergence of Japanese studies in Japan and the United States were emerging differences in intellectual agendas. American researchers tended to choose topics in response to methodological, empirical, and theoretical trends in the national academy, rather than following the interests of their Japanese colleagues.[106] Some dismissed Japanese scholarly writings for their perceived lack of a thesis or argument. (This critique is still frequently heard today.) Meanwhile, as Marius Jansen wrote to Robert J. Smith in 1962, "American Japanology . . . frequently seems to get little more than an amused tolerance from many Japanese, however much they may express appreciation of a different point of view."[107]

The gradual abandonment of modernization as an ideology also undermined the intellectual unity of American and Japanese scholars. During the early phases of the Cold War, professions of faith in modernization knit together academics on both sides of the Pacific. By the 1960s, however, many had begun to question the viability of democracy, capitalism, and peace in the context of

America's increasingly assertive geopolitical ambitions. During this decade, six weeklong summer seminars brought together American and Japanese students of Japan (as well as some scholars from the British Commonwealth) to rethink modernization. At the so-called Hakone Conferences (see chap. 3), many American participants rejoiced in Japan's evident transformation into a bastion of US values. They were "taken aback by the violent reactions" of their Japanese colleagues, who expressed their sense that democracy, capitalism, and peace had yet to be fully achieved.[108] Japanese scholars at Hakone further shied away from declarations that Japan was prepared to lead Asia down its own path, comparing such rhetoric to wartime professions of racial and cultural superiority justifying imperialism. They emphasized the particularity of the Japanese experience, at odds with the universalizing claims of modernization.[109]

Above all, Japanese academics questioned the ways in which modernization had committed their nation to seemingly unstinting support for US global domination. Shunsuke Tsurumi (1922–2015), a historian and philosopher, voiced disapproval of American aggression in his journal *Shisō no kagaku* (The science of thought). Political scientist Masao Maruyama (1914–96) produced a stream of books and articles on the need for a Japanese citizenry capable of withstanding foreign pressure.[110] These scholars did not challenge the ideals of democracy, capitalism, and peace per se but deplored their use in legitimizing the Cold War and the oppression of the developing world. Some Americans found such critiques difficult to accept. Edward Seidensticker recalled of his classmates at the University of Tokyo:

> I was surrounded by very, very intelligent boys, it was clear.... But they were unfriendly and they were opinionated, exceedingly opinionated, exceedingly doctrinaire.... Their view of the world which held America responsible for all of the mischief, all of the ails and all of the sufferings of the world, it just wasn't acceptable.... Their view of the world made me mad, but I think I also felt rather contemptuous of them. It seemed to me that they were misusing their undeniable talents.... I mean, this wasn't a view of the world which was worthy of a first-rate mind.[111]

As Seidensticker's frank remarks made clear, ideological divergence posed an increasingly formidable barrier to binational collaboration in Japanese studies.

Today, with the Cold War more than three decades in the past, Japanese studies has not recovered its early cooperative bent. The original reasons for collaboration have all but vanished: the Japanese studies establishments of both Japan and the United States are fully mature and self-sufficient. However, since a high-water mark in the 1990s, the latter has contracted. Observers have implicated myriad causes in the seeming attenuation of American academic interest in Japan in the twenty-first century. The shrinking population of US undergraduates has prompted universities to retrench in general. The humanities and social sciences, the traditional home of Japanese studies, have suffered from their perceived failure to demonstrate contemporary relevance and to provide marketable job skills to majors. Meanwhile, American strategic and security interests in China and the Middle East have claimed attention and resources formerly focused on Japan. Ongoing recession, now in its fourth decade, has eroded global interest in the Japanese economic model, while the country has failed to cultivate new domains of leadership on issues such as human rights, clean energy, and immigration.

A decade ago, a collection of essays by leading scholars of postwar Japan opened with the sentence "Of course Japan matters"—an explicit rebuttal of the growing academic and public sense that the country had lost its luster as a subject of study.[112] This authoritative pronouncement failed, however, to arrest concerns regarding the future of Japanese studies in the United States—in fact, the debate has since taken an even more apocalyptic turn. A 2019 roundtable at the Association for Asian Studies annual meeting in Denver, Colorado, debated the forthcoming "death of Japan studies," which participants agreed was not too dire a prediction.[113] Should interest in Japan continue to decline, American scholars may be moved to seek greater intellectual integration with their Japanese colleagues—much as their forebears did in the 1950s.

NOTES

1. Jansen, "Stages of Growth," 45.
2. Dower, *Embracing Defeat*, 556.
3. Jansen, "History," 7–15.
4. Cameron, "Far Eastern Studies in the United States," 117.
5. Hardacre, introduction, vii.
6. Cameron, "Far Eastern Studies in the United States," 116.
7. Hardacre, "Postwar Development of the Study of Japanese Religions," 198–99.
8. Bolitho, "Tokugawa Japan," 85.
9. Borton, *Reminiscences*.
10. Bowles, oral history interview, August 23–24, 1980, Marlene J. Mayo Oral Histories, Gordon W. Prange Collection, University of Maryland.
11. Eleanor Hadley, oral history interview, November 4, 1978, Marlene J. Mayo Oral Histories.

12. Eleanor Hadley, oral history interview by George Akita, June 20, 1982, Oral History of Japanese Studies Scholars, 1960s–1980s, Japan Collection, Hamilton Library, University of Hawai'i at Mānoa.

13. John M. Maki, oral history interview, November 3, 1979, Marlene J. Mayo Oral Histories.

14. Key Kobayashi, oral history interview, October 18, 1978, Marlene J. Mayo Oral Histories.

15. Faubion Bowers, oral history interview, July 22, 1982, Marlene J. Mayo Oral Histories.

16. Okamoto, *Man Who Saved Kabuki*.

17. Henderson, "Role of the Shan States," 253–58; Spinks, "Origin of the Japanese Interests in Manchuria," 259–71.

18. Price, *Anthropological Intelligence*, 171–77.

19. Slesnick and Slesnick, *Kanji & Codes*, 2–3, 113.

20. Robert J. Smith, oral history interview by George Akita, December 21, 1978, Oral History of Japanese Studies Scholars, 1960s–1980s.

21. Eleanor Jorden, oral history interview, Apr. 24, 1981, Marlene J. Mayo Oral Histories.

22. Berry, *Japan in Print*; Marcon, *Knowledge of Nature*.

23. Kingsberg Kadia, *Into the Field*, 17.

24. Julian Steward to Fred Eggan, May 17, 1956, file 22, box 5, Fred Eggan Papers, 1870–1991, Archival Biographical Files, Special Collections Research Center, University of Chicago Library.

25. Pelzel, "Japanese Ethnological and Sociological Research," 54.

26. In the most infamous case, the International Military Tribunal for the Far East declined to bring charges against members of the so-called Unit 731, the Kwantung Army biological and chemical weapons development squad responsible for grotesque experiments on human subjects in Manchukuo. SCAP silently restored affiliated doctors to the top of the Japanese medical, pharmaceutical, and academic worlds in exchange for their data. Harris, *Factories of Death*, 215–21.

27. Baerwald, *Purge of Japanese Leaders*, 39.

28. Conrad, *Quest for the Lost Nation*, 82. Altogether, tribunals of the late 1940s purged some two hundred thousand individuals, representing 0.29 percent of the Japanese population. Baerwald, *Purge of Japanese Leaders*, 79.

29. Pelzel, "Japanese Ethnological and Sociological Research," 72.

30. Price, *Cold War Anthropology*, 64. Also facilitating the exoneration of Japan's intellectuals was the fact that the consequences of research in the empire were borne mostly by colonial subjects, whom the Euro-American Allies largely ignored in their pursuit of justice. Totani, *Tokyo War Crimes Trial*.

31. US Cultural Science Mission to Japan, *Report*, 15.

COLD WAR COLLABORATIONS 71

32. Pacific Science Association, *Proceedings*, 7:26–32.

33. Bennett, Passin, and McKnight, *In Search of Identity*, 108.

34. Seiichi Izumi, "Several Impressions of Three Recent Anthropology Meetings," April 25, 1957, file 5314, box 358, series 609, RG 10.1, Izumi Seiichi, Rockefeller Archive Center.

35. Seiichi Izumi, "Toward Understanding the Problem of Acculturation," academic talk, Harvard University, 1956, no. 3, Izumi Seiichi archive, National Museum for Ethnology.

36. Beardsley, *Bibliographic Materials in the Japanese Language*.

37. Watsuji, Yamamoto, and Nishina, *Bibliography of Representative Writings*.

38. Koide, "Following the Road Paved by Naomi Fukuda," 8.

39. Shinobu Iwamura to Charles S. Sheldon, July 16, 1956, box 20, Julian H. Steward Papers, 1842–1976, University of Illinois Archives, University Library, University of Illinois at Urbana-Champaign.

40. Richard K. Beardsley to Julian Steward, April 10, 1956, box 2, Julian H. Steward Papers.

41. Price, *Cold War Anthropology*, xxii.

42. Murdock, "Cross-Cultural Survey," 29–54.

43. Ford, *Human Relations Area Files 1949–1969*, 8.

44. Price, *Cold War Anthropology*, 249.

45. Takakura, *Ainu of Northern Japan*, 5.

46. Beardsley, *Bibliographic Materials*, vii.

47. Richard K. Beardsley to Julian H. Steward, April 10, 1956, Julian H. Steward Papers.

48. Harootunian and Miyoshi, "Introduction: The 'Afterlife' of Area Studies," 1–18; Szanton, "Origin, Nature, and Challenges of Area Studies"; Tansman, "Japanese Studies," 1–33, 184–216.

49. Gluck, "House of Mirrors," 435.

50. Garon, "Rethinking Modernization and Modernity in Japanese History," 346–66.

51. Latham, *Modernization as Ideology*, ix, 4–5, 8, 16.

52. Price, *Threatening Anthropology*, 405–40.

53. Rosenfield, "Japanese Art Studies in America," 165.

54. Erickson et al., *How Reason Almost Lost Its Mind*, 107–32.

55. Kingsberg Kadia, *Into the Field*, 40–66.

56. Speier, "Rise of Public Opinion," 147–67.

57. "John Campbell Pelzel," December 18, 1953, in "Pelzel, John C., 1950–1969," box 37, in Marion J. Levy Jr., 1948–2000. Marion J. Levy Jr. Papers, COU: 985:07:73:01, University of Colorado Boulder Libraries, Special Collections and Archives.

58. Passin, *Encounter with Japan*, 183.

59. Herbert Passin, oral history interview by George Akita, July 22, 1977, Oral History of Japanese Studies Scholars, 1960s–1980s.

60. Despres, "Interview with John W. Bennett," 657.

61. Hirabayashi, *Politics of Fieldwork*, 5.

62. Chartkoff, "Iwao Ishino," 534–537.

63. "Outline of Research Teams," box 5871, Records of the Allied Operational and Occupation Headquarters (RG 331), National Archives at College Park.

64. David L. Sills, oral history interview, April 14, 1979, Marlene J. Mayo Oral Histories.

65. John W. Bennett to Kathryn G. Bennett, August 16, 1949, file 38RRR, box 2A, John W. Bennett Papers (RARE.CMS.119), Rare Books and Manuscripts: Collections, Rare Books and Manuscripts Library, Ohio State University.

66. John W. Bennett to Kathryn G. Bennett, March 24, 1950, file 1, box 1, John W. Bennett Papers.

67. Morris-Suzuki, "Ethnic Engineering," 503.

68. "Ishida Eiichirō," box 5870, Records of the Allied Operational and Occupation Headquarters.

69. Raper, *Japanese Village in Transition*, 12.

70. Raper, *Reminiscences*, 148.

71. John W. Bennett, "Summary of Major Research Problems of the Public Opinion and Sociological Research Division, CIE," file 4, box 1, Records of the Allied Operational and Occupation Headquarters.

72. John W. Bennett to Kathryn G. Bennett, September 13, 1949, file 1, box 1, John W. Bennett Papers.

73. Bennett, "Summary of Major Research Problems."

74. Sills, oral history, 12.

75. Passin, *Encounter with Japan*, 143.

76. John W. Bennett, Journal, May 24, 1949, file 1, box 1, John W. Bennett Papers.

77. Bennett, May 22–23, 1949.

78. Herbert Passin, "Report of Field Trip to Yuzurihara," 1, Herbert Passin Collection, "Field Trip to Yuzurihara Report," Special Collections, DuBois Library, University of Massachusetts at Amherst.

79. Despres, "Interview with John W. Bennett," 653–54.

80. Chartkoff, "Iwao Ishino," 534–37.

81. Hirabayashi, *Politics of Fieldwork*, 159.

82. Beardsley, Hall, and Ward, *Village Japan*, xiii.

83. Beardsley, Hall, and Ward, ix.

84. Smith, interview by Akita.

85. Smith, *Kurusu*, xv.

86. Richard K. Beardsley to Grace Beardsley, July 18, 1950, file "Japan—Tsushima—Plans and Notes, 1950," box 3, Richard K. Beardsley Papers, Bentley Historical Library, University of Michigan.

87. Cornell, "Ainu Assimilation and Cultural Extinction," 304.

88. Sol Tax, Diary of Trip to Asia, December 1958–January 1959, file 1, box 21, Current Anthropology Records, Special Collections Research Center, University of Chicago Library.

89. Tadao Yanaihara, "Opening Address," July 13, 1953, file 1, box 2, American Studies Seminars in Japan Records (SC0266), Department of Special Collections and University Archives, Stanford University Libraries, Stanford, CA.

90. Richard K. Beardsley to Grace Beardsley, July 18, 1950.

91. Raper, *Reminiscences*, 149.

92. Bennett, Journal, May 22–23, 1949.

93. Bennett, "Summary of Major Research Problems."

94. Iwao Ishino to John W. Bennett, June 5, 1951, file 197, box 20, John W. Bennett Papers.

95. Bennett, Passin, and McKnight, *In Search of Identity*, 108.

96. Smith, interview by Akita.

97. Richard K. Beardsley, oral history interview by George Akita, March 5, 1976, Oral History of Japanese Studies Scholars, 1960s–1980s.

98. Passin, interview by Akita.

99. Edwin O. Reischauer, oral history interview, November 1, 1979, Marlene J. Mayo Oral Histories.

100. Crane, "News of the Profession: The First Ten Years," 657; "News of the Profession: Annual Report," 645.

101. Cameron, "Far Eastern Studies in the United States," 126; Jansen, "Stages of Growth," 50–51.

102. Crane, "News of the Profession: The First Ten Years," 651.

103. Massey and Massey, *CULCON Report on Japanese Studies*, 129–30.

104. Steinhoff, *Japanese Studies in the United States and Canada*, 71.

105. Quoted in Jansen, "Stages of Growth," 54.

106. Steinhoff, *Japanese Studies in the United States and Canada*, 8.

107. Marius B. Jansen to Robert J. Smith, August 2, 1962, in "Jansen, Marius B., 1950–1992," box 23, Marion J. Levy Jr. Papers.

108. Beardsley, interview by Akita.

109. Jansen, *Changing Japanese Attitudes*; Koschmann, "Modernization and Democratic Values," 225–50.

110. Bronson, *One Hundred Million Philosophers*; Kersten, *Democracy in Postwar Japan*.

111. Edward Seidensticker, oral history interview, November 10, 1978, Marlene J. Mayo Oral Histories.

AREA STUDIES

112. Gerteis and George, "Revisiting the History of Postwar Japan," 1.
113. Association for Asian Studies annual meeting, March 22, 2019, Denver.

REFERENCES

Archival Collections

Akita, George. Oral History of Japanese Studies Scholars 1960s–1980s. University of Hawai'i at Mānoa Library, Honolulu.

American Studies Seminars in Japan Records (SC0266). Department of Special Collections and University Archives, Stanford University Libraries, Stanford, CA.

Beardsley, Richard K. Papers. Bentley Historical Library, University of Michigan.

Bennett, John W. Papers (RARE.CMS.119). Rare Books and Manuscripts: Collections, Rare Books and Manuscripts Library, Ohio State University.

Current Anthropology Records. Special Collections Research Center, University of Chicago Library.

Eggan, Fred. Papers, 1870–1991. Archival Biographical Files, Special Collections Research Center, University of Chicago Library.

Izumi Seiichi. 1955–57. Series 609: Japan. Rockefeller Foundation Records, Fellowships, Fellowship Files, RG 10.1, 1917–1979. Rockefeller Archive Center.

Izumi Seiichi. Ethnology Research Archives, National Museum for Ethnology, Suita City, Japan.

Levy, Marion J., Jr., 1948–2000. Marion J. Levy Jr. Papers, COU: 985:07:73:01. Special Collections and Archives, University of Colorado Boulder Libraries.

Mayo, Marlene J. Oral Histories. Gordon W. Prange Collection, University of Maryland Libraries.

Passin, Herbert. Collection (MS 565). Special Collections and University Archives, University of Massachusetts Amherst Libraries.

Records of the Allied Operational and Occupation Headquarters (RG 331). National Archives at College Park.

Steward, Julian H. Papers, 1842–1976. University of Illinois Archives, University Library, University of Illinois at Urbana-Champaign.

Published Sources

Baerwald, Hans H. *The Purge of Japanese Leaders under the Occupation.* Berkeley: University of California Press, 1959.

Beardsley, Richard K. *Bibliographic Materials in the Japanese Language on Far Eastern Archaeology and Ethnology.* With John B. Cornell and Edward Norbeck. Ann Arbor: University of Michigan Press, 1950.

Beardsley, Richard K., John W. Hall, and Robert E. Ward. *Village Japan.* Chicago: University of Chicago Press, 1959.

Bennett, John W., Herbert Passin, and Robert K. McKnight. *In Search of Identity: The Japanese Overseas Scholar in America and Japan*. Minneapolis: University of Minnesota Press, 1958.

Berry, Mary Elizabeth. *Japan in Print: Information and Nation in the Early Modern Period*. Berkeley: University of California Press, 2006.

Bolitho, Harold. "Tokugawa Japan: The Return of the Other." In *The Postwar Developments of Japanese Studies in the United States*, edited by Helen Hardacre, 85–114. Boston: Brill, 1998.

Borton, Hugh. *The Reminiscences of Hugh Borton*. New York: Oral History Research Office, Columbia University, 1958.

Bronson, Adam. *One Hundred Million Philosophers: Science of Thought and the Culture of Democracy in Postwar Japan*. Honolulu: University of Hawai'i Press, 2016.

Cameron, Meribeth E. "Far Eastern Studies in the United States." *Far Eastern Quarterly* 7, no. 2 (1948): 115–35.

Chartkoff, Joseph L. "Iwao Ishino (1921–2012)." *American Anthropologist* 115, no. 3 (2013): 534–37.

Conrad, Sebastian. *The Quest for the Lost Nation: Writing History in Germany and Japan in the American Century*. Translated by Alan Nothnagle. Berkeley: University of California Press, 2010.

Cornell, John B. "Ainu Assimilation and Cultural Extinction: Acculturation Policy in Hokkaido." *Ethnology* 3, no. 3 (1964): 287–304.

Crane, Robert I. "News of the Profession: The First Ten Years of the Association for Asian Studies, 1948–1958." *Journal of Asian Studies* 17, no. 4 (1958): 657–78.

Despres, Leo. "An Interview with John W. Bennett." *Current Anthropology* 35, no. 5 (1994): 653–64.

Dower, John W. *Embracing Defeat: Japan in the Wake of World War II*. New York: W. W. Norton, 1999.

Erickson, Paul J., Judy L. Klein, Lorraine Daston, Rebecca Lemov, Thomas Sturm, and Michael D. Gordin. *How Reason Almost Lost Its Mind: The Strange Career of Cold War Rationality*. Chicago: University of Chicago Press, 2013.

Ford, Clellan S. *Human Relations Area Files 1949–1969: A Twenty-Year Report*. New Haven, CT: Human Relations Area Files, 1970.

Garon, Sheldon. "Rethinking Modernization and Modernity in Japanese History: A Focus on State-Society Relations." *Journal of Asian Studies* 53, no. 2 (1994): 346–66.

Gerteis, Christopher, and Timothy S. George. "Revisiting the History of Postwar Japan." In *Japan since 1945: From Postwar to Post-bubble*, edited by Christopher Gerteis and Timothy S. George, 1–9. New York: Bloomsbury, 2013.

Gluck, Carol. "House of Mirrors: American History-Writing on Japan." In *Imagined Histories: American Historians Interpret the Past*, edited by Anthony

Molho and Gordon S. Wood, 434–54. Princeton, NJ: Princeton University Press, 2018.

Hardacre, Helen. Introduction to *The Postwar Developments of Japanese Studies in the United States*, edited by Helen Hardacre, vii–xxviii. Boston: Brill, 1998.

———. "The Postwar Development of the Study of Japanese Religions." In *The Postwar Developments of Japanese Studies in the United States*, edited by Helen Hardacre, 198–99. Boston: Brill, 1998.

Harootunian, H. D., and Masao Miyoshi. "Introduction: The 'Afterlife' of Area Studies." In *Learning Places: The Afterlives of Area Studies*, edited by Masao Miyoshi and H. D. Harootunian, 1–18. Durham, NC: Duke University Press, 2002.

Harris, Sheldon H. *Factories of Death: Japanese Biological Warfare, 1932–1945, and the American Cover-Up*. New York: Routledge, 1994.

Henderson, Clarence. "Role of the Shan States in the Japanese Conquest of Burma." *Far Eastern Quarterly* 2, no. 3 (1943): 253–58.

Hirabayashi, Lane Ryo. *The Politics of Fieldwork: Research in an American Concentration Camp*. Tucson: University of Arizona Press, 1999.

Jansen, Marius B., ed. *Changing Japanese Attitudes toward Modernization*. Princeton, NJ: Princeton University Press, 1965.

———. "History: General Survey." In *Japanese Studies in the United States, Part I: History and Present Condition*, edited by the Japan Foundation, 7–15. Ann Arbor, MI: Association for Asian Studies, 1988.

———. "Stages of Growth." In *Japanese Studies in the United States, Part I: History and Present Condition*, edited by the Japan Foundation, 16–55. Ann Arbor, MI: Association for Asian Studies, 1988.

Kersten, Rikki. *Democracy in Post-war Japan: Maruyama Masao and the Search for Autonomy*. New York: Routledge, 2013.

Kingsberg Kadia, Miriam. *Into the Field: Human Scientists of Transwar Japan*. Stanford, CA: Stanford University Press, 2020.

Koide, Izumi. "Following the Road Paved by Naomi Fukuda." *Journal of East Asian Libraries* 145 (2008): 5–10.

Koschmann, Victor. "Modernization and Democratic Values: The 'Japanese Model' in the 1960s." In *Staging Growth: Modernization, Development, and the Global Cold War*, edited by David C. Engerman, Nils Gilman, Michael E. Latham, and Mark H. Haefele, 225–50. Amherst: University of Massachusetts Press, 2003.

Latham, Michael E. *Modernization as Ideology: American Social Science and "Nation Building" in the Kennedy Era*. Chapel Hill: University of North Carolina Press, 2000.

Marcon, Federico. *The Knowledge of Nature and the Nature of Knowledge in Early Modern Japan*. Chicago: University of Chicago Press, 2015.

Massey, Elizabeth T., and Joseph A. Massey. *CULCON Report on Japanese Studies at Colleges and Universities in the United States in the Mid-70s*. New York: Japan Society, 1977.

Morris-Suzuki, Tessa. "Ethnic Engineering: Scientific Racism and Public Opinion Surveys in Midcentury Japan." *positions: east asia cultures critique* 8, no. 2 (2000): 499–529.

Murdock, George P. "The Cross-Cultural Survey." In *Readings in Cross-Cultural Methodology*, edited by Frank W. Moore, 29–54. New Haven, CT: Human Relations Area Files Press, 1961.

"News of the Profession: Annual Report of the Association for Asian Studies, 1963–1964." *Journal of Asian Studies* 23, no. 4 (1964): 645–67.

Okamoto, Shiro. *The Man Who Saved Kabuki: Faubion Bowers and Theatre Censorship in Occupied Japan*. Translated by Samuel L. Leiter. Honolulu: University of Hawai'i Press, 2001.

Pacific Science Association, ed. *Proceedings of the Seventh Pacific Science Congress of the Pacific Science Association*. Vol. 7, *Anthropology, Public Health and Nutrition, and Social Sciences*. Christchurch, New Zealand: Pegasus, 1953.

Passin, Herbert. *Encounter with Japan*. New York: Kodansha America, 1982.

Pelzel, John C. "Japanese Ethnological and Sociological Research." *American Anthropologist* 50, no. 1 (1948): 54–72.

Price, David H. *Anthropological Intelligence: The Deployment and Neglect of American Anthropology in the Second World War*. Durham, NC: Duke University Press, 2008.

———. *Cold War Anthropology: The CIA, the Pentagon, and the Growth of Dual Use Anthropology*. Durham, NC: Duke University Press, 2016.

———. *Threatening Anthropology: McCarthyism and the FBI's Surveillance of Active Anthropologists*. Durham, NC: Duke University Press, 2004.

Raper, Arthur F. *The Japanese Village in Transition*. Tokyo: General Headquarters, Supreme Commander for the Allied Powers, 1950.

———. *The Reminiscences of Dr. Arthur F. Raper*. New York: Oral History Research Office, Columbia University, 1971.

Rosenfield, John. "Japanese Art Studies in America since 1945." In *The Postwar Developments of Japanese Studies in the United States*, edited by Helen Hardacre, 161–94. Boston: Brill, 1998.

Slesnick, Irwin Leonard, and Carolyn Evelyn Slesnick. *Kanji & Codes: Learning Japanese for World War II*. Bellingham, WA: I. L. and C. E. Slesnick, 2006.

Smith, Robert J. *Kurusu: The Price of Progress in a Japanese Village, 1951–1975*. Stanford, CA: Stanford University Press, 1978.

Speier, Hans. "The Rise of Public Opinion." In *Propaganda and Communication in World History*, vol. 2, *Emergence of Public Opinion in the World*, edited by Harold

D. Lasswell, Daniel Lerner, and Hans Speier, 147–67. Honolulu: University of Hawai'i Press, 1980.

Spinks, Charles Nelson. "Origin of the Japanese Interests in Manchuria." *Far Eastern Quarterly* 2, no. 3 (1943): 259–71.

Steinhoff, Patricia G. *Japanese Studies in the United States and Canada: Continuities and Opportunities.* Tokyo: Japan Foundation, 2007.

Szanton, David L. "The Origin, Nature, and Challenges of Area Studies in the United States." In *The Politics of Knowledge: Area Studies and the Disciplines,* edited by David L. Szanton, 1–33. Berkeley: University of California Press, 2004.

Takakura, Shin'ichirō. *Ainu of Northern Japan: A Study in Conquest and Acculturation.* Translated by John A. Harrison. Philadelphia: American Philosophical Society, 1960.

Tansman, Alan. "Japanese Studies: The Intangible Art of Translation." In *The Politics of Knowledge: Area Studies and the Disciplines,* edited by David L. Szanton, 184–216. Berkeley: University of California Press, 2004.

Totani, Yuma. *The Tokyo War Crimes Trial: The Pursuit of Justice in the Wake of World War II.* Cambridge, MA: Harvard University Asia Center, 2009.

US Cultural Science Mission to Japan. *Report of the United States Cultural Science Mission to Japan.* Seattle: Institute of International Affairs, University of Washington at Seattle, 1949.

Watsuji Tetsurō, Yamamoto Tadaoki, and Nishina Yoshio, eds. *A Bibliography of Representative Writings on Japanese Culture and Science.* Tokyo: Cultural Affairs Division, Office of Public Relations, Foreign Office, 1947.

AUTHOR BIO

MIRIAM KINGSBERG KADIA is Professor of History at the University of Colorado Boulder. She is author of *Moral Nation: Modern Japan and Narcotics in Global History* (2014) and *Into the Field: Human Scientists of Transwar Japan* (2020).

THREE

—ᵐ—

DEBATES ON MODERNIZATION THEORY AT THE HAKONE CONFERENCE

Discrepancies in Value Systems and Perspectives on History

MASAKI FUJIOKA

TRANSLATED BY DANIEL ROY PEARCE

INTRODUCTION

One of the earliest opportunities for Japan to engage with American modernization theory was at the Hakone Conference. Held from August to September 1960, the conference was attended by a total of thirty-four scholars of Japanese studies from the United States, the United Kingdom, Australia, and Japan, including Masao Maruyama and Masaaki Kōsaka. On the part of the US, there was an intention to seek "guidance for underdeveloped countries... through examination of Japan's historical experience of modernization" as a country that had transformed itself from an "unmistakably backward nation" in the nineteenth century to its postwar position as "perhaps the only country in the non-Western world to have succeeded in modernization and industrialization."[1] By extension, the American participants in the Hakone Conference intended to have the Japanese scholars (1) conduct "objective" research into the modernization of Japan, (2) model Japan's process of modernization and strategically export the model to underdeveloped countries, and (3) recommend to the Japanese government policies to maintain their rate of economic growth while acting in concert with the free world, with the US as the leader.[2] In fact, Edwin O. Reischauer, professor of Japanology at Harvard University and participant of the Hakone Conference, after his appointment as ambassador to Japan, engaged in discussion with Hitotsubashi University economist

79

Ichirō Nakayama through the magazine *Chūō Kōron*, concluding that "overall the Japanese model was a tremendous success, and should serve as an 'example' for underdeveloped countries."[3] This perspective of Reischauer's persisted. After leaving his ambassadorial post, he explained his intentions for the Hakone Conference in an article for the *Mainichi Shimbun* newspaper. By raising awareness among Japanese scholars of the "greatest aspect of Japanese modern history," he claimed that "Japan succeeded in modernizing itself more than any other Asian power." American scholars intended to present a countertheory to the Marxist view of history, which continued to exert influence on Japanese intellectuals.[4]

As can be inferred from the above, modernization theory as presented by the American attendees at the Hakone Conference differed from modernization theory as developed by Walt W. Rostow and colleagues at the Massachusetts Institute of Technology's Center for International Studies (MITCIS). According to Ken Kakiuchi's research, there were two distinct schools of thought regarding the theories of modernization that were brought to Japan. One was modernization theory as a Cold War strategy of the United States, with its roots in Russian and Soviet studies in World War II.[5] This theory began to be studied in earnest at MITCIS in 1954 and gave rise to such modernization theories as Rostow's *Stages of Economic Growth* (1960).

The second school of thought was developed by Egerton Herbert Norman, Reischauer, and other Canadian and American Japanologists.[6] It was this modernization theory that was tabled at the Hakone Conference, and it had been developed primarily by American Japanology scholars on the basis of their postwar observations of the history of Japan's modernization. In addition, the American scholars harbored an ambition to develop their theory of modernization into a model that could be applied to other countries throughout Asia and the world.[7] This chapter will focus on this latter modernization theory and examine the debates between Japanese and American researchers on the topic during the 1960s, as well as the discrepancies in their relative historical perspectives that engendered the debates.

Here, I would like to touch on the previous research related to this chapter. First, J. Victor Koschmann, a Japanologist who has been active in the field since the late 1960s, has penned several articles that referred to the Hakone Conference. The most comprehensive of these was "Modernization and Democratic Values" (2003).[8] Also taken up in this chapter are Sannosuke Matsumoto's *The Intellectual State of Modern Japan* (1974) and Tsutomu Tsuzuki's *Intellectuals in Postwar Japan* (1995), which, in contrast to Koschmann's focus on the Hakone Conference itself, place emphasis on the context of Japanese intellectual history before the conference and attempt to understand the situation at and around the conference with respect to this context.[9] Matsumoto and Tsuzuki point out that the American scholars perceived the Japanese researchers as, overall, being strongly influenced by Marxist theory, although this was not actually the case. Although some "Japanese intellectuals committed to the 1960 protest against the Japan-US Security Treaty" participated in the Hakone Conference, not all of them were adherents of Marxism.[10] For instance, in an article for the *Asahi Shimbun* after the Hakone Conference, Reischauer claimed that "Japanese scholars have a tendency, at times, [to] swallow uncritically established theoretical systems such as Marxism."[11]

More recent studies include Samon Kinbara's *Turns and Historical Narratives on the Theory of Modernization* (1999) and *The Subleader of Japanese Modernity* (2005), as well as Ken Kakiuchi's "Japan Studies and Modernization" (2010) and "Masao Murayama's Changing View of Modernization" (2009). These later works differ from both Koschmann, who focused primarily on the Hakone Conference, and Matsumoto and Tsuzuki, who examined the context preceding the conference in addressing the debate on modernization theory between Japanese and American scholars that followed the conference.[12]

Furthermore, previous studies such as Naoko Kōda's *The United States and the Japanese Student Movement, 1948–1973* (2020) have emphasized the importance of the "Reischauer offensive," which included interactions with both intellectuals and workers, as well as prolific writing in a concerted effort by Reischauer to introduce modernization theory into Japan in the 1960s and 1970s.[13] However, Kinbara points out that "after Reischauer's resignation from his post as US Ambassador to Japan, he began to criticize White House policy on Asia" and also became increasingly critical of the modernization theory that he and others had sought to import into Japan.[14] At the same time, Kinbara also argues that key individuals in this chapter, such as American Japanology scholars and modernization theorists John W. Hall and Marius B. Jansen, came under criticism from other American scholars of Japanese studies, including John Dower, during the 1960s and 1970s and had "begun to rethink their methodologies of Asian studies."[15] Kakiuchi also points out that "when looking at American scholars of Japan, there is a generational divide: Reischauer and Norman, who were active during the war, were part of the first generation; Hall and Jansen, actively involved in the 1960s, were the second generation; and the third generation, who began their research in earnest after the Vietnam War." Kakiuchi adds that "John Dower and the rest of the New Left Generation (the third generation)" vehemently opposed Hall, who spoke as president of the

82   AREA STUDIES

Association for Asian Studies (AAS) in January 1968; their objections were so strong that Hall is reported as stating, "We should turn our ears to [Dower]'s generation."[16]

The review of the previous studies makes it clear that (1) the modernization theory that was brought to Japan by Hall, Jansen, and other American scholars at the Hakone Conference and later in the 1960s was not readily accepted by the Japanese scholars and rather became a seed of debate between the Americans and the Japanese that would continue throughout the decade, (2) the Japanese scholars were skeptical of American modernization theory, and the Americans' utter rejection of Communism, which at the time had widely permeated the Japanese scholarly community, inflamed the debate, and (3) from the late 1960s onward, modernization theory as proposed by Hall and colleagues came to be rejected by the younger generation of scholars in American academic circles, including John Dower. This chapter is concerned primarily with points 1 and 3—namely, with what resonances or sympathies can be found between the arguments of the Japanese scholars of the Hakone Conference and of the 1960s and the critiques made by American Japanology scholars such as Dower during the late 1960s and the 1970s.

This chapter aims to examine the aforementioned resonance of ideas between the Japanese scholars at the Hakone Conference and the American scholars of Japanese studies in the latter half of the 1960s through historical analysis of the written work of the parties involved with modernization theory.

DEBATES AT THE HAKONE CONFERENCE

Background of the Hakone Conference and Its Participants

The organizers of the Hakone Conference were University of Michigan professor John W. Hall and the Conference on Modern Japan, established with the support of the Ford Foundation and the AAS.[17] The conference had been proposed and approved at the annual conference of the AAS held in New York in April 1958, and it was subsequently established at the University of Michigan in November, with Hall as representative and with Marius B. Jansen among the five other members. The purpose of the conference was to systemically accumulate and consolidate the results of Japanese studies at universities and research institutions and to explore the possibility of research with new and stimulating ideas and approaches to modern Japan.[18] The conference was intended to formulate a five-year plan along the lines of five research themes, with plans to conduct annual seminars and publish their proceedings. The conference itself was held in Hakone, Kanagawa Prefecture, from August 29 to September 2, 1960, as a preliminary to the five yearly international seminars.[19] According to discussions with Jansen, Hall's initial motivation for founding the Conference on Modern Japan was to bring together the "exotic" aspects of Japanology and unify them into one academic discipline labeled Japanese studies. According to Kakiuchi and Helen Hardacre, "among other things, Hall and Jansen aimed to reform the 'exotic, stereotypical image of Japan and the Japanese,' which was prevalent in the first generation of Japanologists whose work originated in wartime enemy studies" and to revamp the predominant "cultural essentialist research framework."[20] In the previous chapter, Miriam Kingsberg Kadia has already indicated that the second-generation scholars held such impressions regarding the first-generation Japanologists.

In the 1960s, the Ford Foundation, sponsor of the Conference on Modern Japan, was attempting to develop area studies in line with the Central Intelligence Agency (CIA) through financial support for universities. The US government viewed Japan's historical economic experience in particular as a potential model for developing countries.[21] In eventuality, as mentioned in the introduction, the American participants at the Hakone Conference had essentially internalized the intentions of the Ford Foundation and the US government, which guided their objectives at the conference.

It was with these intentions that the Hakone Conference was convened in late August 1960. The main participants of the conference were as follows (the "Proceedings of Preliminary Seminars at Hakone, Japan"):[22]

Ronald Dore (University Reader of Sociology, London School of Economics)

John Hall (Professor of History, University of Michigan)

Marius Jansen (Professor of Modern History, Princeton University)

Shūichi Katō (Associate Professor of Literary Criticism and French Literature, University of British Columbia)

Takeyoshi Kawashima (Professor of Civil Law and Sociology of Law, Faculty of Law, The University of Tokyo)

Masaaki Kōsaka (Professor of Philosophy, Faculty of Letters, Kyoto University)

Marion Levy Jr. (Professor of Sociology, Princeton University)

Masao Maruyama (Professor of Political Science and History of Political Thought, Faculty of Law, The University of Tokyo)

Tsutomu Ōuchi (Professor of Agricultural Economics and Finance, Faculty of Economics, The University of Tokyo)

Edwin Reischauer (Professor of History and Literature, Harvard University)

Yoshio Sakata (Professor of Meiji History, Institute for Research in Humanities, Kyoto University)

Shigeki Tōyama (Professor of History and Modern History, Faculty of Literature and Science, Yokohama City University)

In addition to the twenty-eight researchers, two observers and a Japanese steering committee (including interpreters) of four members, of whom Sadako Nakamura—graduate student at the University of California, Berkeley (later Sadako Ogata, United Nations high commissioner for refugees)—was a participant as an interpreter.[23]

The Nine Criteria for Modern Societies

August 30, 1960, marked the opening of the Hakone Conference. Hall, who chaired the conference, stated in his opening remarks that the theme of the three-day conference would not be "the presentation of individual studies on Japan's modernization" but rather "the concept of modernization and Japan." Unusually for an international conference, it was decided that Japanese would be the "official language," with English used when necessary. On the morning of the first day of the conference, Hall presented the criteria for evaluating modern societies from his paper *Japanese within the Concept of Modernization*, prepared before the conference.[24] Within the paper, the nine essential features of modern societies (hereafter, the nine criteria for modern societies) were as follows:

1. A comparatively high degree of urbanization
2. Widespread literacy
3. Comparatively high per capita income
4. Extensive geographical and social mobility
5. Relatively high degree of commercialization and industrialization within the economy
6. An extensive and penetrative network of mass communication media
7. Widespread participation and involvement by members of the society in modern social and economic processes
8. A relatively highly organized bureaucratic form of government with widespread involvement by members of society
9. An increasingly rational and secular orientation of the individual to his environment based on the growth of scientific knowledge[25]

These nine criteria were both an ingestion and reflection of the modernization theory research being conducted in the US at the time, evidenced by Hall's "statement that typified the American effort to present modernization as an objectively measurable, universal process of which the United States was the prime example," said Koschmann.[26] In fact, the first seven of these criteria were borrowed from Gabriel Almond and James Coleman's *The Politics of the Developing Areas* (1960).[27] On the other hand, these criteria were also established as part of an effort to develop a "conceptual method of analysis that encompasses the process of modernization, cognizant of various historical changes."[28] In other words, Hall and the American participants had an interest in elevating the phenomenon of modernization to a universal theory of social change, and this interest in turn intensified the debate at the Hakone Conference.[29]

The participants at the conference were already aware of Rostow's theory and appeared to show interest in theories of modernization. However, many of the Japanese scholars harbored doubts toward the "overly objectivist . . . approach" of Hall and the American researchers.[30] According to the "Proceedings of Preliminary Seminars at Hakone, Japan," Tsutomu Ōuchi was the first to object to Hall's proposed nine criteria. He argued that, "if we put too much focus on Japan, we must think of the modernization process as a capitalist process" and that, as a result, Hall's categories for modernization necessarily exclude socialist societies.[31] Ōuchi's remarks drew attention to the internal problems with Hall's theory, as he adroitly pointed out that the nine criteria had been established for the sole purpose of discussing the modernization of Japan, and thus it was "not possible to apply the criteria to discussions of world history as a whole."

Such modernization theory (i.e., Hall and colleagues' attempt to simplify as much as possible the indices for measuring modernization and to construct a universal theory applicable to all regions) drew opposition not only from Ōuchi but also from Masao Maruyama and Masaaki Kōsaka.[32] Spearheading the criticism, however, was Takeyoshi Kawashima, scholar of the Civil Code and its social implications and professor in the Faculty of Law at the University of Tokyo. According to the conference proceedings, "in response to Ōuchi's identification of the problems in this approach to modernization, which limits the issue to capitalism with a specific focus on Japan, Kawashima made a number of important comments."[33] First, in an attempt to clarify Hall's position, Kawashima remarked, "It seems to me that you are attempting to position Japan within the context of the processes of change in world history on a global scale, including the near and Middle East." In addition, he stated that

86   AREA STUDIES

the Japanese scholars sought not a "theory that can only be applied to Japan, but something more universal."[34]

Perceiving that Kawashima was suggesting that the nine criteria were far from adequate as a universal model, Jansen, a close ally of Hall's, made the following response in defense of Hall's objective of developing a universal standard for assessing modernization: "As scholars, is it not true that we are compelled to develop theory from fact? You [Kawashima] have said that the Japanese standpoint is different, and while our experiences may indeed be different, are not our interests as scholars the same? I would like to discuss the issue of whether or not capitalization is an appropriate concept of modernization, methodologically speaking, without emphasizing the difference in positions between the Americans and the Japanese."

In response, Kawashima simply replied, "That was my intended meaning." When this debate continued into the years that followed the conference, however, critical remarks regarding Hall's approach began to emerge from both Japanese and American scholars.[35]

"Democracy" and the Problem of Defining Political Terms

The debate between the Japanese and American scholars began to stray off course after the immediate, unexpected opposition to Hall's nine criteria. However, criticism of the criteria was not the only issue raised on the first morning—also brought to the table was the problem of defining political terms to be used in the discussions. Marion Levy Jr., professor of sociology at Princeton University, who described himself as being "particularly fastidious with definitions," remarked that the "difference in approaches between the Japanese and American scholars" was not necessarily problematic. Rather, he criticized, the Japanese researchers took "highly general concepts such as capitalism, feudalism, and revolution amongst others" as if they were givens, while he thought "these concepts themselves must be defined more precisely."[36] The minutes of the first morning of the conference conclude with this statement of Levy's, although Kawashima's article "Essay on Social Science Research regarding Modern Japanese History," (hereafter, "Essay") published after the conference in April 1961, provides further information.[37]

In "Essay," Kawashima notes that the conflict occurred in a context in which Japanese researchers' "conceptual frameworks were not necessarily clear" to the Americans. For instance, the American researchers recall that "the concept of feudalism, as used by the Japanese, was simply a symbol of the 'negative' or 'undesirable'" and thus an emotionally laden concept to be avoided. He also notes an instance in which an American scholar "rather tersely" demanded of the Japanese researchers to "answer the question of whether you are problematizing democracy itself, or not."[38] Kawashima argues that this difference in perceptions of political concepts between the Japanese and American scholars was a reason the Hakone Conference diverged from the theme of Japan's modernization.

In the afternoon session, when the conference resumed, *democracy*, specifically, was taken up from among a number of political terms whose definitions were proving to be problematic, and the discrepancy in perceptions of democracy between the two groups became apparent. As mentioned above, Hall and colleagues' intention was to "analyze Japan's modern history" while "refining and universalizing the concept of 'modernization.'"[39] In the afternoon session, as the issue of defining political terms and the question of whether or not democracy should be viewed as an indicator of modernity became intertwined, the debate "devolved into a rather disorderly process."[40] However, even in the midst of such "disorderly" discussions, the debate on democracy became more distinct, and the discussion converged on "another approach to the topic of modernization."[41]

Masao Maruyama, a political scientist and professor in the University of Tokyo's Faculty of Law, became central to the discussion. He began with "apologies for speaking in the abstract," before raising the question of "why modernity should be problematized."[42] According to Tsutomu Tsuzuki, primarily the American scholars had attempted to satisfy themselves with criteria for the modernization theory that included such elements as urbanization, the spread of literacy, and rise in personal income, and therefore, while Hall and colleagues sought to develop quantitatively comparable criteria within a research framework for the "evaluation and measurement of modernization," their modernization theory did not address value judgments. In response, Maruyama perceived a need to deepen the discussion of issues such as ideologies and ethos.[43]

As a matter of fact, upon close scrutiny, Maruyama's awareness of these issues was already evident on the morning of the first day. As mentioned above, in the morning session, Hall had asked the participants to consider what elements of his nine criteria were insufficient and to deepen the discussion of the interconnections between the individual criteria, to which Maruyama, encouraging a shift in the subject matter from the surface-level aspects of modernization toward value systems, raised the following question: "In my opinion, the [nine criteria] are too sociological. For example, the rational orientation of individuals towards the environment is ultimately a matter of consciousness and attitude. In this dimension, is it not necessary to address the issue of individuals' value systems?"[44]

88

AREA STUDIES

In response, Hall admitted that "the nine criteria do not provide much clarity [on indicators of an individual's value system]." Maruyama continued to criticize the criteria: "By including only one ethos [as a value system]," the criteria "seem arbitrary and haphazard."[45] Hall rebutted by stating, "I wrote the ninth criterion as just such an attempt to point to the value systems and ethos that you have mentioned. If there is a clearer manner of conceptualizing this, we can add it," although Hall avoided giving specific examples of what could be "added."[46]

It was Yoshio Sakata, professor at Kyoto University's Institute for Research in Humanities, who responded to Maruyama and Hall's exchange over value systems. Sakata pointed out that "if we consider what has changed qualitatively, the clearest element is the value system" and that "in considering the relationship between Japanese traditions and modernization, it is precisely systems of value that are important." With this statement, Sakata argued that Hall's criteria did not "necessarily deal with issues of individual consciousness" and that it was important to deepen the discussion of value systems in the debate on modernization.[47] Professor Masaaki Kōsaka of Kyoto University's Faculty of Letters, in agreement with Maruyama, attempted to redirect the debate to the question of value systems from the perspective of the modern man: "In terms of modernization, I think notions of rationality and progress will become relevant, and thus I believe it is appropriate to problematize ideological aspects. In other words, the issue is man, and thus it is modern man who is of interest to us. I would like to add him to the theoretical definition of modern society."[48]

Maruyama, Sakata, and Kōsaka were not the only participants to focus on the notion of value systems as a necessary component of modernization. Tsuzuki pointed out that "it goes without saying that Marxists such as Tsutomu Ōuchi and Shigeki Tōyama opposed the lumping together of capitalism and socialism under one concept of modernization."[49] He also highlighted the point that "on the Japanese side, Maruyama and many others criticized the view prepared by the American researchers for downplaying the issue of changes in values and value consciousness, which are the root of all social change," and that these criticisms of Hall and colleagues' modernization theory were formed in a way that transcended ideological differences.[50]

The Japanese scholars expressed concern regarding the nine criteria in this manner because they had borne witness to both the suppression of speech in the 1930s and defeat in the war. They also experienced the radical dissent surrounding the Treaty of Mutual Cooperation and Security between the United States and Japan (US-Japan Security Treaty) of June 1960. According to Kawashima, "For the Japanese, modernization has been a practical issue since the Meiji era, and especially after the 1930s, a real issue for Japanese intelligentsia as a means of breaking away from autocracy and realizing democratic principles. As a result, many Japanese social scientists, when facing the issue of modernization, were both *motivated by* and *interested in* such practical necessities, which also guided their approaches."[51]

While the American scholars "relatively highly evaluated Japan's achievements in modernization," it was "difficult for [the Japanese scholars] to accept" that the American researchers placed so little importance on the "key issue of the shifting of value consciousness."[52]

Nevertheless, the American scholars attempted to dismiss the Japanese scholars' claim that the issue of their value systems (e.g., democratic political institutions and individual democratic attitudes) in modernization was essential to the development of the indicators of modernization theory. It was Jansen who came to Hall's defense in the debate among Hall, Maruyama, Sakata, and Kōsaka, arguing that Maruyama's concepts of individual consciousness and attitudes "[did] not fall within the nine criteria," as they were consequential phenomena resulting from "national and political participation achieving a certain level of development," and the issue was rather "the process of modernization, which takes place in [all] nation states."[53] American researchers, or perhaps modernization theorists in general, apparently believed that the issue of democracy should be shelved until developing countries achieve economic development and stability as independent nations, which they thought should be given higher priority.

In this way, the Hakone Conference did not achieve its goal of elevating the nine criteria for modern societies to a universal theory, based on the modernization of Japan, that could be applied to the rest of the world. According to Koschmann, the Hakone Conference "took a different, political turn" from the intentions of the American organizers, toward the issue of "whether democracy was, or was not, an integral part of modernization."[54] In a roundtable discussion with Ryūichi Narita, Chizuko Ueno, and Yūko Nishikawa in 2006, Koschmann succinctly summarized the problem with the Hakone Conference: "The Japanese side consistently raised the issue of democracy, and while Masao Maruyama argued that achieving democracy was impossible without first developing the modern man, and thus, that modernization means not only the development of democratic institutions, but also human development, the Americans were completely unable to grasp why this was an important issue."[55] As a result, for Japanese researchers, the Hakone Conference will be remembered as a conference that fostered conflict with American scholars over

DEBATES IN THE LITERATURE AFTER
THE HAKONE CONFERENCE

John W. Hall's "The Modernization of Japan," and Takeyoshi
Kawashima's Essay on the 1960 Hakone Conference

The magnitude of the discrepancy between the Japanese and American researchers at the Hakone Conference was symbolized through the ensuing debate in the literature between John W. Hall and Takeyoshi Kawashima. In January 1961, John Hall penned an essay for the editorial *Shisō*, titled "The Modernization of Japan," in which he spoke negatively about the conference, describing it as "very inefficient" and adding that he "looks back on it with a certain degree of skepticism" and that, "in fact, a conference of thirty participants is indeed very inefficient as an intellectual organism."[57] Hall further complains that "a number of articles on the Hakone Conference in Japanese newspapers [referring, presumably, to the contributions of Shigeki Tōyama and Ronald Dore's 'Mondai ishiki no sōi' to the *Mainichi Shimbun*] discussed in great detail the fundamental differences in perspective that separated the Japanese and the Western scholars" and that he did not want "the differences that emerged at Hakone to be explained away on an ethnic basis alone."[58] In the first place, according to Hall, "the question that has troubled American scholars is whether it is possible to arrive at a general theory of modernization, taking into account all the many phenomena of the developing societies of the world."[59] Hall was dissatisfied that the nine criteria presented at the conference "ended up not being given proper consideration" and that "many differences of perspective were implied but remained unresolved or even undebated," noting that it was "impossible . . . to achieve an ideal state of equilibrium between the participants in terms of individuality, specialization, and research background."[60]

Hall states that his understanding was that, at the Hakone Conference, they were not necessarily dealing with "a process that automatically entails achieving 'better lives' . . . in other words, the values of democracy, civil liberties, or economic equality are not necessarily a part of the modernization process itself."[61] Within the same paper, however, Hall proposes a revision of the criteria that "went undebated" at the Hakone Conference and presents the "Seven Criteria of Modern Society."[62] Hall, demonstrating his tenacity in both setting and justifying evaluative criteria, writes, "As was so often expressed at the [Hakone] conference, the conditions for 'modernity' must be considered as applying to a holistic organic process, and [the "Seven Criteria of Modern Society"] must be seen as interrelated components within this organic process. In their interconnectedness, these criteria form the overall condition of society in a way that is qualitatively different from other nonmodern conditions, as some of the conference participants pointed out."[63]

On the other hand, Kawashima voiced doubts about the modernization theory introduced by Hall and other American researchers. In his "Essay" article, published in *Shisō* in April 1961, three months after Hall's "The Modernization of Japan," he writes:

> Of course, for some people or some states "democracy" may not constitute a major problem in the process of modernization. But, at a conference in which "modernization" was conceived of as a process which would affect every society . . . each in its own time and at its own speed, a process which would embrace the social revolutions of Soviet Russia, Communist China and Asia and Africa, that [democracy] was not brought up for discussion at all left me most dissatisfied. . . . As for me, I would like to know whether the values of "democracy" or the *social and political structure* which goes under the name of "democracy" should be included within the "working hypothesis" of the process of modernization.[64]

In his article "The Meaning of Modernization," published in *Shisō* in 1963, Kawashima further pushed the issue by directly challenging Hall and colleagues' modernization theory: "What is the purpose, in this late age, of using a single term . . . to envelop a diverse range of historical changes into a single concept?"[65] Kawashima draws from his analysis of the debate over the definition of political terms that took place at the Hakone Conference and concludes that *capitalism* is "a term used for civil society" and that "modernization . . . when referring to places other than the West is . . . intended theoretically to hold the West (especially Britain) as a model or even an ideal," a sentiment that resonates with Tsutomu Ōuchi's arguments at the conference.[66] Kawashima continues to say that "if Hall and colleagues aim to elevate modernization theory to a universal theory, it is curious that they do not take into consideration the political phenomenon of democracy."[67]

In regard to this flippancy toward the value of democracy, Kochmann touches on the duplicity of the American researchers; from the perspective of American scholars, Japan was simultaneously seen as a "model of modernization success that is worthy of imitation by other . . . non-Western regions" and as "a non-Western country at risk of falling under the sway of the communists."[68]

92 AREA STUDIES

This was in part due to the discrepancy in the two countries' perspectives on history.

Hall's Rebuttal of Kawashima

In "Changing Conceptions of the Modernization of Japan," in *Changing Japanese Attitudes toward Modernization*, edited by Jansen and published in 1965, John W. Hall reflected on the Hakone Conference, reiterating his opposition to Kawashima and reaffirming the lack of necessity of including democracy in the nine criteria for modern societies or in the "Seven Criteria." First, Hall outlines his intent to present modernization theory as a "more comprehensive" set of criteria, noting that "the work of the modern social scientist has been confined pretty much to his limited disciplinary interest. The problem of creating a unified concept of modernization has received scant attention."[69] Hall cites Shūichi Katō, assistant professor at the University of British Columbia, to demonstrate the reasons for presenting the comprehensive modernization theory and for wishing to examine the connections between the criteria: "As Mr. Kato put it, criteria of the sort we have just listed are like the symptoms of a disease in an individual. 'In treating an illness we do not start with just any manifestation of disorder but consider the several symptoms and their relationships in a syndrome so as to obtain a complete picture. Such a unified approach to modernization recommends itself by its elegance.'"[70]

However, discussions at the Hakone Conference focused on "questions of spirit and values," and Hall was disappointed that the theme of modernization had taken "a different and more political turn, becoming associated with the question of whether or not democracy was an essential element of modernization."[71] Hall further quotes from Kawashima's "Essay," which was a leading proponent of the claim that "democracy is an essential element of modernization" (part of the following has already been cited above, but for clarity, Hall's quotation of Kawashima is included here):

> "Democracy" is as we all know a matter of greatest concern to Japanese. . . . Of course, for some people or some states "democracy" may not constitute a major problem in the process of modernization. But for a conference which took as its objective the discussion of "modernization in Japan," not to take under consideration such an important question was, in my opinion, unduly one-sided. This is not all. At a conference in which modernization was conceived of as a process which would affect every society . . . each in its own time and at its own speed, a process which would embrace the social revolutions of Soviet Russia, Communist China and Asia and Africa, that [democracy] was not brought up for discussion at all left me most dissatisfied.

If in analyzing the historical changes which affect Asia, Africa and Latin America today we ignore the value of "democracy" or its *motive power* we will end in having no true analysis and, I believe, we will be mistaken in our assessment of the future of these societies.[72]

Hall's fixation on Kawashima can be inferred from his lengthy quotation of "Essay." In rebuttal to Kawashima, Hall states that the American group had pointed out that "a fundamental reason why our era is so unsettled and turbulent is simply that the attraction of democratic ideals has come to be felt everywhere in the world" and that it is nothing other than "the democratic dream that is keeping the world on edge." Hall then argues that "what dominated the Hakone Conference" was, rather than an embrace of uncritical optimism for democracy, "an air of skepticism" that made the "Western participants feel hesitant [to discuss democracy within the criteria of modern society]."[73]

Hall continues to rebut Kawashima: "The question of democracy can be resolved into whether rationalization of the political and social aspects of society necessarily leads 'in the long run' to the adoption of democratic values," a question "which the Western scholars at Hakone found difficult to answer on empirical grounds alone" and "which is difficult to discuss without reference to political issues."[74] Even at this stage, Hall remained intent on formulating his criteria for addressing the problem of modernization without addressing the value systems of democracy as a criterion.

CRITICISM FROM THE "THIRD GENERATION" OF AMERICAN JAPANOLOGISTS

As we have examined above, the modernization theory, as proposed by Hall and the other American researchers at the Hakone Conference, lacked from the beginning, in the criteria for measuring modernization, any indices related to democracy or individualism, considered to be prerequisites for a modern society, and this point formed the core of the Japanese scholars' criticisms. However, such criticisms of modernization theory were not accepted by the American researchers until the late 1960s. Kakiuchi points out that Hall's attitude did not change until the latter half of the decade, when the Council for Modern Japanese Studies (i.e., American scholars of Japanese studies) began to "reflect on the preexisting research frameworks."[75]

At this point, it is pertinent to reflect on the fact that the generation preceding Hall and colleagues, the so-called first generation of Japanology, had been under the pressure of anti-Communism and McCarthyism. Here, I would like to focus on E. Herbert Norman, Canadian diplomat and prominent Japanologist, whose works include *Japan's Emergence as a Modern State* (1940), *Soldier and Peasant in Japan* (1943), and *Andō Shōeki and the Anatomy of Japanese Feudalism* (1949). According to Mataji Miyamoto, Norman thought, in *Japan's Emergence as a Modern State*, that "the Edo period was an obstacle, and a negative one toward modernization."[76] Norman argued that although "the people, particularly the peasantry and city poor," wrestled with "the destruction of Tokugawa feudalism" and "extend[ed] the anti-feudal movement by action from below," "the new Government set itself... firmly against any demand for further reform on the part of the lower orders."[77] Norman regarded the Edo period as a time of societal corruption that should be disavowed and held the view that the Meiji government "required a powerful state-machine, a centralized government with a considerable constabulary or military force at its proposal."[78] In addition, the "Meiji government... initiated industrialization and created army." Furthermore, Miyamoto reports that Norman continued: "There was a civil liberties movement in the early 1880s that was completely dismantled by police force and government strategy, and that this suppression of Japanese democracy continued until the day of surrender in 1945."[79]

Norman's take on Japan's history thus negatively evaluated the modernization of Japan from the Edo period through the Meiji Restoration until defeat in the Pacific War. Needless to say, this perception of history stood in stark contrast to that held by the American scholars who participated in the Hakone Conference. Much as Norman did, Reischauer, another of the first generation of Japanology scholars, argued in *Japan: Past and Present* (1946) and *The United States and Japan* (1951) that "it is necessary to point out the imperfections and strains in the history of Japan's modernization, and to consider the reasons for them, but even more imperative now is the need to study why modernization was possible."[80] Reischauer also believed that Japan had developed a feudal system similar to that of Europe; that "this feudalism passively allowed, rather than actively fostered, modernization"; and that "although feudal society had many negative aspects, there was something about it that allowed for a new direction, a modernization." In other words, for Reischauer, "the Edo period was not a prior stage in the negative sense of the word, but an active precursor," one to be affirmed.[81]

In the 1950s, it was the so-called second generation of scholars, including Hall, who took the lead in Japanese studies. For more information on this topic, we can refer to Miyamoto's work; the US occupation forces' vision of modernizing Japan by their own hand "gave way to a sense of mission to subjugate the Communist Party," and Norman was swept up in the storm of anti-Communism and driven to suicide in Cairo in 1957. In other words, Miyamoto points out that, owing to the political climate of anti-Communism, Norman—who, without fully appreciating the Edo and Meiji eras and the Pacific War, regarded the modernization of Japan as having occurred through a revolution from below—was deprived of not only his academic achievements but also his own life.[82]

John Dower, in an article in the special edition of *Shisō* titled "E. H. Norman: Twenty Years after His Death," published in April 1977, wrote, "In the 1960s, [Norman's] discipline itself was stigmatized and distorted, and his modernization theory was almost entirely devoured by the garish machinations of the academic world."[83] Dower continued:

> We will never be able to enter the mind of Norman in those last agonizing days, to know fully what it was that made him take his own life. But we can say with some certainty that it was McCarthyism that ultimately destroyed his will to live.... In retrospect, the neglect of Norman's writings and the vilification of them must also be attributed to the rigorous and pervasive intellectual legacy of McCarthyism in America. This legacy consisted of two things: the indelible fear of political retribution and the involvement of anti-Communism stemming from genuine liberalism and, by that very same token, of an anti-Marxist crusade.[84]

As Dower argues, from the 1950s to the 1960s, Norman and the first generation of Japanese studies scholars were labeled as Communist and Marxist in their view of history. In contrast, the second generation, including Hall and Jansen, embraced the self-perception that they had been trained academically in the creeds of "value neutrality" and "objectivity." In his presidential address to the AAS annual conference in Philadelphia in March 1968, almost eight years after the Hakone Conference, Hall described his academic stance as follows: "For our part, we are annoyed by accusations based on political bias. I also firmly believe that our postwar generation, nurtured by the academic methodology of area studies, has been able to consider an objective approach to foreign studies."[85]

Hall appeals to the second generation of Japanese studies scholars (including himself) as having the academic foundation to measure Japan's modernization with "objective" indicators, and to establish a universal modernization theory.

On the other hand, Hall was unable to ignore the criticisms that came from the American Japanese studies scholarship.[86] According to Hall, "Recently, we have been criticized for holding an 'imperialist bias.' . . . Those leveling such criticisms are clearly the same group of people who are critical of the Japanese government's [Meiji] centennial project. But such accusations are not solely coming from these people. One could discount politically motivated criticism, but even removing political motivation, there are many glaring differences between the academics of [the United States and Japan], that should give us pause for thought."[87]

Hall also points out that critics came from among both Marxist-inspired Japan and the third generation of Japanese studies scholars, intellectual successors of Norman's.

At the 1960 Hakone Conference, Hall's objective was to "measure the degree of modernization through the employment of objective criteria." However, as we have seen in this chapter, the Japanese researchers criticized a lack of value-judgment indicators regarding political concepts such as feudalism, capitalism, and democracy. At the time, Hall countered that, "strictly speaking, these general terms should not be applied to the explanation of modernization's various causes."[88]

However, during this talk, Hall admitted that his and his colleagues' modernization theory had "little to say about the process [necessary for an analysis of modernization]."[89] He acknowledged that it was important to take into account skepticism about political and social problems, such as the fear of nuclear war and population explosion that became significant issues throughout the 1960s; "we also need to pay heed to the position that modernization does not necessarily lead to an ideal society," he said.[90]

Hall's change in stance stems from his experience of direct involvement with the political and social changes of the 1960s, which led him to the realization that "we cannot ignore the fact that ideals closely related to the 'social habitat' define, in a decisive way, the character of each academic discipline."[91] Reischauer, also, "after resigning his post as ambassador to the United States, as if casting off his allegiance to the White House, and as a liberal, actively stoked the fires of idealism. Around 1967 or 1968 he began to criticize the White House's 'imperialist' policy in Asia."[92] In other words, the despair over US foreign policy after the quagmire of the Vietnam War made American Japanese studies scholars critical of the modernization theory of Hall and colleagues.

Kakiuchi points out that the third-generation critics of modernization, such as John Dower, to whom Hall referred at the end of his address, were responsible for Hall's change in direction. Kakiuchi adds that Hall's stance that their arguments should be given due heed was a result of their "considerably intense" criticism of him.[93] In his April 1977 article in *Shisō*, Dower describes the generation before him as "a generation educated to accept with little question, such ideas as academic 'objectivity' non-political and non-ideological 'empiricism,' 'learning free from value judgments,' and the 'free market of ideas,' ... without any rigorous association with bourgeois values, capitalist structures, or social stratification and inequality."[94] And while the second generation of Japanese scholars feel that it is a virtue to be a discipline "free from value judgments" and "unquestioning of bourgeois society," the belief *"that academia should be free from value judgments"* has, on the contrary, brought about a "mass technocratic class of academics" that is "harmful" in the sense that "its indifference to the moral issues it produces and to the higher and more humane ideals of liberalism runs counter to reality," and this was "manifested in a most criminal extreme" during the Vietnam War. Eminent social scientists such as Samuel Huntington of Harvard University, for example, have argued that since "urbanization" is a sign of "modernization," the declining population of the rural Vietnamese townships and the densification of the cities are actually accelerating "Vietnam's progress toward modernity."[95]

Furthermore, Dower borrows Jansen's statement to argue, "What matters is *that people read*, not *what they read*. It is the participation in the generalized yesterday of mass society, not whether we do so as free individuals."[96] Dower also critically points to the fact that "these views were expressed in the early 1960s in a matter-of-fact manner among American scholars."[97] And Dower views the Hakone Conference as an extension of such "liberal academic [pursuit]," free from value judgments, actively or passively embracing McCarthyism, and says that "the separation of state and university has been largely discarded ... and this is now the intellectual caricature of the liberal social sciences."[98]

At the Hakone Conference, which Dower sees as taking place at the height of the modernization theory craze, modernization theory was adopted as the basic framework for Western Japanese (studies) research and was the guiding academic orthodoxy in 1960. For Dower, modernization theory was nothing more than "a lengthy shopping list diligently compiled of its various ingredients," which was, "after all, remarkably simplified." Hence, Dower defined the essence of modernization—and thus the proper focus of academic study—within modernization theory at the Hakone Conference as consisting of "beliefs of rationalization, mechanization, and progress." These three basic principles of modernization theory were invoked with an almost evangelical fervor and became the idols of the liberalists. However, Dower argues that when the Vietnam War caused "contemporary social science research to support and foster the expansionist and counter-revolutionary activities of the United States and the so-called 'free world,' Western scholarship on Japan in the 1960s aided and abetted in the emphasizing the rhetoric of the 'success' of

98 AREA STUDIES

Japanese modernization through the gradual, non-revolutionary methods by which it was accomplished."[99]

Dower also mentions that after the Hakone Conference, the Conference on Modern Japan held six major conferences with the theme of Japan's modernization in the 1960s.[100] While Dower acknowledged that these efforts had broadened and refined Western understandings of Japan and that the topics addressed and the research methods employed had become considerably more diverse, he did not overlook the enormous sums of money that had been invested in this effort, which "brings about its own problems" in "the complex interrelationships between universities, foundations, and governments."[101] Dower says, "If my own impressions within the field of Japanese Studies are correct, many Western scholars of Japan now [in 1977] look back on the general scholarly achievements of this period with bewilderment and disappointment." This is because of "the proof in the literature of the basic anti-Marxist character of modernization theory, or rather that it is a counter-ideology rather than a theory."[102]

Some twenty years later, in 1995, Dower published in *Shisō* an article titled "Sizing Up (and Breaking Down) Japan," in which he summarized the modernization theory of the 1960s. First, Dower writes, "from the mid-1950s, as Japan came to be seen as an indispensable ally of America's in the Cold War in Asia, English-speaking scholarship on Japan changed dramatically," and as a result, "Western scholars, under the overwhelming influence of modernization theory, came to see pre-war state repression and aggression as a kind of temporary derailment." Dower argues that, under modernization theory approaches, "the authoritarian regime of the Meiji period was underestimated . . . and the firm sense that it had given rise to the tyranny and militarism of the 1930s was discarded . . . the pre-war economy was seen as having made intrinsically sound and excellent progress toward achieving 'modern economic growth,'" an inheritance of Norman's view.[103]

Furthermore, Dower sees the modernization theory "exported" to Japan in the 1960s as "reflecting an anti-Marxist and highly autonomist theoretical model" in the Cold War setting. In this theory, according to Dower, "all non-Communist states, as they 'modernized' capitalistically, became more and more like the developed countries of Europe and the US, and the premise was that this was how it should be." In short, modernization theorists have internalized "the ways in which the trajectory of modern social, political, and economic development in Japan is such that the trajectory of modern development in the country 'converges' with the Western model," he concludes. In other words, Dower was aware that modernization theory introduced by

Hall and colleagues was more Eurocentric than "universal." Dower criticizes Hall's modernization theory as "rife with arrogance in a double sense" because such modernization theory did not "merely assume that Japan would develop in basically the same way and in the same direction as the other advanced Western countries" but also included the presupposition that "Japan would never actually 'catch up' with the United States." In Dower's words, Japan was "more than just a late developer" for the US but was forever destined to play the role of "it" in a game of tag. As such, Japan was a country that was "fitting for Americans to treat with patience and tolerance."[104] At the time of the Hakone Conference, the Japanese scholars were acutely aware of the intellectual "arrogance" of the American researchers, who sought to separate Japan's pre–Pacific War history from that of the Pacific War era and thereby to induce Japan to Eurocentricity through modernization theory, while simultaneously attempting to establish the universality of modernization as a theory, and this awareness engendered a discrepancy that could not be reconciled at the Hakone Conference.

CONCLUSION

John W. Hall did not take seriously the criticisms of his and his colleagues' modernization theory as raised by the Japanese scholars at the Hakone Conference in 1960, and he argued against them in a dismissive manner. In the latter half of the 1960s, however, he was able to reconcile the criticisms of the so-called third generation of American Japanese studies scholars. Reischauer, in the immediate aftermath of the Hakone Conference, had a keen insight into the discrepancies that intensified the debate:

> [At the Hakone Conference] there was an interesting contrast between the attitudes of Japanese and Western scholars, in that Japanese scholars have experienced the process of Japanese modernization firsthand and are therefore more likely to consider the process in terms of values.... The Western researchers, on the other hand, tend to consider the modernization more objectively, as to them, [Japanese modernization] has not been such a personal experience. I reserve judgment in terms of right and wrong regarding what has happened in the past century, but merely attempt to describe and analyze the events.... [Nevertheless] this contrast [in attitudes] is a natural one. Western scholars, who study Japanese history from the outside, predictably first compare Japanese history with the modern history of other peoples, develop theoretical frameworks, and then measure the facts against them.[105]

The Western scholars, studying Japanese history from the outside, tended to "lay out the theoretical frameworks and then measure the facts against them," and, for Hall and Reischauer at the Hakone Conference, such an approach was only natural. On the other hand, the Japanese researchers, who attached importance to the value systems of feudalism and socialism, capitalism and democracy, could not possibly accept the American stance of withholding judgment. Furthermore, the American assumption that Japanese researchers were generally under the influence of Marxism was also a reason for not addressing any of the Japanese arguments at the Hakone Conference or in the debates that followed.

However, this was not the only discrepancy between the sides in the debate over modernization theory. In his 1978 article for *Shisō*, Jansen, an ally of Hall's, argued that while their modernization theory "is seen as a pernicious conspiracy by the [American] government, foundations, and universities to maintain the Japanese system that exists today and to add another pillar to prop it up and under the auspices of US-Japan cooperation," this argument was already raised in Japan in the 1960s, and "they [the Japanese scholars] now hear the echoes of their theories among the young American scholars of the late 1960s."[106] The opposite, however, was true, and the American researchers who participated in the Hakone Conference, along with Hall, Jansen, and others, were now paying heed to the "echoes" of criticism emanating from the Japanese researchers at the Hakone Conference in 1960 and in the following years; they were hearing the resonance of arguments of the Japanese scholars who attended the conference, emanating now from the third generation of Japanese studies scholars. The Japanese scholars believed that, in considering and theorizing Japan's modernization, it was impossible to ignore Japan's past, from the Edo period through to the Meiji Restoration, the militarism and oppression of the 1930s, and the defeat in the Pacific War, and therefore, in discussions of the modernization of Japan, democracy, among other value systems, should necessarily be included in indices of modernization theory. However, Hall and colleagues' focus was set determinedly on postwar Japan; no matter the severity of Japan's past experiences, it only needed to modernize economically for "the future." This was the very idea that suggested, as Dower observed, that "Japan was a mere 'latecomer,'" that "Japan would never actually 'catch up' with the US," and that it was "fitting for Americans to treat with patience and tolerance."[107] This idea was also the substrate of the debate that arose in the 1960s over the modernization theory of the American Japanese studies scholars, and at the root were discrepancies in perceptions of the value system of democracy, as well as perceptions of the history of Japan leading up to the Pacific War. An understanding of these discrepancies is the key to understanding the modernization theory debate of the 1960s.

—⚭—

ACKNOWLEDGMENTS

I wish to express my gratitude to Kengo Suzuki for his insights into the "Proceedings of Preliminary Seminars at Hakone, Japan" and the previous research, and to Hiroaki Yoshikawa and Shōtaro Shindo for their advice on the literature on postwar Japanese intellectuals. Aya Ogata aided in the collection of materials. Finally, I wish to express my appreciation to the students of the Lecture on Multicultural Society 1 course at Kyoto University in 2020, whose comments were extremely insightful.

NOTES

1. Harada, "Nihon no kindaika to keizai hatten," 117.
2. Koschmann, "Modernization and Democratic Values," 226.
3. Reischauer and Nakayama, "Nihon kindaika no rekishiteki hyōka," 97.
4. Reischauer, "Tōzai 'kangaekata' no kōkan: Hakone kaigi ni sanka shite" *Mainichi Shimbun*, 7; Kakiuchi, "Nihon kenkyū to kindaikaron," 4.
5. Kakiuchi, 4.
6. Kakiuchi, 4.
7. Reischauer's "modernization theory" explains the process of modernization using a four-quadrant diagram, with the y axis describing the political situation from "total democracy" to "absolute autocracy" and the x axis describing the economy, ranging from "totally controlled economy" to "total free market economy." Reischauer and Nakayama, *Nihon kindai no atarashii mikata*, 130–60. As will be touched upon later in the chapter, this "modernization theory" was employed rather inflexibly by its proponents.
8. For instance, Koschmann, "Intellectuals and Politics," 412–14.
9. Matsumoto, *Kindai Nihon no chiteki jōkyō*; Tsuzuki, *Sengo Nihon no chishikijin*.
10. Tsuzuki, *Sengo Nihon no chishikijin*, 389.
11. Raischauer, "Tōzai 'kangaekata' no kōkan," 7.
12. Kinbara, *Kindaikaron no tenkai to rekishi jojutsu*; Kinbara, *Nihon kindai no sabu rīdā*; Kakiuchi, "Nihon kenkyū to kindaikaron"; Kakiuchi, "Maruyama Masao no kindaikaron no henyō ni tsuite," 13–26.
13. See, for instance, Kōda, "Reischauer Offensive," chapter 5; Koschmann, "Modernization and Democratic Values," 237–42; Kakiuchi, "Nihon kenkyū to kindaikaron," 4–6. According to Masaru Ikei, when it came to intellectuals,

Reischauer spoke only with ideological allies such as Ichirō Nakayama and Tokyo University professor Kentarō Hayashi. However, he also made contact with the Japan Socialist Party, the Democratic Socialist Party, the General Council of Trade Unions, and leaders of affiliated unions, such as the National Railway Workers' Union, the Coal Miners' Union, the General Post Office, the All NTT Workers' Union, and the Railway Workers' Federation, among others, and succeeded in getting them to visit the United States. Ikei, "Amerika no tainichi seisaku," 72–73.

14. Kinbara, *Kindaikaron no tenkai to rekishi jojutsu*, 40.

15. Kinbara, 41.

16. Kakiuchi, "Nihon kenkyū to kindaikaron," 8.

17. Koschmann, "Modernization and Democratic Values," 227. The Ford Foundation disbursed to the Conference on Modern Japan a total of US$35,000, which was paid in one lump sum in 1960, the first year of the conference. Kakiuchi, "Nihon kenkyū to kindaikaron," 2.

18. Hall, foreword to *Changing Japanese Attitudes toward Modernization*, v.

19. Kakiuchi, "Nihon kenkyū to kindaikaron," 1–2; Kakiuchi, "Maruyama Masao no kindaikaron no henyō ni tsuite," 14.

20. Kinbara, *Nihon kindai no sabu rīdā*, 185; Kakiuchi, "Nihon kenkyū to kindaikaron," 3; Hardacre, "Chogen," 7.

21. Cumings, "Boundary Displacement," 271; Koschmann, "Modernization and Democratic Values," 227.

22. In the order of participants as listed in Hall, Kanai, and Tanabe, "Proceedings of Preliminary Seminars at Hakone, Japan."

23. Koschmann, "Modernization and Democratic Values," 228.

24. Hall, Kanai, and Tanabe, "Proceedings of Preliminary Seminars at Hakone, Japan," 1.

25. Hall, Kanai, and Tanabe, 1–2.

26. Cited Koschmann, "Intellectuals and Politics," 413.

27. Hall, "Changing Conceptions of the Modernization of Japan," 17–18; Kakiuchi, "Nihon kenkyū to kindaikaron," 11.

28. Hall, Kanai, and Tanabe, "Proceedings of Preliminary Seminars at Hakone, Japan," 9–11.

29. Kakiuchi, "Maruyama Masao no kindaikaron no henyō ni tsuite," 14.

30. Koschmann, "Intellectuals and Politics," 413.

31. Hall, Kanai, and Tanabe, "Proceedings of Preliminary Seminars at Hakone, Japan," 3.

32. Kakiuchi, "Maruyama Masao no kindaikaron no henyō ni tsuite," 16.

33. Hall, Kanai, and Tanabe, "Proceedings of Preliminary Seminars at Hakone, Japan," 9.

34. Hall, Kanai, and Tanabe, 9–10.

35. Hall, Kanai, and Tanabe, "Proceedings of Preliminary Seminars at Hakone, Japan," 10.

36. Hall, Kanai, and Tanabe, 10–11.

37. Kawashima, "Zuisō," 107–12.

38. Kawashima, 108–9.

39. Tsuzuki, *Sengo Nihon no chishikijin*, 390.

40. Hall, Kanai, and Tanabe, "Proceedings of Preliminary Seminars at Hakone, Japan," 11–12.

41. Hall, Kanai, and Tanabe, 20.

42. Hall, Kanai, and Tanabe , 21.

43. Tsuzuki, *Sengo Nihon no chishikijin*, 390; Kakiuchi, "Maruyama Masao no kindaikaron no henyō ni tsuite," 14.

44. Hall, Kanai, and Tanabe, "Proceedings of Preliminary Seminars at Hakone, Japan," 7–8 (parentheses in the original).

45. Hall, Kanai, and Tanabe, 7–8.

46. Hall, Kanai, and Tanabe, 8.

47. Hall, Kanai, and Tanabe, 8.

48. Hall, Kanai, and Tanabe, 8.

49. Hall, Kanai, and Tanabe, 8.

50. Tsuzuki, *Sengo Nihon no chishikijin*, 390.

51. Kawashima, "Zuisō," 108 (emphasis in original).

52. Tsuzuki, *Sengo Nihon no chishikijin*, 390–91.

53. Hall, Kanai, and Tanabe, 8.

54. Koschmann, "Modernization and Democratic Values," 232–33.

55. Narita, Koschmann, Ueno, and Nishikawa, "Zadankai," 252.

56. Koschmann, "Modernization and Democratic Values," 236.

57. Hall, "Nihon no kindaika," 40–41.

58. Dore, "Mondai ishiki no sōi," 7.

59. Hall, "Nihon no kindaika," 41.

60. Hall, 41.

61. Hall, 44.

62. Hall, 41–45.

63. Hall, 45.

64. Kawashima, "Zuisō," 108–9.

65. Kawashima, "'Kindaika' no imi," 3.

66. Kawashima, 3.

67. Kawashima, 4.

68. Koschmann, "Modernization and Democratic Values," 235.

69. Hall, "Changing Conceptions of the Modernization of Japan," 11.

70. Hall, 20.

71. Hall, 27.

72. Kawashima, "Zuisō," 108–9; Hall, "Changing Conceptions of the Modernization of Japan," 27–28.

73. Hall, 29.

74. Hall, 30.
75. Kakiuchi, "Nihon kenkyū to kindaikaron," 7.
76. Miyamoto, "Gairon," 15–16.
77. Norman, "Japan's Emergence as a Modern State," 115.
78. Norman, 115.
79. Miyamoto, "Gairon," 17.
80. Miyamoto, 17.
81. Miyamoto, 17.
82. Miyamoto, 16.
83. Dower, "E. H. Norman," 121.
84. Dower, "E. H. Norman," 123–24.
85. Hall, "Kindai Nihon hyōka no taido," 110.
86. Kakiuchi, "Nihon kenkyū to kindaikaron," 7.
87. Hall, "Kindai Nihon hyōka no taido," 109–10.
88. Hall, "Nihon no kindaika," 47.
89. Hall, "Kindai Nihon hyōka no taido," 112.
90. Hall, 113–14.
91. Hall, 112–13.
92. Kinbara, *Kindaikaron no tenkai to rekishi jojutsu*, 40.
93. Kakiuchi, "Nihon kenkyū to kindaikaron," 8.
94. Dower, "E. H. Norman," 122.
95. Dower, 123 (emphasis in original).
96. Dower, 123 (emphasis in original).
97. Dower, 123.
98. Dower, 125.
99. Dower, 121.
100. Dower, 121.
101. Dower, 121.
102. Dower, 121.
103. John. W. Dower, "Nihon wo hakaru," 69–70.
104. Dower, 69–70.
105. Raischauer, "Tōzai 'kangaekata' no kōkan," 7.
106. Jansen, "Kindaikaron to higashi Ajia," 29.
107. Dower, "Nihon wo hakaru," 69–70.

REFERENCES

Primary Sources

Dore, Ronald P. "Mondai ishiki sōi" Sekaiteki na kenchi to minzokuteki na kenchi to; 'Kokusai kaigai no muzukashisa: "Nihon no kindaika: Sono mondaiten to hōhō" no kaigi kara'" [Differences in problem consciousness: Global and ethnic perspectives and the difficulty of international conferences; From the conference "Japan's modernization: Problems and methods" (2)]. *Mainichi Shimbun*, September 10, 1960, 7.

Dower, John W. "E. H. Norman to jiyūshugiteki gakumon no gendaiteki kiki" [E. H. Norman and the crisis of modern liberal learning]. Translated by Genji Ōkubo. *Shisō* 634 (April 1977): 121.

———. "Nihon wo hakaru (1): Eigokenni okeru Nihon kenkyū no rekishi jujutsu" [Sizing up (and breaking down) Japan]. Translated by Naoyuki Umemori. *Shisō* 885 (September 1995): 69.

Hall, John W. "Nihon no kindaika: Gainen kōsei no shomondai" [The modernization of Japan: Problems in conceptual constructions]. Translated by Madoka Kanai and Kiyomi Morioka. *Shisō* 439 (January 1961): 40–48.

———. "Kindai Nihon hyōka no taido." Translated by Kenichirō Shōda. *Chuo Koron* 84, no. 1 (January 1969): 102–15.

Hall, John W., Madoka Kanai, and Tatsurō Tanebe. "Proceedings of Preliminary Seminars at Hakone, Japan." Tokyo, 1961.

Jansen, Marius B. "Kindaikaron to higashi Ajia: Amerikano gakkai no baai" [The theory of "modernization" and East Asia: The case of the American scholarly organizations]. Translated by Toru Haga. *Shisō* 646 (April 1978): 25–27.

Kawashima, Takeyoshi. "Zuisō, kindai Nihonshi no shakaigakuteki kenkyū: 1960 Hakone kaigi no kansū" [Essay on social science research regarding modern Japanese history: Reflections on the 1960 Hakone Conference]. *Shisō* 442 (April 1961): 107–12.

———. "'Kindaika' no imi" [The meaning of modernization]. *Shisō* 473 (November 1963): 3.

Norman, E. Herbert. "Japan's Emergence as a Modern State." In *Origins of the Modern Japanese State: Selected Writings of E. H. Norman*, edited by John W. Dower, 115. New York: Pantheon, 1975.

Reischauer, Edwin O. "Tōzai 'kangaekata' no kōkan: Hakone kaigi ni sanka shite" [Exchanging 'ways of thinking' between East and West: On attending the Hakone Conference]. *Asahi Shimbun*, September 11, 1960, 7.

Reischauer, Edwin O., and Ichirō Nakayama. "Nihon kindaika no rekishiteki hyōka" [Historically evaluating Japan's modernization]. *Chūō Kōron* vol. 76, no. 9 (September, 1961): 84–97.

———. *Nihon kindai no atarashii mikata* [A new look at Japanese modernity]. Tokyo: Kōdansha, 1965.

Tōyama, Shigeki. "Kokusai kaigai no muzukashisa: 'Nihon no kindaika: Sono mondaiten to hōhō' no kaigi kara" [The difficulty of international conferences: From the conference "Japan's modernization: Problems and methods" (1)]. *Mainichi Shimbun*, September 8, 1960, 7.

Secondary Sources

Cumings, Bruce. "Boundary Displacement: The State, the Foundation, and Area Studies during and after the Cold War." In *Learning Places: The Afterlives of Area Studies*, edited by Masao Miyoshi and H. D. Harootunian, 261–302. Durham, NC: Duke University Press, 2002.

Hall, John Whitney. "Changing Conceptions of the Modernization of Japan." In *Changing Japanese Attitudes toward Modernization*, edited by Marius B. Jansen, 7–41. Princeton, NJ: Princeton University Press, 1965.

———. Foreword to *Changing Japanese Attitudes toward Modernization*, edited by Marius B. Jansen, v–vii. Princeton, NJ: Princeton University Press, 1965.

Harada, Mikio. "Nihon no kindaika to keizai hatten" [Japan's modernization and economic development]. In *America no Nihon kenkyū* [American studies on Japan], edited by Mataji Miyamoto, 116–32. Tokyo: Tōyō Keizai, 1970.

Hardacre, Helen. "Chogen" [Introduction]. Translated by Hirofumi Ichikawa and Kenji Hatanaka. *Kikan nihon shisōshi* [*Japan Intellectual History Quarterly*] 61 (2002): 6–15.

Ikei, Masaru. "Amerika no tainichi seisaku: Reischauer taishi no yakuwari wo chūshin toshite" [American policy on Japan: The role of Ambassador Reischauer]. *Hōgaku Kenkyū* [*Study of Law*] 43, no. 7 (1970): 54–87.

Kakiuchi, Ken. "Maruyama Masao no kindaikaron no henyō ni tsuite: Hakone kaigi no giron wo chūshin ni" [Masao Murayama's changing view of modernization: A focus on the Hakone Conference]. *Social and Cultural Studies* 25 (2009): 13–26.

———. "Nihon kenkyū to kindaikaron: Kindai Nihon kenkyu kaigi wo chūshin ni" [Japanese studies and modernization theory: Focusing on the Conference on Modern Japan]. *Social and Cultural Studies* 27 (2010): 1–13.

Kinbara, Samon. *Kindaikaron no tenkai to rekishi jojutsu; Seiji hendōka no hitotsu no shigakushi* [Turns and historical narratives on the theory of modernization: One "history of history" in light of political change]. Yokohama: Chūo Daigaku Shuppanbu, 1999.

———. *Nihon kindai no sabu rīdā: Rekishi o tsukuru tatakai* [The subleader of Japanese modernity: The battle to write history]. Tokyo: Nihon Keizai Hyōronsha, 2005.

Kōda, Naoko. "The Reischauer Offensive: Promoting a Different Kind of Past." In *The United States and the Japanese Student Movement, 1948–1973: Managing a Free World*, chap. 5. Lanham, MD: Rowman and Littlefield, 2020.

Koschmann, Victor. "Intellectuals and Politics." In *Postwar Japan as History*, edited by Andrew Gordon, 412–14. Berkeley: University of California Press, 1993.

———. "Modernization and Democratic Values: The 'Japanese Model' in the 1960s." In *Staging Growth: Modernization, Development, and the Global Cold War*, edited by David C. Engerman, Nils Gilman, Mark H. Haefele, and Michael E. Latham, 225–49. Amherst: University of Massachusetts Press, 2003.

Matsumoto, Sannosuke. *Kindai Nihon no chiteki jōkyō* [The intellectual state of modern Japan]. Tokyo: Chūō Kōronsha, 1974.

Miyamoto, Mataji. "Gairon: Amerika no Nihonshigaku" [Introduction: American history of Japan]. In *America no Nihon kenkyū* [American studies on Japan], edited by Mataji Miyamoto, 3–80. Tokyo: Tōyō Keizai, 1965.

Narita, Ryūichi, J. Victor Koschmann, Chizuko Ueno, and Yūko Nishikawa. "Zadankai" [Roundtable discussion]. In *Rekishi no kakikata 2: Sengo to iu chiseigaku* [Mapping history 2: The geopolitics of the postwar era], edited by Yūko Nishikawa, 245–68. Tokyo: University of Tokyo Press, 2006.

Tsuzuki, Tsutomu. *Sengo Nihon no chishikijin: Maruyama Masao to sono jidai* [Intellectuals in postwar Japan: Masao Maruyama and his time]. Yokohama: Seori Shobō, 1995.

AUTHOR BIOS

MASAKI FUJIOKA is a part-time lecturer at Kyoto University and has been researching the formation of academic knowledge and disciplines at US universities in the Cold War era. His book *Organizing of Soviet Studies at American University* (2017) traces the history of Soviet studies in the United States.

DANIEL ROY PEARCE is a lecturer and foreign-language teacher trainer at Shitennoji University. He is author of *Plurilingual Education in a Monolingualized Nation: Innovations in Language Teaching in Japan* (2024).

FOUR

THE DAWN OF KOREAN STUDIES AND KNOWLEDGE PRODUCTION ON KOREA DURING AND AFTER THE PACIFIC WAR

SOMEI KOBAYASHI

INTRODUCTION

K-pop, a musical genre through which many people have come to enjoy Korean culture, has developed a massive following around the world over the last two decades. Samsung and Hyundai have become leading companies, and the "Miracle on the Han River" is now a famous success story. Korea is now the world's fourteenth-largest economy and an OECD member, and former president Kim Dae-Jung was renowned for receiving the Nobel Peace Prize in 1998. In international society, South Korea (the Republic of Korea, or ROC) is now commonly referred to as Korea, and a large amount of information on the country now circulates all over the world. However, until the mid-twentieth century, Korea was not a focus of major interest for many countries, excepting perhaps its near neighbors, Russia, China, and Japan.

When the Pacific War erupted in December 1941, US universities, government agencies such as the State Department, and intelligence circles did not have much knowledge of Korea, which had been under Japanese colonial rule since 1910. The outbreak of war made the US government recognize that gathering and analyzing information on Korea was quite essential for countering Japanese aggression.

During the Pacific War, a large body of knowledge about East Asia was produced and stored by US government agencies, including the Coordinator of Information (COI), the Office of Strategic Services (OSS), and the Office of War Information (OWI). Not a few eminent scholars focused on East Asia answered the calls of these agencies and contributed by analyzing the situation in Japan, China, and Korea and producing numerous reports on the region.

The knowledge relating to East Asia was thus produced by the cooperation of scholars and government agencies as part of the large-scale war efforts against Japan. Bruce Cumings, citing McGeorge Bundy's words, remarked that it was a curious fact of academic history that the first great center of area studies was in the OSS.[1]

Whereas Chinese and Japanese studies shifted to more academic foci after the Pacific War, Korean studies, which also shifted in part, uniquely retained a "hot war" element due to continued hostilities in the region, and such knowledge became institutionalized as Korean studies within the discipline of area studies in US universities.

This chapter aims to describe the dynamism of knowledge production on Korea in the US, from the outbreak of the Pacific War through to the early 1950s, by addressing three questions. First, how was knowledge about Korea accumulated, produced, and circulated between academic circles and government agencies in the US during the Pacific War? In the area of Korean knowledge, George McAfee McCune played a significant role, producing knowledge that was circulated within and stored by the above-mentioned agencies. This first question will be examined through a focus on the role of McCune during the war. Second, how was the knowledge about Korea that was produced during the Pacific War organized, or institutionalized, as Korean studies in US academia? After the end of war, McCune returned to the University of California (UC), Berkeley, and endeavored to open courses and programs for Korean studies. Charles Burton Fahs provided significant help in his efforts. Fahs had been McCune's superior at the OSS and had transferred to the State Department and then to the Rockefeller Foundation after the war. The second question will be considered through an examination of the work of McCune at UC Berkeley and the role of Fahs at the State Department and the Rockefeller Foundation. This examination will show that the human network that was formulated during the war provided significant resources for developing Korean studies in the Cold War era. Third, how was knowledge about Korea accumulated and produced in the postwar US through intellectual exchanges with Korea? In addressing this question, the chapter focuses on a correspondence project launched by the Rockefeller Foundation in 1947 as a new project for intellectual exchange between American and Korean professors. The correspondence project was carried out for two years by the American Council of Learned Societies (ACLS) and was supported by the Rockefeller Foundation, with assistance from McCune's wife, Evelyn Becker McCune, a key individual in the project. The correspondence project will be outlined by examining the following points: Evelyn McCune's efforts and the financial support the Rockefeller

Foundation provided for her research. An examination of the project will reveal an aspect of the process of generating knowledge about Korea through intellectual exchanges between US and Korean academics in the postwar era. In fact, through this project, Korean professors gained access to numerous sources of knowledge about the US, as well as about the latest trends in academic fields. The project also provided American professors with a significant opportunity to take an interest in Korea, as well as to know and understand Korean affairs.

Here, it is pertinent to briefly explore the backgrounds of two key figures on whom this chapter is centered, the already briefly introduced George M. McCune and Evelyn B. McCune. George (1908–48) was born in Pyongyang, Korea, before the Japanese annexation in 1910. He was the firstborn son of George Shannon McCune (1873–1941), an American Presbyterian educational missionary in Korea. The two sons of the elder McCune became academics specializing in Korean issues. George M. McCune created the McCune-Reischauer romanization system, published in 1939 with Edwin Oldfather Reischauer, and as an expert on Korean language and history, he is known as a pioneer of Korean studies in the US.[2] The second McCune son, Shannon Boyd-Bailey (1913–93), also contributed to the development of Asian studies, especially Korean studies, and gained a reputation as a skilled geographer.[3]

George M. McCune received his elementary education in Korea under Japanese colonial rule. In March 1919, a series of Korean uprisings for independence broke out across the Korean Peninsula. According to Kim Seo-Yeon's interview with McCune's daughter, Heather McCune Thompson, McCune left Korea for the US in 1920 because of heart disease, and in 1922, he was admitted to Huron Academy in South Dakota.[4] Records show that he attended the academy from 1926 to 1927, when he transferred to Rutgers University. A year later, McCune moved to Occidental College in Los Angeles, where he obtained his BA in 1930. Later the same year, he returned to Pyongyang to teach at Union Christian College, which had been founded by a Presbyterian missionary in 1905. After teaching there for two years, he again returned to the US, this time to enroll in graduate study at Occidental College. He obtained his master's degree in 1935 and began working on a PhD dissertation on Korean history at UC Berkeley, with a focus on the period of the Chosun dynasty. As part of his PhD research, he conducted fieldwork in Korea from 1936 to 1937. In 1939, McCune was appointed assistant professor in the Department of History at his alma mater, Occidental College, and he received his PhD in Asian history from UC Berkeley in 1941.

Evelyn B. McCune (1907–2012) was also born in Pyongyang, Korea, to an American Methodist missionary. Her life course was similar to her husband's:

she received her primary education at Seoul Foreign School from 1922 to 1926 and then moved to the US for higher education. Evelyn graduated from two colleges and one university: Albion College in 1927, Agnes Scott College in 1928, and UC Berkeley in 1930. She then returned to Korea and served at Seoul Foreign School as both a teacher and a vice principal from 1930 to 1932. In 1933, she married George in Korea, after which they moved to the US. Before and during the Second World War, Evelyn taught at Occidental College as a lecturer in Oriental art (1940–41) and at Polytechnic School in Pasadena as an art instructor (1941–42). In July 1945, she was employed by the Roberts Commission as a research assistant.[5] Records show that her interest in studying Far Eastern art, and Korean art in particular, had been a constant since her high school years, which she spent in Korea.[6] After the Pacific War, Evelyn McCune worked at the University of California Press and conducted graduate research on Korean art history at UC Berkeley.

As mentioned above, George was a pioneer of Korean studies in the US, and Evelyn contributed greatly to the development of Korean studies during the Cold War. During the same period, Reischauer was a key figure in Japanese studies and shared a similar experience with McCune at the OSS. Reischauer was to become one of the founding fathers of East Asian (especially Japanese) studies in the postwar US, and he would become one of the central architects of the Cold War US-Japan relationship.[7] Many scholarly works on the politics of knowledge production in postwar area studies in the Japan field have given special attention to the role of Reischauer. However, as Takashi Fujitani has pointed out, although critical scholarship on Cold War modernization theory has already unveiled its ties to US imperialism, much less attention has been given to the transwar linkages between this theory and the US plans for hegemony in Asia that were already being hatched during the Pacific War.[8]

Compared with the wealth of literature on the politics of knowledge production from the perspective of area studies, and Japanese studies specifically, the establishment and development of Korean studies in American academia has not been sufficiently explored.[9] In 2009, Ahn Jung-cheol examined the institutionalization process of Korean studies in the US and the American perception of Korea, focusing on George M. McCune's activities before and after the Second World War.[10] Ahn's work, published in Korean, is an extremely important analysis of the historical development of Korean studies in the US. However, the historical sources treated in his study are limited to published materials such as articles and newspaper reports—unpublished documents, such as personal papers, private foundation records, and official records, were not included in the analyses. Furthermore, no attention was given to actors outside of academia and policymaking groups, such as private foundations like the Rockefeller Foundation. Thus, although significant, Ahn's study shed light on only a part of the knowledge-production process. In 2020, the book *Peace Corps Volunteers and the Making of Korean Studies in the United States* was published in the US. This book discusses the role of the Peace Corps in the formation of Korean studies in the US, beginning in the 1960s. However, as the 1940s and 1950s did not fall under the scope of this volume, the development of Korean studies during the Pacific War and early Cold War remains underexplored. While many remarkable studies concerning George M. McCune have been conducted in both the US and Korea, few have used his personal papers to analyze his role in the OSS, and his relationship with the Rockefeller Foundation has similarly not been given much attention. Moreover, despite being a prominent scholar of Korean studies, Evelyn B. McCune is virtually invisible in the extant literature, except in references to her as George's wife.[11] While other studies on the OSS and OWI shed some light on knowledge production regarding Korea, George M. McCune's role in the production process of such knowledge has often been overlooked.[12]

To address the limitations in the extant literature, this chapter used three types of primary sources: (1) official records and documents at the National Archives of Records Administration (NARA), such as the OSS records; (2) records of private foundations, such as the Rockefeller Foundation; and (3) personal papers, such as the McCune Collection at the Center for Korean Studies, University of Hawai'i at Mānoa.

This chapter aims to describe a short history of the formation of Korean studies in the US by analyzing the activities of George M. McCune, Evelyn B. McCune, and the Rockefeller Foundation. Although it is a limited history, covering only the period from the mid-1940s to the early 1950s, it should nevertheless help to illuminate "the still-present Cold War frame of knowledge" by furthering the examination of the inseparable relationship between the Cold War and knowledge in the context of East Asia.[13]

GEORGE M. MCCUNE AND US GOVERNMENT AGENCIES IN THE 1940S

Production of Knowledge Relating to Korea during the Pacific War

Before the outbreak of the Pacific War between the US and Japan in December 1941, US president Franklin D. Roosevelt had ordered the creation of a government agency for intelligence and propaganda, which was established as the COI in July 1941. McCune was recruited by the COI to assist in the war effort against Japan because of his wealth of knowledge about Korea and its neighbors and his linguistic abilities in Korean, Chinese, and Japanese. He was offered the position of social science analyst at the Research and Analysis Branch of the COI, which he accepted, beginning his engagement in war service.

In June 1942, Roosevelt ordered that the COI be split into two agencies—namely, the OSS and OWI. McCune joined the OSS. From February 24, 1942, to August 27, 1943, he engaged in research on East Asia, mainly Korea, as a senior research analyst at the Research and Analysis Branch of the Far East Division, where he was involved in the gathering and analysis of extensive information on Korea and the drafting of many intelligence reports.[14] On March 10, 1942, Carl F. Remer, chief of the Far East Division, instructed McCune to prepare a report on the "recognition" of Korea by the US government, including alternatives to potential legal recognition of the Korean Provisional Government in exile.[15] On April 24 of the same year, McCune completed the report, titled *Potentialities of Korean Help against Japan*, which was submitted to Remer.[16] The report presented his analysis of the Korean leaders and organizations in the US campaigning for independence. However, it failed to include adequate alternatives to legal recognition of the Korean Provisional Government. Limitations of the report were mentioned in the submission, which stated that, while the main thread of the analysis was accurate, it lacked important details owing to the shortage of information on Koreans in China.[17] Fully aware of these limitations, when McCune presented the report to Remer, he had already started gathering more information on Korea by interviewing American citizens, such as Christian missionaries and their families, engineers, and entrepreneurs who had been in Korea before the outbreak of the war with Japan.[18]

During his tenure as an analyst at the COI and OSS, McCune also compiled at least four reports. The first, titled *The Korean Independence*, dated April 25, 1942, a companion volume to the above-mentioned *Potentialities of Korean Help against Japan*, provided information on the historical background of the Korean independence movement in Korea, China, and the US.[19] The second, dated June 15, 1942, analyzed the Korean independence movement in China.[20] His third report, dated August 2, 1943, was a concise account of the historical development and structure of the Korean Provisional Government in Chongqing.[21] The fourth report, a lengthy document totaling 128 pages, released on August 5, 1943, examined the Korean economic situation with an analysis of economic data and the state of infrastructure in colonial Korea.[22] The content of these reports highlights McCune's production of knowledge about Korea primarily from political and economic perspectives—a reflection of the COI's and OSS's interest in the Korean situation. Indeed, the COI and OSS commissioned the reports for two purposes: First, they aimed to provide information on the status of the Korean independence movement to facilitate informed consideration of the US position regarding recognition of the Korean Provisional Government in China—the COI and OSS sought to answer the question of which of the competing Korean leaders the US government should support, given due consideration to American national interests. Second, information on the Korean economy was collected and analyzed for the purpose of informing other US government agencies of the economic conditions in Korea because the COI and OSS believed that such knowledge could be of significant help not only in evaluating the military strength of Japan but also in establishing policy in postwar Korea.

The OSS and COI focused primarily on the aspects of politics and economics in Korea and did not devote much attention to other areas, such as Korean history, culture, and people. However, these areas interested McCune, as can be seen in his research topics in the closing phase of the Pacific War in 1945.

In August 1943, McCune resigned from the OSS and took a new appointment at the Board for Economic Warfare (BEW), where his younger brother Shannon McCune was already employed. As a senior economic researcher, McCune worked for a few months at the Office of Economic Warfare Analysis, Enemy Branch, Economic Potential Division, Asiatic Axis Section. On December 7, 1943, he transferred to the State Department, where he was a specialist in Korean affairs, as well as the Japan desk officer. A year and a half later, just before the end of the Pacific War, he left the Department of State.[23] A letter he sent to Erle R. Dickover, division chief of Japanese Affairs, dated July 10, 1945, included the following: "It is with considerable reluctance that I have decided to resign from the Department in view of my continued ill health in as much as it appears inadvisable for me to remain at work in Washington during the coming winter." Although McCune was forced to abandon his work at the State Department owing to his health condition, he expressed regret about this circumstance in the same letter: "It is my hope that after a period of rest and recuperation I may again serve my country in questions which relate to Korean affairs."[24]

McCune's war service at the COI/OSS, BEW, and the State Department was praised by his colleagues. Professor F. Theodore Cloak of Lawrence University, who served with the OSS from 1943 to 1945, expressed his gratitude to George as follows: "The abrupt ending of the war and the sudden cessation of our activities here at the Far East Orientation School prevented my telling you personally how deeply we appreciated your contribution to the success of the school."[25]

Cloak admired McCune for his important role in acquainting so many people with the current problems and future issues in the Far East, recognizing that this could not have been achieved without him. Professor John Fairbank, a well-known specialist on China at Harvard University who was enlisted by the government to serve in the OSS and OWI during the war, also evaluated the quality of McCune's work as outstanding. Further, he nominated him to be a recipient of the Rockefeller Foundation fellowship program for research on Korea.[26] McCune was expected to become a leading scholar on Korean affairs in the postwar era; during his time as an OSS analyst, his work was managed under the direction of Charles Burton Fahs, chief of the Far East Division, who likewise both praised and respected him. In 1946, after the end of the war, Fahs was appointed as assistant director of the Humanities Division at the Rockefeller Foundation, and he was promoted to the position of director by 1950. The shared experiences of McCune and Fahs in the OSS resulted in a close relationship between the two in the postwar period, a relationship that became a significant resource for the development of Korean studies in the US and mutual understanding between the US and Korea.

The outbreak of war with Japan served as an opportunity for the US government to analyze Korean affairs. Before the war, knowledge relating to Korea in the US was virtually nonexistent. The resulting knowledge was largely produced by McCune, an academic scholar on Korea who transferred from academia to the government sector for the war efforts of the US; knowledge of Korea had been generated and organized by stimulating intellectual interactions between academia and the government, although driven by the demands of the latter. Thus, at least during the war, it was difficult to develop intellectual autonomy in the knowledge-production process.

The Close Relationship between George M. McCune and
Charles Burton Fahs during and after the Pacific War

On April 14, 1945, shortly before the defeat of the Nazis, the Rockefeller Foundation informed McCune that he had been awarded a Postwar Fellowship in the Humanities for a period not to exceed twelve months, to begin at any time from the date of the notification through December 31, 1948, and that the fellowship would provide a total of US$2,500 as a grant.[27] Under the grant, McCune planned a brief but comprehensive survey of Korean history, from the early modern period to the contemporary mid-1940s.[28] His selection as a recipient of the fellowship was backed by the strong recommendations of prominent experts. On August 21, 1944, Fairbank informed the Rockefeller Foundation of the outstanding quality of McCune's work and recommended that he should be funded to continue writing about Korea, given that he could not be expected to both teach and write at the same time.[29] McCune was also recommended by Robert Joseph Kerner, professor of history at UC Berkeley and an expert on Slavic and Russian history.[30]

In his resignation letter, McCune intimated a desire to further contribute, and he did, in fact, maintain close ties with the State Department.[31] In December 1945, the State Department held the Moscow Conference of Foreign Ministers to discuss the future of a Korea liberated from Japanese colonial rule. At the conference, the Moscow Agreement statement was made that Korea would be put under trusteeship of the four powers of the US, USSR, UK, and China for up to five years before it could attain independence. On January 4, 1946, Elwrin Withat from the State Department asked McCune for comments or suggestions regarding not only the proposed trusteeship but also the economic conditions in Korea, including inflation, Japanese assets, and foreign trade. While it appears that McCune responded to this request, no documents containing his comments or suggestions could be found among the records of the McCune Papers and the Department of State at the National Archives and Records Administration.

On March 16, 1946, McCune wrote to Fahs, who was still working at the State Department, proposing the establishment of a program to train specialists on Korea and asking for any comments or suggestions. On April 8, Fahs responded that such a program seemed "very sensible and quite essential," remarking that there would likely be members of the State Department's staff willing to join the program if it should prove administratively possible for the department to permit its establishment. Moreover, Fahs told McCune that there would be a stable demand (i.e., at least ten or fifteen serious students) among the State Department, the army, the navy, and universities. However, Fahs stated that, owing to ongoing strife regarding leadership within the State Department, they were not yet in any position to implement new long-term programs.[32] Nevertheless, Fahs understood the program's significance, and he made clear his own willingness to support its establishment.

Fahs attempted to explain the significance of this program to personnel of the American Council of Learned Societies (ACLS), a private nonprofit federation of seventy-five scholarly organizations in the humanities and social sciences, and to the Rockefeller Foundation. He met with both Mortimer Graves, administrative secretary of ACLS, and John Marshall, associate director of the Humanities Division of the Rockefeller Foundation. They discussed the desirability of encouraging a few graduates of the US Navy Japanese Language School and Oriental Language School at Boulder or of the Military

Intelligence Service Language School at Fort Snelling to take up Korean as a second language. At the discussion table, Fahs pointed out the need for a stable demand for Korean studies from the Department of State, the army, the navy, and universities, to which both Graves and Marshall expressed that they were interested in the program.

On April 8, 1946, Fahs wrote to McCune, explaining the details of his talks with Graves and Marshall and asking him to find talented Boulder graduates who might aspire to work with him. Fahs also expressed his confidence that if McCune could do so, he would readily secure scholarship or fellowship assistance from the ACLS and the Rockefeller Foundation.[33]

Meanwhile, McCune had also sent a letter sounding out the program to Edwin M. Martin, chief of the Division of Japanese and Korean Economic Affairs at the Department of State. On March 29, 1946, Martin replied, "I am in complete sympathy with the idea and feel that it is the only answer to the present great dearth of professional persons with any real regional knowledge of Korea."[34] Fahs and Martin both understood the significance of a program that would train professionals in Korean affairs. However, Martin mentioned in his reply to McCune that both he and Fahs recognized obstacles to the procurement of State Department funds and the assignment of State Department employees to such an endeavor. Nevertheless, Martin explicitly told George, "It is such a sound proposal that I am sure somehow something will be worked out, although it is hard to say when."[35]

In support of the program, Fahs left the State Department to join the Rockefeller Foundation as assistant director of the Humanities Division in the fall of 1946. During his tenure as director, he lobbied to broaden university programs in the humanities and social sciences, especially encouraging growth in area studies.[36] Also, at the foundation, Fahs played a crucial role in fostering the development of these academic departments and programs at US colleges and universities. In 1961, he resigned from the Rockefeller Foundation, after which he engaged in diplomatic duty as minister-counselor for cultural and Pacific affairs at the US Embassy in Tokyo until 1967.

The close ties between McCune and Fahs, established during the war, helped lay the foundation for the development of knowledge relating to Korea in the postwar era. This production of knowledge was supported not only by their personal relationship but also by their shared passion for training specialists in Korean affairs. As a result, the received knowledge of Korea, which the two attempted to develop, was characterized by the following two points: First, knowledge was produced to meet the demands of the government sector— government agencies required specialists to fill a knowledge gap on Korean affairs, not only in the wartime period but also in the postwar era. Second, they aimed to produce and store knowledge of Korea to institutionalize Korean studies within the discipline of area studies. To achieve the latter of these aims, McCune attempted to open a course on Korean issues at UC Berkeley after the end of the war, and the next section discusses his efforts for the scholarly development of Korean knowledge in academia.

Challenges in Opening the Korean Program at UC Berkeley in the Late 1940s

In 1946, McCune left the State Department and accepted a new appointment as lecturer in the Department of History at UC Berkeley. UC Berkeley provided him with not only an excellent springboard for his research but also an opportunity to educate students interested in Korean matters. UC Berkeley began its fall term in early October, and, as part of their curriculum, McCune took responsibility for a full-year undergraduate course on Korean history with six registrants and a graduate seminar with four registrants. He was expecting to turn the focus of his graduate seminar to Korean history and culture. He believed that he and his staff would be able to make genuinely relevant contributions to the study of Korean affairs and to the training of students interested in Korea.[37]

In addition to his above duties, McCune also prepared to open an intensive language course in Korean in the Extension Division, slated for launch on October 14.[38] The reasoning for the establishment of the Korean-language course was given as follows: "Korea's strategic position in international politics and in future Far Eastern commercial activity has given a new importance to an understanding of the country's political and social thought. This development has created a widespread need for fluency in the Korean language and grounding in political and cultural history."[39]

As a university extension course, the one-year program consisted of three fifteen-week terms. The program, which adopted the methods for language training developed by the army and navy schools at Boulder and Ann Arbor during the Pacific War, aimed to provide students with a basic knowledge of Korean history, geography, and culture and to cultivate the ability to speak and read the Korean language.

In developing the Korean-language courses, McCune intended to rely on the support of Florence Walne Farquhar, associate professor of Japanese at UC Berkeley. Farquhar was regarded as a distinguished leader in the field of Japanese studies, and, as McCune relayed to Fahs, Farquhar's report of her visit to various institutions in the East was useful in planning his course on Korea.

Farquhar had also shared with McCune her experience, at Yale University, of establishing a class for Korean-language study that was attended by students from the Presbyterian and Methodist Boards.[40] American Presbyterian and Methodist missionaries had shown interest in Korea since their missions in the early twentieth century, and this interest remained steady until at least the mid-1940s.

Farquhar had been born in 1895 in Japan to American Baptist missionaries. After graduating from Harvard and Radcliffe College, she answered the navy's call for the organization of a Japanese Language School at Berkeley, to be funded simultaneously with other schools projected elsewhere. She had extensive experience in course planning and the teaching of Japanese, not only at universities but also at educational institutions of the navy.[41] Although eager to exploit Farquhar's experience, McCune was deprived of her assistance because she died from illness in October 1946. Thus, he turned to a young Korean, Frank Youngjung Lee, for assistance. Lee had taught Japanese language at Stanford University in the army training program and was qualified to handle instruction in Korean.[42] McCune highly evaluated Lee's classes in the extension course at UCB. Thus, he attempted to expand them and established a special Korean language course for students who had already taken Japanese. McCune was also aware of five or six advanced students at UC Berkeley who were interested in taking his proposed course. Among them were ex-American soldiers formerly stationed in Korea.[43] At the early stage of the Korean program at UC Berkeley, in McCune's opinion, only missionaries and ex-military personnel showed interest. While he was passionate and put a great deal of effort into establishing a Korean-related course at UC Berkeley, progress on his research project under the Postwar Fellowship in Humanities was less than stellar.

On September 29, 1946, McCune wrote to David H. Stevens, director of the Humanities Division of the Rockefeller Foundation, to inquire about the possible use of his fellowship as a means for the development of Korean studies. On October 2, on behalf of Stevens, Fahs responded with an approval—McCune was permitted to use the Postwar Fellowship in Humanities grant not only for his own research but also for the development of education materials on Korean studies. However, progress on the research continued to fall short of expectations.

In a letter to Fahs in early November 1946, McCune wrote of his frustration: although the preparation for his lectures on Korean history at the university formed an excellent starting place for his studies, the work needed to be expanded considerably, and teaching and clerical duties prevented him from devoting his full time to the completion of the research project. He appealed to Fahs to delay the initial plan of commencement of January 1, 1947, until September 1, 1947.[44]

At the time, McCune was faced with more difficulties than stalled research; when Stevens and Fahs interviewed him in April 1947, they saw that he was in good spirits, but he was emaciated, and his lips were blue. Nevertheless, in spite of his health condition, he was seen as clearly the most competent among the three or four Korean experts available, and thus they believed he should be given every possible assistance to produce both research and successors in Korean studies scholarship.[45] The Rockefeller Foundation regarded McCune as a promising scholar who had the potential to initiate the development of Korean studies in the US. However, illness prevented him from conducting his own research effectively, and he passed away in November 1948. His goal for the development of Korean studies was succeeded by his wife, Evelyn B. McCune, and Fahs and the Rockefeller Foundation began to support her work after George's death.

EVELYN B. MCCUNE AND THE CORRESPONDENCE PROJECT

Assistance for the Project and Support for Research

In July 1947, Fahs traveled to East Asia and stayed in South Korea for a week, during which time he visited universities in Seoul and met with many friends of George and Evelyn McCune.[46] During his stay, he was struck by the isolation felt by the Korean professors he met.[47] Through this experience, Fahs realized the importance of establishing personal correspondence between Korean and American professors in similar fields to raise the morale of the former and to stimulate them along new lines of research and teaching. Fahs understood that it would not be easy to realize this correspondence project without the continued efforts of someone familiar with the educational institutions in both countries. Given her experience in Korea and her wealth of knowledge on the country, Fahs believed that Evelyn B. McCune's assistance was necessary to overcome the difficulties in undertaking a correspondence project.

The Rockefeller Foundation determined that McCune's knowledge of the Korean language and of personnel in Korea made her the most suitable person available to undertake the correspondence program between Korean and American professors. The program was called the "correspondence project," and it clearly had its roots in the idea that Fahs conceived of during his stay in Korea. Indeed, immediately after Fahs returned from his tour of East Asia, he consulted with McCune by letter about both the feasibility of the correspondence project and her own interest in taking part. At the time, McCune held a job with the University of California Press as an editor of the official publications of all campuses. Fahs inquired as to her interest in attempting to stimulate such correspondence and asked if it would be possible to pay her a part-time salary for doing so, including necessary small expenses for stationery, postage, and occasional small gifts of books or other printed materials to be provided by the Rockefeller Foundation. Moreover, he requested her opinion on the following three points: (1) whether she thought the proposal would be helpful for the development of university scholarship in Korea; (2) whether she herself would be interested in undertaking the project; and (3), if she was interested, what proportion of her time she thought she could fairly devote to the project without neglecting her duties to George and the family.[48] In a letter dated August 19, 1947, McCune expressed agreement in principle with his proposal, which she deemed a meaningful scheme to raise the morale of Korean professors in a practical way. McCune believed that the project would work if care was taken to avoid patronage associated with other organized benevolences—she was sensitive to the possibility of interference in the correspondence between Korean and American scholars by organizations outside the Rockefeller Foundation.[49]

Additionally, Evelyn B. McCune expressed some concerns about the correspondence project, particular in relation to the American scholars' motivation to engage with the project. To adequately evaluate any offer of assistance to the project, McCune asked Fahs for specific details regarding her salary and some costs for the project. At the time, she was receiving a salary of US$2,800 for full-time work at the University of California Press. She was reluctant to leave this post because she felt she had no suitable alternatives, particularly given her preference for "a job that [she] could discharge at home, with a more flexible schedule." Nevertheless, she was willing to work on the correspondence project in a part-time job and informed Fahs that her minimum financial needs would be about US$40 a week. She stated that she could spend five to six hours a day on the project, or more than half of a full-time workload. Moreover, she asked for expenses for stationery, postage, and gifts, amounting to about US$50 a month, as well as funds for translating and other incidental services.

McCune also inquired as to whether she could combine the correspondence work with advanced studies in Korean art or literature; she expressed an eagerness to assist in the project, but only under the conditions that her financial needs were met and that she could conduct her own research, for which she would also require financial support.[50]

In his reply, Fahs expressed his gratitude for McCune's understanding and addressed her expectations regarding financial and research concerns. As a practicable solution, he offered her one of the Rockefeller Foundation's regular training fellowships for her research project: the fellowship would include a stipend of US$175 per month for twelve months. Fahs also informed her that it might be possible to arrange a further US$100 per month, through an ACLS grant-in-aid, for stenographic assistance, postage, books, and other expenses incurred. He emphasized that it would be possible for McCune to manage both her research and the correspondence project on a fairly satisfactory basis.[51] Thus, Fahs acquiesced to her financial and research requests and asked her, if she was satisfied with the conditions of the offer, to fill out and return an application for the fellowship.[52]

On September 30, 1947, McCune sent her application form for the Rockefeller Foundation fellowship along with related documents, including a proposed research plan. As had been indicated in the correspondence with Fahs, McCune was awarded the fellowship by the Rockefeller Foundation in advance because Fahs required her assistance in the project and because he recognized that she would become a significant scholar in the development of Korean studies in the future. Her proposed research plan for the fellowship had two objectives. First, regarding educational aims, her study sought to develop specific training in art research techniques as well as in the use of Chinese texts—several classes and seminars on the history of Chinese art, Buddhist art, Korean history, Chinese culture, and language had begun in the fall semester of 1947. These had been prepared to fulfill the requirements for a master's degree in the Department of Art at UC Berkeley, toward the ultimate goal of a doctorate.[53] Furthermore, she attempted to include a class on Korean art in the coursework for MA and PhD studies. Second, McCune intended to undertake original research in the special field of Korean art. She planned to study the history of Korean art, focusing specifically on the fifth and sixth centuries. According to her explanation, art from this period was represented particularly by the tomb paintings of Koguryo and the sculptures of Silla; her research aimed to trace their varied origins, in an effort to determine the routes, methods, and agencies of transmission. She believed that such a study would contribute not only to the body of knowledge of early Buddhist art but also to development of a clearer picture of early Japanese art in all its phases.[54]

On November 5, 1947, Fahs had a telephone discussion with Graves about the project. Graves mentioned the desirability of having the work in the correspondence project linked with the ongoing development of a guide to Korean studies by George and Evelyn McCune and argued determinedly that the

ACLS should be the agency to handle the project. Therefore, Fahs decided to recommend a grant from the ACLS be made for US$900, which would provide US$200 per month for Evelyn McCune's salary and US$100 per month for stenography, postage, and other expenses to cover the period from November 1, 1947, to January 31, 1948.

On November 7, 1947, Fahs wrote to Cornelius Kruse, executive director of the ACLS, and to Evelyn B. McCune. Kruse was informed that Fahs was proceeding to recommend a grant-in-aid of $900 to McCune, who would carry out the correspondence project.[55] A few days later, Kruse responded that the ACLS would be happy to handle the project.[56] McCune also received a letter from Fahs stating that complications had made it necessary to revert to the original idea that funding be handled as a grant-in-aid rather than a fellowship; Fahs explained that the ACLS would be able to manage this grant-in-aid for her.[57]

On November 13, 1947, the Rockefeller Foundation approved the grant-in-aid of US$3,255 to the ACLS to cover McCune's salary and expenses for her advanced study in Oriental art and for the development of correspondence between Korean and American professors. As Fahs had mentioned, the Rockefeller Foundation, as a whole, confirmed that she would be the most suitable person available to undertake a project for developing contact between Korean and American professors.[58]

Originally, Fahs had intended to provide McCune with financial support through a fellowship. However, as McCune, employed by University of California Press, could not receive a salary from more than one institution or organization, this was changed to a grant. The Rockefeller Foundation was of the opinion that the grant would make it possible for her to give up her editorial position and to spend two-thirds of her time in advanced study, which would enhance her usefulness in the field of Korean studies; the rest of her time would be devoted to the development of the correspondence project. The grant approved by the Rockefeller Foundation was meant to cover three months, although the foundation expected that a further grant would be made in January to carry this project through the remaining eleven months of 1948.[59] Fahs notified her of the Rockefeller Foundation's decision in a letter dated November 18.[60]

On the same day, McCune also sent a reply to Fahs's November 7 letter; she explained that after having received the prior correspondence and in anticipation of carrying out the research, she had cut her hours at the press to half-time in October and was finishing her work there, as the press had found a replacement for her. She had also prepared to begin her studies at UC Berkeley to obtain a graduate degree and had revised her research plan to have a greater focus on knowledge production and a reduced emphasis on training and educational

124 AREA STUDIES

aspects. Thus, the research had two main objectives: the writing of sections on Korean art in George M. McCune's history of Korea and in the Korean volume of the United Nations series, which George McCune was editing, and the preparation of a handbook on Korean art. Evelyn thought that such a program of research and study would be especially useful for the further development of Korean studies. Moreover, in the letter, she mentioned the correspondence project, asking for hasty notification upon the securing of funds to begin operations.[61] The content of this letter indicates that Fahs's and Evelyn McCune's correspondence had crossed in the mail.

In January 1948, the Rockefeller Foundation approved the ACLS grant, which covered the salary of US$200 and expenses of US$100 per month for Evelyn McCune's advanced study in Oriental art and for the development of correspondence between Korean and American professors. The grant was available until December 31, 1948.[62]

The Correspondence Project as Intellectual Exchange

The correspondence project was carried out as an ACLS project sponsored by the Rockefeller Foundation to initiate correspondence between Korean and Americans professors who were willing to help their Korean counterparts in an informal manner by sharing information about up-to-date methods of teaching and new, inexpensive materials.[63]

On April 4, 1948, McCune reported on the status of the correspondence project to Graves. She had set herself a quota for the year, intending to establish correspondence between 150 Korean professors and their opposite numbers in the US. After liberation from Japanese colonial rule, South Korea was governed by the XXIV Corps of the US Army, which established the US Military Government in Korea (USMGIK). US administration continued for three years until the establishment of the Republic of Korea in August 1948.

In the spring of 1948 in South Korea, there were twenty-seven colleges and universities, including agricultural and technical schools, employing a total of around 1,200 to 1,300 instructors. McCune mentioned that of this number, she would be satisfied if she had 150 in established correspondence with American professors by the end of the year.[64] She also expressed satisfaction with the responses from American professors, although she noted that they were all slow in responding to letters; she surmised that the professors were likely overwhelmed with too much work. Further, McCune outlined obstacles to the project in South Korea, which included the Korean professors' preoccupation with local problems, lack of command of English, hostility to Americans in general, or fear or suspicion of being connected with an enterprise of correspondence with "foreigners."[65] In spite of these hurdles, she noted that the project had seen the best response from medical professionals teaching in the medical school of Seoul National University, followed by history professors of the same institution. Interestingly, she pointed out that no fewer than three well-known history professors with "liberal" tendencies, to whom she had written, had disappeared since the summer of 1947. In July 1946, the Department of Education, USMGIK, had announced its policy for the nationalization of Keijō Imperial University, which had been founded under Japanese colonial rule—the department sought to establish Seoul National University by rebuilding Keijō Imperial University. In the process of nationalization, not a few professors had been purged by the USMGIK because they were regarded as Communists, Communist sympathizers, or sympathizers to the North Korean regime. The purge continued for two years until 1948—the "liberal" professors McCune referred to may well have been purged. Meanwhile, she surmised that the army in South Korea was indifferent to the correspondence project itself.[66]

Fahs was also informed of the progress of the correspondence project. He recognized that both Evelyn and George M. McCune had been prudent and imaginative in instructing possible Korean correspondents to avoid political discussion and concentrate on questions relating to their fields of scholarship. Through Evelyn's report, he found that the American professors were generally cooperative.[67]

Evelyn McCune also frequently sent reports to ACLS and the Rockefeller Foundation. In July 1948, she made a report to Graves explaining the status of the project. In the summer of 1948, she had names of 177 Korean professors and half that number of Americans participating in the project. Popularity for the project was highest among professors of medicine and English, according to the report. For Korean professors specializing in art and archaeology, the American books and journals received through the correspondence project were the most fruitful for their research.[68]

According to McCune's reports, the correspondence project had been progressing well. In September 1948, the American professors who had been contacted had almost unanimously consented to participate. She had already established 35 to 40 correspondence partnerships, indicating 70 to 80 names, with a further 50 to 60 partnerships in preparation, indicating 100 to 120 names.[69] She was approaching her target of 150 correspondents. McCune observed that the idea of raising the morale of professors in Korea through correspondence was inspired; American professors were cooperative, and the Korean professors were willing to participate as soon as contact had been established for them.[70]

McCune also referred to gifts that had served to bolster the significance of the correspondence project. She had arranged for the purchase and shipment of over two hundred gifts, ranging from small contributions such as soap, buttons, and needles to larger items such as textbooks, schoolroom supplies, records, and subscriptions to professional journals in the fields of medicine, engineering, religion, and literature.[71] As return gifts from Korean professors, writings in Hangul were delivered to American professors. McCune noted that these gifts from Korea were looked upon as curiosities by American professors but nevertheless aroused interest.[72] The letters and gifts promoted the exchange of mutual knowledge and interest between South Korea and the US and enhanced appreciation for the project.

The grant-in-aid for the correspondence project and Evelyn B. McCune's research covered the period from November 1947 to January 1948. Before it expired, she wrote to Fahs, requesting a renewal. George M. McCune died on November 5, only a few days after Evelyn's letter to Fahs. Fahs and Charles E. Odegaard sympathized with her, and the two expressed positive attitudes toward the renewal of her grant-in-aid to enable her to continue the correspondence project and her own studies in 1949, if she so desired. The Rockefeller Foundation and ACLS were considering renewal of the grant, but no decision had been made because Fahs first needed to confirm Evelyn's desire to continue with the project.[73] She replied to Fahs that the correspondence project should be continued for another year but that she did not expect to have the time to work on it over the next few months. Fahs asked her to suggest a possible candidate to carry on the project.[74] Several days later, she wrote a letter to Fahs and Odegaard, suggesting her father, Arthur L. Becker, as a possible candidate. Becker was a Methodist educational missionary to Korea and had also served as president of Busan University during the US occupation. She emphasized that he had outstanding work experience in the educational field, in support of USMGIK efforts, and that he was already interested in the project. Moreover, Becker was willing to carry out an extended project of this nature and would do so without remuneration if the usual funds were unavailable.[75] The negotiation process during this period cannot be clarified owing to a lack of records; further archival research should be conducted. Nonetheless, McCune herself ultimately received the grant-in-aid again, and she engaged in not only her own research but also the correspondence project until the end of 1949.

She prepared a final report on the correspondence project and submitted it to Odegaard, who forwarded it to Fahs. In the report, she described the status of the project as follows: "Much effort was probably wasted, of course, owing to the great troubles most Korean teachers have been having in financial matters—some of them finding it prohibitive to buy stamps and stationery. However, some Koreans have responded to the gifts sent to them under this project with return gifts of Korean books, and have opened up vigorous correspondence with not only one but several Americans. There are about fifty names in this 'live' group."

She pointed out that gifts, particularly books, stimulated the exchange of mutual knowledge and interest between Korean and American professors and promoted intellectual interactions. The report also reviewed statistical data on the correspondence project. Through the project's two-year run, correspondents were established in eleven Korean institutions: Seoul National University (four departments); Ewha Women's University (seven departments); Yonsei University (three departments); Dankook University (one department); the National Museum (of which one participant was also an instructor in anthropology at Korea University); the Dramatic Art Section of the Department of Education; Severance Medical College; Korea University (five departments); Daegu Medical College; Seoul Presbyterian Theological Seminary; and Iri Agricultural College. She also introduced some of the correspondence partnerships she found most interesting:

> Dr. Paul Dudley White (Harvard Medical School) with Dr. Ri Tonhi, on the subject of cardiovascular diseases
>
> Dr. Elliot Newman (Johns Hopkins Hospital) with Dr. Suh Soonku, on various aspects of cardiology and neurology
>
> Dr. Frank N. Wilson (Heart Station, University Hospital, Ann Arbor, Michigan) with Dr. Lee Jongju, on heart disease
>
> Professor A. Cox (Law School, Harvard University) with J. S. Yoon (Korea University), on labor law
>
> Professor W. H. Coates (University of Rochester) with Dean J. O. Lee (Literary College, Korea University), on the philosophy of history
>
> Professor Kelsen (Political Science, University of California) with S. D. Whang (Law School of Korea University), on international law and aspects of the philosophy of law
>
> Professors J. M. Clark and W. C. Michell (Columbia University) with C. S. Hahn (Department of Economics, Korea University), on the teaching of economics
>
> Professor N. T. Dowling (Law School, Columbia University) with Dean J. O. Yoo (Law School, Korea University), on constitutional law

Professor Allan B. Cole (Department of History, Pomona College) with Sangi Kim (Seoul National University), on the teaching of Oriental history

Professors Wangaard and Hess (School of Forestry, Yale University) with C. S. Shim (College of Agriculture, Seoul National University), on forest utilization

Professor K. W. Aschenener (Department of Philosophy, University of California) with H. Pak (Korea University), on the philosophy of science

Professor G. R. Stewart (novelist, Department of English, University of California) with D. S. Suk (Department of English, Korea University)

The affiliations of the Korean professors who participated in the correspondence project were not limited to Seoul but included other rural areas, such as Daegu, North Gyeongsang Province, and Iri, North Cholla Province. The participants also had varying fields of expertise; they belonged to departments of medicine, law, economics, philosophy, history, English, French, chemistry, physics, metallurgy, art, music, home economics, education, psychology, physical education, dramatic arts, theology, anthropology, archaeology, political science, and agriculture. The correspondence project aimed to develop intellectual interactions between Korean and American professors in all manner of academic fields, and gifts of media for the exchange of knowledge made the project valuable for those involved.

Most of the gifts were books, of which over three hundred were sent out during 1948. Some of these books were new, others were secondhand, and some of the more expensive medical volumes were gifts from various US doctors themselves. One-year subscriptions to periodicals were also gifted to Korean professors, including the *Journals of the Institute of Metals* (American Institute of Physics, London), *Journal of Urology, Journal of Biological Chemistry, Far Eastern Quarterly* (eight subscriptions), *Newsweek, Reader's Digest,* and *Popular Science.* Moreover, McCune and the American professors sent a number of simple medical supplies, clothes (shirts, socks, shoes, ties, several secondhand suits), one projector, some pens and watches, scissors, paper, binders, other small items, and some Harvard Vocarium recordings to be used in teaching English literature. These gifts were mostly sent care of missionaries who had Army Post Office (APO) numbers at the time and a Korean who also had an APO number, although some items were sent directly.

In the report, McCune expressed her impressions of South Korea during her management of the correspondence project. First, she noted the shortage of instructors at every level of education and a decided drop in standards since the colonial era; available instructors had often moved up a rung in the hierarchy during the reorganization upon the departure of the Japanese: grammar school teachers taught high school, and high school teachers had taken college positions. Second, she addressed the overcrowding of schools, poor equipment, inflation, and "purging" of radical teachers, which made the morale of Korean instructors further lowered. Third, she mentioned the attitudes of the Korean people: according to McCune, many Koreans were hesitant to write to Americans for fear of exposing either their ignorance or their lack of English ability. Nevertheless, in conclusion, she reaffirmed the significance of the correspondence project: "About 150 professors have been introduced to each other, friendships have been started, scientific reprints exchanged, helpful advice offered and received, and some real profit has come of this."

McCune understood the meaning of intellectual interaction through the promotion of knowledge exchange between the US and Korea. Therefore, she personally intended to have ten professors on her own list of correspondents; she had not met any of them, but they had, by their letters, induced her to continue correspondence with them indefinitely.

However, she did not display any overt understanding of how the project was linked to the Cold War. When the Rockefeller Foundation conducted projects on Korean affairs, it did not pay much heed to the situation of the Cold War emerging in Europe before the outbreak of the (hot) Korean War in 1950.

The Korean War provided a critical opportunity for McCune to define her academic and political position on Korean issues. After she obtained her master's degree in history at UC Berkeley in 1950, she was dispatched to Seoul for a salvage mission of the US Army that would transfer art treasures from the National Museum in Seoul to Busan, the provisional capital of South Korea. From 1951 to 1952, she worked at the Library of Congress as Korean Section chief, during which time she visited Korea again in 1952 as a mission member for the Library of Congress and the Department of State to investigate damage to the books and art treasures at libraries and museums in South Korea. Through these experiences, McCune discovered the significance of the duties of government agencies, such as the army and the State Department, and of cooperating with them. In the 1960s, she worked at the State Department as an analyst of North Korean affairs; for Evelyn, the Korean War became a great inspiration for research topics from the 1950s to 1970.

CONCLUSION

This chapter traced the process of knowledge production on Korea from the mid-1940s to the early 1950s, and then several distinctive aspects were observed.

First, knowledge on Korea began to be produced, circulated between, and stored by academic and government agencies as part of a larger strategy to ensure US victory over Japan in the Pacific War: George M. McCune intended to research and analyze the conditions of Korea not only for academic purposes but as a part of the war effort. Therefore, knowledge production assumed a strong character of policy science. Knowledge about Korea came to be called Korean studies in the postwar era; in the US, the development of Korean studies was based on wartime resources and furthered by collaborative work between scholars and government agents from the mid-1940s at the latest.

Second, George M. McCune attempted to shift the scope of knowledge production on Korea from military to civil purposes after the end of the Second World War; he made great efforts to open courses on Korea at UC Berkeley for students who were interested in Korean affairs, and he sought to institutionalize knowledge about Korea produced during the Pacific War as Korean studies in US universities. Fahs understood and supported McCune's effort to produce such knowledge, both when he worked at the OSS and during his time at the Rockefeller Foundation. The Rockefeller Foundation itself encouraged the advancement of not only Korean studies but also area studies generally. Through the process of institutionalization, the character of knowledge on Korea gradually shifted from policy science to the generation of academic resources for Korean studies.

Third, the Rockefeller Foundation supported Evelyn B. McCune in her efforts, both for her own research and for her role in the correspondence project between Korean and American academics. Evelyn B. McCune, in turn, intended to utilize the foundation for her own research; through the correspondence project, she established a win-win relationship with the foundation. The correspondence project also became an opportunity for Americans to learn about various aspects of Korea through intellectual interactions and contribute to the continuing development of Korean studies in the US.

The Korean War accelerated the development of Korean studies in US universities. Facing a shortage of Korean experts, some major universities, including Stanford and Harvard, opened many courses and programs relating to Korean affairs for the training of specialists. In the 1950s, the Ford Foundation and Carnegie Endowment for Peace began to support the launch of similar courses and programs, as did the Rockefeller Foundation. This chapter has explored the nature of Korean studies knowledge, which originated as a Pacific War strategy, as well as the interim period between the liberation of Korea up until the next hot war, but the character of Korean studies knowledge after the

Korean War and the way this knowledge developed in light of the global Cold War remain areas that warrant further exploration.

NOTES

1. Cumings, *Parallax Visions*, 173.

2. Ahn, *Birth of Korean Studies*; Wilbur, "McAfee McCune."

3. S. McCune, *Mansei Movement*.

4. Kim S.-Y., "Life of George McAfee McCune," 249.

5. Rockefeller Foundation, Personal History and Application for a Fellowship in Far Eastern History, August 10, 1956, McCune, Evelyn Becker, 1956–1957, 1966, series 200: United States, subseries 200, E: Fellowships, Scholarships, Training Awards, box 14, Rockefeller Foundation Records, Fellowships, Fellowship Files, SG 10.1 (FA244), Rockefeller Archives Center (hereafter RAC).

6. Rockefeller Foundation.

7. Fujitani, *Race for Empire*, 101

8. Fujitani, 231.

9. See Cumings, *Parallax Visions*.

10. Ahn, *Birth of Korean Studies*.

11. Kim S.-Y., "Life of George McAfee McCune."

12. Ahn, *Birth of Korean Studies*; Kim S.-Y., "Life of George McAfee McCune"; Yu, *OSS in China*; R. S. Kim, *Project Eagle*; Katō, *Origin of Symbolic Emperor System*.

13. Yoneyama, *Cold War Ruins*.

14. These intelligence reports are stored in box 19, folder 5, George M. McCune Papers, McCune-Becker Collection, Center for Korean Studies, University of Hawai'i at Mānoa (hereafter UHM).

15. Report on *Potentialities of Korean Help against Japan*, George M. McCune to Remer, April 24, 1942, box 20, folder 1, George M. McCune Papers, UHM.

16. Report on *Potentialities of Korean Help against Japan*, report 41a, April 25, 1942, box 7, Reports and Studies, 1942–1949, UD177, RG 226, National Archives and Records Administration (hereafter NARA).

17. Report on *Potentialities of Korean Help against Japan*, McCune to Remer.

18. Kobayashi, "US Intelligence Agencies," 139–50.

19. Korean Independence Movement, April 25, 1942, COI, Research and Analysis Branch, Far Eastern Section, Office of Strategic Service, RG 226, NARA.

20. Unification of Korean Independence Groups, June 15, 1942, OSS, Far Eastern Section, R&A 298, Office of Strategic Service, RG 226, NARA.

21. Recent Korean Documents Relating to the Korean Provisional Government in Chungking, August 2, 1943, OSS, Research and Analysis Branch, R&A 1028, Office of Strategic Service, RG 226, NARA.

AREA STUDIES

22. Economic Survey, August 5, 1943, OSS, Far Eastern Section, R&A 774, Office of Strategic Service, RG 226, NARA.

23. Box 19, folder 5, George M. McCune Papers, UHM.

24. George M. McCune to Erle R. Dickover, July 10, 1945, box 19, folder 5, George M. McCune Papers, UHM.

25. F. Theodore Cloak to George M. McCune, August 30, 1945, box 19, folder 5, George M. McCune Papers, UHM.

26. George McCune, recommended by John Fairbank, August 21, 1944, Rockefeller Foundation Records, Fellowships, Fellowship Files, SG 10.1 (FA244), series 200, box 14, RAC.

27. Norma S. Thompson to George M. McCune, April 14, 1945, Rockefeller Foundation Records, Fellowships, Fellowship Files, SG 10.1 (FA244), series 200, box 14, RAC.

28. George M. McCune to Charles B. Fahs, November 2, 1946, Rockefeller Foundation Records, Fellowships, Fellowship Files, SG 10.1 (FA244), series 200, box 14, RAC.

29. G. McCune, recommended by Fairbank.

30. Memo, July 19, 1945, Rockefeller Foundation Records, Fellowships, Fellowship Files, SG 10.1 (FA244), series 200, box 14, RAC.

31. G. McCune to Dickover, July 10, 1945.

32. Charles Burton Fahs to George M. McCune, April 8, 1946, box 19, folder 5, George M. McCune Papers, UHM.

33. Fahs to McCune.

34. Edwin M. Martin to George M. McCune, May 29, 1946, box 19, folder 5, George M. McCune Papers, UHM.

35. Martin to McCune.

36. Online Collection and Catalog of Rockefeller Archive Center, s.v. "Charles B. (Charles Burton) Fahs."

37. George M. McCune to David H. Stevens, September 29, 1946, Rockefeller Foundation Records, Fellowships, Fellowship Files, SG 10.1 (FA244), series 200, box 14, RAC.

38. G. McCune to Fahs, November 2, 1946.

39. Intensive Instruction in the Korean Language, Rockefeller Foundation Records, Fellowships, Fellowship Files, SG 10.1 (FA244), series 200, box 14, RAC.

40. G. McCune to Fahs, November 2, 1946.

41. University of California, "In Memoriam."

42. George M. McCune to Charles B. Fahs, October 7, 1946, Rockefeller Foundation Records, Fellowships, Fellowship Files, SG 10.1 (FA244), series 200, box 14, RAC.

43. G. McCune to Fahs, November 2, 1946.

44. G. McCune to Fahs.

DAWN OF KOREAN STUDIES AND KNOWLEDGE PRODUCTION   133

45. Charles B. Fahs, interview, April 11, 1947, Rockefeller Foundation Records, Fellowships, Fellowship Files, SG 10.1 (FA244), series 200, box 14, RAC.

46. Charles B. Fahs to George M. McCune, August 1, 1947, 200R, American Council of Learned Societies—Korean Studies, 1947–1950, 1955, series 200, box 264, Rockefeller Foundation Records, Projects, RG 1.2 (FA387), RAC.

47. C. B. Fahs to Cornelius Krause, November 7, 1947, 200R, American Council of Learned Societies—Korean Studies, 1947–1950, 1955, series 200, box 264, Rockefeller Foundation Records, Projects, RG 1.2 (FA387), RAC.

48. C. B. Fahs to Evelyn B. McCune, August 1, 1947, 200R, American Council of Learned Societies—Korean Studies, 1947–1950, 1955, series 200, box 264, RAC.

49. Evelyn B. McCune to C. B. Fahs, August 19, 1947, 200R, American Council of Learned Societies—Korean Studies, 1947–1950, 1955; Letter from C. B. Fahs to Evelyn B. McCune, September 12, 1947, Series 200, Box 264, RAC.

50. Rockefeller Foundation Records, Fellowships, Fellowship Files, SG 10.1 (FA244), series 200, box 14, RAC.

51. E. McCune to Fahs, August 19, 1947; Fahs to E. McCune, September 12, 1947.

52. E. McCune to Fahs, August 19, 1947; Fahs to E. McCune, September 12, 1947.

53. Proposed Study Plan, 200R, American Council of Learned Societies—Korean Studies, 1947–1950, 1955, series 200, box 264, RAC.

54. Proposed Study Plan, RAC.

55. C. B. Fahs to Cornelius Kruse, November 7, 1947, 200R, American Council of Learned Societies—Korean Studies, 1947–1950, 1955, series 200, box 264, RAC.

56. Cornelius Kruse to C. B. Fahs, November 12, 1947, 200R, American Council of Learned Societies—Korean Studies, 1947–1950, 1955, series 200, box 264, RAC.

57. C. B. Fahs to Evelyn B. McCune, November 7, 1947, 200R, American Council of Learned Societies—Korean Studies, 1947–1950, 1955, series 200, box 264, RAC.

58. Grant-in-Aid to the American Council of Learned Societies, November 13, 1947, RF46142, 200R, American Council of Learned Societies—Korean Studies, 1947–1950, 1955, series 200, box 264, RAC.

59. Grant-in-Aid to the American Council of Learned Societies, RAC.

60. C. B. Fahs to Evelyn B. McCune, November 18, 1947, 200R, American Council of Learned Societies—Korean Studies, 1947–1950, 1955, series 200, box 264, RAC.

61. Evelyn B. McCune to C. B. Fahs, November 18, 1947, 200R, American Council of Learned Societies—Korean Studies, 1947–1950, 1955, series 200, box 264, RAC.

62. Grant-in-Aid to the American Council of Learned Societies, January 7, 1948, RA H4808, 200R, American Council of Learned Societies—Korean Studies, 1947–1950, 1955, series 200, box 264, RAC.

134 AREA STUDIES

63. Evelyn B. McCune to Charles E. Odegaard, June 28, 1949, 200R, American Council of Learned Societies—Korean Studies, 1947–1950, 1955, series 200, box 264, RAC.

64. Evelyn B. McCune to Mortimer Graves, April 4, 1948, 200R, American Council of Learned Societies—Korean Studies, 1947–1950, 1955, series 200, box 264, RAC.

65. E. McCune to Graves.

66. E. McCune to Graves.

67. Excerpt from C. B. Fahs Trip to the Far East, April 14, 1948, 200R, American Council of Learned Societies—Korean Studies, 1947–1950, 1955, series 200, box 264, RAC.

68. Evelyn B. McCune to Mortimer Graves, July 23, 1948, 200R, American Council of Learned Societies—Korean Studies, 1947–1950, 1955, series 200, box 264, RAC.

69. Evelyn B. McCune to C. B. Fahs, September 11, 1948, 200R, American Council of Learned Societies—Korean Studies, 1947–1950, 1955, series 200, box 264, RAC.

70. E. McCune to Fahs.

71. Evelyn B. McCune to Mortimer Graves, September 26, 1948, 200R, American Council of Learned Societies—Korean Studies, 1947–1950, 1955, series 200, box 264, RAC.

72. E. McCune to Graves.

73. C. B. Fahs to Evelyn B. McCune, December 6, 1948, 200R, American Council of Learned Societies—Korean Studies, 1947–1950, 1955, series 200, box 264, RAC.

74. C. B. Fahs to Evelyn B. McCune, December 14, 1948, 200R, American Council of Learned Societies—Korean Studies, 1947–1950, 1955, series 200, box 264, RAC.

75. Evelyn B. McCune to C. B. Fahs, December 19, 1948; Charles E. Odegaard to C. B. Fahs, December 23, 1948, 200R, American Council of Learned Societies—Korean Studies, 1947–1950, 1955, series 200, box 264, RAC.

REFERENCES

Primary Sources

Rockefeller Foundation Records, Fellowships, Fellowship Files, SG 10.1 (FA244), Rockefeller Archives Center (RAC).

Rockefeller Foundation Records, Projects, RG 1.2 (FA387), RAC.

George M. McCune Papers, McCune-Becker Collection, Center for Korean Studies, University of Hawai'i at Mānoa (UHM).

Office of Strategic Service, RG 226, National Archives and Records Administration (NARA).

Secondary Sources

Books

Ahn, Jung-cheol. *The Birth of Korean Studies in the US Institutions and the US Perception of Korea: The Case Study of George M. McCune. Korean History in the World,* Lee, Taejin, eds. [In Korean.] Seoul: Daehakusa, 2009.

Cumings, Bruce. *Parallax Visions: Making Sense of American–East Asian Relations at the End of the Century.* Durham, NC: Duke University Press, 1999.

Fujitani, Takashi. *Race for Empire: Koreans as Japanese and Japanese as Americans during World War II.* Berkeley: University of California Press, 2011.

Katō, Tetsurō. *The Origin of Symbolic Emperor System: Japan Plan in US Psychological Warfare.* [In Japanese.] Tokyo: Heibonsha, 2005.

Kim, Robert S. *Project Eagle: The American Christians of North Korea in World War II.* Lincoln: Potomac Books, 2017.

Kim, Seung-kyung, and Michael Robinson, eds. *Peace Corps Volunteers and the Making of Korean Studies in the United States.* Seattle, WA: Center for Korea Studies, 2020.

McCune, Shannon Boyd-Bailey. *The Mansei Movement, March 1, 1919.* Honolulu: University of Hawai'i Press, 1976.

Yoneyama, Lisa. *Cold War Ruins: Transpacific Critique of American Justice and Japanese War Crimes.* Durham, NC: Duke University Press, 2016.

Yu, Maochun. *OSS in China: Prelude to Cold War.* New Haven, CT: Yale University Press, 1996.

Articles

Kim Seo-Yeon. "The Life of George McAfee McCune and His View on Korea." [In Korean.] *Journal of Korean History* (Korea University) 18 (2018): 237–66.

Kobayashi, Somei. "US Intelligence Agencies and George McAfee McCune during the Pacific War: Gathering Information on Korea from Missionaries through the Office of Coordination/Office of Strategic Service." [In Japanese.] *Journal of Korean History* (Chōsen-Shi Kenkyūkai) 58 (2020): 127–58.

Wilbur, C. Martin. "McAfee McCune (June 16, 1908–November 5, 1948)." *Far Eastern Quarterly* 9, no. 2 (February 1950): 185–91.

Online Resources

Online Collection and Catalog of Rockefeller Archive Center, s.v. "Charles B. (Charles Burton) Fahs." Accessed October 31, 2020. https://dimes.rockarch.org /agents/8fgdhQozzVZpzKucKCQP9W.

University of California. "In Memoriam, 1946: Florence Walne Farquhar, Japanese; Berkley, 1895–1946." Accessed October 31, 2020. http://texts.cdlib .org/view?docId=hb300004ss&chunk.id=div00003&brand=calisphere&doc .view=entire_text.

AUTHOR BIO

SOMEI KOBAYASHI is Professor at Nihon University College of Law. He is author of *Media Space of Koreans in Japan: Newspapers during the Allied Occupation of Japan* (2007) and many articles on East Asian history in the Cold War era and Korean studies.

PART II

SCIENTIFIC KNOWLEDGE

FIVE

THE EMERGENCE OF CHINA'S NUCLEAR RESEARCH

Between the Civil War and the Cold War

YUKO SATO

INTRODUCTION

With the rapid deterioration in US-China relations in recent years, the US government has taken measures seemingly intended to shut Chinese companies out of US markets and has come to regard US-based Chinese scientists as akin to spies, clearly reflecting the perceived threat of the possible development of international scientist networks that include the Chinese. The Chinese government's ambitious Thousand Talents Plan, which aims to have a great number of Chinese scientists undergo training outside the country and subsequently return as experts, is likely viewed as a threat by many countries, with the foremost being the US.

Even when the People's Republic of China (PRC) was still a much weaker country than it is now, it surprised the world with its first successful nuclear weapon test only fifteen years after the proclamation of the PRC's establishment. The Chinese scientists who led their country's nuclear development project to success continue to be praised by Chinese citizens today for their devotion to China, particularly for their decision to give up staying in the West, where they could have earned higher salaries, and return to China to secretly participate in the project. After the PRC's establishment and subsequent intervention in the Korean War, Chinese scientists who repatriated to the PRC were shut out of Western scientist networks for many years. During the postwar years, Chinese scientists had to face a life-changing decision of whether to remain in the West, where they could maintain high professional standards as experts in their field, or repatriate and devote themselves to their country.

Repatriating the few international Chinese scientists, recruiting other scientists domestically, and fostering a younger generation of scientists were all important to both Nationalists and Communists. They did not only contribute to the development of science and technology in the country but their expertise was also of critical importance for respective research institutes that were politically at risk of being weakened on the fringes of the rivalry between Nationalists and Communists.

Research on Chinese students studying in the US since the final years of the Qing dynasty has been conducted by Stacey Bieler.[1] However, Bieler's research did not focus specifically on China's nuclear research or on the Chinese government's recruitment of natural scientists. In fact, there have been almost no historical treatments of the emergence of China's nuclear research from the perspective of the Chinese government's call for repatriation as a measure to secure enough researchers for its nuclear project—perhaps because researchers have not generally recognized this period as the dawn of modern Chinese science and technology. Many biographies and oral histories of the scientists concerned have been published in the Chinese language.[2] However, few have been compiled with broad, objective perspectives, and, when compared with one another, some reveal inconsistencies. This chapter thus examines such biographies and oral histories from the perspective of China's efforts to formulate its nuclear research program, which had begun at some point between the Chinese Civil War and the Cold War.

Nuclear development requires several thousand workers. As the number of surviving biographies and oral histories fall far short of those numbers, they reflect merely a fragment of China's emerging nuclear program. Nevertheless, in 1959, looking back to a decade earlier, Qian Sanqiang—a key physicist in the PRC's nuclear development program who is credited as the father of China's atomic bomb—stated that, in 1949, China only had about ten people who could be called nuclear physicists.[3] Although one should take this statement with a grain of salt, the number of available physicists nevertheless clearly fell far short of several thousand, and the success of measures to repatriate Chinese scientists, even just a handful, must have made a great difference. Success in repatriating prominent natural scientists, including physicists and other researchers, and having them participate in its nuclear development project would have been of great promotional value and could have inspired a snowball effect, encouraging more scientists to return, as well as attracting new recruits, which was of utmost importance to the PRC at its dawn of existence. From these perspectives, this chapter examines the measures taken by both the Chinese Nationalists and the Communists to develop China's

THE EMERGENCE OF CHINA'S NUCLEAR RESEARCH

networks of scientists and promote their nuclear development programs, the purposes for which they used the networks, and the reactions they elicited from the Chinese scientists.

NUCLEAR HUMAN RESOURCES UNDER
THE NATIONALIST GOVERNMENT

China's Approach to US Nuclear Research

The Chinese Nationalist government, led by Chiang Kai-shek, became particularly interested in the power of the atomic bomb in August 1945 when it learned of Japan's defeat. The Nationalist government, having witnessed the strength of the Japanese army when its capital, Nanjing, fell into Japanese hands, was shocked by the emergence of the atomic bomb—the weapon that defeated Japan and ended World War II. Subsequently setting its sights on the future development of its own atomic bomb, the Nationalist government began formulating plans to mobilize the country's resources. Still in the early stages of developing the nation's electric power system and lacking foreign currency because of severe inflation after the war, China first needed to cultivate human resources and identify the natural resources it could exploit.

In the autumn of 1945, Chen Cheng, the minister of war, summoned physicist Wu Dayou, mathematician Hua Luogeng, and chemist Zeng Zhaolun to the Ministry of War office located in Chongqing and ordered them to select five promising young scientists to carry out research into developing an atomic bomb. Wu and the two other scientists explained to Chen that their country lacked adequate funds, electricity, engineers, and physicists and then suggested that the Ministry of War first allow them to study in the US along with a number of young scientists; Chen approved.[4] Wu decided to take Li Zhengdao (also known as T. D. Lee) and Zhu Guangya with him, Hua Luogeng took Sun Benwang, and Zeng chose Tang Aoqing and Wang Ruixin, also known as Wang Jui Hsin.[5]

On January 13, 1946, Hua Luogeng visited Mei Yiqi, a physicist who was also the president of Tsing Hua University at the time, to tell him that the Ministry of War was sending a research delegation to the US.[6] In the same year, on June 13, Mei met with Qian Changzuo, Wu Youxun, and Sa Bendong at Academia Sinica to hear their thoughts on the Ministry of National Defense's research proposal.[7] Qian had just become director of the Sixth Office of the Ministry of National Defense when the Ministry of War was reorganized as the Ministry of National Defense on June 1, and the Sixth Office of the Ministry was charged with gathering scientists and conducting military research, including atomic bomb development. Wu, in addition to being president of the National Central University, was a physicist, who some officials suggested could be more suited than others for the US-bound research delegation, a view elaborated upon below. Sa, the then secretary-general of Academia Sinica, was also a physicist and had previously taught at Ohio State University. Two days later, on June 15, Gu Yuxiu, another physicist and then director general of the Shanghai Municipal Education Commission, who had an official trip to the US scheduled for the following month, visited Mei to discuss matters relating to his trip. He expressed his hope to gain cooperation from the US on behalf of Tsing Hua University in the scientific fields essential for national defense, including aviation, radio physics, and atomic physics.[8] Having previously received Vannevar Bush's supervision during study abroad in the 1920s, Gu met with Bush during his trip and asked for help with the Nationalist government's nuclear development project.[9]

By March 1946, the US Department of State knew of the Chinese Ministry of War's plan to send its delegation including Wu, Hua, and Zeng in the autumn of the same year. In addition, the State Department was also aware of the Nationalist government officials' opinions of their delegation, according to which Wu was selected unanimously, while some officials questioned Hua and Zeng's political loyalty and intelligence and suggested that they instead send older and more experienced physicists like Wu Youxun and H. C. Zen.[10]

In July 1946, shortly before the departure of the Ministry of War's delegation, the US conducted an atomic bomb test at Bikini Atoll. Several international representatives from the Soviet Union and China, among other countries, were invited to observe the test, code-named Operation Crossroads. The representatives for China were Chao Chung-Yao, professor and physicist at the National Central University, and Hou Teng, a military attaché to the US. Chao was ordered to visit the US and bring back an accelerator, and he was provided with US$125,000 for its acquisition. However, the allowance was insufficient, and the order was impossible to follow without violating the US embargo. Chao instead purchased parts, which he brought home with him. Chao extended his stay in the US, and in March 1947, during Zhu Kezhen's visit, he often enjoyed meals with Zhu and other Chinese US residents, while also conducting nuclear research at the California Institute of Technology and Massachusetts Institute of Technology (MIT). Chao finally returned to the PRC in 1950.[11]

Wu Youxun, whom the Nationalist government had assessed as more politically loyal and intelligent than the members of the delegation, was also sent on an official trip to the US in December 1947. The overt purpose of Wu's trip was to attend a UNESCO conference, but another likely goal was to meet with Vannevar Bush as a representative of the Chinese government to convey its requests to the US State Department.[12] Wu had previously studied at the University of Chicago's Department of Physics under Arthur H. Compton, before Compton became leader of the Manhattan Project's Metallurgical Laboratory at the University of Chicago and recruited key project figures, including Enrico Fermi.[13] Wu asked Compton to write a letter of introduction addressed to Bush. Although Bush eventually canceled their meeting, he apologized for the last-minute change and offered to reschedule if Wu was still in the US. However, Bush also explained to Wu that although he understood from Compton's letter that the Chinese government desired formal discussions with the US State Department over certain issues, he could not engage under his own initiative unless the government raised such issues directly. In response to this, Wu requested a meeting with Bush the following week and wrote that while he understood Bush's position on Compton's letter, he wanted to explain his circumstances when they met.[14] This correspondence exchange indicates two facts: (1) Bush regarded Wu as an unofficial representative who had not been delegated any authority by the Chinese government, and (2) Wu's strategy to approach Bush was to ask Compton to act as a mediator.

Wu was not the only person who turned to a connection developed while abroad for intermediary help in approaching members of the Manhattan Project. As mentioned above, Gu Yuxiu also relied on his former instructor Vannevar Bush.

In the early summer of 1949, Gu and his family moved to Taiwan, following the Nationalist government. Later that summer, Gu received an invitation from MIT to teach as a guest instructor of electrical engineering. He accepted the invitation and moved with his family to the US the following year. In 1952, before the expiration of his contract with MIT, Gu asked Bush for help in finding another job in the US, and in 1955, Bush was contacted by an electric power company as a reference and was asked about the degree of loyalty and intelligence Gu had demonstrated while working at the University of Pennsylvania. This reference call suggests the possibility that Gu was trying to avoid moving back to the Republic of China (ROC) by asking Bush for help building a career in the US.[15]

Wu Dayou was still in his thirties when he was sent to the US in 1946. While the Ministry of War initially planned to call its delegation back after about two years, the Chinese Civil War caused a dramatic change of plans, and, after earning his degree at the University of Michigan, Wu remained in the US as an instructor, teaching at several universities. In September 1949, at the age of forty-one, Wu became an associate research officer of the Chalk River Laboratories' nuclear power project, which was an essential part of the nuclear power development plan being administered by Canada's National Research Council. Over the following two years, Wu was promoted to junior research officer and then to head of the newly established Theoretical Physics Department as the senior research officer.[16]

Wu remained in Canada for about a decade after joining the Chalk River Laboratories' project, during which time he was reunited with Zhou Peiyuan, a physicist who was sent twice by the PRC to attend the Pugwash Conferences on Science and World Affairs, once in 1957 and again the following year. Wu and Zhou had previously represented the ROC together at the tercentenary celebration of the birth of Isaac Newton, held in July 1946, the year before Wu moved to the US. On his second visit to Canada, Zhou stayed at Wu's home for three nights along with Chen Xingshen (also known as S. S. Chern), who was working at the Institute for Advanced Study, located in Princeton, New Jersey, and whom Zhou had contacted in advance by telegram. The three discussed the future of China's science and international relations, focusing primarily on the technological development of the PRC and issues underlying its technology. Zhou was not directly involved in the PRC's nuclear development project.[17] However, he served both as chief and vice-principal of Peking University's Physics Department and was already known as having a close relationship with Zhou Enlai—a relationship based on favoritism and protection.[18]

In 1950, Chao Chung-Yao, who had been pursuing nuclear power research at the California Institute of Technology, decided to return to the PRC. However, much as Qian Xuesen, a missile engineer colleague, had been detained while trying to board their ship bound for China, Chao was also detained by US forces in Japan when the ship stopped at the Port of Yokohama. This detainment infuriated the government of the PRC, who encouraged the repatriation of Chinese scientists at the California Institute of Technology. However, when a representative of the Nationalist government came to bail Chao out, he declined the representative's offer, refusing to be taken back to Taiwan. Subsequently, Chao was released after a little over ten days and returned to mainland China. The US State Department was unconcerned with the PRC's incensed reaction but nevertheless regarded Qian and Chao's case as exceptional and thus did not see any need to regard all other Chinese scientists working at the California Institute of Technology as suspect.

After being released and returning to China, in 1951, at a welcome-back party held for him by Li Siguang, introduced in the next section of this chapter, Chao Chung-Yao said that the US government had decided to allocate 90 percent of its atomic-physics budget to developing atomic bombs, practically forcing scientists to work on developing nuclear weapons; he added that, because of

THE EMERGENCE OF CHINA'S NUCLEAR RESEARCH   145

this, some physicists at the California Institute of Science and Technology had given up working in their area of expertise and switched to pursuing biological research instead.[19]

The Competition over Recruiting Li Siguang

Li Siguang (1889–1971) was a geologist well known for his achievements in geomechanics, which are claimed to have been of great help to China in achieving its long-cherished goal of discovering oil, with the Daqing Oil Field find in 1959. In the mid-twentieth century, subterranean resources such as uranium and oil held greater significance in terms of national power than they do today. With reliable methods of identifying their distribution patterns just beginning to be developed, Li, whose recognition was already growing by the time of the Chinese Civil War, also saw growing competition for his loyalty between the Nationalists and Communists, who were each trying to sway him with better incentives.

Li had first studied in Japan, and after the 1911 Revolution, in 1913 he moved to the UK, where he studied mining engineering and geology before returning to China in 1919. At the time, research in the fields of geology and physics was more advanced in the UK than in the US. In 1928, Academia Sinica, comprising research institutes dedicated to geology, physics, and the social sciences, was established in Nanjing and welcomed Li as director of the Institute of Geology, located in Shanghai.

For another two years from 1934, Li studied in the UK, and after returning, he refused to follow Chiang Kai-shek's request for the institutes to evacuate to Chongqing in the face of the Sino-Japanese War. Instead, Li relocated the Institute of Geology to Guangxi Province. Other institutes, dedicated to physics, psychology, and the social sciences, also relocated to Guangxi. Because of insufficient funds, Li's institute had to limit its research into geological mineral resources in Guangxi and the neighboring province of Hubei.[20] However, as a serendipitous result of this unfortunate situation, in 1943, while conducting a geological survey in Guangxi Province, Li's subordinate Nan Yanzong discovered uranium ore, and the following year Nan published a paper on the discovery, jointly authored with Wu Leibo, who assisted in the survey.[21] The paper opened with an acknowledgment expressing gratitude to Li.[22]

By 1945, Li had moved to Beipei, located about sixty kilometers north of Chongqing, and in summer that year, when recovering from an illness, he was paid a visit by Wang Shijie, then head of the Nationalist government's Ministry of Foreign Affairs, who offered to provide some nutritious food to help Li recuperate. However, recognizing Wang's political position, Li politely declined his offer. A few days later, T. V. Soong, premier of the ROC, visited Li and offered him the post of ambassador to the UK, but once again, Li declined.[23] Subsequently, that same summer, representing the Communists, Zhou Enlai visited Li twice and urged him to gather Zhu Kezhen and H. C. Zen to form what would be officially established on July 6 as the Chinese Scientific Workers Association.[24]

In this way, Li was considered of great significance by both the Nationalists and Communists not only for being an established scientist but also for having played a part in the discovery of uranium ore, as credited in Nan and Wu's tribute. At the time, many countries were focusing strategic attention on underground resources, and reflecting this trend, in May 1948, the Nationalist government appointed Weng Wenhao—geologist and then head of the Nationalist Government Resources Committee—as premier of the ROC. With China's nuclear development project, including the development of the atomic bomb, still at the stage of locating new underground resources for military use, the Chinese government needed geologists to cooperate with politics.

In 1948, Li revisited the UK to attend an international conference and, considering his country's situation, decided to remain in the UK for a while. His paper "Introducing *Military and Political Consequences of Atomic Energy*" is generally considered to have been written during this visit, as he mentions that the book he introduces within—*Military and Political Consequences of Atomic Energy* by P. M. S. Blackett—was published "this year in February." In his paper, Li examines the political and social impact of the atomic bomb produced under the Manhattan Project, which was participated in by seven University of Chicago scientists and physicists, including James Franck. Li also discusses the Franck Report, produced by the Franck Committee, which recommended against using the atomic bomb without prior warning.[25] Seen as the most essential geologist in China's developing self-sufficiency in uranium ore, Li attracted the attention of both Nationalist and Communist top officials and must have been well aware—as is interpretable from his paper—that the government expected him to serve as a key to its nuclear development project.

The government's aim in calling Li and other Chinese scientists to repatriate to advance the country's nuclear research was capitalized on by Academia Sinica. The academy believed that if it could get Li to return and thereby help the government achieve its aim, his presence would lead to more funding. Early in the summer of 1949, Academia Sinica learned that Li, who was in the UK, taking shelter from the Civil War, would finally be returning. The institute hoped to secure Li as a project representative to increase its chances of securing research funds. Wu Youxun, deputy head of the National Academy of Beiping—who at the time was in Shanghai, seeking shelter from the war—told Zhu Kezhen, a meteorologist, that Academia Sinica planned to telegram Li to ask him to return precisely for the above reason. Tao Menghe, who was listening to Wu share the academy's plan with Zhu, subsequently told Zhu that Li had promised, in a letter, to return and that he would take a route that passed through Turkey.[26] In late September, the ROC's ambassador to the UK sent officials to search for Li and found his wife. However, according to her, Li was somewhere outside the UK on a geological survey, and although the officials' mission included gifting Li US$5,000, his wife declined the offer.[27]

On October 1, immediately after the PRC's proclamation ceremony, the State Council of the PRC appointed Li, in absentia, alongside Wu Youxun, Zhu Kezhen, Chen Boda, and Tao Menghe, as vice presidents of the country's newly established Chinese Academy of Sciences, to serve under Guo Moruo as president. In November, some time after Li had embarked on his trip back to China via eastern Europe, Zhou Enlai, then premier of the State Council, contacted Wang Jiaxiang, ambassador to the Soviet Union, and Wu Wendao, Xinhua News Agency's Prague branch president, to tell them that Li had already secretly entered eastern Europe. Zhou said that they must find a way to establish contact with Li and also negotiate with Czechoslovak government officials before he reached Czechoslovakia, to secure help in getting him safely into the country.[28]

In 1950, traveling back from the UK via Hong Kong, Li finally reached Nanjing in April and then Beijing in May. Guo Moruo greeted Li at his hotel in Beijing. On the following day, Li was visited by Zhou Enlai, and the two spoke for almost three hours. Li told Zhou about the changes he had witnessed abroad in the scientific community under capitalism and said that he wanted to return to Nanjing someday to pursue geological research. Zhou then explained the urgent demand of their newborn country and asked Li to aid Guo at the Chinese Academy of Science with research in an area related to the natural sciences and also to lead the efforts of the nation's geologists, aimed at helping the country lay its scientific foundations. Zhou and Li exchanged some basic ideas on what kinds of functions the envisioned geological research institute would need.[29] The reason Zhou willingly went through the trouble of arranging for Li's safe return must have been Li's invaluable expertise and connections, and arranging for the return of this geologist, for whom the government had high political expectations, indeed helped Academia Sinica secure the funds it needed.

Securing Foreign Currency and Organizing
Underground Communist Party Members

As with scientists pursuing research funding, the Communists were also extremely enthusiastic about securing foreign currency, and to them, talented scientists were their golden geese.

The Communists provided party members who had studied abroad under the Nationalist government's programs with financial support in US dollars. To do so, they asked those who had passed the Nationalist government's self-funded study-abroad examination, and who had therefore been granted the right to purchase foreign currency at government official prices, to make such purchases on their behalf. In other words, the Communists took advantage of scientists to obtain foreign currency and viewed studying abroad as a way to not only learn about the values of the Western world but also acquire something with practical value—foreign currency.

In 1940, telecommunications and electrical engineer Luo Peilin joined the Chinese Communist Party. Under the recommendation of Qian Xuesen, then teaching at the California Institute of Technology, Luo was granted the right to study abroad at the university and received hundreds of US dollars as funding from the Communist Party. When he studied abroad in the US, in the fall of 1948, Luo was thirty-five years old. According to Luo, others besides himself— including Zhang Daqi, an electrical machinery specialist—received financial support from the Communist Party to study abroad. When Zhang passed the Nationalist Party's self-funded study-abroad examination, the Communists asked him to make a purchase of foreign currency on their behalf.[30]

At the time, securing foreign currency was a chronically critical issue for both the Nationalists and the Communists. In fact, in January 1948, the cost of foreign currency even caused a temporary suspension of the Nationalist government's study-abroad examination.[31] Those without international passports were deprived of the right to make US-dollar savings withdrawals from the People's Bank of China, and in early 1949, after a series of military losses by the Nationalist government and the relocation of its bank to Guangzhou, US-dollar savings could only be withdrawn in Guangzhou City.[32]

In March 1949, when the Communists occupied Beiping (Beijing), they seized the Nationalist government's foreign currency reserves left behind in the national treasury. Qian Sanqiang, director of the Institute of Atomic Energy, asked Li Weihan, head of the Department of United Front of the Chinese Communist Party, for permission to use part of this foreign currency—about US$50,000—for a deal he would make with Frederic Joliot-Curie on buying from him in April some material on nuclear research at a World Peace Council conference in Paris; foreign currency was also a means of acquiring new weapons and technologies.

Chinese scientists studying abroad would often keep track of one another's whereabouts, share meals and free time with one another, and, in regions where rents were high, split the cost by living together. In addition, those who

THE EMERGENCE OF CHINA'S NUCLEAR RESEARCH   149

returned from studying abroad would participate in regular gatherings of the Western Returned Scholars Association (an alumni association for those who had studied in the West), including general meetings that would last for several days. However, on the other hand, there also were cases in which Chinese scientists would not return, so in around 1948, the Communists began organizing efforts to encourage their repatriation.

According to Qian Baogong's recollection of the efforts he put into establishing an association for Chinese students pursuing natural science studies in the US, he—inspired by the establishment of two Chinese Scientific Workers Associations, the first of which was established in the UK in 1948, the second in China—said the first thing he did was seek Xue Baoding's advice, on the basis of which he chose New York as the location for a science students' association named the Association of Chinese Scientific Workers in the US. In the winter of 1948, after returning to the US, Xue informed his Chinese counterparts in every state he passed through of Qian and his plan to establish the association in New York. Subsequently, Qian contacted Tang Aoqing, chair of the Columbia University Chinese Students and Scholars Association, and the Association of Chinese Scientific Workers in the US came into existence. In the winter of 1948, the association held its first preparatory meeting at Columbia University. The meeting welcomed twenty to thirty participants, to whom Qian explained the association's significant purpose of unifying the large number of Chinese scientists studying abroad in the US under the single aim of returning to their country to apply the cutting-edge scientific expertise they would acquire. Members at the meeting decided to have Tang Aoqing (physics and chemistry), Sun Benwang (mathematics), Yang Keqin (medicine), and Qian Baogong (science) form a small preparatory group and have Qian serve as secretary in charge of coordinating communication between members both inside and outside New York City; the association thus had, as key members, two of those who had been part of the research delegation sent by the Nationalist Ministry of War—Tang and Sun.

Another version of the story is relayed in Wang Jianzhu's recollection, which suggests greater interference by the Communists in the establishment of the association.[33] According to Wang, shortly before the Communists' victory in the Civil War, they sent an underground party member, Hou Xianglin, to the US to attend MIT as a graduate student pursuing a doctoral degree. In the winter of 1948, Hou transferred from Boston to Chicago, immediately after which he received an order from the Communist Party to establish an organization to unify natural science students through patriotic education and to make necessary preparations to ensure that such students would return to mainland

China. Hou contacted other underground party members and founded, in Chicago, the Association of Chinese Scientific Workers in the US in January 1949. Within a year of its foundation, the association had set up thirty-two branches with more than seven hundred members across the US and regularly held meetings to keep members up-to-date on circumstances in China.

At the end of 1949, a message titled "An Open Letter to Classmates Studying Abroad in the US" was published in the association's bulletin and signed by fifty-two members in proclamation of their determination to repatriate. First to sign the open letter was the then twenty-three-year-old Zhu Guangya. As a former member for the Nationalist Ministry of War's delegation, Zhu's signature on the open letter attracted great attention. In November and December 1949, under the name of the association, Zhu and Cao Xihua held multiple roundtable discussions for Chinese international students in Ann Arbor, home to the University of Michigan, where they espoused the significance of returning to China to help meet the demands of their home country.

THE PRC'S LIMITED HUMAN RESOURCES
IN ITS EARLIER YEARS

Uranium Mining by the Soviet Union and Human Resources in China

In addition to keeping track of Chinese scientists abroad, both the Nationalists and Communists closely observed Japanese scientists in mainland China, as did the Soviet army. Sent by the Japanese government in 1943, Tadayoshi Hikosaka, a physicist known for his research into the structure of nuclei, was working at the Lushun University of Technology, where according to one of his students, "On August 15, 1945, the Soviet army contacted Dr. Hikosaka with an easy-money deal. The Soviet Union seemed to believe that Dr. Hikosaka's mission as assigned by the Japanese government was to construct an atomic reactor and bomb with the uranium lying beneath the ground of Korea and Manchuria."[34]

The Nationalist government, displeased by the Soviet Union's invasion and conducting of uranium mining operations in its territory after the Japanese army's retreat from the area, compounded with the already frustrating circumstances of a civil war whose future was uncertain, officially announced that it was under threat by the Soviet army, and this fact—uranium mining being conducted by the Soviet Union in the Ashan district of Xinjiang—also appears in a US State Department report dated April 19, 1949. In the report, the State Department declared that the Chinese government had already been rendered powerless and recommended that the US treat the Chinese government's request for help with caution and with consideration of the unfolding of events.[35]

The uranium mining by the Soviet Union remained an issue even after the foundation of the PRC. Premier Zhou Enlai, in telegrams sent to Wang Zhen, secretary of the Xinjiang branch of the Central Committee of the Chinese Communist Party, and Peng Dehuai, chair of the Northwest China Military and Administrative Commission in August 1950, stated that he had inquired of Luo Shen (Chinese transliteration of Nikolai V. Roshchin), the Soviet Union's ambassador to China, whether the mining organization in the Ashan district (now Altay Prefecture) of Fuhai County had been established as part of the Sino-Soviet Metals Company.[36]

The Nationalist government relied on Japanese scientists. This can be seen in the movement of Sixth Office of the Nationalist government's Ministry of National Defense, which prevented Tōru Tomita—the geologist who made the first discovery of uranium ore in China—from returning to Japan and forced him to adopt a Chinese-sounding name, Fu Zhida, and to continue pursuing research in China. In addition, to attract to its nuclear research project more Japanese scientists, including those who returned after the war as well as others who had never been to the country before then, the Nationalist government was prepared to offer salaries equivalent to those of its own scientists and looked into researchers at the Institute of Physical and Chemical Research and the Research Institute for Iron, Steel and Other Metals, Tohoku University (both located in Japan), paying particular attention to their fields of expertise.[37]

The Chinese government continued to largely rely on Japanese scientists even after the foundation of the PRC. For instance, as late as 1950, eight of the fourteen scientists who were working at the Dalian Institute of Chemistry and Physics were Japanese.[38] In fact, in 1946, Hikosaka, mentioned above, was contacted and asked for help by the Chinese Economic Construction Society, a Nationalist organization. Also, Soviet authorities "kept an eye on him as a specialist of atomic nuclei" while he taught Chinese students as a professor at Dalian University (which had then just been founded), from 1947 to October 1949.[39] In its earlier days, the PRC lacked sufficient Chinese scientists for its projects and thus needed to continue relying on Japanese scientists.

Scientists Who Never Returned

Between 1946 and 1948, during the Civil War, many students and researchers were sent to study abroad. As of August 30, 1950, there were 5,541 Chinese students studying abroad, of whom 3,500 were in the US, 1,200 in Japan, and 443 in the UK. Efforts to repatriate these students and researchers to the PRC

152 SCIENTIFIC KNOWLEDGE

succeeded in getting about 2,000 to return between 1950 and 1953.[40] In other words, despite the call, more than half did not return to mainland China.

One such researcher was Wu Chien-Shiung, a physicist whom both the Nationalists and Communists hoped would return to join their respective parties. Wu was known for her participation in the Manhattan Project, and Wu Dayou was ordered by the Nationalists to ensure that she, along with other scientists, would return to join their party. In fact, the Nationalist Government's Office of Secretariat had stated in a report published in October 1947 that China had the necessary personnel to develop an atomic bomb, albeit on the supposition that a number of specific scientists, including Wu Chien-Shiung, would be returning.[41] The Communists had also based their selection of members for the Chinese Academy of Sciences' 1950 research project on the premise that she would be returning soon. However, Wu refused to return on the grounds that her husband's profession (he was also a scholar) required them to remain in the US.[42]

More scientists besides Wu refused to repatriate for family reasons. According to Chen Shiyi, who returned from Paris in 1950, Cai Bolin (a son of Cai Yuanpei) and Qin Guoxian, both of whom were affiliated with Frederic Joliot-Curie's laboratory, were unable to leave France for family reasons.[43] Their inability to return was not due to external causes, such as being detained by the government; instead, they remained of their own volition, deciding to prioritize their own lives as scientists.

Refusal to Relocate and Fear of the Communists

With the Nationalist military losing all three major military campaigns, beginning with the first in the autumn of 1948, and with its head count shrinking, the scientists' movement to refuse relocation to Taiwan intensified.

On January 13, 1949, eleven scientists affiliated with Academia Sinica's Institute of Geology, including Xu Jie, Zhao Jinke, Si Xingjian, and Sun Dianqing, gathered at the home of Zhang Wenyu and took the following oath to refuse to relocate their laboratory: "In light of the respect for academic research to be independent and free from political rule and of the likelihood that should we relocate to where only harsher living conditions await, we unanimously agree to stay in either Nanjing or Shanghai, and should anyone violate this oath, he/she shall be expelled from the geological academe in perpetuity." Li Siguang, director of Academia Sinica, who was still in the UK at the time, was informed of the oath by mail.[44]

In March 1949, the Communist army conquered Beiping, and in April, Nanjing. In May, the Shanghai Municipal Police pointed out to Academia Sinica, located at the time in Shanghai, that, despite having been ordered for quite some time by the ROC government to relocate to Taiwan through Guangzhou, it still had not complied.[45]

Because the Nationalist government had been weakened by the time it made a similar relocation request, the scientists were able to refuse to comply. However, they did not have any idea of how the Communists assuming power viewed them or what scientific policies they would introduce. While the Communists continued to expand their occupation of China, Academia Sinica sounded out the Communists' policies on science. In early June 1949, Academia Sinica in Shanghai decided to send representatives to Beijing to contact the Central Committee of the Chinese Communist Party to learn about the Communists' scientific research policy.[46] A few days later, Academia Sinica was requisitioned by the Military Control Commission. The commission had introduced a number of new policies, one of which was to eradicate reactionary organizations, but had not yet established any details on how it would treat scientists, a fact that caused those under this requisition great distress.

One of the Communists' missions was to confiscate all materials left behind by the Nationalist government, including those related to nuclear research. Zhou Enlai is known to have often led missions of this type. For instance, Zhou instructed Ye Jianying, secretary of the South China branch of the Central Committee of the Chinese Communist Party, to loot all materials that the Nationalists had gathered in Guangzhou for transportation to Taiwan. Zhou specifically said that, among the materials, the library resources that the Nationalist Ministry of National Defense had gathered for general reference purposes must be recovered and preserved if they still remained in Guangzhou.[47] In addition, Zhou ordered the recovery of documents, maps, graphs, account books, and archives stored at diplomatic establishments abroad, stating that rewards would be given to those who greatly contributed to this effort and that if former diplomatic mission staff wished to continue their careers, the State Council would employ them.[48]

SCIENTISTS UNDER THE COMMUNIST PARTY

The Defeated Nationalist Government and Prevailing Communists

In early September 1949, the Western Returned Scholars Association (Western Society) held a reunion over several days, during which the Standing Committee of the Preparatory Committee for the National Assembly of Natural Scientists held a meeting with Zeng Zhaolun as chairman.[49] The Association of Chinese Scientific Workers in the US, the organization that had encouraged Chinese students studying abroad to return to mainland China, was represented by Zhu Guangya, Ma Shijun, Tang Aoqing, and Xu Xianxiu. Wu Dayou had moved to Canada, T. D. Lee remained at the University of Chicago along with Chen Ning Yang (also known as Yang Zhenning), and Zeng Zhaolun had returned to mainland China. In 1950, serving as promoter, Hua Luogeng released a statement urging US-based international Chinese students to repatriate.[50] None relocated to Taiwan in the early 1950s with the Nationalist government, with the exception of Wu Dayou, who was a member of the delegation of young scientists sent abroad by the Ministry of War (or the Ministry of National Defense when sent to the US) and who returned to the ROC in Taiwan in the 1960s.

Among the scientists who were the first to go to Taiwan or move to other countries, some found reasons to return to mainland China. Weng Wenhao—geologist, former uranium mining negotiator in charge of negotiations with the US and Switzerland, and premier of the ROC, who had been taking shelter in Paris—requested permission to return to mainland China after the PRC had been founded. Weng's request was granted under the conditions, laid down by Zhou Enlai, that he cross the border through Guangzhou via Hong Kong when entering the mainland and that he also, after arriving in mainland China, make a declaration of abandonment of his previous political status. Zhou was extremely cautious in accepting Weng, as reflected by these conditions, which he organized into a letter that he addressed to Li Kenong, then head of the Central Military Commission Intelligence Department.[51]

In October 1948, Chen Xingshen (S. S. Chern) received an invitation to the US from J. Robert Oppenheimer, who worked at the Institute for Advanced Study, located in Princeton, New Jersey. Around the same time, Jiang Lifu, then director of the Institute of Mathematics of Academia Sinica, who was Chen's supervisor as well as his former mathematics teacher at the National Southwestern Associated University, received a telegram from the Chinese government, ordering him to immediately report to Nanjing and prepare to move to Taiwan. Jiang packed his books at the Institute of Mathematics, sent them to Taiwan, and subsequently arrived in Taipei himself in February 1949. However, in September, Jiang reconsidered his mission and, coming to the belief that his work was on the mainland, under the pretense of illness returned to Guangzhou, where he would spend the rest of his life. As for Chen, he took a Pan American Airways flight from Shanghai on New Year's Eve, 1948, landing in San Francisco on New Year's Day, 1949, to head for Princeton.

In June 1950, after helping Li Siguang safely return in May, Zhou Enlai ordered Wu Wendao, president of Xinhua News Agency's Prague branch, to similarly aid another scientist, Huang Zhangfeng, a physicist in his third year studying abroad in France, during which time he had written a doctoral dissertation on nuclear power, and the nephew of Huang Yanpei, then vice-premier of the State Council. At the time, Huang Zhangfeng was on his way to eastern Europe to return home via the Soviet Union. Zhou's order to Wu was to help Huang follow the necessary procedures when he reached eastern Europe.[52]

In June 1950 when the Korean War broke out, Li Siguang, reminded of the scale of destruction the US could bring if it declared nuclear war, emphasized China's need to devote greater effort to nuclear research and development. In a paper he contributed to *Kexue Tongbao* (Chinese science bulletin) titled "Voices of Resonance and Dissonance with Nuclear War," Li strongly denounced the US, arguing, "The *American Empire* is trying to use its atomic bombs to threaten the citizens of China and North Korea. However, it has chosen the wrong countries and dealt with them in the wrong way."[53] At the time, the Chinese People's Volunteer Army had not yet been mobilized. However, Li's statement reflects the growing fear that Chinese scientists felt about the possibility of atomic bombs also being dropped on China. After the publication of this editorial, Li paid multiple visits to Qian Sanqiang, who was now director of the Institute of Modern Physics, to observe the institute's research progress and also help Qian effectively allocate newly returned scientists.[54]

Zhu Kezhen and the PRC's Nuclear Development

In September 1951, a telegram from the US Embassy in Delhi to Bruce Hamilton of the US Department of State introduced an article titled "Nuclear Power Research in China," which had appeared a few days earlier in *Eastern Economist*, an Indian newspaper. The article stated, "While not much is known about the level of importance the Chinese Communists place on nuclear power research, it has at least been pursued in China since the days of the Nationalist government's rule." It then went on to say, "A regional specialties exhibition recently held in Hankou highlighted uranium ore," before emphasizing that the Russian News Agency TASS had reported some time earlier, "Two professors at the Russian Academy of Sciences, Abram Ioffe and Dmitri Skobeltzyn, along with a French professor, Joliot-Curie, a former high-commissioner of the French Alternative Energies and Atomic Energy Commission, were welcomed by the Chinese Physical Society as honorary members."[55]

In March 1952, Military Secretary Lei Yingfu and staff officer Wei Ming, under orders from Premier Zhou Enlai, visited Zhu Kezhen to inquire as to when they could expect to see the creation of the atomic bomb, which they referred to cryptically as *sunburst*. In response, Zhu pointed out that creating an atomic bomb required more funds and human resources. Three days later, he borrowed an English-language book titled *The Effects of Atomic Weapons,* presumably authored by Los Alamos scientists, from Chao Chung-Yao.[56]

Although Zhu was the vice president of the Chinese Academy of Sciences, he was foremost a meteorologist. Why would he be turned to for matters related to creating an atomic bomb? Along with Li Siguang, Zhu was known to have a strong interest in atomic bombs. Zhu kept a diary, in which he often wrote about his discussions with nuclear physicists, including Wang Ganchang—who had been his colleague ever since he had served as president at Zhejiang University—and Qian Sanqiang and Peng Huanwu, who were affiliated with the Institute of Modern Physics, Chinese Academy of Sciences. Wang gave Zhejiang University students a lecture on nuclear power in late August 1945, and from September 1947, during the Civil War, with funds he received from the United Service to China, he studied abroad at the University of California, before subsequently returning in January 1949.

At Zhejiang University, Zhu had taken up what would become his lifelong hobby of extensively reading and keeping notes on atomic bombs. For instance, in February 1948, while reading H. H. Arnold's "Air Force in the Atomic Age," published in *One World or None*, Zhu took notes on J. Robert Oppenheimer's estimates.[57] In addition, in November 1950, after reading the August issue of the British journal *Atomic Scientist*, Zhu requested that the library purchase a US journal, the *Bulletin of the Atomic Scientists*, the eighth edition of *American Men of Science*, and the *New Advanced Atlas*, and in the evening of the same day, he invited a number of prominent physicists to dinner, including Wang Ganchang; Wu Youxun; Qian Sanqiang's wife, He Zehui;[58] and Peng Huanwu.[59] Around this time, Zhu seemed to have been interested in the Franck Report, as he made daily mention of it in his diary.[60]

Shedding Some Light on Qian Sanqiang

After returning from the Soviet Union at the end of 1952, Qian Sanqiang immediately revisited the USSR in February 1953, this time leading a delegation of experts to study its science and technology. Immediately after returning in July, he reported to Gao Gang, chair of the State Planning Commission of the PRC and concurrently a vice-chair of the Central People's Government Council. Gao maintained a strong military presence in the Northeastern Greater Administrative Area, but by this time he had left the region and moved to Beijing, where he had assumed the aforementioned positions. The

THE EMERGENCE OF CHINA'S NUCLEAR RESEARCH 157

State Planning Commission oversaw the formulation of China's five-year plans; therefore, Qian reported to Gao immediately upon return to have him incorporate nuclear research into the First Five-Year Plan, which was under development at the time. Qian explained to Gao the need to promote nuclear science and nuclear projects. In response, Gao said that although the nation's economy was facing great difficulty, and thus promoting nuclear projects immediately would be impossible, Qian's ideas would certainly be forwarded to their superiors.[61]

In August 1954, Peng Dehuai, minister of national defense, invited Qian to his residence to explain the structure and mechanism of atomic bombs.[62] Peng was invited to visit the Soviet Union's atomic bomb test the following month.

Also in 1954, in Haicheng, Liaoning Province, after Tōru Tomita and his colleagues' discovery, and in Guangxi Province, after that of Nan Yanzong, a geological survey team under the command of Li Siguang discovered uranium ore. The ore extracted from Haicheng was of low quality. However, a sample discovered in Guangxi Province was placed in a case, given the title "the Starting Ore," and presented at the expanded meeting of the Central Secretariat of the Chinese Communist Party in January 1955 to show the radioactivity of the ores in Guangxi Province. In front of the leaders of the Chinese Communist Party, including Mao Zedong, Qian Sanqiang used a Geiger counter to demonstrate the radioactivity of the Starting Ore.

After demonstrating the sample ore's radioactivity at the expanded secretariat meeting, Qian again visited the Soviet Union in April and stayed for almost a year. This visit was arranged secretly, and at one point it attracted the interest of Japan's Cabinet Research Office. For a month between May and June 1957, a delegation of Japanese physicists was invited to the PRC by the Chinese Academy of Sciences. Subsequently, after returning, the physicists were summoned by the Cabinet Research Office and peppered with questions primarily concerning the status of China's nuclear research. The office's questionnaire, handed to Mokichirō Nogami, one of the physicists, comprised many questions of the following sort: Did there seem to be any influence by other nations (primarily the Soviet Union) on the research institutes you visited? How would you describe the present state of China's mineral mining operations relating to its nuclear project and the outlook for such operations? Did Chinese scientists seem to be cooperating with the People's Liberation Army, and if so, in what ways? Nogami responded that the delegation knew nothing more than what was reported in the newspapers. Hearing this, the office followed up with more questions, specifically asking whether they saw any building near the Temple of Heaven, or *Tiantan*, in Beijing that could have been a nuclear center and whether they had heard anything about Qian Sanqiang's whereabouts during 1955, the year in which he had disappeared.[63]

The Cultural Revolution and Closer US-PRC Relations

The PRC celebrated its first successful nuclear test in October 1964, upon which the Chinese scientists who had returned from the West and played a significant role in their country's nuclear development project were summarily dismissed from their positions—the successful test had lowered their value. In addition, during the Cultural Revolution, which broke out in May 1966, scientists in all organizations came into conflict with one another. In spite of their great contribution to the state nuclear project, the repatriated nevertheless came to be viewed as suspect precisely because of their Western educational and occupational backgrounds.

The Cultural Revolution also gave rise to the theft of nuclear information. This took the form of the direct theft of confidential documents and the wiretapping of long-distance calls between nuclear development bases located in rural areas and in Beijing. The thefts were undertaken by paramilitary groups of students, called the Red Guards, usually led behind the scenes by political leaders, while countermeasures to prevent wiretapping and the stealing of confidential information were overseen by the then premier Zhou Enlai.[64]

The US-PRC rapprochement in the early 1970s saved the returnee scientists from their predicament. People's attitudes toward those with a Western education suddenly changed, and while this did reflect one aspect of the contemporary PRC, in that value was entirely politically determined, it also highlighted the extremely small segment of the country's population that had or valued an international academic background. Therefore, although the Communists expended much effort in the competition with the Nationalists over recruitment of scientists who had left China during or before the Civil War, thereafter there was no new supply of personnel with Western academic backgrounds—this was the result of the PRC's severing of nearly all relations with the West during the Cold War. Thus the older scientists with Western educational backgrounds who had previously helped develop the atomic bomb came to be highly regarded again.

Physicist Chen Ning Yang had moved to the US in 1946 and obtained US citizenship while pursuing research at the University of Chicago. Another physicist, T. D. Lee, despite being urged to return, had also chosen to stay in the US; together, the two conducted research for which they were awarded the Nobel Prize in Physics in 1957. In July 1971, President Richard Nixon shocked the world by revealing that Henry Kissinger, his national security adviser, had secretly visited the PRC and that he planned to visit again in February of the following year. The PRC government completely reversed its attitude and began welcoming US-based Chinese scientists; notably, the government immediately approved Yang's request to visit the PRC, welcoming his temporary return to the country at the end of July 1971. The government's sudden shift to enthusiastically welcome their expatriate counterparts dissatisfied the previously repatriated Chinese scientists, who, after having returned on the request of the Communists and contributed to their nuclear development project, nevertheless had to suffer hardships imposed by the Cultural Revolution.

For instance, Wu Youxun received a visit by Ke Ting-Sui, who came to tell him about Yang's return being featured in the newspapers and expressed dissatisfaction at Zhou Enlai's open-armed welcome. Ke was dissatisfied all the more because whereas Yang, who had betrayed China and adopted US citizenship, was being welcomed warmly, he himself had been detained for several months along with an acquaintance who was arrested for having connections to the Yin Ju-keng administration (the pro-Japanese local government during the Sino-Japanese War) and the Central Club Clique (a powerful faction within the Nationalists that held sway over the party management and intelligence activities). Ke also lamented that it was unfair that Chao Chung-Yao, despite having returned because of his love for China, continued to be detained and stated that the country's old intellectuals must also be unhappy with this situation.[65]

However, there was at least one scientist, Deng Jiaxian, whose situation changed for the better because of his acquaintance with Yang. According to a thank-you letter to Yang penned by Deng's wife, Deng was being held back from work despite having contributed to the nuclear development project. Yang subsequently inquired as to how his longtime friend was doing at work, which led to Deng's workplace allowing him to return.

There was also a situation where the US delegation was dominated by Chinese physicists who had graduated from Tsing Hua University, and Niu Manjiang, a biologist from Peking University, could not take part. Niu did subsequently find another opportunity, although he had to do so with little help from the Chinese Academy of Sciences. Yet another episode shows the impact of the US delegation on Chinese scientists living in China. Huang Jiqing, a geologist who became seriously ill during the Cultural Revolution and was not provided with proper treatment, had little hope for the same governmental attention as Deng Jiaxian had received, his friends suspected, because there was no geologist in the US delegation who might have inquired into Huang's state of affairs.[66]

CONCLUSION

China's nuclear research began under the Nationalist government, and, despite being conducted without sufficient funds or electricity, the program's existence was internationally recognized even at an early stage. China's method of cultivating researchers was dependent on other countries, and under the Nationalist government, the rare few Chinese scientists with international experience served in key positions in the government and helped facilitate its negotiations by requesting help from their former academic advisers and by applying their study-abroad experience in the West in other ways. Sending off scientists to study abroad was an effective way to cultivate professional personnel and also a means for the Communists to secure foreign currency under the Nationalist government's rule.

Nearly half of the international students sent abroad during the Civil War, when subsequently faced with the life-changing decision of whether to return to help the reconstruction of their war-torn homeland—personally risking the possibility of their family members losing their jobs and themselves never being able to resume their own research—chose to either return to or remain in mainland China and refused to relocate to Taiwan.

When the Nationalists were hurriedly relocating to Taiwan, conflict over the ownership of nuclear research documents and human resources arose between the Nationalists and the Communists. Noteworthy also is the tale of geologist Li Siguang; when the Nationalists asked Li to return, they offered him special privileges and rewards. Li refused the lure of the money and other benefits and agreed to return only after the Communists took power. The Nationalists and the Communists both exerted great effort to secure the scientists essential to their country's nuclear research; for example, efforts led by Zhou Enlai were aimed at ensuring the safe return of Li, a uranium mining operations member who had also published papers on nuclear power, and Huang Zhangfeng, a physicist who was pursuing nuclear research at Joliot-Curie's laboratory in France.

However, such political expectations, and the recruitment conditions initially promised, shifted frequently under the influence of domestic scientific communities and connections. They eventually lost all meaning once China's nuclear development succeeded and the subsequent Cultural Revolution broke out, upending the situations of many scientists and often negatively affecting their status. Scientists became renewed targets of political attention after the US-China rapprochement. Although China still had a number of years to go before its economic reforms would begin, immediately after the establishment

THE EMERGENCE OF CHINA'S NUCLEAR RESEARCH   161

of closer US-China relations, the US and China resumed interactions in the scientific community, with the returnee scientists from the US playing a leading role in this process. Although the preferential treatment of physicists and graduates of Tsing Hua University persisted, Chinese scientists were welcomed back to the international scientist network that they had been part of before the start of the Cold War.

NOTES

1. Bieler, *"Patriots" or "Traitors"?*

2. Iris Chang wrote an English biography, *Thread of the Silkworm*, of Qian Xuesen, who later returned to China in 1955. For examples of biographies and memoirs in Chinese, see Gu and Zhu, *Women de fuqin Zhu Guangya*; Wang C., *Liebian zhi guang*; Wu, *Huiyi*.

3. Hiramatsu, *Chūgoku no Kakusenryoku*, 128.

4. American Consulate General Kunming, Yunnan, China, to Walter S. Robertson, Esquire, Chargé d'Affaires ad interim, American Embassy, Chungking, March 11, 1946, no. 26 Secret, Subject: Plans of Chinese Government to Acquire Information on Development of Atomic Energy, attached to office memorandum, US Govt. to U, Mr. Gullion, from FC, Jack D. Neel, October 1, 1947, General Records of the Department of State, Office of the Secretary, Special Asst. to Sec. of State for Atomic Energy and Outer Space General Records relating to Atomic Energy Matters, 1948–1962, box 46, folder 21, "China, Nationalist," RG 59, National Archives II, College Park.

5. Wu, *Huiyi*. In addition, some argue that Hua Luogeng also chose Xu Xianxiu (also known as Shien-siu Shu), who had already been in the US. After graduating from Tsing Hua University, Xu had been studying applied mathematics at Brown University as late as March 1947. See the diary of Zhu Kezhen, who had been in Europe and the US for half a year and met with Xu in the US. *Zhu Kezhen Quanji*, 10:399–400.

6. *Mei Yiqi riji*, 197.

7. *Mei Yiqi riji*, 227.

8. *Mei Yiqi riji*, 227.

9. Sato, "Developing Uranium Deposits."

10. American Consulate General Kunming, Yunnan, China, to Walter S. Robertson. Ren made an inspection tour of the US at the request of China Foundation for the Promotion of Education and Culture from July 1947 to February 1948. Zhao, "Ren Hongjun nianpu," 41.

11. *Zhou Peiyuan wenji*, 514–15.

12. "Xingzhengyuanzhang Song Ziwen (T. V. Soong) han guoming zhengfu wenguanchu wei pai Kang Liwu wei lianheguo jiaoyu kaxue wenhua zuzhi

di'erjie dahui Zhongguo daibiaotuan zongdaibiao Zhao Yuanren Yan Yangchu Li Shuhua Wu Youxun Chen Yuanwei daibiao qing chuan Chen lingpai," September 1, 1947, Guoming Zhengfu, Guoji gexing huiyi daibiao renmian (4), Historia Sinica, 001-032137-00028-038.

13. Nakazawa, *Oppenheimer*.

14. Folder 2948, box 121, Vannevar Bush Papers, Library of Congress.

15. July 31, 1950; October 16, 1951; Y. H. Ku to Bush, February 18, 1952; T. L. Cole, General Electric Company, to Bush, June 21, 1955. All are in folder 150, box 63, Vannevar Bush Papers, Library of Congress.

16. Middleton, *Physics at the National Research Council of Canada*, 185–86.

17. *Zhou Peiyuan Wenji*, 480.

18. On the patron-client relations between Zhou Enlai and Zhou Peiyuan, see Sato, "Criticizing Einstein."

19. Ma, Ma, and Ma, *Li Siguang nianpu xubian*, 327.

20. Xu Shubin and Li Lin, *Shijigengqianqiu: Huiyi Li Siguang*, 3–26.

21. Nan Yanzong and Wu Leibo. "The Discovery of Uranium Ore in FuHeZhong District in Guangxi." Dizhi Lunping, 1 (1944): 85-92.

22. The above-mentioned book, a memoir by Li's wife Xu Shubin and daughter Li Lin, did not address the discovery of uranium. For the precise story of Nan's discovery of uranium, see Sato, "Criticizing Einstein."

23. Ma, Ma, and Ma, *Li Siguang nianpu xubian*, 247; Chen et al., *Li Siguang chuan*, 167.

24. Ma, Ma, and Ma, *Li Siguang nianpu xubian*, 248.

25. Ma, Ma, and Ma, 269–84.

26. *Zhu Kezhen Quanji*, 11:453–54, entry for June 5, 1949. The National Academy of Beiping was at 395 Route Ferguson, Shanghai.

27. Ma, Ma, and Ma, *Li Siguang nianpu xubian*, 290.

28. Zhonggong Zhongyang wenxian yanjiushi, *Jianguo Yilai Zhou Enlai Wengao*, 1:533.

29. Chen et al., *Li Siguang chuan*, 193–94.

30. "Luo Peilin," 96–101.

31. Wang and Liu, "1950 niandai guiguo liumei kexuejia," 70.

32. *Zhu Kezhen Quanji*, 11:433, 443.

33. Wang J., "'Kelifulan zongtonghao,'" 38–41.

34. Editorial Committee, *Mokuren no hana*, 137.

35. "Uranium in Sinkiang," 500 Natural Resources (mines and minerals), DOS Memorandum of Conversation, April 19, 1949, folder "Top Secret (1949)," box 15, lot 56, D 151, 1949, Top Secret Subject file, 1945–50, RG 59, National Archives at College Park.

36. Zhonggong Zhongyang wenxian yanjiushi, *Jianguo Yilai Zhou Enlai wengao*, 3:201.

THE EMERGENCE OF CHINA'S NUCLEAR RESEARCH 163

37. Sato, "Developing Uranium Deposits."

38. *Zhu Kezhen Quanji*, 18:39–40, entry for February 16, 1966. The entry was written when Zhu reread his own diaries of 1949, 1950, and 1964 ahead of the business trip to Dalian.

39. Editorial Committee, *Mokuren no hana*, 158–59.

40. Duan, *Zhongguo Jinxiandai Keji Sichao*, 52.

41. On the instruction to Wu and the secretariat's report, see Sato, "Developing Uranium Deposits."

42. As Qian's chronology suggests, Wu Jianxiong and Zhang Wenyu had been supposed to return to China. Wu chose to stay in the US, and Zhang did not return until 1956, as a result of negotiations at the Geneva Conference. Ge, *Qian Sanqiang nianpu changbian*, 146.

43. *Zhu Kezhen Quanji*, 12:230, entry for November 29, 1950. According to physicist Zou Guoxing, who would return from France in May 1966, they expected that Cai Bolin would not be able to return to China because he had been engaging in highly classified research on atomic bombs and because he had become a French citizen to match his French wife. See *Zhu Kezhen Quanji*, 18:107, entry for May 8, 1966.

44. Ma, Ma, and Ma, *Li Siguang nianpu xubian*, 285.

45. *Zhu Kezhen Quanji*, 11: 437, entry for May 9, 1949.

46. *Zhu Kezhen Quanji*, 11:453, entry for June 4, 1949.

47. Zhonggong Zhongyang wenxian yanjiushi, *Jianguo Yilai Zhou Enlai wengao*, 1:563.

48. Zhonggong Zhongyang wenxian yanjiushi, 2:23–24.

49. *Zhu Kezhen Quanji*, 11:517, entry for September 3, 1949.

50. However, after Hua returned to Tsing Hua University, he was treated coldly because of factional rivalry among the powerful Zhou Peiyuan and other professors, and thus he was not able to secure a promotion to director of the Department of Mathematics at the university. An oral history of Xu L., "Wo suo zhidao de Hua Luogeng yu Chen Xingshen," 23–24.

51. Zhonggong Zhongyang wenxian yanjiushi, *Jianguo Yilai Zhou Enlai wengao*, 2:340.

52. Zhonggong Zhongyang wenxian yanjiushi, 2:464.

53. Li, "Voices of Resonance and Dissonance with Nuclear War."

54. Ma, Ma, and Ma, *Li Siguang nianpu xubian*, 326.

55. Andrew V. Corry, New Delhi, India, to J. Bruce Hamilton, September 16, 1951, folder 21, box 46, RG 59, Atomic Energy and Disarmament Lot Files, Office of the Secretary Office of the Special Assistant to the Secretary of State for Atomic Energy and Outer Space: General Records Relating to Atomic Energy Matters, 1948–1962, National Archives at College Park.

56. *Zhu Kezhen Quanji*, 12:764.

164   SCIENTIFIC KNOWLEDGE

57. *Zhu Kezhen Quanji*, 11:31.

58. He Zehui had conducted research on uranium nuclear fission with Qian Sanqiang at Joliot-Curie's laboratory, and she later returned to China with Qian as her husband. She established a sufficiently high reputation for her research that her name was included in the Secretariat of the National Government report as one of the reliable talents for building an atomic bomb. See Sato, "Developing Uranium Deposits."

59. *Zhu Kezhen Quanji*, 12:226.

60. *Zhu Kezhen Quanji*, 12:229.

61. Ge, *Qian Sanqiang nianpu changbian*, 216.

62. Ge, 246; Y. Wang, *Peng Dehuai nianpu*, 575.

63. Nogami, "Naikaku chosa shitsu jiken no keika houkoku," 32–37.

64. Zhonggong Zhongyang wenxian yanjiushi ed., *Zhou Enlai nianpu*, 2:57, 75.

65. *Zhu Kezhen Quanji*, 20:457–58, entry for August 21, 1971.

66. *Zhu Kezhen Quanji*, 21:154, entry for July 22, 1972.

REFERENCES

Primary Sources

"Guomin Zhengfu," Digitized materials at Academia Historica, Taipei, Taiwan.

RG 59, Atomic Energy and Disarmament Lot Files, National Archives at College Park.

RG 59, Top Secret Subject File, 1945–50, National Archives at College Park.

Vannevar Bush Papers, Library of Congress, Washington, DC.

Secondary Sources

Bieler, Stacey. *"Patriots" or "Traitors"? A History of American-Educated Chinese students.* Armonk, NY: M. E. Sharpe, 2004.

Chang, Iris. *Thread of the Silkworm.* New York: Basic Books, 1995.

Chen, Qun, Duan Wanti, Zhang Xianglong, Zhou Guojun, and Huang Xiaokui, eds. *Li Siguang chuan.* Beijing: Renmin chubanshe, 2009.

Duan, Zhiwen. *Zhongguo Jinxiandai Keji Sichao de xingqi yu bianqian.* Zhejiang: Zhejiang daxue chubanshe, 2012.

Editorial Committee for Hikosaka Tadayoshi tsuitōbunshū, ed. *Mokuren no hana: Hikosaka Tadayoshi tsuitō bunshū.* Tagajo: The Editorial Committee for Hikosaka Tadayoshi tsuitōbunshū, 1991.

Ge, Nengquan, ed. *Qian Sanqiang nianpu changbian.* Beijing: Kexue chubanshe, 2013.

Gu, Xiaoying, and Mingyuan Zhu. *Women de fuqin Zhu Guangya.* Beijing: Renmin chubanshe, 2009.

Hiramatsu, Shigeo. *Chūgoku no Kakusenryoku* [China's nuclear power]. Tokyo: Keiso Shobo, 1996.

Li Siguang. "Voices of Resonance and Dissonance with Nuclear War." *Kexue tongbao* [Chinese science bulletin] 1, no. 8 (December 1950): 515–18.

Luo Peilin. "Luo Peilin: Dang pai wo qu liuxue, Wo yao duideqi dang." Edited by Delu Wang. *Zhonggong Danshi Yanjiu*, no. 1 (2011): 96–101.

Ma, Shengyun, Yue Ma, and Lan Ma, eds. *Li Siguang nianpu xubian*. Beijing: Dizhi chubanshe, 2011.

Mei Yiqi. *Mei Yiqi riji: 1941–1946*. Compiled by Huang Yanfu and Wang Xiaoning. Beijing: Tsing Hua daxue chubanshe, 2001.

Middleton, William Edgar Knowles. *Physics at the National Research Council of Canada: 1929–1952*. Waterloo, Ontario: Wilfrid Laurier University Press, 1979.

Nakazawa, Shiho. *Oppenheimer: Genbakuno chichi ha naze suibaku kaihatsu ni hantai shitaka*. Tokyo: Chuko Shinsho, 1995.

Nogami, Mokichirō. "Naikaku chosa shitsu jiken no keika houkoku (Hoka Nihon Butsurigaku daihyo dan'in no hōkoku sonota: sononi)" Supplement, *Soryushiron Kenkyu* 17 (1958): 32–37.

Sato, Yuko. "Criticizing Einstein during the Cultural Revolution." *Kokusai Seiji* [International relations] 179 (2015): 126–41.

———. "Developing Uranium Deposits in China: Nationalist China's Early Nuclear Development and the International Politics." *Kokusai Seiji* [International relations] 197 (September 2019): 26–41.

Wang Chunjiang. *Liebian zhi guang: Ji Qian Sanqiang*. Beijing: Zhongguo Qiannian chubanshe, 1990.

Wang, Delu, and Zhiguang Liu. "1950 niandai guiguo liumei kexuejia de guicheng ji mingyun." *Kexue Wenhua Pinglun* 9, no. 1 (2012): 68–87.

Wang Jianzhu. "'Kelifulan zongtonghao' Zhongguo liumei kexuejia de guiguo lichen." *Dangshi tiandi*, no. 3 (2007): 38–41.

Wang, Yan, ed. *Peng Dehuai nianpu*. Beijing: Renmin chubanshe, 1998.

Wu Dayou. *Huiyi* [A memoir]. Beijing: Zhongguo Youyi chuban gongsi, 1984.

Xu, Lizhi. "Wo suo zhidao de Hua Luogeng yu Chen Xingshen-Xu Lizhi xiansheng fangtanlu." *Shuwu*, no. 5 (2007): 16–24.

Xu, Shubin, and Lin Li. *Shijigengqianqiu: Huiyi Li Siguang*. Shanghai: Shanghai wenyi chubanshe, 1978.

Zhao, Huizhi. "Ren Hongjun nianpu (xu)." *Zhongguo Keji Shiliao* 10, no. 2 (1989): 39–55.

Zhonggong Zhongyang wenxian yanjiushi, ed. *Jianguo Yilai Zhou Enlai wengao*. Vols. 1–3. Beijing: Zhongyang wenxian chubanshe, 2008.

———, ed. *Zhou Enlai nianpu: 1949–1976*. Vol. 2. Beijing: Zhongyang wenxian chubanshe, 1997.

Zhou Peiyuan. *Zhou Peiyuan wenji*. Beijing: Beijing Daxue chubanshe. 2002.

Zhu Kezhen. *Zhu Kezhen Quanji*. Vols. 10–12, 18, 20, 21. Shanghai: Shanghai Keji Jiaoyu chubanshe, 2006–11.

AUTHOR BIO

YUKO SATO is a part-time lecturer at Faculty of Law, Komazawa University in Japan. Her research area is China's political and diplomatic history with a focus on interactions between science and politics.

SIX

THE MICHIGAN MEMORIAL PHOENIX PROJECT AND TAIWAN

Nuclear Technological Aid by a US Public University

YUKA TSUCHIYA MORIGUCHI

INTRODUCTION

In the previous chapter, Yuko Sato illuminated the tug-of-war between the Communist and Nationalist regimes over talented Chinese scientists who had Western educational backgrounds. This chapter also addresses the transnational migration of scientists and engineers, who inevitably take with them scientific knowledge. More concretely, this chapter focuses on how technological knowledge about nuclear energy nurtured in a US public university was used in the US government's overseas aid program and how implementing such knowledge in foreign lands (in this case, Taiwan) was a complicated business, as knowledge traversed national and political borders. It is generally understood that the US aid for Taiwan intensified with the Mutual Security Act of 1951 and ended in 1965; the nuclear technological aid discussed in this chapter also took place during that period. However, it was not a simple one-way transfer of knowledge from the US to Taiwan, because Chinese scientists and engineers who aligned with neither the People's Republic of China (PRC) nor the Republic of China (ROC) and had been trained in the US played important roles in the program.

The first half of this chapter sheds light on the process through which scientific knowledge nurtured in a US university was diverted to the state overseas aid program. From the late 1950s to mid-1960s, scientists affiliated with the University of Michigan visited twenty-two countries—most of which were developing countries—as "consultants" on nuclear science education and operational plans for research reactors. This program was based on a contract between the Michigan Memorial Phoenix Project (the Phoenix Project) and the

International Cooperation Administration (ICA), a US government agency later renamed the Agency for International Development (AID). The American scientists assisted developing countries where US research reactors were provided as part of President Dwight Eisenhower's Atoms for Peace program. By 1960 in Asia, Japan (1955), Taiwan (1955), the Philippines (1955), Korea (1956), Thailand (1958), South Vietnam (1959), and Indonesia (1960) had concluded bilateral agreements with the US that included the provision of research reactors, either US$350,000 in financial aid or half the price of the reactor, and technical assistance. The University of Michigan scientists aided these countries in installing and activating reactors, managing research institutes, and training engineers.

The Phoenix Project, established by the Regents of the University of Michigan in 1948 as a memorial to students and alumni who had died in World War II, originally had little to do with overseas aid programs; its purpose was to support faculty research on peaceful uses of nuclear energy. The project was financed by donations from alumni, local industries, and philanthropic organizations. In 1953, Ford Motor Company donated a research reactor to the university, and the US Atomic Energy Commission (AEC), a government agency overseeing both civilian and military uses of nuclear energy, provided reactor fuel. The Phoenix Project developed into a well-established on-campus science program, and by 1960, it was supporting 341 research projects led by the university's faculty.[1]

So, what brought about the "international turn" of the Phoenix Project? This chapter will explore how and why a public university's on-campus grant-in-aid program was converted to a government-contracted, overseas technological aid program. First and foremost, such a transformation reflected the process under which scientific knowledge became a weapon of the Cold War battle to win over the "hearts and minds" of the Third World elite. To strengthen technological and psychological ties with developing countries, the US government exported research reactors, even to countries lacking a solid foundation of science education; consequently, the US government needed to send American scientists and engineers to help install and operate the research reactors safely and efficiently in those countries. To recruit scientists and engineers for overseas dispatch, the US government set eyes on the Phoenix Project, which had established prior experience in research reactor operation. In 1956, the ICA approached leading professors of the Phoenix Project and organized a contract with the University of Michigan to send faculty members overseas as nuclear technological consultants.

Second, the transformation of the Phoenix Project corresponded to the environment in which postwar US science was situated. The Second World War,

THE MICHIGAN MEMORIAL PHOENIX PROJECT AND TAIWAN   169

the Korean War, and the Cold War had drawn science and state power into a significantly closer relationship, and greater numbers of university laboratories were engaged in large-scale, interdisciplinary research projects funded by government agencies. The University of Michigan–ICA contract was part of this general trend in US science and academia.

Third, the "international turn" of the Phoenix Project was an indirect outcome of strong demand from developing countries. To these countries, nuclear power appeared to be a dream technology that promised boundless energy and food supply and that would even open a path toward nuclear armament. They sent trainees to, and invited consultants from, not only the US but also the UK and the Soviet Union. However, the US attracted the largest number of Third World trainees, and the University of Michigan was one of their favored destinations. To understand more about this third point, the demand from developing countries, the latter half of this chapter explores the Phoenix Project's foreign aid program for the ROC as a case study and examines how various actors in the ROC interacted with US aid providers.

According to science historian J. Megan Greene, in the early 1940s, the Kuomintang (KMT) in China already viewed modern science and technology as a cornerstone of nation building—Sato's argument in chapter 5 supports such a thesis too. However, in the wake of the KMT's retreat to Taiwan in 1949, the KMT government's interest in science and technology in general waned as efforts were concentrated on "retaking" China. According to Greene, "the one area in which the state took an active interest in promotion of science and technology" was nuclear physics, ostensibly because the KMT sought its military applications to retake China.[2] Lee Wei-Chen also explains that nuclear power generation was the area of greatest focus for the US in its technological aid programs for the ROC, with much of the aid funds being allocated to the Tai Power Company, a former Japanese colonial company.[3] Furthermore, the case study in this chapter will show that it was not only for weapons development and energy generation that the KMT government pursued nuclear technology; it also aimed to strengthen scientific research and education to prove its authenticity as a legitimate successor to Chinese academic activities.

By examining the historical records produced in three locations—Michigan; Washington, DC; and the National Tsing Hua University in Taiwan—this chapter will highlight the power of the US state to mobilize science and technology, as well as its limitations. The government exploited scientific knowledge originally produced in a US university for diplomatic goals, and such scientific knowledge assumed hegemonic influence over foreign societies. However, this chapter will also reveal the limitations of state power to control the transnational migration of scientists and scientific knowledge, a fact that complicates the understanding of the US aid program as a simple unidirectional and unilinear transplantation of knowledge.

The existing scholarship on Cold War US foreign aid includes not only Burton I. Kaufman' seminal work (1982) but also many newer books and articles published over the past few decades. On Asia in particular, David C. Engerman's research into the development programs for India, Nick Cullather's discussion of agricultural aid programs for increased food production, Bradley R. Simpson's research focusing on Indonesia, and Jessica Elkind's exploration of the development of South Vietnam are some examples. In the Japanese language also, many important works based on meticulous primary source research, including Shōichi Watanabe's edited volume, have appeared in the past few decades.[4] However, there are scarcely any academic works on nuclear technological aid seen from the Asian perspective, with an exception of Shinsuke Tomotsugu's work on the Asia Nuclear Center.[5]

On the other hand, there is a wealth of literature on President Eisenhower's Atoms for Peace, some of which deals with developing countries' reactions to the campaign. Probably the single most important, and a fairly recent scholarly work in this field, is Jacob Darwin Hamblin's well-researched book on the global US Atoms for Peace programs and their consequences. Before this, John Krieg focused on international conferences as opportunities to arouse Third World leaders' desire for nuclear modernity, and, in a similar vein, Ran Zwigenberg examined the background of the 1955 Atoms for Peace exhibition held in Hiroshima. Kenneth Osgood dealt with Atoms for Peace as an example of Eisenhower's propaganda campaign, and Shinsuke Tomotsugu explored nonaligned nations' interest in nuclear energy.[6] None of these works, however, focus on the Phoenix Project; as far as the author is aware, there has as yet been no scholarly work on the University of Michigan–ICA contract.

As for the history of US-ROC relations, James Lin's pioneering works should be mentioned.[7] In the Japanese language, the above-mentioned chapter by Lee Wei-Chen and a recent article by Shunsuke Shikata are also noteworthy.[8] In the field of science history, in addition to Greene's book, Audra Wolfe discusses the Asia Foundation's aid in the publication of science textbooks in Taiwan in a chapter of her book.[9] However, there are no secondary sources in either English or Japanese that detail the nuclear technological aid for Taiwan. This chapter explores the grossly under-studied theme of the Phoenix Project's nuclear technological aid for Taiwan, relying chiefly on US primary sources stored at Bentley Historical Library at the University of Michigan (including detailed reports by Phoenix Project consultants who visited Taiwan) and at the National Archives (including telegrams and other exchanges between Washington, Tokyo, and Taipei). In addition, the author visited National Tsing Hua University in Taiwan in May 2023 and collected information on the history of the nuclear facility there.[10] Although the author's limited proficiency in Chinese language presented an obstacle to the full understanding of the Taiwanese side of the story, my visit to Tsing Hua and discussions there have tremendously improved my understanding of the atmosphere of the university in the early years of nuclear technology.

Upon this background, this chapter illuminates the process in which US science and scientists were exploited for the Cold War state project and assumed a hegemonic status in developing countries. At the same time, it challenges the stark dichotomy between "provider" and "recipient" of technological aid by drawing attention to the transnational movement of scientists and their knowledge. In short, this chapter demonstrates both the state's ability to exploit scientific knowledge and its inability to keep scientific knowledge completely under state control.

THE MICHIGAN MEMORIAL PHOENIX PROJECT AND THE ICA CONTRACT

When the Phoenix Project was established as the University of Michigan's World War II memorial, "over 7,500,000 US dollars were contributed by alumni, friends of the University, and industry" to support studies on the peacetime applications of atomic energy. The Phoenix Project provided "equipment, supplies, laboratory assistance, travel money, publication funds, and other research support" for hundreds of projects led by the university's faculty members. The funds were intended to be seed money to support projects in their initial stages, before financial assistance from foundations or government agencies was available.[11]

In the 1950s, an increasing number of US universities were introducing programs in nuclear science, and some built research reactors on campus. The University of Michigan, to whom the Ford Motor Company donated a reactor in 1953, was one of the earliest examples. Ralph A. Sawyer, director of the Phoenix Project and dean of the Horace H. Rackham Graduate School, was enthusiastic about the introduction of a research reactor.[12]

Around the same time, the US government was seeking out universities and industrial laboratories that could offer training courses for foreign engineers. President Eisenhower's Atoms for Peace speech at the UN General Assembly on December 8, 1953, had spurred the National Security Council (NSC) to draft a policy paper, NSC 5431, "Cooperation with Other Nations in the Peaceful Uses of Atomic Energy," in August 1954. NSC 5431 proposed that the US government should aid in the construction of small-scale reactors and provide fissionable material and training programs to other countries.[13] Initially, these activities were intended as an "interim" measure for "a year or longer" until the launch of the International Atomic Energy Agency (IAEA), which would assume the role. In reality, however, the US continued these activities for much longer than one year. In March 1955, the NSC drafted another policy paper, NSC 5507/2, "Peaceful Uses of Atomic Energy," which argued that offering small research reactors and technical training to foreign countries would be a "natural step" toward the future development of nuclear power generation and would provide the US with "great psychological advantages" over the Soviet Union.[14] In short, reactors and training would cultivate future markets for US reactors and also provide the US a winning edge against the Soviet Union in the battle to captivate the hearts and minds of developing countries. By the end of 1960, the US had concluded bilateral nuclear agreements with thirty-seven countries and provided them with research reactors. Naturally, these countries needed trained engineers to operate the newly introduced reactors; to train foreign engineers, the AEC established the International School for Nuclear Science and Engineering (ISNSE) in March 1955 at the Argonne National Laboratory on the outskirts of Chicago.[15] Although the ISNSE accepted more than four hundred trainees from all over the world between 1955 and 1960, that number was nevertheless insufficient to cultivate the large cohort of engineers necessary to fill all the vacant positions in the thirty-seven countries.

The first contact from the US government to the University of Michigan was made in January 1956, when Jack Kaufman of the AEC's Reactor Division telephoned Sawyer to inquire as to whether the Phoenix Project could dispatch consultants to developing countries. To discuss the matter in detail, Kaufman visited the university campus and met with Sawyer, Phoenix Project assistant director Henry J. Gomberg, and Vice President Marvin L. Niehuss. Sawyer later recommended to Niehuss that the Phoenix Project and the University of Michigan should accept the work if the university could hire additional staff to spare the extra burden on the existing faculty members.[16] He suggested to Niehuss that "three staff members be added on a half-time teaching basis to the Engineering Faculty" with the "understanding that the other half of their time [would] be available for consulting service." After securing some financial and logistic assistance from the Fund for Peaceful Atomic Development, the university authorized the Phoenix Project to officially enter into negotiations with the AEC.[17] Kaufman told Sawyer that he was "anxious to receive a proposal" and mentioned that if a proposal was submitted within two weeks, a contract could be signed in about two months. Sawyer submitted a proposal but did not hear back from the AEC for the next four months.

The AEC's abrupt cessation of communications was related to conflicting opinions within the organization. Some argued that the AEC had access to "most of the best nuclear engineering and scientific talent in the United States," that "the breadth of competent sources of consultants [was] more readily available to the AEC than to the University of Michigan," and that the Phoenix Project's service would "result in substantially greater costs" than if consultancy were carried out by the AEC. Apparently, this rivalry between the AEC and the Phoenix Project lasted for years; even after a few years of the Phoenix Project actually providing the consulting service, some AEC officers would refer to a "long-standing dispute" regarding whether it should be the AEC or the Phoenix Project providing such services to developing countries.[18]

In the meantime, Gomberg was approached by the ICA. In June 1956, Gomberg was participating in a meeting of the Organization for European Economic Cooperation (OEEC, predecessor to the Organization for Economic Cooperation and Development, or OECD) Working Party on the Special Committee on Nuclear Energy as an adviser on technician training. The US government was planning to contribute funds to the OEEC nuclear training center, and Gomberg was appointed as one of the US advisers. Eugene W. Scott, ICA's chief of the Nuclear Energy Division, Office of Industrial Resources, was also present at the meeting. He was impressed with Gomberg's presentation on the Phoenix Project and forwarded the presented paper to the AEC and the Department of State. Scott also asked Gomberg to "come to Washington for a conference on the contract proposal sometime soon."[19] Gomberg explained that they had submitted a proposal to the AEC but received no response for four months. He sent a copy of the proposal to the ICA and expressed that the university would be pleased to discuss it further.[20]

Consequently, on November 6, 1956, a contract was concluded between the ICA and the University of Michigan. The contract mandated the university to "provide technical and advisory services to ICA" for training and demonstration in the uses of nuclear energy. Concretely, the university was to "study the technical resources of the countries," "survey the possibility of power developments using atomic energy," and assist the US Operations Mission (USOM)[21] in "carrying out meetings designed to provide information on the practical uses of radioisotopes and radiation in industry, medicine, agriculture, and other fields of technology." For these purposes, the University of Michigan was to appoint a project supervisor who would be responsible for receiving and coordinating instructions and directions from the ICA, a secretary to assist the director, six regular consultants who would serve as technical advisers to the designated countries, and special consultants who would provide miscellaneous and special advisory services. The Phoenix Project was responsible for submitting quarterly progress reports to the ICA. All consulting services were "under the over-all direction of ICA," and the staff was to "operate under the administrative supervision" of the USOM in the designated countries. William Kerr, professor of nuclear engineering at the University of Michigan, was appointed project supervisor.[22] Special consultants were later divided into two categories: "Special Consultants," mature specialists who could "use their knowledge in the solution of practical problems in the overseas missions," and "Miscellaneous Consultants," a group of young interns who supported senior specialists and worked in cooperation with foreigners while at the same time gaining experience and developing as "trained career men" to sustain US foreign aid programs in the future.[23]

The University of Michigan perceived the ICA-contracted overseas aid program as an opportunity to promote the university's prestige, but for the US government, the contract was a foreign policy measure: On June 11, 1955, President Eisenhower, in his address at the Centennial Commencement of Pennsylvania State University, announced that the US government would provide research reactors, nuclear fuels, and technical training to friendly nations and would cover either US$350,000 or half of the reactor's price.[24] The president's announcement was a concrete embodiment of policy papers NSC 5431 and NSC 5507/2. The AEC, the Department of State, and the ICA decided which countries to offer research reactors strategically—choosing key countries and regions of importance in the defense of the "free world" against the Communist threat, among which, as this chapter will later demonstrate, the ROC was a prime example. The US government tapped into the Phoenix Project's rich resources for promoting foreign policy objectives. In January 1957, the ICA, the Department of State, and the AEC invited Kerr and Gomberg to an interagency meeting held in Washington, DC, and briefed them on the government's expectations.[25] Kerr and Gomberg were told that the Phoenix Project researchers would act "as consultants to the local Mission [USOM]" and that their reports would be "surveyed by both the State Department and AEC," in addition to the ICA. When their consultation terms ended, they would go through "de-briefing in Washington."[26] James C. Meem, acting chief (later chief) of the Nuclear Energy Staff, Office of Industrial Resources, ICA, was the officer in charge of the Phoenix Project.

The Phoenix Project leaders became increasingly committed to the ICA project. Kerr wrote to another Michigan professor that the project was "not only to perform a vitally useful service to our State Department, but also gives us an unparalleled opportunity to gain an insight into the problems and possibilities in the peacetime application of nuclear energy."[27] On November 6, 1959, near the end of the first three-year contract period, Sawyer and Kerr strongly advocated the renewal of the contract.[28] By this time, the Phoenix Project had produced a fifteen-page booklet titled *A General Atomic Energy Program*, a compilation of know-how for developing countries to introduce nuclear technologies. The booklet was authored by Kerr and G. Hoyt Whipple, a regular consultant of the project and professor at the School of Public Health, and was originally presented at the Second UN Conference on Peaceful Uses of Atomic Energy in 1958 (more information on this conference will be provided later).[29]

By March 1960, the ICA–Phoenix Project program had developed into a full-fledged overseas technological aid project. Table 6.1 shows a list of countries visited by Phoenix Project consultants until February 1960.[30] The ICA widely promoted the availability of the Phoenix Project consulting service to USOM worldwide, and by 1963, project consultants had made a total of thirty-six visits to twenty-two countries.[31] The consultants came from departments of nuclear engineering, chemical engineering, chemistry, physics, zoology, public health, medicine, and biophysics. In addition, professors from the law department offered on-campus consultation for foreign visitors.[32]

At the request of the AEC, the University of Michigan also offered training courses for foreign engineers. On December 5, 1956, W. Kenneth Davis, director of the AEC's Division of Reactor Development, inquired of President Harlan Hatcher whether the University of Michigan could offer a one-year graduate program in nuclear technology to foreign students. Since enrollment at the ISNSE was limited by space, the AEC was asking universities to operate a "one-year graduate course in nuclear energy technology comparable to the ISNSE program."[33] The University of Michigan accepted a small number of foreign trainees on an irregular basis, beginning with two German researchers who held doctoral degrees in physics and were to have supervisory responsibility for operating a newly built research reactor. Initially, the university only collected US$300 per semester from foreign trainees. However, as the number of overseas applications increased and "the long range demand became evident," the university could no longer afford to subsidize the training and decided to charge US$3,000 per trainee.[34] In the fall semester of 1957, thirty-three foreign nationals of the following nations were enrolled in the nuclear engineering department (number of students in parentheses): Belgium (1), Burma (1), Chile (1), China (1), Czechoslovakia (1), England (1), France (2), Greece (1), Hungary (1), India (2), Japan (2), Jordan (1), Korea (1), Mexico (4), Norway (1), the Philippines (2),

Table 6.1 Countries Visited by Phoenix Project Consultants up to 1960

Country visited	Date	Consultants
[illegible]	April–May 1957	William Kerr
Turkey	June 1957	William Kerr
Lebanon	June 1957	William Kerr
Pakistan	October 1957	William Kerr G. Hoyt Whipple
Iraq	October 1957	William Kerr
Iran	October 1957	G. Hoyt Whipple
Colombia	January 1958	Henry J. Gomberg W. Wayne Meinke
Indonesia	March 1958	Lloyd Brownell Charles Simons
Ecuador	April 1958	Henry J. Gomberg
Korea	April 1958	G. Hoyt Whipple
Puerto Rico	June 1958	G. Hoyt Whipple
Japan	August 1958	Henry J. Gomberg
Korea	August 1958	Henry J. Gomberg
Yugoslavia	September 1958	G. Hoyt Whipple
Tunisia	September 1958	Charles Simons
Greece	January 1959	Henry J. Gomberg
Turkey	February 1959	Charles Simons
ROC	March 1959	Ralph A. Sawyer William Kerr
Philippines	March 1959	William Kerr
ROC	July–August 1959	Henry S. Frank
Pakistan	August 1959	W. Wayne Meinke
Greece	October 1959	Henry J. Gomberg
IAEA Headquarters (Austria)	October 1959	Henry J. Gomberg
Israel	February 1960	G. Hoyt Whipple

Source: Prepared by the author and based on the table attached to the correspondence from Kerr to Gomberg, March 29, 1960, box 21, MMPP.

Spain (2), Switzerland (1), Thailand (4), Turkey (2), and Uruguay (1); this list, however, may include regular, degree-seeking graduate students in addition to "trainees."[35]

The University of Michigan also accepted trainees who had completed the ISNSE course. After seven months of training at the ISNSE, a number of students enrolled in the university's graduate school for further training in using the Ford reactor. They chose the University of Michigan because their home countries were seeking to introduce reactors of the same type as the Ford reactor—that is, the "swimming pool" type. As the ISNSE did not have this type of reactor, the AEC asked the University of Michigan to accept former ISNSE trainees who wished to build experience with swimming pool reactors.[36]

The University of Michigan–ICA contract was terminated in January 1965. During the life of the project, nineteen consultants, fifteen of whom were University of Michigan faculty members, provided various forms of assistance in twenty-two countries. Of these countries, the ROC was the most frequently visited: Kerr and Sawyer visited the ROC in March 1959, Frank in July 1959, Kerr and Sun in October 1960, Ricker in April 1961, and Sun in August 1961. The second most visited countries were Greece, Pakistan, Thailand, and Turkey; each was visited three times by regular consultants.[37] Of the five most visited countries, three were in Asia, which reflected both the demand from Asian countries for nuclear technological assistance and the importance the US government placed on the region.

THE EMERGENCE OF NUCLEAR ENGINEERING AS A NEW ACADEMIC DISCIPLINE

The "international turn" of the Phoenix Project was linked to the emergence of nuclear engineering as a new academic discipline. The University of Michigan's top administration, as well as the Department of Engineering, wished to gain national and international prestige in this promising new field. Gomberg, in his speech at the Deans of Engineering conference, stressed the urgent need for the establishment of the new discipline of nuclear engineering. He quoted AEC commissioner William Libby, saying that "50,000 engineers and scientists would be needed by the Atomic Energy program" in the near future, and emphasized that US universities should produce more nuclear engineers; "the market is there and growing," he appealed to the deans, and he encouraged them to establish nuclear engineering programs.[38]

At the Second UN Conference on the Peaceful Uses of Atomic Energy, held in Geneva in 1958, Whipple and Kerr presented a paper titled "A Generalized

Atomic Energy Program," which was also included in the proceedings of the conference.[39] The paper covered topics such as "administration," "survey of available resources," "choice of purpose," "schedule for introduction," "training," "health and safety," "radioisotope facilities," "research reactor," and "power reactor" and introduced various kinds of research reactors, with an emphasis on the importance of choosing an appropriate reactor type, with consideration given to the intended purpose, cost, location, and staff availability. Further, the authors gave a cautious but unambiguous message of encouragement for nuclear power generation. Although they did "not believe that atomic energy [was] a panacea for all the ills of the world," they were "convinced that among the benefits which atomic energy [would] ultimately bring to the world there are many that can be of great value if properly selected and integrated into the development of a country."[40] As mentioned in the previous section, this paper was later compiled into a brochure and distributed to developing countries. Presenting a paper at the Geneva Conference undoubtedly helped to legitimize the Phoenix Project's status as a leader in nuclear technological aid.

As well as the prestige of the university, financing was also an important factor. The personnel newly hired by the university for the ICA program spent one semester (five months) as regular teaching staff and the rest of the year on the ICA program. The addition of teaching staff helped "fill the need developed by the expansion of Nuclear Engineering and Science programs." The university bore only "the cost that would normally be incurred in hiring additional teachers," while the ICA covered "all of its own costs," including salaries and travel expenses for the consultants. Therefore, "by pooling and rotating the personnel," the university received "the benefit of a more diversified staff" of "proven quality and ability" at lower-than-normal expense.[41] This was a good deal for the university, especially when it was in the midst of expanding its nuclear engineering program.

The Phoenix Project was faced with one serious problem—ensuring the safety of reactor operations in developing countries. Although the AEC carried out safety studies in the subject countries before initiating Phoenix Project consulting services, such studies alone did not constitute the ultimate approval of reactor operations. Kerr was concerned that the Phoenix Project would "take on what may prove to be a rather fearsome responsibility" if a final approval was issued casually. To ensure that proper precautions would be taken, Kerr proposed establishing the position of "Research Reactor Project Director," which would be responsible for the operational integrity of each reactor.[42] Training research reactor project directors became an important part of the Phoenix Project consulting service.

Another issue that perturbed Kerr was potential nuclear weapons proliferation. In his letter to the ICA, Kerr warned that "the implications of assisting countries in the installation of research reactors are definitely of a long-term nature," and one "vitally important implication" was that "in spite of the most peaceful of objectives," the training or equipment provided to recipient countries would be "potentially useful in developing a military program."[43] The US government had shown little concern about nuclear weapons proliferation during the 1950s, but concern about the issue mounted during the 1960s. This concern became a reality in October 1964, in the form of a successful test by the PRC. As the Nonproliferation Treaty (NPT) was being discussed, the idea of exporting nuclear reactors to developing countries to win their hearts and minds became outdated. During the eight years and two months of its operation, however, the Phoenix Project and the ICA left concrete marks on technological knowledge in developing countries. The next section will provide a detailed analysis of the reception of US nuclear technological aid, through the example of the ROC.

THE CASE OF THE NATIONAL TSING HUA UNIVERSITY IN THE ROC

As already mentioned, of the twenty-two countries to which the Phoenix Project sent consultants, the ROC was the most frequently visited. The main site of the Phoenix Project consulting service was the National Tsing Hua University. The university's origin was Tsing Hua Yuan, established in 1909, "where an office was established . . . for selecting and sending Chinese students to the United States for a college education on an indemnity returned by the U.S. government to China." It became Tsing Hua Imperial College in 1911 and was renamed Tsing Hua College after the inauguration of the ROC in 1912. It became National Tsing Hua University in 1928. During the Sino-Japanese War, the university was relocated to Hunan, and thereafter to Kunming, Yunnan, where it united with two other universities.[44] When the Second World War ended, reconstruction of the university started in Beijing but was taken over by the PRC when the Communists took power and the Nationalists retreated to Taiwan in 1949. Mei Yiqi, who had been Tsing Hua's president since 1931, migrated to the US, where he administered the Tsing Hua Endowment (later renamed China Foundation). However, in 1955 he moved to Taiwan by the request of the Nationalist government. The China Foundation became the primary funding source to reestablish the National Tsing Hua University in Hsinchu, located about forty miles south of Taipei.[45] In the meantime, the PRC also reestablished Tsing Hua University in Beijing.

The emergence of the two Tsing Hua Universities and Mei's migration to Taiwan were symbolic of the Cold War in East Asia, which also divided knowledge, education, and technology. As Yuko Sato described in chapter 5, the KMT and the Communist Party engaged in a tug-of-war over Chinese scientists, especially those educated in the US or the UK. Because of this background, reconstructing Tsing Hua University as a cutting-edge academic institute and making it the home for East Asia's first nuclear reactor meant validating the university as a legitimate successor of Chinese science and technology. As soon as the US-ROC bilateral agreement was concluded in 1955, the ROC sent engineers to the US to study reactor construction technology and to determine the most suitable type of reactor. Such quick action was possible because Mei himself was a physicist, as Yuko Sato pointed out, and he had been involved in the Nationalists' initiative to send a delegate of young scientists to the US since 1945. In the end, a swimming pool reactor, designed by General Electric Company (GE) and fueled by enriched uranium, was selected by the ROC engineers. GE would furnish the components necessary for construction of a research reactor and provide assistance in its construction and start-up. Tsing Hua University would be "responsible for construction of the reactor and for putting it into operation."[46]

However, there was a desperate shortage of skilled engineers, and the ROC relied heavily on the US for their training. As Sato pointed out, many of the Chinese scientists who studied abroad during the Civil War of 1946–48 stayed in Western countries and did not repatriate. When Tsing Hua University's Institute of Nuclear Science was launched in 1956, there were only twelve staff members, including Zheng Zhen-Hua (also known as Victor Cheng), Ye Xi-Rong, Chu Shu-Kung, Chien Ji-Peng, Ge Bao-Shu (also known as Ko Paoshu), Yang Yu-Dong (also known as Rudy Yang), and Li Ming-Li. All except Ye and Chu were "loaned" from Tai Power Company and had received training in the US.[47] For example, Victor Cheng, who participated in the fourth session of ISNSE, was introduced in a monthly magazine of the Argonne National Laboratory (where the ISNSE was housed) as "a good companion, a hard worker, and a competent scientist." In the interview with the magazine, he said that "(1) first-hand knowledge about nuclear engineering; (2) fostering of the spirit of international cooperation; and (3) experience with the American democratic way of life" were some of the assets he accumulated at the ISNSE.[48]

One of the US-educated scientists who played an important role in the ROC was Sun Kuan-Han, who was born in mainland China in 1914 and graduated from Zhejiang University. In 1937, he was awarded a Tsing Hua University scholarship to study abroad and enrolled in Pittsburg University. There he received a PhD in physics in 1940 and became an engineer at Westinghouse Electric Corporation, where he stayed for thirty years, later heading the company's Radiation and Nucleonics Laboratory.[49] In 1959, he was invited to the ROC to become a member of the committee chaired by Mei to prepare for the reactor construction. This was the first time he was involved in the ROC's reactor project. In 1960 and 1961, he revisited the ROC as a Phoenix Project consultant and even headed the Institute of Nuclear Science at Tsing Hua University. Sun was called the father of Taiwanese nuclear science and was a respected public intellectual and writer. He also became known as a supporter of democracy and human rights as he worked hard to release writer Bo Yang, who had been arrested and imprisoned for his political thoughts by the Nationalist government. After retiring from Westinghouse, Sun lived on the Tsing Hua University campus as adviser to the Institute of Nuclear Science and spent the rest of his life in Taiwan. To honor him, his laboratory was preserved long after his retirement.[50]

Other committee members invited by Mei included Rudy Yang, Chien Ji-Peng, C. H. Wong (also known as David Wong), and Ko Paoshu. All had graduated from the ISNSE, and Chien and Wong had spent six more months at the University of Michigan. The ROC had sent engineers to every ISNSE session except the first.[51] In sum, Tsing Hua University's reactor program almost entirely relied on US-trained engineers and Chinese engineers living in the US. Subsequently, more Chinese scientists were invited from the US or Canada as visiting professors or short-term residence scholars, but no one contributed to Tsing Hua University as much as Sun.

From the US government's perspective, the nuclear development program in the ROC was part of a larger nuclear policy toward Asia. After President Eisenhower announced the intent to offer research reactors to friendly nations, the AEC opened branch offices in London, Brussels, Buenos Aires, and Tokyo. The Tokyo office, established in the US Embassy on November 15, 1957, was the hub of US nuclear policies toward Asian nations. Herbert W. Pennington, who had previously worked for private companies such as DuPont, Monsanto Chemical, and Westinghouse, directed the office, while concurrently serving as a science attaché to the US Embassy.[52] The US nuclear technological aid to other Asian countries, including the ROC, the Philippines, Vietnam, Thailand, and Burma, was coordinated by Pennington's Tokyo office.

When the ground was broken for the Tsing Hua research reactor on December 7, 1958, Pennington flew to the ROC. At Tsing Hua University, Pennington observed that "staffing [was] still a problem," but "all in all the future prospects look[ed] somewhat better." An increasing number of students were applying for the Fulbright and IAEA scholarships, and the ISNSE consistently accepted trainees from the ROC. Most ISNSE graduates went on to receive additional training at US universities, and Tsing Hua University's new graduates had already begun to receive training in the US. Pennington's report also pointed out that "publicity" of the fact that a reactor was being built in the ROC would attract overseas Chinese engineers.[53] Pennington's report indicates that the US intended to attract overseas Chinese to Taiwan in the field of nuclear science.

Pennington's report also indicated that the AEC and the ROC government had been discussing nuclear power generation from an early stage. The AEC thought that the ROC should "first exploit the research bilateral before negotiating a power agreement," but it did not object to the ROC introducing nuclear power in the near future.[54] During his visit, Pennington met with the president and vice president of Tai Power Company, together with a representative of J. G. White Engineering, a US construction company specializing in dams and power plants. They agreed that 1967 would be the "tentative target" for building a nuclear power plant. The Tai Power Company had already sent employees to the US for training in nuclear power technology. For example, Ko Paoshu, after completing the third session of ISNSE, spent a year working on the Experimental Boiling Water Reactor (EBWR) at Argonne National Laboratory. Victor Cheng, after the fourth session of the ISNSE, spent six months working on the CP-5 reactor and another six months working on the KEWR reactor at Argonne National Laboratory. In addition, there were "two Tai Power participants in the 7th session of ISNSE and one in the 8th session," and an application had been submitted to Oak Ridge National Laboratory for two seventh ISNSE session members to attend the "Reactor Supervisors and Reactor Hazards Evaluation courses." If not accepted by Oak Ridge, they were planning to gain experience with operating power reactors at Shippingport and Dresden nuclear power plants.[55] Such prolific participation of Tai Power engineers in US training programs indicates the consensus between the US and ROC governments that the ROC would sooner or later build a US-designed nuclear power reactor. It is noteworthy that many Tai Power employees, including Ko and Cheng, became faculty members of Tsing Hua University. For many years thereafter, Tai Power and Tsing Hua University cooperated with each other to achieve the goal of nuclear power generation.

As Tsing Hua University was planning to introduce a GE reactor, the ROC's Atomic Energy Commission (CUSA), USOM, and Mei discussed the urgent need to send trainees to GE's Atomic Power Equipment Department in San Jose, California. They decided to send Lee In-king and Tsing Der-ling, both ISNSE graduates, to GE's Reactor Training Course in June and July 1958.[56]

CUSA, USOM, and Mei also decided to send Yang, Cheng, Chien, and Wong to GE's training course, and four other trainees attending the seventh session of ISNSE were also instructed to participate in GE's training course.[57]

To their disappointment, however, GE soon stopped accepting new foreign trainees. Since the US government's conclusion of bilateral agreements with more than thirty countries, trainees from those countries began to fill up both the ISNSE and private companies' training courses toward the end of the 1950s. GE's Reactor Training Course also became fully booked by the end of 1959. USOM bemoaned the fact that they had "received 4 negative replies from the 6 companies contacted," including GE, to their request to accept trainees from the ROC. USOM reluctantly sent trainees to Westinghouse, despite the fact that the company did not provide training with a swimming pool reactor.[58] The increasingly restricted training opportunities in the US highlighted the significance of the Phoenix Project, insofar as it would dispatch experts to the ROC for consulting service.

The Phoenix Project consultation service officially commenced in early 1959, although the ROC had in fact already been receiving unofficial consultation since 1957.[59] From March 17 to April 3, 1959, Sawyer and Kerr visited the ROC as the first official Phoenix Project consultants. They were expected to advise on "technically and economically feasible" nuclear programs for the ROC, "equipment and facilities being considered for purchase," a training program for such a project, and "graduate study in the fields of mathematics, chemistry, physics, and biology" at Tsing Hua University.[60] The ICA in Washington had instructed Sawyer and Kerr to travel to Japan and meet with Pennington before going to Taipei. On March 16 and 17, Sawyer and Kerr met with Pennington, director of the USOM in Japan D. H. Thibodeaux, and other ICA staff at the US Embassy in Tokyo. They were briefed on the problems of the ROC's "energy sources" and activities in the nuclear energy area. Thibodeau explained that the ROC would need to rely on nuclear energy as a power source "in the very near future." They flew to Taiwan the following day.

As the Phoenix Project consultants submitted detailed reports to the ICA and their copies are included in the records of the Phoenix Project stored at the University of Michigan, it is possible to grasp, in substantial detail, their experiences in Taiwan. According to the report of the visit by Sawyer and Kerr, Tsing Hua University desperately needed more teaching staff. Two visiting faculty members from the US, Sun Kuan-Han and Lee C. Teng, could not stay long because of their regular commitments in the US. Sun, as already introduced, occupied an important position in Westinghouse, and Teng was an accelerator specialist of the Argonne National Laboratory. Teng was born and raised in

China and left for the US in 1947 to enroll in the University of Chicago, where he earned a doctoral degree in high-energy physics in 1951, and subsequently became an internationally renowned scientist in accelerator technology. Teng joined the Argonne National Laboratory in 1955, and in December 1961, he was appointed director of Argonne's Particle Accelerator Division.[61] Just like Sun, Teng was a US-based scientist of Chinese origin. In addition to Sun and Teng, there were six part-time professors who spent only one day per week at Tsing Hua University. The full-time staff comprised five people: one full professor and four assistant professors. Of these, only one had a PhD—the others were young scientists. Furthermore, three of the staff, Chien, Wong, and Yang, were "heavily involved in reactor design and construction" and therefore could not spare much time for education.[62] The staffing difficulty was related, at least to some degree, to low salaries and poor living conditions. One young scientist trained at the California Institute of Technology returned to the PRC, but he was invited to Taiwan to hold a research position there. However, he was "very unhappy" with his salary and living conditions; since the ROC and the PRC were competing to acquire foreign-educated Chinese scientists, such a situation posed a serious problem.[63]

Second, Sawyer and Kerr's report pointed out a major problem in the management of the nuclear reactor facilities: the lack of clear leadership responsibilities. They recommended the "appointment of a construction project director" and suggested Sun Kuan-Han for the position. They also recommended the appointment of a laboratory director, reactor supervisor, and reactor operating staff and further advised that "there were certain responsibilities which should reside outside the group that [was] making use of the research reactor and its products," such as regulations for safety.[64]

Third, Sawyer and Kerr interviewed various parties to evaluate the possibility and desirability of nuclear power generation. R. Smith, an employee of J. G. White Engineering Company, told them that Tai Power Company was "keeping abreast of nuclear power developments," although economic feasibility was a problem. A Tai Power Company representative explained that although a nuclear power plant would have "considerable political impact," this was not within the purview of Tai Power; it was a governmental concern. On another occasion, the US ambassador in Taipei mentioned that "the political consideration" concerning nuclear power was "unimportant at the present time" and that a "nuclear power plant should be built on Formosa only when it becomes economically feasible."[65] Their interviews indicate that all parties were in basic agreement on the commencement of nuclear power generation, sooner or later. The "political consideration," presumably referring to the possibility of nuclear weapons proliferation, was not a serious concern at that time, although all involved were likely aware that nuclear power generation would produce plutonium that could be processed to fuel nuclear weapons.[66]

In May 1959, Henry S. Frank, chemistry professor at the University of Pittsburgh, joined the ICA–Phoenix Project team in the ROC as a special consultant.[67] In the prewar years, Frank had taught at Lingnan University in Canton, China, and was well known among Chinese scientists; some of the Tsing Hua faculty were his former students. Frank also knew Dean Chen Ker-Chung of Tsing Hua University very well, as they had spent many years together in China. Because of this unique background, Frank was invited to Tsing Hua University to help solve the staffing problem.[68] He proposed the establishment of "a recruitment center in the United States" that would "canvass the whole field of nuclear science in the United States (and beyond) for possible candidates for appointment." He also advised that "special steps should be taken to overcome the extreme financial disadvantages" under which faculty were working. Frank emphasized the importance of financial assistance from the ICA, AEC, and Fulbright Program and believed that such support would be "in the national interests of the United States."[69] For Frank, "national interests" meant prevailing in the competition with the PRC; he explained that the PRC was developing "an effective nuclear program" with Soviet assistance and that, to counter this, "an active and imaginative program of research in nuclear science" would make a valuable contribution to "showcase" the ROC's technological achievement. Frank further warned that the "striking discrepancy" in the standards of living between the ROC citizens and the Americans living there should be corrected. Since "American visiting professors or technical experts should stand in an especially close and cooperative relationship to their Chinese counterparts on the same campus," glaring differences in treatment could disrupt the "group effectiveness" of the organization, according to Frank.[70]

In October 1959, Sun Kuan-Han's contract with Tsing Hua University expired, and he returned to Westinghouse.[71] The staffing situation at Tsing Hua University did not improve rapidly; according to Pennington, although young engineers who received training in the US were returning, the university had not been able to secure "someone of the stature of Dr. Sun."[72] Moreover, President Mei fell ill, and, bereft of his charismatic persona, the morale of the ROC scientists waned. Harry C. Schmid, chief ICA officer in Taipei, invited Kerr and Sun to the ROC again to receive their assistance.[73] Schmid expected that Mei would try to convince Sun to leave Westinghouse and take over his position as director of the Institute of Nuclear Science.[74] Sun expressed concerns about the "low morale of the Institute staff," as some faculty members were "more interested in material comfort than scholastic endeavor." He recommended that "a vice president or acting vice president of the University must be found to lead the university on the day-by-day basis" and that Victor Cheng should be appointed as acting assistant director of the Institute of Nuclear Science. Sun also advised securing a larger budget for recruitment to secure quality faculty members.[75] Kerr's confidential report to the ICA endorsed Sun's concerns, pointing out the inefficiency of the decision-making process, lack of long-term goals, and need for more senior staff.[76]

Perhaps as a result of Sun's and Kerr's strong expressions of concern, when Kerr revisited Tsing Hua on his way home from his consulting mission to Thailand three months later, the situation was somewhat ameliorated.[77] Kerr observed that the reactor start-up preparation seemed to be progressing smoothly, and the university was expecting to receive two engineers from GE to assist. Also, University of Michigan reactor physicist professor Ricker was invited to aid in the start-up process. Pennington, too, flew from Tokyo to contribute. With the support of all of these US specialists, the research reactor achieved criticality on April 13.

Before he left the ROC, Ricker had advised Schmid that Sun would be a prime candidate for the position of director of the Institute, judging from his "reputation as a scientist and administrator and the high regard which the Chinese hold for him," and recommended making every effort to acquire his service.[78] Schmid and Kerr agreed, but it was not practical to ask Sun to give up his position at Westinghouse. Kerr thought that President Mei should "make the best offer [he] could" to recruit Sun.[79] In June 1961, President Chiang Kai-shek invited Sun to attend a conference in Taipei, presumably to persuade him to direct the institute.[80] Ultimately, Sun accepted the director's position while he remained in his position at Westinghouse. He stayed at Tsing Hua University in 1962 and 1964 for two months each year and also served as an adviser to the ROC's representative to the IAEA.

Around the same time, however, a discouraging brain drain took place at Tsing Hua University. Chien Ji-Peng, a founding member of the Institute of Nuclear Science and one of the few experienced full-time faculty members, was planning to leave the ROC to "take a teaching position at a small school in the United States." According to Kerr, Chien's primary objective was not "obtaining further scientific training" but "earning sufficient funds to allow him to pursue advanced scientific training at some later time." This incident reveals that even though US science and technology had hegemonic power in Taiwan, the US government could not control the transnational migration of scientists or prevent brain drain.[81]

Although the ICA–Phoenix Project consulting service in the ROC began to be phased out in 1964 and was officially terminated in January 1965, US and ROC historical records indicate that AID, successor to the ICA, assumed responsibility for the consulting service. In 1965, AID arranged and funded an agreement of cooperation between Tsing Hua University and Argonne National Laboratory. With the AID funds, Argonne provided books, articles, and experimental devices and sent consultants to Tsing Hua University. These consultants included Lee C. Teng, director of Argonne's Particle Accelerator Division, who, as mentioned above, had been visiting faculty at Tsing Hua in 1959.[82] In 1965, however, the US aid to the ROC in general was heading toward cessation, and AID was also planning to discontinue all its activities in the ROC. The US decision was partly attributable to the ROC's rapid expansion of exports, at a rate of as much as 22 percent a year.[83] The US Congress felt that there was no more need for financial aid to the ROC, especially in light of the tremendous military budget necessary to continue the war in Vietnam.

However, the Tsing Hua–Argonne agreement was extended for at least one more year. In 1965, AEC chair and Nobel Prize–winning chemist Glenn Seaborg visited Tsing Hua University. After meeting with Chiang Kai-shek and university faculty members, he penned a letter to the director of AID, urging him to reconsider the decision to terminate its assistance to the ROC. He reminded the director that there was "considerable merit to continuing" the Tsing Hua–Argonne partnership program: "Despite Taiwan's progress, funds for science and education are still scarce, and I feel that continued US assistance to this project for the longest time possible consistent with US national policy would pay dividends far in excess of the modest investment which would be required to continue this arrangement."

On the basis of his observations of the efficacy of the sister laboratory agreement in Turkey, Seaborg argued that "similar long-term US assistance to [Tsing Hua]" would be "the solution to a potentially grave problem."[84] What "grave problem" could be solved by long-term nuclear technological assistance? Although Seaborg did not mention it explicitly, the US government was deeply concerned about the ROC's pursuit of nuclear weapons development, especially given the PRC's successful test in the previous year. The Central Intelligence Agency (CIA) suspected that Chiang Kai-shek had ordered scientists of the Chung-shan Institute of Science and Technology (CIST) to develop nuclear weapons.[85] In this context, Seaborg was likely suggesting continuation of the US commitment to the ROC's nuclear program as a means to forestall nuclear weapons development. Ultimately, the agreement with Argonne was extended, although it is not clear whether Seaborg's letter influenced the decision.[86]

188   SCIENTIFIC KNOWLEDGE

Even as US aid was petering out after 1965, partnership between the ROC and the US in nuclear technology continued, as the ROC purchased Westinghouse and GE power reactors from the US. The Tai Power Company declared its intention to commence nuclear power generation in 1964 with the cooperation of Tsing Hua University.[87] The AEC renewed its bilateral agreement with the ROC in 1972, offering a six-hundred-megawatt power reactor and enriched uranium. Consequently, the ROC commenced commercial nuclear power generation in 1978.[88]

This case study of the ICA–Phoenix Project consulting service to the ROC reveals a constant shortage of qualified engineers and educators in nuclear technology and an equally constant flow of engineers to the US to receive training. The ROC's nuclear science almost entirely depended on US aid. However, it should be noted that some of the "US" consultants to the ROC, such as Sun and Teng, were US-based scientists of Chinese origin. As Greene points out, it had been a long-standing practice of the KMT to employ foreign-educated scientists.[89] Reliance on American scientists of Chinese origin such as Sun and Teng, therefore, may have been a natural and acceptable part of the government policies. Such a practice reminds us that, while individual scientists may have nationalities, knowledge itself does not bear a national flag. Douglas B. Fuller and Murray A. Rubinstein point out the importance of "tacit knowledge" that is "embedded in individuals" in the international flow of science and technology. Individuals are "key for knowledge transfer" as they engage in internal cooperation and various organizational activities.[90] Although case studies in Fuller and Rubinstein's edited volume primarily concern post–Cold War information technology industries, this chapter has demonstrated that scientific knowledge, embedded in individuals, traversed national borders even within the confinement of the Cold War diplomacy. The US and ROC governments may have had their own interests and objectives, such as creating a modern and prosperous "free China" or developing nuclear weapons, but neither could completely hold sway over individual scientists or scientific knowledge.

CONCLUSION

A close examination of the development of the ICA–Phoenix Project consulting service revealed a process under which academic knowledge generated in a public university was mobilized for the Cold War. The US government tapped into the expertise that the University of Michigan had accumulated through the Phoenix Project and employed that expertise for diplomatic purposes—that is, to strengthen the free world and win the hearts and minds of the Third World science elite. The University of Michigan professors, for

THE MICHIGAN MEMORIAL PHOENIX PROJECT AND TAIWAN 189

their part, accepted the government invitation for various reasons, including enhancing the prestige of the university, gaining eminence in the new academic field, ensuring a pipeline for government funding, and securing employment of faculty members from diverse fields. In other words, the ICA and the Phoenix Project found each other to be useful partners, albeit for different purposes. In this government-academic alliance, knowledge of nuclear engineering held hegemonic power, with which the US would expand its cultural and scientific sphere of influence.

Developing countries held great expectations for nuclear technology but lacked both skilled engineers and the means to train them. The ROC demonstrated an almost total reliance on US technological aid to cultivate their own engineers. In this sense, US scientific knowledge was indeed hegemonic, as almost all ROC engineers in nuclear science sought training in the US, and ROC university laboratories consulted US experts. However, "US consultants" included US-based scientists of Chinese origin, and their existence complicates a binary understanding of the "giver" and "receiver" of technological aid. After all, knowledge is not differentiated by the nationalities or residences of those who acquire it. Moreover, the ROC government, senior scientists, and younger US-trained engineers all had different dreams and objectives, such as nuclear weapons development, nuclear power generation, the establishment of modern science education, and personal fulfillment, including better salaries or advanced education—such diverse motives further complicate the labeling of scientific knowledge in terms of nationality.

Nevertheless, it is hard to deny the long-term influences of US nuclear technology on the recipient countries. The ROC's science community was firmly tied to US science and technology through training and consulting services. The very first research reactor introduced in the ROC was a GE product, and Sun, a Westinghouse engineer, directed the Institute of Nuclear Science. This may explain why all of the ROC's nuclear power plants installed GE or Westinghouse nuclear reactors. US science and technology in the early Cold War era, therefore, had hegemonic power in developing countries, but at the same time, scientific and technological knowledge maintained an elusiveness, as it belonged to individual scientists who could both live and work transnationally.

NOTES

1. "Michigan Memorial–Phoenix Project," n.d., box 20, Records of the Michigan Memorial Phoenix Project, Bentley Historical Library, University of Michigan (hereafter MMPP). I would like to express my sincere gratitude to the librarians and archivists at the Bentley Historical Library, University of

190 SCIENTIFIC KNOWLEDGE

Michigan. Without their help, I could not have accessed the precious historical sources on the Phoenix Project.

2. Greene, *Origins of the Developmental State in Taiwan*, 7.

3. Lee, "Amerika-gasshūkoku no enjo to Taiwan," 282–85.

4. Kaufman, *Trade and Aid*; Engerman, *Price of Aid*; Cullather, *Hungry World*; Simpson, *Economists with Guns*; Elkind, *Aid under Fire*; Watanabe, *Reisen henyō-ki no kokusai-kaihatsu enjo to Asia*.

5. Tomotsugu, "Ajia genshiryoku center kōsō to sono zasetsu."

6. Hamblin, *The Wretched Atom*; Krige, "Techno-Utopian Dreams"; Zwigenberg, *Hiroshima*; Osgood, *Total Cold War*; Tomotsugu, "Bandung Conference."

7. Lin, "Sowing Seeds and Knowledge"; James Lin, "Martyrs of Development."

8. Shikata, "1950 nendai ni okeru beikoku no taiwan seisaku to kakyō."

9. Wolfe, *Freedom's Laboratory*, chap. 7.

10. I am deeply thankful to Professor Peir Jinn-Jer of National Tsing Hua University's Nuclear Science and Technology Development Center, who introduced me to the history of the Tsing Hua nuclear reactor and showed me precious photos and publications by the university and its faculty members. My sincere appreciation also goes to Professor Lan Shichi of National Chengchi University, who enabled my visit to Tsing Hua University and introduced me to its distinguished faculty, including Dean Li Cho-ying, Professor Wang Hsien-chun, and Professor Shen Diau-Long, to whom I owe a precious opportunity to learn about the history of Taiwan. I also thank Patrick Yeh and Lin Yuting, who aided my research at Tsing Hua University.

11. "Michigan Memorial–Phoenix Project," n.d., box 20, MMPP.

12. Director Ralph A. Sawyer to T. W. Bonner, Department of Physics, Rice Institute, September 2, 1955, box 20, MMPP.

13. Document 238, "National Security Council Report: NSC 5431/1 Note by the Executive Secretary to the National Security Council on Cooperation with Other Nations in the Peaceful Uses of Atomic Energy," August 13, 1954, and enclosure titled "Statement of Policy by the National Security Council on Cooperation with Other Nations in the Peaceful Uses of Atomic Energy," *Foreign Relations of the United States* (hereafter *FRUS*), *1952–1954*.

14. Document 14, "National Security Council Report: NSC 5507/2, Peaceful Uses of Atomic Energy," March 12, 1955, *FRUS*, *1955–1957*.

15. Hilberry to Flaherty, "Appendix A, Background and Discussion," September 30, 1954, RG 326, ANL Miscellaneous Correspondence and Reports, box 17, National Archives at Chicago. More on the ISNSE in Moriguchi Tsuchiya, *Science, Technology*, chap. 4.

16. Sawyer to Regent Roscoe O. Bonisteel, January 19, 1956, box 21, MMPP.

17. Sawyer to Vice President Marvin L. Niehuss, January 28, 1956, box 21, MMPP.

18. James C. Meem, Chief, Nuclear Energy Staff, Office of Industrial Resources, to Kerr, January 29, 1959, box 21, MMPP.

19. Scott to Gomberg, July 6, 1956, box 21, MMPP.

20. Gomberg to C. W. Flesher, Director, Office of Industrial Resources, ICA, June 29, 1956, box 21, MMPP.

21. USOM was the ICA's overseas office, which simultaneously functioned as the US economic mission in that country.

22. "Contract between International Cooperation Administration and the University of Michigan," November 6, 1956, box 21, MMPP. The "Special Consultants" at that point were H. J. Gomberg, professor of nuclear and electrical engineering and assistant director of Michigan Memorial Phoenix Project; L. E. Brownell, professor of chemical and metallurgical engineering and supervisor of the Fission Products Laboratory; H. A. Ohlgren, professor of chemical and metallurgical engineering; John Villella, research associate, parasitology, use of irradiation in arresting development of parasites; Wayne Meinke, assistant professor of chemistry.

23. Arthur G. Stevens, Director of Personnel, ICA, to President [of the university], November 12, 1958, box 21, MMPP.

24. Eisenhower, "Address at the Centennial Commencement."

25. "University of Michigan–ICA Nuclear Energy Project ICA-W-209; Quarterly Progress Report No. 1," February 21, 1957, box 21, MMPP.

26. Kerr to Frank, July 31, 1959, box 21, MMPP.

27. Kerr to Robert L. Williams, January 22, 1957, box 21, MMPP.

28. Ralph A. Sawyer to Leonard J. Saccio, Acting Director, ICA, June 12, 1959, box 21, MMPP.

29. Kerr and Whipple, *A General Atomic Energy Program*, n.d., box 21, MMPP.

30. Kerr to Gomberg, March 29, 1960, and attached table, box 21, MMPP.

31. ICA (Saccio) to USOM, November 12, 1959, box 21, MMPP.

32. Wayne Meinke to H. D. Bengelsdorf, Division of International Affairs, AEC, January 7, 1963, box 15, MMPP.

33. W. Kenneth Davis, Director, Division of Reactor Development, AEC, to Harlan Hatcher, December 5, 1956, box 21, MMPP.

34. Henry J. Gomberg, Assistant Director, MMPP, to Theodore J. Wilson, Assistant Chief, Training and Technical Aids Division, Office of Industrial Resources, ICA, November 17, 1959, box 21, MMPP.

35. "Enrollment Breakdown for Fall Semester (1957)," box 15, MMPP.

36. Gomberg to R. G. Taecker, Director, International School of Nuclear Science and Engineering, Argonne National Laboratory, October 4, 1957, box 15, MMPP; Kerr to Gomberg, January 19, 1959, box 20, MMPP; I. E. Wallen, Acting

192   SCIENTIFIC KNOWLEDGE

Chief, Training and Education Branch, Division of International Affairs, AEC, to Sawyer, November 22, 1957, box 21, MMPP.

37. "The University of Michigan A.I.D. Nuclear Energy Project, AID-W-209: Final Report," December 1965, box 22, MMPP.

38. H. J. Gomberg, "Nuclear Engineering: The Impact on Engineering Education," Conference on Science and Technology for Deans of Engineering, September 9–12, 1957, box 20, MMPP.

39. "Phoenix Project Assistance to the United States Atoms-for-Peace-Program," n.d., box 21, MMPP.

40. G. Hoyt Whipple and William Kerr, "A Generalized Atomic Energy Program: Submitted for Inclusion in the Second International Conference on the Peaceful Uses of Atomic Energy, Geneva, Switzerland," September 1–13, 1958, box 21, MMPP.

41. Gomberg to Edmund A. Cumminskey, November 6, 1956; "Approved Budget February 1, 1962–January 31, 1963, Contract No. AID-W-209," box 21, MMPP. For example, the ICA (AID) budget for the Phoenix Project consultants for the one-year period from February 1, 1962, to January 31, 1963, was US$75,000.

42. Kerr to Ralph J. Strom, Nuclear Energy Staff, Office of Industrial Resources, ICA, August 2, 1957, box 21, MMPP.

43. Kerr to Richard B. Palmer, Assistant Deputy Director for Operations, Interregional Operations Staff, ICA, July 7, 1961, box 22, MMPP.

44. *National Tsing Hua University Bulletin, 1984–1985*, 5.

45. Huang, *Nuclear Energy and Tsing Hua*, 2.

46. Ralph A. Sawyer and William Kerr, "Report on Visit to Formosa," May 1959, box 21, MMPP. The 1955 bilateral agreement was amended on March 4, 1959, to permit the transfer of special nuclear materials, including "260 grams of plutonium to be used in preparing plutonium-beryllium sources, and enough enriched uranium for construction of a fission chamber for use in the research reactor."

47. Huang, *Nuclear Energy and Ting Hua*, 9. Tai Power Company (also known as the Taiwan Power Company) is a state-owned company established in 1946 by unifying the Japanese colonial power programs in Taiwan. Chinese names are spelled in alphabetical letters as they were shown in US government records in those days, which may differ from present-day Pinyin.

48. "ISNSE Alumni: Victor Chen-hua Cheng," *Argonne News Bulletin* 4, no. 1 (January 1962): 9.

49. National Tsing Hua University Library website, accessed October 6, 2020, http://archives.lib.nthu.edu.tw/sun/life.htm.

50. Professor Peir Jinn-Jer, interview with the author, May 5, 2023, National Tsing Hua University.

51. Sawyer and Kerr, "Report on Visit to Formosa." Zheng was later "loaned" to Japan for six months to work on the JRR-2 (the first Japanese research reactor) and CP-5 (a US reactor imported to Japan).

52. "AEC Tokyo jimusho o kaisetsu: Shochō niwa Pennington shi" [AEC opens Tokyo office: Mr. Pennington appointed director], *Atomic Industrial News* [*Genshiryoku Sangyo Shimbun*], November 25, 1957.

53. Pennington to A. A. Wells, Director, Division of International Affairs (TOAEC 19), January 14, 1959, box 23, MMPP.

54. Sawyer and Kerr, "Report on Visit to Formosa."

55. Pennington to Wells, January 14, 1959.

56. In-king Lee to George F. Mahoney Jr., Project Manager, Industrial Training Division, ICA, June 21, 1958, RG 469, Entry P185, box 2, National Archives at College Park (hereafter NACP).

57. Haraldson, ICA Taipei, to ICA, June 12, 1958; In-king Lee to George F. Mahoney Jr., ICA, August 18, 1958; In-king Lee to George F. Mahoney Jr., ICA, May 10, 1959, RG 469, Entry P185, box 2, NACP.

58. George F. Mahoney Jr., "Note for File," September 24, 1959, RG 469, Entry P185, box 2, NACP. The four companies that declined the ICA's application were General Electric Company, AMF Atomics, the Babcock & Wilcox Company, and Atomic International.

59. Sawyer and Kerr, "Report on Visit to Formosa."

60. H. C. Schmid, ICA Taipei, to ICA Washington, January 21, 1959, box 23, MMPP.

61. *Argonne News Bulletin International* 4, no. 2 (April 1962): 2, 8.

62. R. A. Sawyer and W. Kerr, "Recommendations Concerning the Nuclear Science Program at Tsing Hua University," (draft), n.d., box 23, MMPP.

63. Sawyer and Kerr, "Report on Visit to Formosa."

64. Sawyer and Kerr.

65. Sawyer and Kerr.

66. Kerr to Schmid, May 19, 1959, box 23, MMPP.

67. Kerr to Harry C. Schmid, Chief, Education Division, ICA Mutual Security Mission to China, May 29, 1959, box 23, MMPP.

68. Schmid to Kerr, June 19, 1959, box 23, MMPP; Henry Frank, "Report on Visit to Formosa," October 13, 1959, box 21, MMPP.

69. Frank, "Report on Visit to Formosa"; Frank, "Recommendations concerning the Staffing Problem of the Institute of Nuclear Science, National Tsing Hua University," and cover letter from Frank, Consultant to ICA, to William Newfeld, Acting Chief Education Adviser, August 25, 1959, box 21, MMPP.

70. Frank, "Report on Visit to Formosa."

71. Schmid to Kerr, October 27, 1959, box 23, MMPP.

72. Herbert Pennington to A. A. Wells, Director, Division of International Affairs, AEC, December 9, 1959, box 23, MMPP.

73. Schmid to Kerr, August 16, 1960, box 23, MMPP.

74. Schmid to Kerr, September 12, 1960, box 23, MMPP.

75. K. H. Sun, ICA Consultant to Taiwan, University of Michigan Contract, Manager, Radiation and Nucleonics Lab., Westinghouse Electric Corporation, to Harry C. Schmid, November 4, 1960, box 23, MMPP.

76. Kerr to Schmid, "Preliminary Report on Visit to Taiwan," October 17, 1960, box 23, MMPP.

77. Kerr to Schmid, December 29, 1960, box 23, MMPP.

78. Charles W. Ricker, IAEA/ICA Consultant, to Harry C. Schmid, Chief, ICA, May 2, 1961, box 23, MMPP.

79. Kerr to Schmid, May 17, 1961, box 23, MMPP.

80. Kerr to Schmid, June 15, 1961, box 23, MMPP.

81. Kerr to Schmid, June 15, 1961.

82. Huang, *Nuclear Energy and Tsing Hua*, 11, 14.

83. "Letter from the Ambassador to the Republic of China (Wright) to the Assistant Secretary of State for Far Eastern Affairs (Hilsman)," December 19, 1963, *FRUS, 1961–1963*, document 197.

84. Chairman, AEC, to David E. Bell, Administrator, AID, November 2, 1965, RG 59, China Affairs box 4 FSE1301 Nuclear Power Development, NACP.

85. "Nationalist China: Science," April 1974, (CIA, National Intelligence Survey), Digital National Security Archives, accessed May 8, 2020, https:// search.proquest.com/dnsa_ci/docview/1679088447/FFCF1444A0C34E28PQ /3?accountid=11929.

86. Huang, *Nuclear Energy and Tsing Hua*, 14.

87. Huang, 201, 218.

88. "United States and Republic of China Sign Agreement for Cooperation concerning Civil Uses of Atomic Energy," April 4, 1972, RG 59, China Affairs box 14 SE—Atomic Energy Agreement, NACP.

89. Greene, "KMT and Science and Technology," 8.

90. Fuller and Rubinstein, *Technology Transfer*, 2–4. For the influences of overseas Chinese engineers on the development of the IT industry in Taiwan, see Yu Zhou and Jinn-Yuh Hsu (chap. 5), "Divergent Engagements: Comparing the Roles and Strategies of Taiwanese and Mainland Chinese Returnee Entrepreneurs in the IT Industry."

REFERENCES

Primary Sources

Eisenhower, Dwight D. "Address at the Centennial Commencement of Pennsylvania State University." June 11, 1955. American Presidency Project. https://www.presidency.ucsb.edu/documents/address-the-centennial -commencement-pennsylvania-state-university.

Foreign Relations of the United States (FRUS), 1952–1954. Vol. 2, part 2, *National Security Affairs.* Washington, DC: Government Printing Office, 1984. https://history.state.gov/historicaldocuments/frus1952-54v02p2.

Foreign Relations of the United States (FRUS), 1955–1957. Vol. 20, *Regulation of Armaments; Atomic Energy,* Washington, DC: Government Printing Office, 1990. https://history.state.gov/historicaldocuments/frus1955-57v20.

Foreign Relations of the United States (FRUS), 1961–1963. Vol. 22, *Northeast Asia.* Washington, DC: Government Printing Office, 1996. https://history.state.gov/historicaldocuments/frus1961-63v22.

Michigan Memorial Phoenix Project records: 1947–2003, Bentley Historical Library, University of Michigan.

RG 59, General Records of the Department of State, National Archives at College Park.

RG 326, Records of the Atomic Energy Commission, National Archives at Chicago.

RG 469, Records of the US Foreign Assistance Agencies, National Archives at College Park.

Secondary Sources

Cullather, Nick. *The Hungry World: America's Cold War Battle against Poverty in Asia.* Cambridge, MA: Harvard University Press, 2010.

Elkind, Jessica. *Aid under Fire: Nation Building and the Vietnam War.* Lexington: University Press of Kentucky, 2016.

Engerman, David C. *The Price of Aid: The Economic Cold War in India.* Cambridge, MA: Harvard University Press, 2018.

Fuller, Douglas B., and Murray A. Rubinstein, eds. *Technology Transfer between the US, China and Taiwan: Moving Knowledge.* London: Routledge, 2013.

Greene, J. Megan. "The KMT and Science and Technology, 1927–1980." In *Technology Transfer between the US, China and Taiwan: Moving Knowledge,* edited by Douglas B. Fuller and Murray A. Rubinstein, 7–24. London: Routledge, 2013.

———. *The Origins of the Developmental State in Taiwan: Science Policy and the Quest for Modernization.* Cambridge, MA: Harvard University Press, 2008.

Hamblin, Jacob Darwin. *The Wretched Atom: America's Global Gamble with Peaceful Nuclear Technology.* New York: Oxford University Press, 2021.

Huang, Jun-Ming, ed. *Nuclear Energy and Tsing Hua.* Hsinchu, Taiwan: National Tsing Hua University Press, 2011.

Kaufman, Burton I. *Trade and Aid: Eisenhower's Foreign Economic Policy, 1953–1961.* Baltimore: Johns Hopkins University Press, 1982.

Krige, John. "Techno-Utopian Dreams, Techno-Political Realities: The Education of Desire for the Peaceful Atom." In *Utopia/Dystopia: Conditions of Historical Possibility,* edited by Michael D. Gordin, Helen Tilley, and Gyan Prakash, 151–75. Princeton, NJ: Princeton University Press, 2010.

Lee Wei-Chen. "Amerika-gasshūkoku no enjo to Taiwan: Keizai jiritsuka no michi o tadotte" [The US aid and Taiwan: The way toward economic independence]. In *Reisen henyō-ki no kokusai-kaihatsu enjo to Asia: 1960-nendai o tou* [Overseas development aid and Asia in the Cold War in transition: Inquiry into the 1960s], edited by Shōichi Watanabe, 273–96. Kyoto: Minerva Shobo, 2017.

Lin, James. "Martyrs of Development: Taiwanese Agrarian Development and the Republic of Vietnam, 1959–1975." *Cross-Currents: East Asian History and Culture Review* 9, no. 1 (2020): 67–106.

———. "Sowing Seeds and Knowledge: Agricultural Development in the US, Taiwan, and the World, 1949–1975." *East Asian Science, Technology and Society (EASTS)* 9 (June 2015): 127–49.

Moriguchi Tsuchiya, Yuka. *Science, Technology, and the Cultural Cold War in Asia: From Atoms for Peace to Space Flight*. London: Routledge, 2022.

National Tsing Hua University. *National Tsing Hua University Bulletin, 1984–1985*. Hsinchu, Taiwan: National Tsing Hua University, n.d.

Osgood, Kenneth. *Total Cold War: Eisenhower's Secret Propaganda Battle at Home and Abroad*. Kansas City: University Press of Kansas, 2006.

Shikata, Shunsuke. "1950 nendai ni okeru beikoku no taiwan seisaku to kakyō" [The US policy for Taiwan in the 1950s and overseas Chinese]. *Amerikashi Kenkyu* [American history] 45 (2022): 97–116.

Simpson, Bradley R. *Economists with Guns: Authoritarian Development and U.S.-Indonesian Relations, 1960–1968*. Stanford, CA: Stanford University Press, 2008.

Tomotsugu, Shinsuke. "Ajia genshiryoku center kōsō to sono zasetsu: Eisenhower Seiken no tai Ajia gaikō no ichi danmen" [The Asia Nuclear Center plan and its collapse: One aspect of the Eisenhower administration's Asia diplomacy]. *Kokusai Seiji* [International relations] 163 (January 2011): 14–27.

———. "The Bandung Conference and the Origins of Japan's Atoms for Peace Aid Program for Asian Countries." In *The Age of Hiroshima*, edited by Michael D Gordin and John Ikenberry, 109–28. Princeton, NJ: Princeton University Press, 2020.

Watanabe, Shōichi, ed. *Reisen henyō-ki no kokusai-kaihatsu enjo to Asia: 1960-nendai o tou* [Overseas development aid and Asia in the Cold War in transition: Inquiry into the 1960s]. Kyoto: Minerva Shobo, 2017.

Wolfe, Audra J. *Freedom's Laboratory: The Cold War Struggle for the Soul of Science*. Baltimore: Johns Hopkins University Press, 2018.

Zwigenberg, Ran. *Hiroshima: The Origins of Global Memory Culture*. Cambridge: Cambridge University Press, 2014.

AUTHOR BIO

YUKA TSUCHIYA MORIGUCHI is Professor of American History at Kyoto University. She is author of *Science, Technology and the Cultural Cold War in Asia: From Atoms for Peace to Space Flight* (2022) and many other books and articles on US cultural/science diplomacy during the Cold War.

SEVEN

REDISCOVERY OF A COLD WAR SPACE

The Politics of Science in the DMZ
Ecological Survey

MANYONG MOON

TRANSLATED BY REBECCA LEE PATERSON

INTRODUCTION

After its liberation in 1945 and subsequent division in the wake of the Korean War (1950–53), the Korean Peninsula found itself situated on the front lines of the Cold War.[1] The Korean War served as a catalyst that brought the Cold War from the imagined into a tangible reality.[2] In fact, nowhere was the impact of the Cold War more intense or destructive than on the Korean Peninsula.[3] In spite of this, South Korea took advantage of the geopolitical conditions created by the Cold War to achieve rapid economic growth. Amid these events, South Korea's science and technology also demonstrated quantitative growth over a short period of time, owing to aggressive government policies.[4] It was the scientists themselves who played a central role in this process; they stressed the importance of science and technology promotion even before the government rolled out a full-fledged science and technology policy, and actively worked to develop their own sectors and institutions in line with government policy trends. As they turned their aspirations and government policies into reality, the international environment, or, in other words, scientific collaboration, also proved to be an important factor, both directly and indirectly.[5] Support for science and technology, both practical support and the provision of know-how, was in many cases proposed and promoted against the backdrop of the Cold War. The Cold War is now widely viewed in terms beyond the arms and propaganda races of the US and the Soviet Union, in that it also encompassed education, scholarship, art, knowledge production, and interpersonal exchange—a "cultural turn" had occurred.[6] Under this framework, science and technology have also come to be understood in a new light.[7]

In reality, after the Second World War, science and technological development, much more so than any other field, assumed a central role in capturing the hearts and minds of people, not only in South Korea but in many Third World countries.[8] However, particularly in South Korea, which, as a divided state, was at the forefront of the Cold War, this legacy persists and has left numerous traces in science and technology. For instance, among the scientists featured in Audra Wolfe's recent works on science and the Cold War is Harold Jefferson Coolidge (1904–85), who headed the Pacific Science Board of the US National Academy of Sciences and is a well-known figure in the field of biological sciences in South Korea.[9]

This chapter traces the history of the US–South Korean collaborative ecological survey of the demilitarized zone (DMZ), which began with ties to Coolidge, and through this, attempts to clarify the different positions taken by the South Korean and American biologists, as well as the perspective from which the distanced North Korea viewed the region. In her recent ethnographic fieldwork in the South Korean DMZ, Eleana J. Kim has shed light on the complex interactions between humans and the nonhuman ecology.[10] Lisa Brady has emphasized the environmental and scientific value of the DMZ, claiming that the scientific fieldwork, which began in 1965, transformed it into a scientific landscape.[11] Jaehwan Hyun has suggested paying attention to the complex politics revealed in the collaborative project and noting the dissonance between the American and Korean scientists during the ecological survey.[12] Their arguments resonate strongly with the author, who would therefore like to focus on the intentions of Korean biologists and the different perspectives of the two Koreas over the ecological space called the DMZ. Up until this point, there have been numerous studies on South Korean science and technology against the backdrop of the Cold War. By focusing on the particular scientific discipline of biology, and in particular, the joint US-Korean DMZ ecological survey, which came to be one part of public relations and diplomacy of the 1960s, I hope to add one more narrative to further the understanding of the relationship between the Cold War and South Korean science.

THE SOUTH KOREAN SCIENTISTS'
POSTCOLONIAL DESIRES

Upon their liberation in 1945, the South Korean people launched various initiatives to rebuild their nation. Predictably, science and technology experts emphasized that the promotion of their disciplines was of utmost priority. It was feared that even if the country appeared to achieve independence, if this was not backed with technology, the nation would, in actuality, be relegated to a colony-like position. While their arguments consisted of slightly different initiatives, a common thread ran through them: the desire to establish an administrative structure capable of systematically promoting science and technology policies, to establish facilities for research and development, and to strengthen science and technology education.[13]

However, in reality, the issue of science was not a high priority among the government's policy concerns. Scientists' plans for the promotion of their fields were largely detached from reality, appearing somewhat ivory-towerish and idealistic in character, and as such, somewhat distant from the more immediate concerns of a government in the midst of social disorder and economic hardship. Nevertheless, because the development of personnel with high-level expertise in science and technology had been greatly restricted during the period of Japanese colonial rule, the US military government and the South Korean government prioritized the expansion of science and technology in higher education, establishing national universities with departments of science and engineering.

On June 8, 1948, with the foundation of a government imminent, leading scientists gathered together to hold a roundtable discussion on the science and technology needed for the new government's national reconstruction and its future, as well as on the societal role of scientists and engineers. They pointed out that science in South Korea was lagging behind the international standard and emphasized that its promotion was essential, above all else, for rebuilding the nation. The National Science Museum's butterfly specialist Seok Ju-myeong, participating in this discussion, showed remarkable confidence in saying, "When it comes to fauna and flora, there is a local quality to them. So, while this may sound ridiculous, it is unlikely even after 10 or 20 years that foreign scholars in the physics and chemistry fields will view Korean scientists as 'teachers,' and pose questions to them. However, at least in biology, there would be much for visiting foreign researchers to ask us, and to learn from us."[14]

Seok's confidence was based on his accumulation of remarkable research findings.[15] As the biologists were handling the fauna and flora of their native country, they had a fundamental sense of pride in their work when compared to experts in other fields. The participants of the discussion responded with mirth to Seok's statement. However, his personal visions for the future were never realized, as he passed away two years later at the height of the Korean War.

By the mid-1950s, despite continued demands by the scientific and technological community to the government for the promotion of science and technology as part of restoration efforts to repair the damage of the Korean War, government responses left much to be desired. After President Dwight Eisenhower's "Atoms for Peace" speech, South Korea concluded a nuclear cooperation agreement with the US, and while they pushed ahead with nuclear power projects, the South Korean government's expectations for nuclear power were more directed toward practical aims such as the generation of energy.[16] In addition, through the Minnesota Project, and with support from the International Cooperation Administration (ICA), education and research in the faculties of medicine, engineering, and agriculture in Seoul National University took strides in switching to a US-style system.[17] However, because there was a lack of support and policies for basic science, which was considered to be of less practical value, a relative sense of deprivation among the basic scientists began to grow. For example, Seoul National University zoologist Kang Young Sun (1917–99), in his appraisal of scientific circles in 1957, revealed the following regarding the pitiable state of the basic sciences that had not managed to benefit from oversees support from enterprises such as the Minnesota Project: "We should say that the basic branches of natural sciences in our country, having no opportunities to receive foreign aid in terms of equipment amongst other aspects, and not being included in plans for national restoration, have been left in ruins by the Korean War. As a consequence, the scientists working in these areas have been placed in unprecedented adversity."[18] Because of such circumstances, in South Korea basic scientists, including biologists, had to search for their own funding.

In the 1960s, full-scale economic development was promoted, and support for science and technology gradually increased. However, the field of biology, having little to do with industry, fell outside the scope of support. As a result, biologists had to seek new solutions. Among these was to make use of their personal international networks and obtain research grants through international organizations.

Kang Young Sun, regarded as a luminary in zoological circles in South Korea, took advantage of various international networks such as the US Smith Mundt exchange program, the Asia Foundation, the International Atomic Energy Agency (IAEA), the Rockefeller Foundation, and the US National Academy of Sciences to secure a variety of study opportunities and research funding. Through such means, his research trajectory progressed through cytology, human genetics, the genetics of fruit flies, and cancer cell research to expand to wider areas of cell sciences such as fish cell biology.[19] A recent study points out that the research experiences utilized by Kang came from the networks he built during his time studying at the Faculty of Zoology at Hokkaido Imperial University and argues that, as such, he remained unable to rid himself of the legacy of colonialism.[20] However, during Kang's active collaboration with overseas academics, he acquired diverse subject knowledge and know-how, and by passing these on to younger scholars, he strengthened the foundations of South Korean zoology.

In addition, ornithologist Won Pyong-Oh (1929–2020), having shown Coolidge his collection of bird samples and research data during the latter's visit to South Korea in 1960 and having received zealous encouragement, was advised to participate in the twelfth conference of the International Council for Bird Preservation in Japan. Owing to this, Won began academic collaborations with Japanese academics and obtained his PhD from Hokkaido University. In addition, under the supervision of Sidney Dillon Ripley (1913–2001), chair of the International Council for Bird Preservation, he carried out his postdoctoral research.[21] At the time, he was approached by an official of the US State Department inquiring about whether South Korea should be included in a US government–sponsored research project on migratory birds. In response, Won asserted that since most migratory birds traveling south from Manchuria and Siberia pass through Korea, it was natural that the country should be included. As a result, after his return to South Korea, he received funding support from the US for seven years while on the faculty of Kyunghee University. During this time, Won attached aluminum tracking tags to the legs of two hundred thousand birds, spanning 135 species. He recollected that "it was the Japanese academics who helped me brush up on my basic academic skills, and the American scholars who broadened the world of learning."[22] In addition to these examples, there were in fact many cases of biologists embracing new knowledge obtained during overseas training and study, with the overwhelming majority of these biologists heading to the US for these opportunities. Of course, this was not a phenomenon seen only among biologists; it was similar for experts in other fields of science.[23]

In 1963, biologists and geologists organized the Korean Commission for Conservation of Nature and Natural Resources (KCCN). Beginning in 1964 with a comprehensive academic study of Mount Halla, Jeju Island, they surveyed the state of important domestic nature and natural resources and sought to lead the way in their conservation. In 1965, KCCN became a member of the International Union for Conservation of Nature and Natural Resources (IUCN). Participating in the International Biological Program (IBP) from 1965, KCCN planned to make great strides in the biological world by carrying out related research. This is an example of how a group of biologists promoted advances in their discipline through international support projects, rather than at the level of individual scholars.

The IBP was an international research project that aimed to improve biological productivity and the welfare of human beings, and between 1964 and 1974, a total of ninety-seven countries participated, directly or indirectly.[24] In line with this, South Korean biologists founded the Committee for the IBP in South Korea, with Kang Young Sun as representative. Yet, despite attempts to dispatch him to represent the country for the first general meeting, held in Paris in July 1964, he could not secure a travel grant and thus was unable to join. Although the IBP was an international research project, the headquarters did not provide direct financial support for the research activities of each individual country. Consequently, member states had to secure their own research funding. Therefore, to guarantee their budget, the Korean IBP committee had to repeatedly request funding from the South Korean government or the Asia Foundation. Although it did fall short of their anticipated 1966 budget of 3 million won, after a "desperate effort by the scholars," they were able to create a research plan based on a meager yearly budget of 400,000 won (US$1,500). Forming seven subcommittees, the researchers began their activities in 1966. The government required the research by the South Korean IBP to contribute to economic development plans, and as a result, the biologists had to adjust their research plans through negotiations with the government.[25] In spite of their meager budget, they "would do their utmost best to protect the image of South Korea and to contribute to the development of the country through the research development of biological resources," and they had to make every effort to maintain good working relationships with various institutions both at home and abroad to secure sparse research funding.[26]

Beginning with their first publication in 1967, the South Korean IBP recorded their research findings in the annual IBP report. The report, which published a total of seven volumes until 1975, was sent to the IBP headquarters in the UK and distributed to member states all over the world. Furthermore, in addition to holding two large-scale symposia for these projects in South Korea, the committee organized the South Korea–Japan IBP seminar and shared research findings by participating in events such as the IBP general assembly and regional meetings. As a result, the IBP provided a good springboard for Korean biologists to make themselves known to the international academic community and to develop their research activities. One of the background factors that led to the government's continued financial support of the IBP Korea Committee, even if the amount of support was not large, was the DMZ ecological survey.

REDISCOVERING THE DMZ THROUGH
ECOLOGICAL SURVEY

With the ceasefire armistice of the Korean War that came into effect on July 27, 1953, a buffer zone based on the military demarcation line, four kilometers wide—two kilometers each north and south of the line—was established to prevent military escalation. This is known as the DMZ.[27] Contrary to its name, there are many soldiers stationed at guard posts around the clock, and countless numbers of land mines are buried on both sides of the boundary.[28] Because of this, the area has also been nicknamed the "heavily militarized zone" or "secretly militarized zone." As human activity is fundamentally restricted in the DMZ, natural ecosystems have been relatively well preserved. As well as being a base for migratory birds such as the red-crowned crane to spend the winter as they pass through the Korean Peninsula, it is home to various precious natural monuments and endangered species such as the Asian black bear, foxes, Siberian musk deer, long-tailed goral, and the Eurasian otter. Hence, the DMZ is also called the largest nature conservation reserve in Asia.

For almost ten years after the DMZ was created, the majority of media articles on the region were stories about the various military conflicts between the North and South. However, in February 1964, an article titled "Wood, Field and Stream: Wildlife in Korean Demilitarized Zone Is Unlikely to Be Disturbed" was published in the *New York Times*. Six days later, a South Korean newspaper published a translation under the title "The Paradise of the Beasts: The DMZ." The original article's author, Oscar A. Godbout (1926–67), worked as an outdoor columnist for the *New York Times* and published articles introducing nature and wildlife from across the globe. It is not clear whether he visited the DMZ, but his article provided a new perspective on the region—a place to encounter the true world of nature, where fauna and flora, with little direct contact with humans, could flourish in peace. The value of the DMZ, which up until this point had been regarded as a dangerous place—as the location of incidents and accidents caused by conflict between heavily armed soldiers and a place where rare contagious diseases (e.g., epidemic hemorrhagic fever) threatened the lives of military personnel—was being shown in a different light. It is uncertain how large a role this report played in the change of perception regarding the DMZ, but there is a strong possibility that it is one reason for the first ecological survey of the DMZ, which began the very next year.

The ecological survey of the DMZ was the outcome of a continued collaboration between South Korean biologists and Harold Jefferson Coolidge, president of the IUCN. Coolidge was also an executive director of the Pacific

Science Board of the US National Academy of Sciences and maintained an intimate relationship with South Korean scholars and their academic institutions. In November 1965, Seoul National University professor Kang Young Sun acted as a mediator in the conferment of an honorary doctorate to Coolidge at the university, and for both of them, this event became the turning point that led to the idea of conducting an ecological survey of the DMZ.[29] This idea roused a considerable amount of interest not only from South Korean biologists but from those in academic circles in the US as well. The South Korean scholars, who had begun to conduct serious research on natural ecosystems through the KCCN, were able to receive support from abroad, with the DMZ survey providing just such an opportunity. While the necessity of research in ecosystem ecology had come to be widely recognized by the IBP, established in 1964, the US seized the opportunity to promote an ecological survey in a region of military significance.

Coolidge and five South Korean scholars carried out a three-day preliminary survey of the area in December 1965, followed by the first ecological survey in the Panchuk Valley, a western region neighboring the DMZ. The next year, Kang visited the US on a four-week short-term training program, taking the preliminary results of this survey with him. On this occasion, he reached an agreement with the Smithsonian Institution regarding the DMZ survey; it included a two-year preliminary study, fully funded by the US to an amount of US$120,000, and the actual survey was to be carried out by the South Korean researchers. After the two-year preliminary survey, it was decided to proceed with a full five-year study.[30]

Owing to this agreement, an "International Conference for the Conservation of Nature and Ecological Survey of Wildlife in the Demilitarized Zone and the Construction of the South Korean Science Museum" was held, and for this occasion, eighteen scholars from the US visited South Korea. Part of the group was to stay eight months in the country to carry out general research on the local birds, wildlife, and plants. For many of the South Korean biologists, this was their first time conducting a long-term research project in collaboration with foreign scholars. In September of the same year, Kang, participating as the South Korean representative for the Pacific Science Conference held in Japan, proposed to adopt the DMZ as a national park, and this was selected as a formal agenda item for the conference.[31] The DMZ was to make its debut in international academic circles as a subject of ecological research, rather than a site of military conflict.

In October 1966, a survey of the area began. This survey was divided across thirteen subject areas and was carried out until August 1968. According to an article at the time, while there existed three DMZs throughout the world, the Korean DMZ held the most value for academic surveys. It was anticipated that these results would provide invaluable data for the scientific world.[32] However, as the DMZ was such a dangerous place, the researchers participating in the survey had to write memorandums indicating that they understood and accepted the risk of whatever accidents may happen. Furthermore, Won Pyong-Oh, the ornithologist who had migrated to the South during the Korean War, was being urged by North Korean propaganda broadcasts to return to the North, where his father, Won Hong-Gu, still lived, and as a result was subject to around-the-clock monitoring by military personnel.[33]

Helmut Buechner (1918–75), head of the Smithsonian Office of Ecology, visited South Korea in November 1967 and announced that there was a plan to support the survey with funding of US$2.8 million. Buechner revealed that he had requested support from the Korean Ministry of Education, the Ministry of Agriculture and Forestry, the Ministry of Science and Technology, and others and received a grant of 10–20 percent of the total cost required to carry out a comprehensive ecological survey of biology, climate, agriculture, and other items, not only in the DMZ but across the whole of South Korea. The aim of the ecological survey was to measure human effects on the environment using the DMZ as a baseline. Therefore, in addition to the DMZ, surveys had to be conducted in other regions of the Korean Peninsula that had been significantly affected by human activities. Furthermore, a Korean Center for Environmental Studies would need to be established to supervise the plan to promote group education and scientific activities for middle and high school teachers and their students and to provide scholarships and opportunities to South Korean students to study abroad in the US. To achieve such lofty goals, a long-term project of around twenty-five years was inevitable.[34] First, Buechner, other Smithsonian Institution researchers, and Pennsylvania State University entomologist Kim Ke-Chung acted as consultants for the project. They received the five-year research plan from the South Korean researchers and even went as far as to draw up tangible plans for promotion after reviewing a selection of twenty-seven research topics. This indicates that the project was not just an ecological survey of the DMZ but a big-picture attempt to transplant US-style education and research methods in biology in general, including ecology, to South Korea.

However, in 1968, with increasingly frequent military provocation from North Korea, plans for the ecological survey of the DMZ made no further progress; as evidenced by a succession of incidents, including the Pueblo Incident, military tensions had heightened between the North and South. As a result, after the completion of the preliminary survey in September 1968, the Smithsonian canceled the five-year study because of safety concerns for their researchers—the military Cold War had derailed plans for the Cultural Cold War.

However, according to the Smithsonian Institution's yearbook, the issue of securing funding, together with military tensions, caused the cessation of the DMZ project.[35] In 1967, the year the preliminary survey went ahead, the so-called CIA scandal occurred, and the agency's omnidirectional strategy for the Cultural Cold War was exposed to the public.[36] In the aftermath of this incident, the Asia Foundation, the Ford Foundation, and others, which had been prime candidates to sponsor the DMZ ecological survey, became hesitant to provide support. The Smithsonian, unable to find suitable supporters, had no choice but to cancel the DMZ project.

The final report comprising the two-year survey's results was submitted to the Smithsonian in September 1968.[37] In its preface, Buechner intimated that the project was inspired by Coolidge and that he had considered the possibility of converting the area into a national park in the event that North and South Korea were reunified. In part 3 of the report, a compilation of fifteen individual thematic reports by the South Korean scholars who participated in the survey was organized according to discipline. Interestingly, included in the final report, in addition to an evaluation of the project in its entirety, was an extremely harsh evaluation of the individual research reports conducted by the South Korean researchers. Kim Ke-Chung considered the two-year preliminary project to be somewhat disappointing and asserted that the cause of this lay in the South Korean researchers' lack of scientific competence and the Smithsonian's inaccurate judgment of the academic environment at the time.[38] In other words, the assessment was that the Korean academic community was not ready to carry out sufficient preparations to undertake such a project. In fact, what the Smithsonian had anticipated went beyond a simple survey of the biota of the DMZ and was rather a systematic ecological analysis that applied the concepts of ecosystem ecology. However, the understanding of ecology and ecosystem research was not particularly advanced in academic circles in South Korea. Moreover, between the research teams of the US and South Korea there existed not only a gap in academic standards and interests but a difference in culture too; the Americans were perplexed by the strict hierarchy between Korean academic advisers and their students.

Science historian Hyun Jaehwan, who analyzed in detail the letters exchanged between the researchers participating in the ecological survey of the DMZ, revealed that during the process of promoting the project, the cultural gaps manifested between the two sides in various ways, such as the struggle for leadership and the generation gap between the established South Korean biologists who had studied in Japan and the young South Korean biologists who were active in the US.[39] Edwin Tyson (1920–76) of the Smithsonian expressed his dissatisfaction with the political and sectarian nature of the South Korean biologists and with their problems communicating in English during the early stages of the project. To mediate this, Kim Ke-Chung, born in 1934, who was both knowledgeable of South Korean culture and fluent in English, was hired as a curator. After graduating from the Department of Biology at Seoul National University, Kim had studied abroad in the US and had been a student of Kang's during his time in school and thus was unable to make strong or direct requests of his former mentor. Consequently, Kim's position and role in the research team did not go as planned, according to accounts from the American side. Also, the South Korean biologists, who had an abundance of knowledge and experience in South Korean nature, found it difficult to be subjected to unilateral instruction from the American academics. Kang hoped to distribute as equally as possible, among the scientists who participated under his leadership, the research funding he had finally secured. In the eyes of the US scholars, Kang may have appeared to be a stubborn old scholar obsessed with money, but he likely considered himself a representative of South Korean academic circles in which he had great pride. Tyson believed that he could not pass over leadership rights to the South Korean researchers, as the ecological survey of the DMZ was not a foreign aid program but a project for which the Smithsonian held responsibility in the allocation of research funds.[40] Such conflict, in the end, led to a breakdown in the aid that the South Korean government had been willing to provide. This shows that while on one hand the DMZ project was furthered through international collaborative research, on the other hand the project was strongly affected by the mutually divergent interests of those participating.

Recently, sociologist Kim In-soo presented a paper that made clear how the US attempted to control South Korean scholars and academia through their support of research activities in the field of agricultural economics.[41] In his paper, Kim adroitly demonstrates how the asymmetrical academic authority that was Cold War America, armed with intellectual networks, research funding, and opportunities for training, had regulated and controlled, at an internal intellectual level, progress in the social sciences of South Korea and the creation of knowledge in the field. Similarly, many studies have addressed the impact and transforming influence that academic support from private foundations has had on academic knowledge and scholarly discourse in the field of social science and policy and on policymaking itself.[42] In contrast, there has been relatively little of this type of research in the fields of science and technology, including medicine, in South Korea. This is because, first of all, scientific disciplines themselves have rarely become the object of critical analysis. Second, because science and technology are often perceived as universal and objective, developing countries tend to accept science and technology from developed countries so naturally and matter-of-factly that such knowledge transfer itself has rarely been problematized. However, the case in this chapter reveals that the process of US academic aid, even in the field of science and technology, involved forced importation of specific knowledge and methodologies to the Korean academic community; it did not simply introduce advanced science and technology in a smooth, unquestioned manner.[43] This aspect particularly stood out in biology, a field greatly affected by features of the native fauna and flora.[44]

In reality, problems such as delays due to cultural differences during the process of international collaboration in developing countries were not uncommon. However, US and Korean scholars did not take this reality into account when conducting the project for the ecological survey of the DMZ. Moreover, the plan to bring in a curator to act as a mediator was proposed late in the project and the curator did not play an appropriate role given the Korean culture of seniority and the hierarchy of master and disciple. This shows that for overseas technical support to be successful, the recipients' skill in absorbing information is important, but equally important is the providers' ability to communicate.

What were the South Korean biologists trying to achieve through the ecological survey of the DMZ? Even though the survey was not completed, it had presented an opportunity to discover a new aspect of a problematic region: the DMZ had transformed from a conflict zone into an ecological treasure house. Furthermore, by carrying out collaborative research with global institutions, even if they could not receive appraisals that satisfied them, the South Korean biologists were able to demonstrate the value of their research activities to the South Korean government and society at large. With the inauguration of a multinational project like the IBP ahead of them, the biologists, anxious at having been unable to secure financial resources, were fortunate to receive support from the Smithsonian Institution and thereby gain the opportunity to conduct the survey. In contrast to the attempts of the American researchers to use the DMZ survey as an opportunity to convert South Korean ecology and biology to the US style, the South Korean researchers sought to use the survey as an opportunity to mobilize support and social recognition for their research activities.

A DIFFERENT PERSPECTIVE ON THE DMZ

In 1972, the two Koreas announced a joint statement on the terms of agreement for unification, and with this thawing of relations, interest in the DMZ was reignited. The English-language report outlining the results of the DMZ survey to the Smithsonian in 1968 was published in Korean in June 1972. The report was titled "A Study on Natural Resources in the DMZ," and it was the first domestic report of which a large part consisted of information about the fauna and flora and the ecological environment of the areas neighboring the DMZ.[45] The Korean-language version was not a direct translation of the Smithsonian report; it reordered the contents without the analytical results of the ecological survey and focused primarily on listing the fauna and flora that inhabited the DMZ, divided into plant resources, animal resources, and geological surveys. The biologists named their version "A Study on Natural Resources," in place of "the ecological survey," to emphasize the utility of their research. As mentioned above, in their support of the IBP, the government had requested that the biologists participate in developing the economy. The title expressed their intention to respond to such a request. One of the reasons for there being two reports with differing titles and content, although based on the same survey, was that readership would be different, but perhaps the chief reason was that the tone of the Korean version emphasized that research and conservation of the area were of high value because of the abundance of wildlife. Therefore, issues such as changes in the ecological environment fifteen years after the war, and the restoration of devastated plant life, were put off until later.

Kang, named among the report's authors, stated that "in order to solve all problems peacefully, beginning with issue of the unification of the North and South, our first priority is to use the truce line for peace between the two sides."[46] In addition, he insisted that the DMZ was not only academically relevant but also closely related to the livelihoods of the South Korean people, as there was a possibility of finding a species of tree among those that grow in the area that may be suitable for the land in the South. In his conclusion, while he proposed to mobilize North and South Korean scientists to conduct a joint DMZ survey, he also expressed his hopes that South Korea would continue the research alone, should the intended collaboration prove to be impossible.

Soon after, Kang received a request from the Board of National Unification to present an overview of the wild animals in North and South Korea.[47] In this report, he drew on previous studies to produce a list of the mammals, birds, reptiles, amphibians, and freshwater fish inhabiting the two countries and presented the endemic species that could only be found in the two halves of the peninsula. At the time, against the backdrop of the July 4 North-South Korea Joint Statement, the Board of National Unification requested reports about a number of topics for the purpose of preparing for the reunification and promoting understanding of North Korea. The biologists, too, had a role in this. Although awkwardly described as "natural resources," the fauna and flora of North and South Korea soon became a matter of concern for the government; this positive influence was brought about by the ecological survey of the DMZ.

After that, Kang announced more concrete plans for collaborative research between the North and South concerning the natural resources of the DMZ.[48] This included a master plan to develop together the central area of the Mount Taebaek Range connected by Mount Seorak, Hyangnobong Peak, and Mount Geumgang as a national park, to lay the groundwork to create a world-renowned nature preserve, and to conduct a general academic survey lasting for three years. Specifically, the North and South were to form survey teams of eighty-four people each, organized into five groups consisting of twenty-three teams of zoologists, botanists, ecologists, geologists, and landscapers. A plan was proposed to create a joint committee headed by the survey and for group leaders to discuss important matters. This report was the first to incorporate a tangible plan for a joint ecological survey of the DMZ. However, as relations between the North and South once again deteriorated, further discussions became impossible. Half a century later, as of 2024, this proposal has yet to be realized.

However, on the basis of the biologists' proposal for a follow-up survey on the biota of the DMZ, in 1972, the Bureau of Cultural Property of the Ministry of Culture and Information made a request to the KCCN for another study.[49] Accepting this request, thirty-three scholars revisited the four locations surveyed in 1966. The results were published in 1975 under the title "The Report on the Scientific Survey of Areas near the DMZ."[50] The research team considered the DMZ and neighboring areas to be "another world—under strict control and isolated as a closed off area governed solely under the providence of nature," and again emphasized that the region covering Mount Seorak, Hyangnobong Peak, and Mount Geumgang should be designated a national park. Moreover, Kang insisted that research concerning the wildlife surrounding the DMZ become the foundation of the entirety of South Korea's research on wildlife. His claim was that, because the species of a given area show changes when the region is left in its natural state, untouched by humans, the biota of the DMZ was useful for biogeography and biological colony research beyond the dimension of diversity. Of course, the research team also recognized that this area was not completely isolated from human influence, but they nevertheless believed that the DMZ could play a role as a type of ecological testing site and fieldwork laboratory.

In this way, the ecological surveys of the DMZ conducted up until the 1970s received support from the Bureau of Cultural Property of the Ministry of Culture and Public Information and were carried out under promotion by constituent members of the KCCN. Since the ecological environment of the DMZ was preserved in such good condition, the Ministry of Culture and Public Information, which managed natural monuments, accepted both the biologists' argument that it should be managed as a nature reserve and also the need for follow-up research. As a result, the ecological survey of the DMZ achieved the biologists' intended results. The findings also showed a progression from a simple listing of species to research about changes in the ecosystem. Thus, this research tells the story of how the DMZ survey became the foundation that strengthened the research capabilities of South Korean biologists: the DMZ was no longer solely a space marred by violence or a barren wasteland—it had become a place of academic exploration. From 1980 onward, South Korea continuously voiced their opinion, based on this survey, that the DMZ should be preserved as a site of ecological conservation.

However, the view of North Korea, which also held its own side of the DMZ, was one of extreme indifference. North Korea viewed the DMZ through an exclusively dictionary-definition stance, considering it a type of buffer zone on which both sides of a war agree to not station military power. Narratives treating the DMZ as an area of species diversity, ecology, and natural conservation are almost unheard of in the North Korean literature.[51] For North Korea, the DMZ was an outcome of the ceasefire and merely a buffer zone designated to avoid any kind of military conflict. Therefore, it was nothing more than a symbol of ethnic demarcation and a legacy of times of conflict that needed to be removed quickly. As a result, they vehemently oppose the idea of preserving the ecology of the DMZ, regarding it as a criminal attempt to perpetuate ethnic division. For example, in 2004, through talks between spokesmen for the Committee for the Peaceful Reunification of the Fatherland, North Korea made the following criticism of the South Korean government's plans for attempting to register the DMZ as a world heritage site: "[The DMZ] is a symbol of the misery and pain of ethnic division, an area of intense military confrontation between the North and South. To attempt to register this demilitarized area as some kind of 'legacy' is a reckless act of nonsense against the people."[52] The spokesman continued, regarding the attempt to register the DMZ as a world heritage site and to open it as an area for international tourism as "thoughtless conduct against the people and their unification which seeks to eternalize the division of our people" and asserting that "the military line of the DMZ is not a subject for preservation, but an object whose very existence should be done away with as quickly as possible so that our people can freely travel between the North and South."[53] North Korea took the stance that other political issues such as the national sea border at the five islands in the Yellow Sea should be resolved together in order to agree to the preservation of the DMZ. In other words, until the present day, the DMZ has remained solely a subject of political and military discussion to North Korea. They regarded the ecological survey of the DMZ, too, with purely political scrutiny.

Even if North Korea has not connected the DMZ to issues regarding ecosystems, it has nevertheless repeatedly shown interest in the natural environment and the conservation of ecology. In 1992, they joined the Convention on Biological Diversity, becoming a formal member state in 1994. In 1998, in cooperation with the Global Environment Facility, they created and implemented the "Strategy and Action Plan for the Biological Diversity of the Democratic People's Republic of Korea." In 2003, following the six standards for classification set by the IUCN, the North designated conservation areas that, according to data from 2005, comprised a total 234 zones.[54] Furthermore, they joined the Ramsar Treaty in 2018.

Currently, North Korea still does not include the DMZ as a specified area for the conservation of nature. However, the "Anbyon project," [55] which aimed to protect the red-crowned crane, demonstrated North Korea's interest in conservation. So there is much room for North and South Korea to explore ways of working together through the medium of biology, with a particular focus on the DMZ. Even though the two sides' perspectives of the DMZ remain in conflict, it also remains entirely possible for both sides to see eye to eye through a joint project in biology.

CONCLUSION

The DMZ, the legacy of the fierce conflict that was the Korean War, is a prohibited land simmering with military tension. A generation has passed since the end of the Cold War, but the DMZ still bisects the Korean Peninsula. It was because of the ecological surveys that the DMZ, a region previously regarded as a powder keg, began to attract fresh attention due to its ecological value in the latter half of the 1960s. Although the planned large-scale survey did not eventuate, on the basis of the preliminary survey alone, the DMZ found new potential as a treasure house of wildlife and an academic space for ecological research. Owing to this, while visible developments are yet to be made, the DMZ was expected to perhaps become a seed of peace for the future.

The first ecological survey of the DMZ was the outcome of both the South Korean biologists' search for supporters and the Smithsonian's plans to induct South Korean biological research and education into a US-style framework through the medium of ecology. The fact that the US Air Force Office of Scientific Research (AFOSR) provided funding for the preliminary survey suggests that this project could not break away from the grasp of the militaristic Cold War. Through an ecological survey of an area of particular military significance and with the expansion of "ecosystem ecology," the US planned to firmly establish both ecology and biology under American hegemony; they envisioned not a stand-alone survey study but a twenty-five-year project through which the American style of education and research would be introduced and installed. Rooted in the backdrop of such a grand plan by the Smithsonian Institution was the Cultural Cold War.

However, because of mounting military tensions between the North and South, the grand scheme of the joint South Korea–US survey of the DMZ floundered at the planning stage. This is primarily because the military Cold War frustrated plans for the Cultural Cold War. In addition to this, the failure to secure sufficient funds for the project was also a factor; here, the CIA scandal of 1967, too, had an effect on the circumstances that left the Ford Foundation and the Asia Foundation no choice but to become cautious of plans relating to the Cultural Cold War. Furthermore, behind the scenes of the ecological survey of the DMZ, there was the fundamental problem of various power struggles between the South Korean and American scholars, including differences in perception of the ecological survey projects, differences in culture, and intergenerational conflicts, among others. Before the advent of ecosystem ecology anticipated by the US, even basic wildlife surveys were not being conducted in the area, on top of which the South Korean scholars rejected being relegated to merely passive recipients of benefits; as the self-confidence displayed by entomologist Seok Ju-myeong, quoted at the beginning of this chapter, shows, Korean biologists did not shy from conflict with American scholars, bolstered by their familiarity with the "locality" of living creatures. This allows us to see that the transfer of science and technology—knowledge often perceived as objective and universal—and the actual process of knowledge production do not constitute a smooth one-way path.

Interestingly, North Korea, one of the agents directly facing the DMZ, had a completely different understanding of the area. They understood the DMZ literally, as a space symbolizing division, and criticized any ecological surveys, research, or attempts at conservation as plots to solidify the demarcation. To North Korea, the DMZ was only a military stage—an instrument of political negotiation.

In this way, there existed differing perspectives regarding the DMZ, as a space existing in the Cold War, and its ecological surveys, perspectives that continue to differ even into the present day, largely because of the multifaceted politics of science involving the DMZ. Despite this, the ecological value of this space is constantly growing; the possibility remains open for the DMZ to become a useful instrument for improving North-South relations in the future, if it is remembered that the animals and plants inhabiting it are the protagonists of a renewed awareness of the value of a place once filled with military tension. Eleana J. Kim offers a novel perspective by emphasizing the importance of "biological peace" over human-centered political and economic concerns. The ecological surveys of the DMZ, conducted for a short time half a century ago, were a key factor in the growth and development of the field of biology in South Korea. However, the seeds sown by the ecological surveys have yet to bear enough fruit. Through the wildlife that passes to and from the military boundary lines of the DMZ, which are defined by mere signposts, it is hoped that a true ecological survey can be conducted, and perhaps the permanent stability of peace can be realized.

NOTES

The section "Rediscovering the DMZ through Ecological Survey" is an abridged revision of the author's paper "The Meaning and Prospect of the Ecological Survey of the DMZ," *Daedong Munhwa Yeongu* 106 (2019): 37–44.

1. The first draft of this chapter was presented as "The Ecological Survey of the DMZ and the Growth of Biology in South Korea" at the 2017 East Asian Environmental History (EAEH) conference in Tianjin, China. Revised versions have been presented in a workshop on "Public Diplomacy of Knowledge" in Kyoto, January 2020.

2. Masuda, *Cold War Crucible*.

3. In the Korean translated version of his book, Westad cites the simultaneous progression of conflicts of ideology and colonization as major factors contributing to the severity of the impact of the Cold War on the Korean Peninsula. Westad, *Global Cold War*.

4. Campbell, *Technology Policy of the Korean State*.

5. Park, "Roles of the United States and Japan," 206–31.

6. Saunders, *Cultural Cold War*; Kishi and Tsuchiya, *Bunka reisen no jidai*.

7. For instance, recent research has traced the nature and role of Cold War science and technology through international expos during the era. Molella and Knowles, *World's Fairs in the Cold War.*

8. Wolfe, *Competing with the Soviet.*

9. Wolfe, *Freedom's Laboratory.*

10. E. Kim, *Making Peace with Nature.*

11. Brady, "From War Zone to Biosphere Reserve."

12. Hyun, "Brokering Science, Blaming Culture."

13. Moon, "Postcolonial Desire."

14. "A Roundtable Discussion of the Night of a New Science," *Hyeondae gwahak* 8 (1948): 44–51.

15. Moon, "Becoming a Biologist in Colonial Korea."

16. DiMoia, "Atoms for Power?"

17. O. Kim and Hwang, "Minnesota Project."

18. Kang Young Sun, "A General Comment on the 1957 Cultural Circles in Natural Sciences," *Kyunghyangsinmun,* December 23, 1957.

19. Shin and Moon, "Kang Young Sun's Making of South Korean Biology."

20. Hyun, "Making Postcolonial Connections."

21. Coolidge and Ripley knew each other from their time serving together as area specialists and naturalists in the Office of Strategic Services (OSS) during the Second World War. When the ecological survey of the DMZ was being promoted, Ripley was working as a secretary at the Smithsonian Institution. Shin, "'Wildlife Paradise.'"

22. Won, *Saedeuri saneun sesangeun areumdapda,* 80–90.

23. South Korean students' inclination to study in the US can be seen in the majority of academic disciplines. Kim Jongyoung pointed out that South Korean intellectuals who studied abroad in the US enjoyed privileges in their home country and played a role as confederates in the construction of hegemony by American universities. Kim, *Jibaebanneun jibaeja.*

24. Worthington, *Evolution of IBP*; Coleman, *Big Ecology,* 15–88.

25. "Korean National Programme for the IBP," *Report for the IBP* 2 (1968): 5–19.

26. "In the Global Ranks: International Participation of Academia in South Korea," *Kyunghyangsinmun,* January 26, 1966.

27. For comprehensive information about the DMZ, see Brady, "Life in the DMZ."

28. On the basis of the military agreement in 2018, North and South Korea attempted a test removal of eleven guard posts (GPs) in the DMZ and removed ten of them. However, since the breakdown of the Second US–North Korea Summit Conference held in Hanoi in 2019, in the backdrop of worsening relations between the US and North Korea, removal of the remaining GPs

has been suspended. It is currently estimated that 60 South Korean GPs and 150 North Korean GPs remain. Yang Nak Kyu, "Once More Promoting the Dismantlement of the GPs," *Asiagyeongje*, January 21, 2020.

29. Coolidge references the importance of research in the DMZ in the opening of the speech titled "The Role of International Nature Conservation When Protecting Our Natural Environment," which he gave after receiving his honorary doctorate on November 4, 1965, at Seoul National University.

30. US$36,000 of this funding was provided by the US Air Force Office of Scientific Research (AFOSR). Even today, AFOSR provides funding to various basic research projects that the US Air Force has deemed essential for accomplishing missions. Hyun, "Brokering Science, Blaming Culture."

31. "Plans to Adopt the South Korean DMZ as a National Park," *Dongailbo*, September 1, 1966.

32. Apart from the Korean Peninsula, the border between Israel and the United Arab Republic and that between North and South Vietnam were also DMZs. "Inspecting the DMZ with Cross-Sectional Photography," *Dongailbo*, September 12, 1966.

33. Ornithologist Won Hong-Gu was a scientist representing North Korea. With his confirmation of the Daurian starlings in North Korea that his son, Won Pyong-Oh, had released, they met indirectly through a bird. Refer to Endō Kimio's *Ariran no aoi tori* for the story about them.

34. Buechner, "Ecological Study in Korea." This document is a proposal created for the agreement with the South Korean government.

35. Smithsonian Institution, *Smithsonian Year 1968*, 288.

36. De Vries, "1967 Central Intelligence Agency Scandal."

37. Buechner, Tyson, and Kim, *Final Report*.

38. Ke Chung Kim, "Part Two: The Smithsonian Ecology Program in Korea: Reviews and Recommendations," in Buechner, Tyson, and Kim, 1–10.

39. Hyun, "Brokering Science, Blaming Culture."

40. Edwin Tyson to Helmut K. Buechner, November 28, 1966. Smithsonian Institution Archives, Box 16, Folder 3.

41. Kim In-soo, "Cold War and Politics of Intelligence."

42. For instance, Berman, *Influence of the Carnegie*; Wu, "Rockefeller Foundation's Support Projects"; Latham, *Right Kind of Revolution*; Parmar, *Foundations of the American Century*; Hong, *Hanguk sahoegwahagui giwon*; Sin, *Geundaehwarongwa naengjeon jisik chegye*.

43. It is argued in several studies that the transfer of knowledge and technical support from developed countries did not always go well. See, for instance, Wang, "Transnational Science during the Cold War"; Fan, "Global Turn in the History of Science."

44. In a translation of the American middle school biology textbook by the Biological Sciences Curriculum Study (BBCS), promoted as part of the

Cultural Cold War in the projects popularized from abroad, the translators had to the creatures of the recipient region. This confirms the importance of native knowledge in biology. Wolfe, *Freedom's Laboratory*, 145–67.

45. Kang, *Bimujang jidaeui cheonyeonjawone gwanhan yeongu*.

46. Ibid., 1.

47. Kang, *Nambukan cheonyeonjawonui bigyoyeongu*.

48. Kang, *Bimujangjidae gongdonggaebareul tonghan nambukan sanghohyeopjosangui munjejeom mit daechaek*.

49. The KCCN, which promoted the DMZ ecological surveys in 1966, changed their name to the Korean Association for Conservation of Nature (KACN) in 1974.

50. KACN, *Bimujangjidae injeopjiyeok jayeonjonghap haksuljosabogoseo*.

51. For instance, there is no mention of the DMZ by the DPR Korea State of the Environment Project Team, which manages the ecological environment of North Korea, in *DPR KOREA: State of the Environment 2003*; or Ministry of Land and Environment Protection, *Democratic People's Republic of Korea*.

52. "Talks by Spokesmen of the Committee for the Peaceful Reunification of the Fatherland," *Rodongsinmun*, October 5, 2004.

53. "Preserving the Demilitarized Zone: A Plot for Eternal Division," *Rodongsinmun*, October 8, 2004.

54. The Democratic Peoples' Republic of Korea, *Urinaraui jayeonbohojiyeok*.

55. The Anbyon project was launched in 2008 under the initiative of the International Crane Foundation to restore the wintering area, and South Korea did not directly participate in the project. See Healy, "Social Ecologies in Borderlands."

REFERENCES

Berman, Edward H. *The Influence of the Carnegie, Ford, and Rockefeller Foundations on American Foreign Policy: The Ideology of Philanthropy*. New York: State University of New York Press, 1983.

Brady, Lisa M. "From War Zone to Biosphere Reserve: The Korean DMZ as a Scientific Landscape." *Notes and Records* 75 (2021): 189–205.

———. "Life in the DMZ: Turning a Diplomatic Failure into an Environmental Success." *Diplomatic History* 32, no. 4 (2008): 585–611.

Buechner, Helmut K. "Ecological Study in Korea: A Proposal for Research and Education." Smithsonian Institution, November 1, 1967.

Buechner, Helmut K., Edwin L. Tyson, and Ke Chung Kim. *Final Report: A Cooperative Program for Ecosystem Research in Korea, October 1966–September 1968*. Washington, DC: Office of Ecology, Smithsonian Institution, 1968.

Campbell, Joel R. *The Technology Policy of the Korean State since 1961*. New York: Edwin Mellen, 2009.

Coleman, David C. *Big Ecology: The Emergence of Ecosystem Science*. Berkeley: University of California Press, 2010.

United Nations Environment Programme. *DPR KOREA: State of the Environment 2003*. Klong Luang: United Nations Environment Programme, Regional Resource Centre for Asia and the Pacific, 2003.

———. *Urinaraui jayeonbohojiyeok* [Natural conservation regions of our land]. Pyongyang: Democratic Peoples' Republic of Korea, 2005.

de Vries, Tity. "The 1967 Central Intelligence Agency Scandal: Catalyst in a Transforming Relationship between State and People." *Journal of American History* 98, no. 4 (2012): 1075–92.

DiMoia, John. "Atoms for Power? The Atomic Energy Research Institute (AERI) and South Korean Electrification, 1948–1965." *Historia Scientiarum* 19, no. 2 (2009): 170–83.

Endō, Kimio. *Ariran no aoi tori* [The blue birds of Arirang]. Fuwa: Tarui Hinode Printing Office, 2013.

Fan, Fa-ti. "The Global Turn in the History of Science." *East Asian Science, Technology and Society* 6, no. 2 (2012): 249–58.

Healy, Hall, George Archibald, and Arthur H. Westing. "Social Ecologies in Borderlands: Crane Habitat Restoration and Sustainable Agriculture Project in the Democratic People's Republic of Korea." In *The Social Ecology of Border Landscapes*, edited by Anna Grichting and Michele Zebich-Knos, 89–106. London: Anthem, 2017.

Hong Jeongwan. *Hanguk sahoegwahagui giwon* [Origin of Korean social science: Ideology and modernization theory system]. Goyang: Yeoksabipyeongsa, 2021.

Hyun, Jaehwan. "Brokering Science, Blaming Culture: The US–South Korea Ecological Survey in the Demilitarized Zone, 1963–1968." *History of Science* 59, no. 3 (2021): 315–43.

———. "Making Postcolonial Connections: The Role of a Japanese Research Network in the Emergence of Human Genetics in South Korea, 1941–1968." *Korean Journal for the History of Science* 39, no. 2 (2017): 293–324.

Kang Young Sun. *Bimujangjidae gongdonggaebareul tonghan nambukan sanghohyeopjosangui munjejeom mit daechaek* [Problems and measures for mutual cooperation between the two Koreas through joint development of the DMZ]. Seoul: Board of National Unification, 1973.

———. *Bimujang jidaeui cheonyeonjawone gwanhan yeongu* [A study on natural resources in the DMZ]. Seoul: Board of National Unification, 1972.

———. *Nambukan cheonyeonjawonui bigyoyeongu* [A comparative study of natural resources in North and South Korea]. Seoul: Board of National Unification, 1972.

Kim, Eleana J. *Making Peace with Nature: Ecological Encounters along the Korean DMZ*. Durham, NC: Duke University Press, 2022.

Kim In-soo. "The Cold War and Politics of Intelligence: With a Focus on the Formation Circumstances of Park Jin-Hwan's Farm Management Analysis (1966)." *Dongbuga yeoksanonchong*, 61 (2018): 408–65.

Kim Jongyoung. *Jibaebanneun jibaeja: Miguk yukakgwa hanguk elliteuui tansaeng* [The ruled rulers: Studying abroad in the US and the birth of the South Korean elite]. Paju: Dolbegae, 2015.

Kim, Ock-Joo, and Sang-Ik Hwang. "The Minnesota Project: The Influence of American Medicine on the Development of Medical Education and Medical Research in Post-war Korea." *Korean Journal of Medical History* 9, no. 1 (2000): 112–23.

Kishi Toshihiko and Tsuchiya Yuka, eds. *Bunka reisen no jidai: America to Asia* [Decentering the Cultural Cold War: The US and Asia]. Tokyo: Kokusai-shoin, 2009.

Korean Association for Conservation of Nature (KACN). *Bimujangjidae injeopjiyeok jayeonjonghap haksuljosabogoseo* [The report on the scientific survey of areas near the DMZ]. Seoul: Bureau of Cultural Property of the Ministry of Culture and Information, 1975.

Latham, Michael E. *The Right Kind of Revolution: Modernization, Development, and U.S. Foreign Policy from the Cold War to the Present*. Ithaca, NY: Cornell University Press, 2011.

Masuda, Hajimu. *Cold War Crucible: The Korean Conflict and the Postwar World*. Cambridge, MA: Harvard University Press, 2015.

Ministry of Land and Environment Protection, DPRK. *Democratic People's Republic of Korea: Environment and Climate Change Outlook*. Pyongyang: Ministry of Land and Environment Protection, DPRK, 2012.

Molella, Arthur P., and Scott Gabriel Knowles, eds. *World's Fairs in the Cold War: Science, Technology, and the Culture of Progress*. Pittsburgh: University of Pittsburgh Press, 2019.

Moon, Manyong. "Becoming a Biologist in Colonial Korea: Cultural Nationalism in a Teacher-cum-Biologist." *East Asian Science, Technology and Society* 6, no. 1 (2012): 65–82.

———. "The Meaning and Prospect of the Ecological Survey of the DMZ." *Daedong Munhwa Yeongu* 106 (2019): 37–44.

———. "Postcolonial Desire and the Tripartite Alliance in East Asia: The Hybrid Origins of a Modern Scientific and Technological System in S. Korea." In *Engineering Asia: Technology, Colonial Development and the Cold War Order*, edited by Hiromi Mizuno, Aaron S. Moore, and John DiMoia, 165–88. London: Bloomsbury, 2018.

Park, Tae Gyun. "The Roles of the United States and Japan in the Development of South Korea's Science and Technology during the Cold War." *Korea Journal* 52, no. 1 (2012): 206–31.

Parmar, Inderjeet. *Foundations of the American Century: The Ford, Carnegie, and Rockefeller Foundations in the Rise of American Power.* New York: Columbia University Press, 2014.

Saunders, Frances Stoner. *The Cultural Cold War: The CIA and the World of Arts and Letters.* New York: New Press, 2000.

Shin Hyangsuk, and Manyong Moon. "Kang Young Sun's Making of South Korean Biology." In *Je7hoe hanilgwahaksa semina balpyojip* [The proceedings of the 7th Korea-Japan History of Science Seminar], 79–83. Seoul: Korean History of Science Society, 2017.

Shin, Jieun. "'A Wildlife Paradise': International Collaboration on the DMZ Ecology in the 1960s." Smithsonian Institution Archives blog, November 12, 2019. https://siarchives.si.edu/blog/%E2%80%9C-wildlife-paradise%E2%80%9D -international-collaboration-dmz-ecology-1960s#disqus_thread.

Sin Ju Back, ed. *Geundaehwarongwa naengjeon jisik chegye* [Modernization theory and the system of Cold War knowledge]. Seoul: Hyean, 2018.

Smithsonian Institution. *Smithsonian Year 1968.* Washington, DC: Smithsonian Institution, 1968.

Wang, Zuoyue. "Transnational Science during the Cold War: The Case of Chinese/American Scientists." *Isis* 101 (2010): 367–77.

Westad, Odd Arne. *The Global Cold War: Third World Interventions and the Making of Our Times.* Cambridge: Cambridge University Press, 2005.

Wolfe, Audra J. *Competing with the Soviet: Science, Technology and the State in Cold War America.* Baltimore: Johns Hopkins University Press, 2013.

———. *Freedom's Laboratory: The Cold War Struggle for the Soul of Science.* Baltimore: Johns Hopkins University Press, 2019.

Won Pyong-Oh. *Saedeuri saneun sesangeun areumdapda* [The world of birds is beautiful]. Seoul: Daum, 2002.

Worthington, E. B., ed. *The Evolution of IBP.* Cambridge, UK: Cambridge University Press, 1975.

Wu Linchun. "Rockefeller Foundation's Support Projects in Post–Cold War Taiwan." In *Bunka reisen no jidai*, edited by Kishi Toshihiko and Tsuchiya Yuka, 119–40. Tokyo: Kokusai-shoin, 2009.

AUTHOR BIOS

MANYONG MOON is Associate Professor and Vice-Director of the Korean Research Institute of Science, Technology and Civilization at Jeonbuk National

University. He is author of *The Evolution of Science and Technology Research Systems in South Korea* (2017).

REBECCA LEE PATERSON is a PhD student at the Graduate School of Education, Kyoto University. Having completed her undergraduate degree in Japanese studies at the University of Cambridge, she came to Japan to pursue her postgraduate studies in Second Language Acquisition.

PART III

PRACTICING KNOWLEDGE

EIGHT

—ᴍ—

US AID, JOURNALISM EDUCATION IN TAIWAN, AND A TRANSNATIONAL NETWORK OF CHINESE-SPEAKING JOURNALISTS

MIKE SHICHI LAN

INTRODUCTION

China's Civil War resumed shortly after the Second World War and continued well into the Cold War period; as a result, political and ideological rivalry between the People's Republic of China (PRC), established by the Chinese Communist Party, and the Republic of China (ROC), led by the Chinese Nationalist Party (also known as Kuomintang, or KMT), made Taiwan a focal point of Cold War tension.[1] Shortly after the Korean War, the US officially brought Taiwan, where the ROC government had consolidated its regime since 1949, into the global anti-Communist alliance. To enhance US strategic interests, monetary assistance was provided to strengthen the ROC's standing vis-à-vis the PRC.

While US aid to the ROC—and other allies—during the Cold War has drawn significant scholarly attention, most studies have been devoted to its political and economic aspects.[2] In recent years, as scholars have begun to turn their attention to the social and cultural arenas of the Cold War, topics such as popular culture, technology, media, and education have become major areas of inquiry, as the chapters in this volume also demonstrate. This chapter explores the juncture of media and education by looking into the development of journalism education under the ROC government in Taiwan and the role of US aid during the 1950s and 1960s. Furthermore, to examine the effect of this US-supported journalism education, this chapter also analyzes the career paths of a selected group of alumni of National Chengchi University.

US SUPPORT FOR JOURNALISM
EDUCATION IN TAIWAN

Traditionally, most journalists underwent no formal training before starting to work and write for newspapers. However, with the establishment of journalism as an academic discipline at the beginning of the twentieth century, journalism education became a part of the university curriculum—first in the US (University of Missouri, 1908; Columbia University, 1912) and later in places like China, Spain, and Canada—and served as a training ground for professional journalists.[3]

In China, journalism education at the university level began at Peking University in 1918. By 1937, twenty-six out of thirty-two public and private universities in China offered journalism, and most had been established under the influence of US journalism education.[4] After the civil war, journalism education continued at Peking and Tsing Hua Universities under the PRC government. On the other side of the Taiwan Strait, after the ROC government established its regime in Taiwan, journalism education at the university level started in 1954, in conjunction with the "reestablishment" of National Chengchi University (NCCU).

NCCU began its existence as the cadre training school of the KMT, the Central School of Party Affairs, in 1927; transformed itself into the Central School of Politics in 1929; and adopted its current name in 1946.[5] The Chinese Civil War ended the school's operations in China in 1949, and the ROC government "reestablished" NCCU as the first new public university in Taiwan in 1954. It started with four graduate programs, among them the Graduate School of Journalism. In the following year, the Department of Journalism was set up to offer one of the five majors for NCCU's inaugural class of undergraduate students. In comparison to tertiary-level journalism programs in other Asian countries, NCCU's was one of the earliest, especially when considering non-Communist Chinese-speaking territories. As Yang Zhang shows in chapter 9 of this volume, the Chinese University of Hong Kong (CUHK) established its Journalism Department only in 1965, a full ten years after NCCU. In other words, between 1955 and 1965, NCCU in Taiwan offered the only Chinese-speaking journalism program at the university level outside of the PRC.

Since its outset, the Department of Journalism received significant support from the US, from both governmental and nongovernmental sources. On the one hand, journalism education under the ROC government had strong historical ties with American schools of journalism, most notably with the University of Missouri; scholars have recognized that the "Missouri model" of journalism education has been widely adopted in universities across China since the 1920s.[6] Journalism education at Central School of Politics in Nanjing, the predecessor of NCCU, was established in 1934 by Ma Xingye, a graduate of Missouri's School of Journalism and also the first Chinese trained in professional journalism education based on the "Missouri model."[7] When NCCU's journalism education commenced (first with the graduate school) in 1954, it inherited personal and institutional connections to the University of Missouri. For example, in the inaugural school year of 1954–55, both faculty and the library of Missouri's School of Journalism donated a collection of books to NCCU.[8]

More importantly, however, the development of journalism education at NCCU since the 1950s should be understood in the larger context of the US-led global alliance in the ideological war against Communism. Scholars have studied the role of various US government agencies such as the United States Information Agency (USIA) in shaping the ideological war.[9] Nongovernmental agencies have also been thoroughly examined, including in this volume, in which the Ford and Rockefeller Foundations are examined in chapter 1 by Shin Kawashima and chapter 4 by Somei Kobayashi. More specifically in the field of journalism, as Jae Young Cha demonstrates in chapter 10, the US State Department played an active role in promoting pro-American journalists and journalism in South Korea. This chapter further argues that the US aid for journalism education at NCCU also contributed to, and was motivated by, the anti-Communist ideological war.

During this period, to strengthen its faculty and curriculum, NCCU's Department of Journalism continuously hosted visiting professors from the US, including (in order of visit) Carlton Culmsee (Utah State University, 1955, under arrangement by the State Department),[10] Howard Rusk Long (Southern Illinois University, 1957), Charles Clayton (Southern Illinois University, 1961), and John Casey (University of Oklahoma, 1963).[11]

The first visiting professor, Carlton Culmsee (1904–93), was dean of the College of Arts and Sciences at Utah State University during the 1950s. In an introduction to the collection of his private papers, the Culmsees (the dean and his wife) were described as having been "asked by the Nationalist government" to help "reestablish the National Chengchi University" in Taiwan.[12] During his stint at NCCU, Culmsee taught "Propaganda [xuanchuanxue]" and "Public Relations [gonggong guanxi]"; and his wife taught English.[13] It was this visit that enabled Carlton Culmsee to "[publish] numerous articles about Taiwan and the Orient in many regional and national magazines" in the US, "as a result of teaching and the extensive travel to the islands of Quemoy, Matsu, and the Far East."[14]

Culmsee's writing during this period was consistent with the aims and strategies of the ideological war conducted jointly by the US and the ROC. One of his articles, published under the title "Tight Little Island—Off China" in the *New York Times Magazine* in August 1956, shortly before he concluded his visit to NCCU, introduced the island of Quemoy to American readers:[15] "In recent years many exotic names of faraway places have made sudden impact on the consciousness of Americans as they became focal points in the cold war—and then, as the center of the struggle shifted elsewhere, have virtually dropped out of the news. One such name is that of this small, Nationalist-held, wind-swept island that nestles against the southeast coast of Red China—Quemoy."

The timing of Culmsee's article was no coincidence; it was published at the height of ROC-PRC military confrontation over the island of Quemoy, shortly after the PRC's intensive bombardment of Quemoy (later known as the First Taiwan Strait Crisis) in September 1954 and at a time when the US was strengthening its military support to ROC (since the signing of the ROC-US Mutual Defense Treaty in 1954). Writing against this background, Culmsee argued in his article, with a positive and assertive tone in support of the ROC and the US support for the ROC, "It's Quemoy, still a besieged fortress although life is looking up for its people."[16]

Another notable American journalism scholar who came to teach at NCCU was Howard Rusk Long. Long served on the faculty of the University of Missouri for ten years, before moving to Southern Illinois University (SIU) in 1953 to serve as chair of the Department of Journalism.[17] He was known as being "instrumental in the growth of the journalism program at SIU and in the development of the campus newspaper."[18] Long served nine months at NCCU between 1957 and 1958. It is worth noting that newspapers in Taiwan reported that before Long returned to the US, he expressed great concern about the Publication Law in Taiwan.[19] Shortly after Long returned to the US, he published an article in the journal *Quill*, in which he quoted ROC president Chiang Kai-shek saying that the Publication Law in "China" (ROC) was "intended to prevent communism" and that restriction would be reduced once "the conditions allow."[20]

While the information available now is limited, on the basis of the analysis above, it would be fair to argue that the US support to the Department of Journalism at NCCU further strengthened the ROC's anti-Communist ideological war. The US-ROC cooperation was best exemplified by the inauguration of NCCU's Journalism Building, which opened its doors in March 1962. On this occasion, NCCU published a bilingual booklet titled *Special Issue Commemorating the Dedication of the New Journalism Building*, in which the Chinese text was translated word for word into English. Nearly half of the booklet was devoted to a section titled "Messages from Around the World," which comprised congratulatory messages mostly from scholars and leading figures of journalism from the US, including the following:[21]

Benjamin M. McKelway, President, The Associated Press
Frank H. Bartholomew, President, United Press International
Arthur Hays Sulzberger, Chairman of the Board, *The New York Times*
Marshall Field, Jr., President and Publisher, *The Chicago Sun-Times* and the *Chicago Daily News*
Henry R. Luce, Publisher, *Time* and *Life* New York
Frank Luther Mott, Dean, Emeritus, School of Journalism, University of Missouri
Earl F. English, Dean, School of Journalism, University of Missouri
J. T. Salter, Professor of Political Science, University of Wisconsin
Robert Blum, President, The Asia Foundation[22]

The appearance of these names in the booklet effectively demonstrated the close collaboration and mutual support between the US and ROC in promoting journalism education at NCCU. And most notably, the centerpiece of this booklet was "A Message from the President of the United States," with a half-page portrait photo of President John F. Kennedy. In this personal congratulatory message from President Kennedy, the goal of journalism education, as supported by the US and conducted jointly with the ROC government, was clearly stated:[23]

Your university . . . is already well-known in the Far East for the leading role which it has taken in promoting the teaching of journalism throughout the entire non-Communist world. The institution of a free press is a foundation stone of the democratic system of government and a symbol of man's determination to influence his future by expressing his ideas in his own way. I am hopeful that your school of journalism and its freedom-of-information center will be a source of constant inspiration to those who cherish democracy, and an example of the contrast between the freedom of communications which prevails in a free society and the controlled press of the totalitarian system existing on the mainland China.

As NCCU's Department of Journalism, together with the whole university, grew larger during its first decade, US support from another source made a huge contribution and impact—the recruitment of "overseas Chinese students" to study in Taiwan.

US SUPPORT FOR EDUCATION OF "OVERSEAS CHINESE STUDENTS" IN TAIWAN

Since the establishment of the PRC government in 1949, the population of millions of "overseas Chinese" has been the focal point of political battles between the ROC and the PRC. Both "Chinese" governments wished to attract support from these Chinese "compatriots" from afar, hoping to strengthen their political legitimacy both domestically and internationally.[24] As Yuka Tsuchiya Moriguchi shows in chapter 6 of this volume, the ROC and the PRC also competed against each other for overseas Chinese scientists and engineers in the course of developing nuclear technology. Amid the highly intense competition between the ROC and the PRC, both governments considered education a critical means to draw overseas Chinese physically and ideologically closer.

On the ROC side, education of "overseas Chinese students," or *qiaosheng* in Chinese, took off in 1954, with support from the US. Under the consideration of preventing overseas Chinese, mostly in Southeast Asia, from pursuing higher education in Communist China, the US government began to allocate a significant amount of monetary aid to the ROC government in Taiwan, enabling the recruitment of qiaosheng.[25] The US aid continued till 1965, and thousands of qiaosheng completed their study in Taiwan during this period, mostly obtaining college degrees.

The US aid worked in two ways: On the one hand, it provided each qiaosheng with "individual funding," including travel, tuition, and stipends through the ROC's Chinese Overseas Community Affairs Council, to study in Taiwan. On the other, from 1954 to 1962, for each qiaosheng enrolled in Taiwan, the host university received a certain amount of "institutional funding," through the ROC's Ministry of Education, to develop infrastructure (including classrooms, dormitories, cafeterias, libraries, gymnasiums, laboratories, and other equipment) on campus to accommodate the needs of the qiaosheng.[26] From 1954 to 1956, qiaosheng were allowed to enroll only in public universities in Taiwan; therefore, US aid as institutional funding was allocated only to public universities. In 1957, qiaosheng began to be allowed to enroll in private universities in Taiwan, but the majority of qiaosheng studying in Taiwan under US aid continued to enroll in public universities until the final year of aid in 1965.[27] Thus, US aid as institutional funding was allocated mostly to public universities in Taiwan.

Funding from the US was particularly significant to public universities in Taiwan because it arrived at a time when the ROC government was short on financial resources for higher education. While the institutional funding to each university was calculated on the basis of the number of qiaosheng enrolled, it did not only benefit qiaosheng—some dormitories were only available to qiaosheng, but classrooms, cafeterias, and libraries were all shared by qiaosheng and domestic students. Therefore, the US funding to support qiaosheng education in Taiwan turned out to be a significant source of financial support for higher education in general in Taiwan.

Among public universities in Taiwan that hosted qiaosheng, and thereby received US aid as institutional funding, NCCU was exceptional in terms of its timing and curriculum. As mentioned earlier, NCCU was first established in mainland China in 1927, but along with other public universities under the ROC government, it ceased operations in 1949 as a result of the Chinese Civil War. After the ROC government consolidated its rule in Taiwan, it decided to "reestablish" some of those public universities that had once existed in mainland China; NCCU was designated by the Ministry of Education as the first public university to be reestablished in Taiwan. After years of planning, NCCU was reestablished in 1954. While no evidence shows that such a coincidence was planned, NCCU's reestablishment coincided with the inauguration of US aid to qiaosheng education in Taiwan.

NCCU opened its doors in 1954 and received its first batch of undergraduate students the following year. With US aid, and under the efforts of the ROC government, qiaosheng students were only given the opportunity to undertake undergraduate studies (or study at high schools) in Taiwan. While other public universities in Taiwan had begun to host qiaosheng students in 1954, NCCU started one year later. However, US aid as institutional funding under the qiaosheng policy, in terms of its timing, was particularly significant to NCCU. While other public universities in Taiwan that started to receive qiaosheng students in 1954 were based on existing schools (and campuses) from the Japanese colonial period, NCCU was an entirely new "reestablished" school.[28] As it struggled to develop its infrastructure, literally from scratch, with rather limited financial resources from the ROC government, NCCU received a significant amount of US aid as institutional funding, which began to arrive in 1955 with the inaugural class of undergraduate domestic and qiaosheng students. When NCCU planned to build its first cluster of undergraduate classrooms and dormitories, the budget was set at 1.5 million New Taiwan dollars, which was paid for entirely by the "US aid."[29]

In terms of its curriculum for qiaosheng, NCCU was also exceptional. As mentioned above, among universities in Taiwan, NCCU was the first school that offered journalism as an undergraduate major, starting in 1955. It should be further pointed out that at the time, in the Chinese-speaking world, only three universities provided academic training in journalism; the other two were Fudan

232 PRACTICING KNOWLEDGE

and Renmin Universities in the PRC.[30] To overseas Chinese who aspired to study journalism, NCCU was the only non-Communist choice at the time. This situation did not change until the aforementioned CUHK established its Department of Journalism, also under US assistance, in 1965. To put it in the context of the anti-Communist ideological war conducted by the US and its allies such as the ROC, before 1965, NCCU was the only school in the non-Communist world that could train Chinese-speaking journalists and thereafter have them promote anti-Communist ideology to the global Chinese-speaking audience.

When NCCU admitted its inaugural undergraduate class in 1955, under the ROC's official education policy, five majors were offered to undergraduate domestic as well as qiaosheng students: education, political science, diplomacy, frontier administration, and journalism. It was at NCCU's Department of Journalism that US aid for journalism education in Asia and US aid for qiaosheng education converged.

OVERSEAS CHINESE STUDENTS (QIAOSHENG) STUDYING JOURNALISM AT NCCU

Between 1955 and 1965, NCCU expanded its undergraduate majors from five to more than a dozen.[31] Notably, even amid such expansion, journalism constantly ranked among the most popular majors for qiaosheng enrolled at NCCU during this period. As table 8.1 shows, for three consecutive years between 1959 and 1961, the number of qiaosheng freshmen enrolled in the Department of Journalism consistently ranked first among all departments. In 1962, it was a close third; in 1964, third; and in 1965, a close second. In the years underlined, the percentage of qiaosheng freshmen enrolled in the Department of Journalism was particularly high, sometimes exceeding 30 percent.

If we consider the Department of Journalism alone, it becomes clear that qiaosheng constituted a major part of its student population. Beginning with the freshman class of 1955, the number of qiaosheng from Southeast Asia enrolled in the department continued to climb, and throughout the following decade, qiaosheng consistently accounted for nearly half of each intake. For example, of the inaugural class of the department that enrolled in 1954, forty-eight students remained until their final year (1958), twenty-one (43%) of whom were qiaosheng. The fourth intake of 1958 was rather significant; of its total forty-seven students, more than half, twenty-four (51%) to be exact, were qiaosheng.[32] For the next few years, this high percentage of qiaosheng in the Department of Journalism continued, as table 8.2 demonstrates. Between 1959 and 1962 in particular, the qiaosheng freshmen outnumbered their domestic compatriots.

Table 8.1 NCCU's Total Number of Qiaosheng Freshmen and Departments with the Highest Number of Qiaosheng Freshmen, 1958–65

Year: Total	Department and its number of qiaosheng freshmen			
1958: 127	Western languages 35	Diplomacy 28	Education 26	**Journalism 24**
1959: 160	**Journalism 52**	Diplomacy 38	Education 32	
1960: 209	**Journalism 74**	Education 51	Western languages 33	
1961: 119	**Journalism 32**	Education 25	Western languages 22	
1962: 93	Western languages 26	Education 25	**Journalism 24**	
1963: 162	Education 33	Western languages 31	Banking 25	**Journalism/** business administration **22**
1964: 93	Education 31	Western languages 28	**Journalism 26**	
1965: 79	Western languages 28	**Journalism 25**	International trade 21	

Source: Guoli Zhengzhidaxue, "*Guoli Zhengzhidaxue xueze*"; *Zhengda xiaokan*, no. 2, no. 11, no. 19, no. 27, no. 35, no. 43, no. 51. For the total enrollment of qiaosheng, see Xingzhengyuan guoji jingji hezuo fazhan weiyuanhui, *Qiaosheng jiaoyu jihua yunyong Meiyuan chengguo jiantao*, 6.

Note: Underlining indicates years when Journalism was the most popular choice.

Table 8.2 Enrollment by Class of the Department of Journalism, NCCU, 1962

	Total	Qiaosheng	Percentage of qiaosheng
Senior	78	45	57% (*entered in 1959)
Junior	103	68	66% (*entered in 1960)
Sophomore	58	29	50% (*entered in 1961)
Freshman	53	25	47% (*entered in 1962)

Source: *Zhengda xiaokan*, no. 19.

234 PRACTICING KNOWLEDGE

Table 8.3 Annual Enrollment of the Department of Journalism, 1958–65

	Number of qiaosheng	Number of domestic students	Total enrollment	Percentage of qiaosheng in journalism	Number of qiaosheng in journalism and its percentage of total enrollment of qiaosheng at NCCU
1958	85	128	213	39.9%	518, 16.4%
1959	111	113	224	49.6%	632, 17.6%
1960	164	130	294	55.8%	**806, 20.4%**
1961	172	125	297	57.9%	**772, 22.3%**
1962	167	123	290	57.6%	**769, 21.7%**
1963	147	120	267	55%	772, 19%
1964	99	121	220	45%	689, 14.4%
1965	102	131	233	43.8%	661, 15.4%

Source: Zhengda xiaokan, no. 2, no. 11, no. 19, no. 27, no. 35, no. 43, no. 51.

Note: For three consecutive years, the percentage of enrollment in journalism exceeded 20 percent, as shown by numbers in bold.

In addition, among NCCU's dozen or so undergraduate majors, the Department of Journalism continuously attracted a disproportionally high number of qiaosheng. Table 8.3 describes the numbers and percentages.

From 1955 to 1965, qiaosheng who were supported by US aid to study in Taiwan were clearly a major component of NCCU's Department of Journalism. As table 8.3 shows, in each year during this period, near or more than half of the students enrolled in NCCU's Department of Journalism were qiaosheng. This demonstrates that US aid supported the buildup of NCCU's Department of Journalism since 1955 and supported a significant number of qiaosheng receiving journalism education at the university over the subsequent decades. The number (and proportion) and the place of origin of qiaosheng graduates from NCCU's Department of Journalism further illustrate the outcome of this joint US-ROC education effort (table 8.4).

The statistics of graduates shows that in the first eleven graduating classes of NCCU's Department of Journalism, between 1959 (when the first batch of students, including qiaosheng supported by US aid, who began study in 1955, graduated) and 1969 (when the last class of US-aid-funded qiaosheng

Table 8.4 Number of Graduates and Origin of Qiaosheng Graduates, Department of Journalism

Class 19 (graduated in 1959; entered in 1955)*

Total	Qiaosheng	Countries with the most qiaosheng		
43	17	Hong Kong 13	Borneo 1	Indonesia 1

Class 20 (graduated in 1960; entered in 1956)

Total	Qiaosheng	Countries with the most qiaosheng		
52	9	Hong Kong 4	British Borneo/ Sarawak 2	Indonesia 1

Class 21 (graduated in 1961; entered in 1957)

Total	Qiaosheng	Countries with the most qiaosheng		
50	11	Indonesia 3	Malaya/Singapore 3	Hong Kong 2

Class 22 (graduated in 1962; entered in 1958)

Total	Qiaosheng	Countries with the most qiaosheng		
52	21	Hong Kong 8	Indonesia 5	Malaya/ Sarawak/ Singapore 5

Class 23 (graduated in 1963; entered in 1959)

Total	Qiaosheng	Countries with the most qiaosheng		
74	40	Hong Kong 14	Malaysia/Singapore 9	Indonesia 5

Class 24 (graduated in 1964; entered in 1960)

Total	Qiaosheng	Countries with the most qiaosheng		
88	46	Malaysia/ Singapore 21	Hong Kong 10	Indonesia 4

Class 25 (graduated in 1965; entered in 1961)

Total	Qiaosheng	Countries with the most qiaosheng		
38	15	Malaysia 5	Hong Kong 3	Indonesia 3

Class 26 (graduated in 1966; entered in 1962)

Total	Qiaosheng	Countries with the most qiaosheng	
40	14	Malaysia 9	Hong Kong 3

Class 27 (graduated in 1967; entered in 1963)

Total	Qiaosheng	Countries with the most qiaosheng	
53	17	Malaysia 11	Hong Kong 3

(continued)

236   PRACTICING KNOWLEDGE

Table 8.4 (*continued*)

Class 28 (graduated in 1968; entered in 1964)

Total	Qiaosheng	Countries with the most qiaosheng	
59	22	Malaysia 6	Hong Kong 4

Class 29 (graduated in 1969; entered in 1965)

Total	Qiaosheng	Countries with the most qiaosheng	
54	20	Hong Kong 9	Malaysia 8

Source: These numbers are based on Guoli Zhengzhidaxue, *Guoli Zhengzhi daxue Biye Jiniance*; and Guoli Zhengzhidaxue chuanbo xueyuan xinwenxue xi, "Lijie xiyou minglu (daxuebu)."

*The order of graduation classes dated back to the period before 1949, with graduates in 1937 as Class 6. See Guoli Zhengzhidaxue chuanbo xueyuan xinwenxue xi, "Lijie xiyou minglu (daxuebu)."

graduated), there were a total of 603 graduates; among them, 232 were qiaosheng, totaling more than 38 percent. Of the qiaosheng graduates, eighty were originally from the combined areas of Malaysia (Malaya, Sarawak, Sabah) and Singapore, representing nearly one-third of all qiaosheng graduates; seventy-three were from Hong Kong, and twenty-three from Indonesia.

The above findings clearly indicate that the US aid, coupled with an American model of journalism education at NCCU, formed the basis of training a significant number of overseas Chinese in journalism in Taiwan. Among these graduates, some went on to work in journalism, and among qiaosheng graduates, some returned to their home countries and worked for Chinese media there. While we do not have exact figures on the number of graduates who eventually became journalists, the numbers shown above illustrate several major effects of journalism education in Taiwan in the 1950s and 1960s. First, that NCCU's Department of Journalism, as well as its "specialized knowledge" of journalism, partially supported by American money and faculty, did not only serve as the training ground for journalists in the ROC (Taiwan); the "specialized knowledge" of journalism as manifested by the department also helped to train many overseas Chinese journalists who found employment in Southeast Asia, often in Chinese newspapers. Second, this joint effort between the ROC and the US in training overseas Chinese journalists also found its largest target audience in Southeast Asia, most notably in Malaysia, Singapore, and Hong Kong.

The analysis above shows that NCCU's Department of Journalism, in the first decade since it was established in 1954, was the juncture of two separate but related sources of US aid and cultural diplomacy: journalism education and overseas Chinese education. As a result, the department—or rather, what activities these graduates engaged in after graduating from the department—will serve as a focal group to examine the effects of US cultural diplomacy in the field of journalism.

Furthermore, the effect of US cultural diplomacy through NCCU's Department of Journalism extended beyond Taiwan; as students of the department came from both Taiwan and Southeast Asia during this period, they likewise found employment in both Taiwan and Southeast Asia when they graduated. Therefore, the career trajectories of alumni from the department will serve to demonstrate the effects of US cultural diplomacy in the field of journalism in both Taiwan and Southeast Asia.

In the following sections, this chapter will focus on alumni of NCCU's Department of Journalism who went on to work in the field of journalism in Southeast Asia. This group of alumni consists of (1) qiaosheng originally from Southeast Asia who received US aid between 1955 and 1965 (i.e., graduated between 1959 and 1969); and (2) non-qiaosheng students who sought employment in Southeast Asia. The career paths of these alumni show that in addition to working as journalists, a good number went on to teach journalism. This is likely due to the fact that, in the 1950s, NCCU's Department of Journalism was, as pointed out above, one of the very few academic programs of journalism in the Chinese-speaking world, and the only one under a non-Communist regime; many alumni went on to take up teaching positions at academic programs of journalism set up across Southeast Asia in the 1960s and afterward. Thereby, to fully examine the long-term effect in the field of journalism, alumni who *practiced* journalism and alumni who *taught* journalism will be included in the analysis. In particular, the remainder of this chapter will focus on alumni who practiced journalism in Malaysia and the US, two areas in which Chinese newspapers have continued to flourish from the 1960s until today, and alumni who taught journalism in Singapore and Hong Kong—two Chinese-speaking societies in which journalism programs were established in the 1960s and onward.

QIAOSHENG ALUMNI WHO PRACTICED JOURNALISM

From the 1950s to 1970s, the ROC government, having been supported by the US and its Cold War strategies, presented itself internationally as the legitimate "China" (holding the China seat at the United Nations, for example) and concentrated particular effort in conveying this image to the overseas Chinese.

During this period, a number of NCCU qiaosheng journalism graduates found employment in Southeast Asia. Among these alumni, some did contribute to the anti-Communist ideological war and help to sustain the image of the ROC as the legitimate "China" through various overseas Chinese newspapers. However, others chose different paths, ideologically and politically.

Cold War Warriors: Chinese Newspapers in Malaysia

In Malaysia, there are several major Chinese newspapers. One of the largest is *Nanyang Siang Pau* (also known as Nanyang Shangbao), originally established by Tan Kah Kee (Chen Jiageng) in Singapore in 1923. Since the Chinese Civil War and the subsequent establishment of the PRC, Tan Kah Kee and his newspaper have been widely regarded as pro–Beijing government.[33] Its main rival is *Sin Chew Jit Poh* (also known as Xingzhou Ribao), established by brothers Aw Boon Par (Hu Wenbao) and Aw Boon Haw (Hu Wenhu) in Singapore in 1929. Politically, in the 1950s, *Sin Chew Jit Poh* was considered pro–ROC government.[34] The political stance of *Sin Chew Jit Poh* was perhaps best testified by the fact that the paper's name on the front page was displayed in calligraphy written by Chiang Kai-shek, supreme leader of the ROC until 1976.[35]

In addition to *Sin Chew Jit Poh*, another major newspaper, *Kwong Wah Yit Poh* (Guanghua ribao), was supportive of the ROC government. The newspaper was originally founded in Penang in 1910 by Sun Yat-sen, who also founded the KMT and was regarded as the "national father" of the ROC. In addition, *China Press* (Zhongguo bao) was considered pro-ROC in the 1950s.[36] This newspaper was founded in Kuala Lumpur in 1946 by Li Xiaoshi, together with a group of Chinese community leaders who were members of the KMT, in pursuit of "anti-communism and support for the KMT government (of the ROC)."[37] *China Press* openly declared that the paper was founded in response to "disturbance" caused by a "leftist" newspaper in Kuala Lumpur.[38]

Other Chinese newspapers in Malaysia did not show much favor toward either the ROC or the PRC. *Shin Min Daily News* (Xinming ribao) was founded in 1967 by businessman Liang Runzhi and novelist Zha Liangyong (pen name Jin Yong), who was also the publisher of *Ming Pao* (Mingbao) in Hong Kong; it should be pointed out that Zha Liangyong's *Ming Pao* was harshly criticized by "leftist" parties in the 1960s, and Zha himself was considered to be close to the ROC government in the 1970s. In 1973, after his visit to Taiwan and meeting with ROC leaders, Zha personally wrote and published in *Ming Pao* a series of highly positive reports on the ROC.[39]

It came as no surprise that of the qiaosheng who studied journalism at NCCU under US aid and returned to practice journalism in Malaysia in the

1960s, most found employment in the aforementioned pro-ROC newspapers. Several worked as editorial staff and held key positions at various newspapers. For example, Wong Teng Loong (also known as Huang Dinglong), who graduated NCCU in 1962, served as the deputy editor in chief of *China Press*.[40] Liu Yahuang, a 1964 alumnus, worked for several decades in Chinese-language newspapers, including *Kwong Wah Yit Poh*, *Sin Chew Jit Poh*, and *Shin Min Daily News*.[41] Chin Yok Pin (Chen Yuping), who graduated in 1966, worked many years at *China Press*.[42] And Ding Yuzhen, who graduated in 1968, joined *Kwong Wah Yit Poh* in 1975, later becoming editor in chief in 1997.[43] Another notable graduate was Yang Laitian, alumnus of the class of 1959. As reported in the ROC's government newspaper, Yang founded a Chinese newspaper named *East Malaysia Evening News* (Dong Malaixiya wanbao) in 1966.[44]

It should be noted that for the aforementioned NCCU qiaosheng journalism alumni, working for pro-ROC newspapers in itself did not necessarily mean supporting the ROC, the US, or the anti-Communist ideological war. Nevertheless, such alumni surely helped to keep the pro-ROC newspapers running, which for many years supported and helped to sustain the ROC's claim as the sole legitimate government of China, domestically and internationally. However, a few of NCCU's qiaosheng journalism alumni did in fact play a more direct role in fulfilling the expectations of the US-ROC joint effort in journalism education by contributing more directly to the anti-Communist ideological war. One was 1960 graduate Alfred K. Lee (Li Dunqiao), who first worked in his native Sarawak in East Malaysia (or Malaysian Borneo) for the state government news agency from 1960 to 1965 and then moved to work for the East Malaysia–Brunei office of the United States Information Service (USIS) in 1966. Most notably, he was decorated with the medal of Ahli Bintang Sarawak by the Sarawak state government in 1983 for his contribution to the psychological warfare against the "underground insurgence"—allegedly Communist activities—in the 1960s.[45]

Ideological Enemies: Pro-PRC Journalists

From the 1970s, several changes began to occur among these Taiwan-trained overseas Chinese journalists and the Chinese media they worked for. First, a number of alumni who continued to work for Chinese newspapers in Southeast Asia took up key positions as publishers or editors in chief, becoming decision-makers in Chinese media in Southeast Asia. Second, several moved beyond Taiwan and Southeast Asia, most notably to the US, and took up key positions managing Chinese newspapers there. This expanded the role and influence of Taiwan-trained overseas Chinese journalists in the global Chinese community.

A third, and probably more significant, change was that most Chinese newspapers transformed themselves from "Chinese community newspapers" to "Chinese-language newspapers." This signified an identity shift among the overseas Chinese in general, who gradually began to view themselves as ethnic Chinese with nonaligned national and political identities in Southeast Asia, instead of as "Chinese living abroad." Consequently, news coverage of "China," of either the ROC or the PRC, became "international news."[46] In other words, news coverage of "China" no longer represented the identity, or political allegiance to either the ROC or the PRC, of overseas Chinese.

These changes notably coincided with the opening up and subsequent rise of political and cultural influences of the PRC. More and more overseas Chinese media (mostly, but not limited to, newspapers) had begun to provide greater coverage of the PRC, in contrast to the earlier focus on the ROC, and helped the Chinese-reading population across the world to better understand—and probably to further identify with—China under Communist rule. During this process, several overseas Chinese journalists who originally were qiaosheng—supported by US aid to receive an American model of journalism education at NCCU during the late 1950s and early 1960s—took leading roles in overseas Chinese media from the late 1970s and subsequently contributed to shaping a new image of the PRC as the legitimate "China."

Among NCCU's qiaosheng journalism alumni who graduated between 1959 and 1969, several were regarded by the ROC government as outright pro-PRC. One was Chen Yuhan, who graduated in 1963. He worked first for the *China Press* office in Singapore and later for *Shin Min Daily News*. However, in the early 1970s, Chen established *Taiyang Bao* (The sun), which was later suspended by the Malaysian Ministry of Internal Affairs after it reported widely on, and published a special pictorial issue upon, the death of the PRC's supreme leader, Mao Zedong (in 1976).[47]

Another example was James Chan Kai Hang (also known as Chen Juteng), who graduated in 1964 and also later worked for *China Press*. In 1971, the ROC's consulate general in Kuala Lumpur reported to the Ministry of Foreign Affairs that Chan had written an article in *China Press* commenting on ROC government officials' defection to the PRC. Chan allegedly wrote in his article that "[the government in] Taiwan was stupid and impotent in dealing with diplomatic affairs, and hiding fact from its own people; this has brought a huge negative impact on the morale of the society." Furthermore, the Ministry of Foreign Affairs concluded from Chan's case that, "in *China Press*, those who are ideological leaning the most to the 'left' were a group of former qiaosheng" who had studied in Taiwan.[48]

The most notable "pro-PRC" NCCU qiaosheng journalism graduate was probably Eddie K. Soo (Su Guokun), who graduated in 1962 and was recorded in his graduation yearbook as a student from Hong Kong. He was best known for his work with the US edition of *Sing Tao Daily* (*Sing Tao Jih Pao*, Xingdao ribao) in the 1970s.

Sing Tao Daily was established in 1938 in Hong Kong by Aw Boon Haw (Hu Wenhu), cofounder of the aforementioned *Sin Chew Jit Poh*. During the 1970s, *Sing Tao Daily* was run by Aw Boon Haw's daughter, Sally Aw Sian (Hu Xian). Much like her father, and the *Sin Chew Jit Poh* newspaper in Malaysia (and Singapore), Sally Aw and *Sing Tao Daily* showed strong support for the ROC government. Unlike most newspapers in Hong Kong, *Sing Tao Daily* continued to publish under the ROC calendar (which employs the founding of ROC in 1912 as its inaugural year) instead of the Gregorian calendar, which had been adopted by the PRC at its founding in 1949 and which was later widely considered by the Chinese-speaking community as a symbol of political identification with the PRC, at least until 1987.[49] In 1968, *Sing Tao Daily* began to publish its US edition from its New York office; the US edition was said to be an idea originally proposed by Eddie Soo to Sally Aw. In establishing *Sing Tao Daily-USA*, Aw provided 51 percent of the founding capital, and Soo himself provided the other 49 percent, with Soo soon being entrusted to run the US newspaper.[50]

In the early 1970s, Soo and Aw came into conflict over several issues.[51] One of these was the calendar adopted for the newspaper. As discussed above, *Sing Tao Daily* in Hong Kong adopted the ROC calendar to show its support for the ROC government. However, Soo decided to adopt the Gregorian calendar for *Sing Tao Daily-USA* in 1971, a move that coincided with the change of the "China" seat from the ROC to the PRC at the United Nations. Subsequently, the US edition expanded its coverage on the PRC. Soo also invited Chinese American scholar Zhao Hao-sheng (who taught at Yale University) as a columnist for the newspaper.[52] Zhao wrote articles explicitly supportive of the PRC and its policy toward Taiwan, most notably with an article titled "[The PRC's] Liberation of Taiwan [Is] Coming!" in his regular column in *Sing Tao Daily-USA*.[53] Before long, Soo and Zhao were considered "pro-PRC" and *Sing Tao Daily-USA* had become known as a "leftist" Chinese newspaper in the US.[54]

These changes alarmed both the ROC government in Taiwan and Sally Aw in Hong Kong. Under pressure from ROC authorities, Aw met Soo and proposed buying out Soo's share in *Sing Tao Daily-USA*, but Soo turned Aw down.[55] In 1974, after PRC leader Deng Xiaoping's unprecedented visit to the United Nations Headquarters in New York, *Sing Tao Daily-USA* published Deng's speech in its entirety.[56] The ROC authorities considered such an act as "propaganda for the Chinese communist" and again pushed Aw to take action in removing Soo from the newspaper. In 1977, ROC agents allegedly sent death threats to, and physically attacked, the New York office of *Sing Tao Daily-USA*. Later, Aw filed a lawsuit in the US against Soo over the ownership of *Sing Tao Daily-USA*, after which Soo was eventually forced to change the name of the newspaper to *North American Daily* (Beimei ribao), and Aw established a new newspaper using the name *Sing Tao Daily-USA*.[57]

While running the *North American Daily*, which shuttered in 1988, Soo took further action that was conspicuously "pro-PRC."[58] In 1979, Soo was invited, together with Zhao, by the National Tourism Bureau of the PRC to pay a visit to *Beidaihe*, the resort originally reserved for PRC high-ranking officials and military leaders. Soo became one of the first overseas Chinese journalists from the US to visit the PRC since 1949. His visit was arranged under the instruction of the PRC's State Council and was later reported in the official newspaper *People's Daily* as a promotion of "civilian tourism" (though open to "foreign guests" only at the time) to *Beidaihe*.[59]

Considering the education opportunities and resources available to overseas Chinese students in Southeast Asia in the 1950s and 1960s, it would be fair to argue that many benefited from the joint effort between the US and the ROC governments in promoting journalism education and qiaosheng education in Taiwan. The career trajectories of some of these qiaosheng alumni, especially those associated with pro-ROC Chinese newspapers in Malaysia, may be considered as consistent with the political and ideological agenda set out by the US and ROC governments in the 1950s. However, cases such as James Chan and Eddie Soo demonstrated that government policy did not always lead to politically desirable outcomes; some qiaosheng, having had their higher education in Taiwan financially sponsored by the US, later became supporters of the PRC.

Journalism education at NCCU, as supported by the US for more than a decade, was intended to train qiaosheng from across Asia, as well as domestic students from Taiwan, to contribute to the anti-Communist ideological war. Interestingly, and perhaps unexpectedly, this joint educational project also paved the way to promote journalism education in Southeast Asia and Hong Kong.

EDUCATORS: TEACHING JOURNALISM IN SINGAPORE AND HONG KONG

In addition to alumni who went on to practice journalism, a sizable cohort of NCCU journalism alumni who studied during the US aid period from 1955 to

1965 later became journalism scholars. While most were not qiaosheng from Southeast Asia, several made their careers and subsequently trained many professional journalists and journalism scholars in Southeast Asia. In order of graduation, the first was Eddie C. Y. Kuo (Guo Zhenyu), a 1962 graduate. After graduation, he was offered the East-West Center Scholarship by the US State Department in 1964 to study at the University of Hawai'i, where he received a master's degree in sociology. He subsequently obtained his PhD in sociology from the University of Minnesota in 1972, after which he went on to teach at the University of Singapore in 1973.[60] While he was a member of the Department of Sociology, Kuo offered a course on Mass Communication and Social Development, which was considered the first course of mass communication ever offered at a university in Singapore.[61] Kuo later founded the Department of Mass Communication at the National University of Singapore in 1990; the first batch of undergraduate students enrolled in the following year.[62] In 1992, Kuo also established the School of Communication Studies at Nanyang Technological University, where he served as the school's dean until 2003.[63]

Next was Leonard Chu (Zhu Li), who received his master's degree from the Graduate School of Journalism at NCCU in 1969 and later a PhD from SIU. Chu began teaching at the Department of Journalism and Communication at CUHK in 1975, and he served as its chair from 1986 to 1991.[64] As Chu taught for so many years at CUHK, at least four scholars who served as dean of the School of Journalism and Communication of CUHK were his former students.[65]

While Chu was teaching at CUHK, other alumni from NCCU's Department of Journalism joined him as colleagues, including Huangfu Hewang and Lee Chin-chuan (Li Jinquan).[66] Huangfu graduated from NCCU in 1966 and began teaching at CUHK in 1977; he later served as the chair of the Department of Journalism of Chu Hai College of Higher Education in Hong Kong from 2008 to 2016.[67] Lee graduated from NCCU in 1969 and, much like his upperclassman Eddie Kuo, was awarded the East-West Center Scholarship in 1971 to study at the University of Hawai'i, later obtaining his PhD at the University of Michigan. Lee taught at CUHK from 1978 to 1982, and then at the University of Minnesota from 1982 to 2004, during which time he joined CUHK as visiting chair professor from 1994 to 1995 and 1996 to 1998. Lee then taught at the City University of Hong Kong from 2002 until his retirement in 2018.[68] In his own biographical notes, Lee mentions that he taught five different scholars (four at CUHK and one at Minnesota) who later served as deans of the School of Journalism and Communication CUHK.[69]

None of the aforementioned NCCU journalism alumni were qiaosheng, but they nevertheless attended NCCU during the US aid period and consequently benefited from the US double support to journalism and qiaosh-eng education. While these NCCU journalism alumni did not play a direct role in the anti-Communist ideological war, as the US aid program during the 1950s and 1960s had intended, their rich experiences and groundbreaking accomplishments in training journalists in Singapore and Hong Kong could, and should, be recognized as a lasting legacy—and perhaps an unexpected outcome—of the US-ROC joint educational effort during the Cold War.

CONCLUSION

In pursuit of common political interest and Cold War propaganda, the US and the ROC governments worked together to establish journalism education at NCCU in Taiwan. From the mid-1950s to 1960s, the program recruited students from Taiwan, as well as from Southeast Asia, and trained a significant number of Chinese-speaking professional journalists. Some of these NCCU alumni went on to work in journalism, and many of those who did took up key edito-rial positions at news media that were supportive of, or at least sympathetic to, the anti-Communist stance of the US and the ROC in Taiwan, Malaysia, and beyond. However, as this chapter has explored, this joint educational effort designed for Cold War propaganda resulted in two unintended consequences.

First, as seen in both Malaysia and the US, several NCCU journalism alumni became critical of the ROC government in the late 1960s and 1970s. As they continued to play significant roles in Chinese-language news media, such alumni contributed to the shaping and reshaping of the ROC's image, vis-à-vis the PRC, among overseas Chinese communities. In the political and ideologi-cal realm, this change was significant, as the work of these so-called "pro-PRC" NCCU-trained journalists challenged, if not outright undermined, the Cold War propaganda initiatives envisioned by the US and the ROC.

Second, perhaps somewhat separated from the political and ideological front line, several NCCU journalism alumni went on to pursue academic careers; several of them, such as Eddie Kuo and Lee Chin-chuan, were further sup-ported by scholarships from the US State Department. These NCCU graduates became leading journalism scholars in Singapore and Hong Kong in the 1980s, and their influence on journalism education and contributions to training fu-ture generations of journalists in the region continue until the present day.

This chapter, like chapter 9 by Yang Zhang and chapter 10 by Jae Young Cha in this volume, shows that individual recipients of the US aid to journalism education in different Asian countries maintained their own autonomy and acted according to the local conditions in their decisions to adopt, modify, or reject the official agenda set by the US and its allies. As a result, the effect of US-supported education in its allied countries during the Cold War was limited. The political and ideological intentions of the US-ROC joint efforts in promoting journalism education in Taiwan in the 1950s and 1960s were at best only partially accomplished. Rather, these joint Cold War efforts resulted in unintended consequences that were occasionally politically counterproductive and at other times very productive educationally.

NOTES

* The author would like to express his sincere gratitude to the generous support from the research project of "Freedom, Democracy, and Human Rights in Modern East Asia (2018–2019)" at the National Chengchi University (NCCU), Professor Yuka Tsuchiya Moriguchi of Kyoto University, Professor Eddie Kuo of Singapore University of Social Sciences, Dato Jeffrey Low (Liu Wenxing), Mr. Liu Yahuang, Mr. Loke Jack Keng (Lu Jiejing), and all the meticulous efforts of my research assistant Wu Bozhen.

1. This has been the subject of a great deal of scholarship, usually related to the US foreign policy. See S. G. Zhang, *Deterrence and Strategic Culture*; Accinelli, *Crisis and Commitment*; Christensen, *Useful Adversaries*; Garver, *Sino-American Alliance*; Xiao and Lin, "Inside the Asian Cold War Intrigues."

2. These topics have continued to draw scholarly attention for more than half a century. See Chang, "U.S. Aid and Economic Progress in Taiwan"; Jacob, *U.S. Aid to Taiwan*; Winckler and Greenhalgh, *Contending Approaches*; Cullather, "Fuel for the Good Dragon"; Goldman and Gordon, eds., *Historical Perspectives*; Chiang, "U.S. Aid." For a more critical examination of the US role, see Cumings, *Parallax Visions*; Amsden, *Escape from Empire*.

3. Y. Zhang and Li, "Misuli xinwen jiaoyu zai xiandai Zhongguo de yizhi," 321–23.

4. Zhang and Li, 323.

5. Guoli Zhengzhidaxue, "Zhengda xiaoshi."

6. Y. Zhang and Li, "Misuli xinwen jiaoyu zai xiandai Zhongguo de yizhi," 334–36.

7. Guoli Zhengzhidaxue chuanbo xueyuan, "Ma Xingye: yidai xinwen zongshi."

8. *Lianhe bao*, "Misuli xinwen xueyuan zengwo Zhengda tushu."

9. See, for example, Cull, *Cold War*.

10. *Lianhe bao*, "Meixuezhe sanren jianglaitai renjiao."

11. Around this time, from March to May 1959, Hideo Ono, a prominent journalism scholar from the University of Tokyo, also joined NCCU as a visiting professor. See *Lianhe bao*, "Fuzongtong zuoyan Gegusen Keke bingceng jiejian

Xiaoye Xiuxiong"; *Zhongyang she*, "Guoli Zhengzhidaxue xiaozhang Chen Daqi zengjinianpin yu Riben Xiaoye Xiuxiong jiaoshou." It is worth noting that in 1963 Hideo Ono was made NCCU's first honorary professor. See Guoli Zhengzhidaxue chuanbo xueyuan xinwenxue xi, "Dashi ji."

12. Archives West, "Biographical Notes."

13. *Lianhe bao*, "Zhengda yanjiubu zuo zhengshi shangke."

14. Archives West, "Biographical Notes."

15. *Lianhe bao*, "Kong Musi jiaoshou zuo litai fanmei"; Culmsee, "Tight Little Island." The *New York Times Magazine*, which usually features articles longer than the typical newspaper reports or commentary, is the weekly supplementary to the leading American newspaper the *New York Times*.

16. Culmsee, "Tight Little Island."

17. ISWNE, "Howard R. Long Scholarship."

18. Illinois Center for the Book, "Illinois Authors."

19. *Lianhe bao*, "Meiguo Nanyilinuozhou daxue xinwenxi zhuren Lang Haohua zuochen jiushi cheng minhangdui keji lihua feigang zhuanfan Meiguo."

20. *Lianhe bao*, "Zhongguo banxing xin chubanfa zhizai fangfan gongchan zhuyi yiai qingkuang xuke jiyu fangkuan Lang Haohua yinshu zongtong tanhua." *Quill* is the "Society of Professional Journalists' national magazine," which claims to have been "a respected and sought-after resource for journalists, industry leaders, students and educators on issues central to journalism" for more than ninety years. See *Quill*'s official website, https://www.quillmag.com /about/.

21. Guoli Zhengzhidaxue, *Zhengda xinwenguan luocheng jinian tekan*, 25–43.

22. Robert Blum was the founding president of the Asia Foundation's Board of Trustees (1954–62) and the founding president of the Asia Foundation. See Asia Foundation, "Robert Blum."

23. Guoli Zhengzhidaxue, *Zhengda xinwenguan luocheng jinian tekan*, 23.

24. This topic has continued to draw scholars' attention. For recent works, see Oyen, *Diplomacy of Migration*; Kung, *Diasporic Cold Warriors*.

25. For a more detailed study, see Wong, "College Admissions." It should be noted that administratively, the ROC government defined and recruited ethnic Chinese students from abroad in two different categories: "Chinese Overseas students" (*qiaosheng*) and "students from Hong Kong and Macao" (*Gang Ao sheng*). However, during the 1950s and 1960s, US educational aid, allocated either as "individual funding" to each qiaosheng or as "institutional funding" to the host university, applied to both categories of students. Therefore, this chapter makes no distinction between the two categories and considers all of these students as qiaosheng.

26. Qiaowu weiyuanhui yanjiu fazhan kaohechu, *Qiaosheng huiguo shengxue gaikuang*, 24–25.

US AID, JOURNALISM EDUCATION IN TAIWAN   247

27. Qiaowu weiyuanhui yanjiu fazhan kaohechu, 38.

28. Among them were the National Taiwan University, which was built on the foundation of the Tohoku Imperial University, established by the Japanese colonial authorities in 1928, and the Taiwan Provincial College of Engineering (later changed to National Cheng Kung University in 1971), built on the foundation of an engineering school also established by the Japanese colonial authorities in 1931.

29. *Zhongyang ribao*, "Zhengda xinxiaoshe jizhaoshang xingjian ji jiaoshi sushe ge sichuang."

30. Kuo, "My Academic Journey," 3.

31. By 1963, several new undergraduate majors were added, including Chinese language, Eastern languages, Western languages, law, finance, public administration, banking, international trade, accounting, and business administration. See Guoli Zhengzhidaxue, "*Guoli Zhengzhidaxue xueze*"; *Zhengda xiaokan*, no. 27.

32. Guoli Zhengzhidaxue, *Guoli Zhengzhi daxue xiaowu huiyi jilu*.

33. Du, "Baohuang yu geming, qingong yu fangong."

34. Lu, *Xinma huaren de zhongguoguan zhiyanjiu*, 77.

35. Du, "Baohuang yu geming, qingong yu fangong."

36. Lu, *Xinma huaren de zhongguoguan zhiyanjiu*, 77.

37. Du, "Baohuang yu geming, qingong yu fangong."

38. *Zhongguo bao*, "Guanyu women."

39. G. Zhang, "Jin Yong yu *Mingbao* diyige shiwu nian."

40. Yap, *Maxin Baorenlu*, B20; Yap, *Malaixiya huawen baoyeshi*, 173.

41. Liu Yahuang, interview with the author, August 2019, Kuala Lumpur, Malaysia.

42. Yap, *Maxin Baorenlu*, B13.

43. Yap, *Malaixiya huawen baoyeshi*, 191.

44. *Zhongyang ribao*, "Qiaosheng Yang Laitian zaima chuangban wanbao."

45. Lee, *Zhengzhan shiyun you miwu*.

46. Du, "Baohuang yu geming, qingong yu fangong."

47. Yap, *Maxin Baorenlu*, B12.

48. Zhonghua minguo Waijiaobu dangan, "Waijiaobudian zhu Jilongpo zonglingshiguan dianwen." I want to express my sincere gratitude to Mr. Zeng Xinhao, of the Department of History, National Taiwan University, for providing me with this information.

49. Mai, "Hu Xian."

50. *Renmin wang*, "Meiguo huawen chuanmei fazhan zongshu (jiexuan)"; *Shijie xinwenbao*, "Taiwan tewu qiangji Niuyue huawenbao."

51. Y. Li, *Taibei, Xianggang, Niuyue*, 79–81.

52. *Shijie xinwenbao*, "Taiwan tewu qiangji Niuyue huawenbao."

248   PRACTICING KNOWLEDGE

53. Yuan, *Feishi zhitan.*

54. Tang, "Shengming shi xinglu de yingzi."

55. *Shijie xinwenbao,* "Taiwan tewu qiangji Niuyue huawenbao."

56. Deng's speech, "Speech by Chairman of the Delegation of the People's Republic of China, Teng Hsiao-Ping, at the Special Session of the U.N. General Assembly," April 10, 1974, is available at https://www.marxists.org/reference /archive/deng-xiaoping/1974/04/10.htm.

57. *Shijie xinwenbao,* "Taiwan tewu qiangji Niuyue huawenbao"; Tang, "Shengming shi xinglu de yingzi."

58. *Shijie xinwenbao,* "Taiwan tewu qiangji Niuyue huawenbao."

59. Liu, "Liaoyang shengdi de pingminhua zhuanxing"; Shanhaiguanqu zhengxie, "Shanhaiguan gujin."

60. Kuo, "My Academic Journey," 4.

61. Guo, "Chushi Xinjiapo," 44.

62. Guo, "Xinjiapo chuanbo jiaoyu," 62.

63. Kuo, "My Academic Journey," 6–7; Guo, "Xinjiapo chuanbo jiaoyu," 63.

64. Yang, "Zhu Li."

65. Ong, "Zhu Li."

66. Su, "Xishuo Zhongda xinchuan wushi."

67. Zheng, "Yidai xinwen xuezhe Huangfu Hewang"; *Zhuhai xueyuan,* "Fugao."

68. Guoli Zhengzhidaxue chuanbo xueyuan xinwenxue xi, "Li Jinquan."

69. Li J., "Chuanbo zongheng," 145.

REFERENCES

Accinelli, Robert. *Crisis and Commitment: United States Policy toward Taiwan, 1950–1955.* Chapel Hill: University of North Carolina Press, 1996.

Amsden, Alice H. *Escape from Empire: The Developing World's Journey through Heaven and Hell.* Cambridge, MA: MIT Press, 2007.

Archives West. "Biographical Notes." *Carlton Culmsee Papers, 1897–1993.* Accessed July 15, 2022. https://archiveswest.orbiscascade.org/ark:80444/xv21850.

Asia Foundation. "Robert Blum." Accessed August 9, 2020. https://asiafoundation .org/people/robert-blum/.

Chang, David W. "U.S. Aid and Economic Progress in Taiwan." *Asian Survey* 5, no. 3 (1965): 152–60.

Chiang Min-hua. "The U.S. Aid and Taiwan's Post-war Economic Development, 1951–1965." *African and Asian Studies* 13, no. 1–2 (2014): 100–120.

Christensen, Thomas J. *Useful Adversaries: Grand Strategy, Domestic Mobilization, and Sino-American Conflict, 1947–1958.* Princeton, NJ: Princeton University Press, 1996.

Cull, Nicholas J. *The Cold War and the United States Information Agency: American Propaganda and Public Diplomacy, 1945–1989*. Cambridge: Cambridge University Press, 2008.

Cullather, Nick. "Fuel for the Good Dragon: The US and Industrial Policy in Taiwan, 1950–1965." *Diplomatic History* 20, no. 1 (1996): 1–25.

Culmsee, Carlton. "Tight Little Island—Off China." *New York Times Magazine*, August 19, 1956, 188.

Cumings, Bruce. *Parallax Visions: Making Sense of American–East Asian Relations at the End of the Century*. Durham, NC: Duke University Press, 1999.

Du, Jinxuan. "Baohuang yu geming, qingong yu fangong: fenrao Malaixiya huawenbao bainian de 'luxian' zhizheng" [Defending the emperor and revolution, pro-Communist and anti-Communist: One hundred years of conflict over 'approaches' confronting Chinese newspapers in Malaysia]. *Newslens*, December 14, 2019. https://www.thenewslens.com/article /128772.

Garver, John W. *The Sino-American Alliance: Nationalist China and American Cold War Strategy in Asia*. Armonk, NY: M. E. Sharpe, 1997.

Goldman, Merle, and Andrew Gordon, eds. *Historical Perspectives on Contemporary East Asia*. Cambridge, MA: Harvard University Press, 2000.

Guo, Zhenyu [Eddie C. Y. Kuo]. "Chushi Xinjiapo" [First acquaintance with Singapore]. *Yihe shiji* (Singapore), no. 37 (October 2018).

———. "Xinjiapo chuanbo jiaoyu: cong bozhong dao chengyin (shang)" [Communication education in Singapore: From sowing seeds to making a shade (part 1)]. *Yihe shiji* (Singapore), no. 40 (July 2019).

Guoli Zhengzhidaxue [National Chengchi University]. *Guoli Zhengzhi daxue Biye Jiniance* [Graduation yearbook, National Chengchi University], 1959 to 1969.

———. *Guoli Zhengzhi daxue xiaowu huiyi jilu* [Minutes of academic affairs meetings, National Chengchi University]. Taipei: Guoli Zhengzhi daxue, 1958.

———. "Guoli Zhengzhidaxue xueze" [Academic rules, National Chengchi University], January 18, 1957. In *Guoli Zhengzhidaxue. Guoli Zhengzhidaxue xiaowu huiyi jilu* [Minutes of academic affairs meetings, National Chengchi University]. Taipei: Guoli Zhengzhi daxue, 1958.

———. "Zhengda xiaoshi" [University history]. Accessed August 5, 2020. https:// archive.rdw.lib.nccu.edu.tw/history/.

———. *Zhengda xinwenguan luocheng jinian tekan* [Special issue commemorating the dedication of the new Journalism Building, National Chengchi University]. Taipei: Guoli Zhengzhi daxue, 1962.

Guoli Zhengzhidaxue chuanbo xueyuan [College of Communication, National Chengchi University]. "Ma Xingye: yidai xinwen zongshi" [Ma Xingye: The founder of journalism in his generation]. Accessed July 22, 2020. https://comm .nccu.edu.tw/zh_tw/member/link18/retired_teachers/%E9%A6%AC%E6%98

%9F%E9%87%8E-%E4%B8%80%E4%BB%A3%E6%96%B0%E8%81%9E%E5%AE%97%E5%B8%AB-41865033.

Guoli Zhengzhidaxue chuanbo xueyuan xinwenxue xi [Department of Journalism, College of Communication, National Chengchi University]. "Dashi ji" [Chronicle of major events]. Accessed July 15, 2020. https://jschool.nccu.edu.tw/zh_tw/Introduction/chronicle.

———. "Lijie xiyou minglu (daxuebu)" [List of department alumni by year (undergraduates)]. Accessed July 8, 2020. https://jschool.nccu.edu.tw/zh_tw/AL/SuccessiveOutstandingAlumni.

———. "Li Jinquan: shouqu yizhi de Zhonghua chuanbo wenti yanjiu xuezhe" [Lee Chin-chuan: Renowned Chinese communication scholar]. Accessed July 15, 2020. https://jschool.nccu.edu.tw/zh_tw/AL/AlumniOverview/alumni015.

Illinois Center for the Book, Illinois State Library. "Illinois Authors: Howard Rusk Long." Accessed August 8, 2020. http://www.illinoisauthors.org/cgi-bin/illinoisAuthors/getSpecificAuthor.pl?uid=6443.

ISWNE (International Society of Weekly Newspaper Editors). "Howard R. Long Scholarship." February 14, 2012. https://www.iswne.org/foundation/scholarships/howard_r_long/howard-r-long-scholarship/article_61147c06-575f-11e1-9f55-001871e3ce6c.html.

Jacob, Neil Herman. *U.S. Aid to Taiwan: A Study of Foreign Aid, Self-help, and Development.* New York: Frederick A. Praeger, 1966.

Kung, Chien-Wen. *Diasporic Cold Warriors: Nationalist China, Anticommunism, and the Philippine Chinese, 1930s–1970s.* Ithaca, NY: Cornell University Press, 2022.

Kuo, Eddie C. Y. "My Academic Journey." *Chinese Communication Association Newsletter (CCA News)*, December 2012.

Lee, Alfred K. [Li Dunqiao]. *Zhengzhan shiyun you miwu: shouwei Shalaoyue liutaisheng banshiji muen lucheng* [Reminiscence of fifty-year blessed journey through thick and thin by the first Sarawakian graduate from Taiwan]. Malaysia: Alfred K. Lee, 2004.

Li Jinquan [Lee Chin-chuan]. "Chuanbo zongheng: xueshu shengya wushinian" [Crisscrossing communication: Fifty years of academic career]. *Chuanbo yanjiu yu shijian* [Journal of communication research and practice] 9, no. 1 (January 2019): 131–63.

Li, Yong. *Taibei, Xianggang, Niuyue* [Taipei, Hong Kong, New York]. Taipei: Huangguan chubanshe, 1983.

Lianhe bao [United daily]. "Fuzongtong zuoyan Gegusen Keke bingceng jiejian Xiaoye Xiuxiong" [Vice president hosted dinner for (Magnus L.) Gregersen and (Alan) Kirk and met Hideo Ono]. March 5, 1959.

———. "Kong Musi jiaoshou zuo litai fanmei" [Professor Carlton Culmsee left Taiwan and returned to the US yesterday]. August 22, 1956.

———. "Meiguo Nanyilinuozhou daxue xinwenxi zhuren Lang Haohua zuochen jiushi cheng minhangdui keji lihua feigang zhuanfan Meiguo" [Howard Long, chair of the Department of Journalism, Southern Illinois University, left (Republic of) China yesterday morning at nine on Civil Air Transport passenger plane to the US via Hong Kong]. June 16, 1958.

———. "Meixuezhe sanren jianglaitai renjiao" [Three American scholars will come to Taiwan and teach]. September 10, 1955.

———. "Misuli xinwen xueyuan zengwo Zhengda tushu" [University of Missouri's School of Journalism donated books to Chengchi University here]. April 6, 1955.

———. "Zhengda yanjiubu zuo zhengshi shangke" [Graduate school of Chengchi University started its class yesterday]. October 4, 1955.

———. "Zhongguo banxing xin chubanfa zhizai fangfan gongchan zhuyi yiai qingkuang xuke jiyu fangkuan Lang Haohua yinshu zongtong tanhua" [(Republic of) China implemented new publication laws, aiming to prevent Communism; once the condition allows, restrictions will be lifted. Howard Long quoted the president's statement]. July 2, 1958.

Liu, Xinyin. "Liaoyang shengdi de pingminhua zhuanxing" [Transformation of a rehabilitation retreat to civilian use]. *Guojia renwen lish* [National humanities and history], no. 19 (2014). http://reader.epubee.com/books/mobile/fc /fcfbe9e11e0e3a9a29e7dfd308e3b9b6/text00008.html.

Lu, Hu. *Xinma huaren de zhongguoguan zhiyanjiu* [Study of the perception of China among Chinese overseas in Singapore and Malaysia]. Singapore: Centre for Chinese Studies, Singapore University of Social Sciences, 2014.

Mai, Yanting. "Hu Xian: Xu Jiatun tongzhan *Xingdao ribao*" [Aw Sian: Xu Jiatun led united front work targeting Sing Tao Jih Pao]. Radio France Internationale (RFI), May 2, 2018. http://www.rfi.fr/tw/%E4%B8%AD%E5%9C%8B/20180205 -%E8%83%A1%E4%BB%99%E8%A8%B1%E5%AE%B6%E5%B1%AF%E7%B5 %B1%E6%88%B0%E6%98%9F%E5%B3%B6%E6%97%A5%E5%A0%B1.

Ong, Jacqueline. "Zhu Li: jiaoxue sishizai yucai pianji Taigangao" [Zhu Li: Forty years of teaching, fostering talent all over Taiwan, Hong Kong, Macao]. Guoli Zhengzhi daxue chuanbo xueyuan: renwu texie [College of Communication, National Chengchi University: Close-up]. January 7, 2013. https://jschool.nccu .edu.tw/zh_tw/faculty/RetiredTeacher/emeritus017.

Oyen, Meredith. *The Diplomacy of Migration: Transnational Lives and the Making of U.S.-Chinese Relations in the Cold War.* Ithaca, NY: Cornell University Press, 2015.

Qiaowu weiyuanhui yanjiu fazhan kaohechu, ed. *Qiaosheng huiguo shengxue gaikuang* [Overview of overseas Chinese students returning to the home country for study]. Taipei: Qiaowu weiyuanhui yanjiu fazhan kaohechu, 1972.

Renmin wang [People's daily online]. "Meiguo huawen chuanmei fazhan zongshu (jiexuan) [Overview of the development of Chinese media in the US (excerpt)]."

November 4, 2005. http://media.people.com.cn/BIG5/22114/54740/54742/3830015.html.

Shanhaiguanqu zhengxie [Political Consultative Committee of the Shanhaiguan district]. "Shanhaiguan gujin" [Past and present of Shanhaiguan]. August 4, 2008. http://www.shgzx.gov.cn/shownews.asp?id=333.

Shijie xinwenbao [World journal]. "Taiwan tewu qiangji Niuyue huawenbao" [Special agents from Taiwan fired a gun at Chinese newspaper in New York]. December 1, 2006. http://news.sina.com.cn/o/2006-12-01/150910659500s.shtml.

Su, Yaoji. "Xishuo Zhongda xinchuan wushi" [Telling the story of fifty years of journalism and communication at the Chinese University (of Hong Kong) in details]. *Ming Pao*, October 31, 2015. http://www.com.cuhk.edu.hk/zh-TW/about/school-history.

Tang, Yan. "Shengming shi xinglu de yingzi: daonian Lin Bowen" [Life is the shadow of walk: Commemorating Lin Bowen]. *Storm Media*, February 11, 2019. https://www.storm.mg/article/928294.

Winckler, E. A., and Greenhalgh, Susan, eds. *Contending Approaches to the Political Economy of Taiwan*. Armonk, NY: M. E. Sharpe, 1988.

Wong, Ting-Hong. "College Admissions, International Competition, and the Cold War in Asia: The Case of Overseas Chinese Students in Taiwan in the 1950s." *History of Education Quarterly* 56, no. 2 (2016): 331–57.

Xiao, Ruping, and Lin Hsiao-ting. "Inside the Asian Cold War Intrigues: Revisiting the Taiwan Strait Crises." *Modern Asian Studies* 52, no. 6 (2018): 2109–36.

Xingzhengyuan guoji jingji hezuo fazhan weiyuanhui. *Qiaosheng jiaoyu jihua yunyong Meiyuan chengguo jiantao* [Review of the effect of US aid to overseas Chinese education project]. Taipei: Xingzhengyuan guoji jingji hezuo fazhan weiyuanhui, 1966.

Yang, Qianrong. "Zhu Li: wei huaren chuanbo xuezhe daqi goutong qiuaoliang" [Zhu Li: Building bridges for Chinese communication scholars]. Guoli Zhengzhi daxue chuanbo xueyuan: renwu texie [College of Communication, National Chengchi University: Close-up]. November 1, 2010. Accessed August 5, 2020. https://comm.nccu.edu.tw/zh_tw/link18/people10/%E6%9C%B1%E7%AB%8B-%E7%82%BA%E8%8F%AF%E4%BA%BA%E5%82%B3%E6%92%AD%E5%AD%B8%E8%80%85%E6%90%AD%E8%B5%B7%E6%BA%9D%E9%80%9A%E6%A9%8B%E6%A8%91-38723442.

Yap, Koon See, *Malaixiya huawen baoyeshi (1815–2010)* [The Chinese Press in Malaysia]. Selangor, Malaysia: Manland, 2010.

———, ed. *Maxin Baorenlu (1806–2000)* [Who's who in the press, Malaysia and Singapore]. Selangor, Malaysia: Manland, 1999.

Yuan, Richard [Dafang Ruan]. *Feishi zhitan: xiangshidai qiangsheng duilishifuze* [Talk like a nonofficial: To raise a voice to our time and to take responsibility for history]. Taipei: Fengyun shidai chubanshe, 2010.

Zhang, Guiyang. "Jin Yong yu *Mingbao* diyige shiwu nian (1959–1973)" [Jin Yong and *Mingbao* the first fifteen years (1959–1973)]. *Ming Pao*, November 1, 2018. https://news.mingpao.com/ins/%E6%96%87%E6%91%98/article/20181101 /s00022/1541062064564/%E9%87%91%E5%BA%B8%E8%88%87%E3%80 %8A%E6%98%8E%E5%A0%B1%E3%80%8B-%E7%AC%AC%E4%B8%80%E5 %80%8B15%E5%B9%B4%EF%BC%881959-1973%EF%BC%89%EF%BC %88%E6%96%87-%E5%BC%B5%E5%9C%AD%E9%99%BD%EF%BC%89.

Zhang, Shu Guang. *Deterrence and Strategic Culture: Chinese-American Confrontations, 1949–1958*. Ithaca, NY: Cornell University Press, 1992.

Zhang, Yong, and Li Jinquan [Chin-chuan Lee]. "Misuli xinwen jiaoyu moshi zai xiandai Zhongguo de yizhi" [Transplantation of the Missouri journalism education model in modern China]. In *Wenren lunzheng: Minguo zhishifenzi yu baokan* [original title: *Literati cum Political Commentators: Intellectuals and the Press in Republican China*], edited by Jinquan Li, 321–50. Taipei: Zhengda chubanshe, 2008.

Zheng, Mingren. "Yidai xinwen xuezhe Huangfu Hewang" [Journalism scholar of the generation Huangfu Hewang]. *Mingbao*, December 15, 2017. https://m .mingpao.com/pns/%E4%BD%9C%E5%AE%B6%E5%B0%88%E6%AC%84 /article/20171215/s00018/1513275336093/%E4%B8%80%E4%BB%A3%E6%96 %B0%E8%81%9E%E5%AD%B8%E8%80%85%E7%9A%87%E7%94%AB%E6 %B2%B3%E6%97%BA.

Zhengda xiaokan [Bulletin of Chengchi University], no. 2, November 1960; no. 11, December 1961; no. 19, November 1962; no. 27, December 1963; no. 35, December 1964; no. 43, January 1966; no. 51, January 1967.

Zhongguo bao [China press]. "Guanyu women" [About us]. Accessed on August 3, 2020. https://www.chinapress.com.my/%e5%85%b3%e4%ba%8e%e6%88%91 %e4%bb%ac/.

Zhonghua minguo Waijiaobu dangan [Archives of the Ministry of Foreign Affairs, Republic of China]. "Waijiaobudian zhu Jilongpo zonglingshiguan dianwen" [Telegram from the Ministry of Foreign Affairs to the Consulate General, Kuala Lumpur]. In "Dongnanya huaqiao shexian (san)" [Allegations of overseas Chinese in Southeast Asia (part 3)], September 1, 1970–September 26, 1971. Guoshiguan [Academia Historica, Taiwan], file 020-990600-2919.

Zhongyang ribao (Central daily). "Qiaosheng Yang Laitian zaima chuangban wanbao" [Chinese overseas student Yang Laitian founded an evening newspaper in Malaysia]. November 20, 1966.

Zhongyang ribao [*Central Daily*]. "Zhengda xinxiaoshe jizhaoshang xingjian ji jiaoshi sushe ge sichuang" [New school buildings of Chengchi University will be constructed soon as construction bidding began; four buildings each for classrooms and dormitory]. May 2, 1955.

Zhongyang she [Central News Agency]. "Guoli Zhengzhidaxue xiaozhang Chen Daqi zengjinianpin yu Riben Xiaoye Xiuxiong jiaoshou" [President of National

Chengchi University Chen Daqi presented souvenir to Professor Hideo Ono from Japan]. May 11, 1959. August 25, 2022. https://nrch.culture.tw/view.aspx ?keyword=%E5%B0%8F%E9%87%8E%E7%A7%80%E9%9B%84&s=566896 &id=0006449460&proj=MOC_IMD_001.

Zhuhai xueyuan [Zhuhai College]. "Fugao: daonian Huangfu Hewang jiaoshou" [Obituary: In memory of Professor Huangfu Hewang]. *Zhuhai xueyuan: xiaonei xinwen* [Zhuhai College: Campus news], December 14, 2017. https://www .chuhai.edu.hk/zh-hant/news/%E8%A8%83%F5%91%8A%EF%BC%9A%E6%82 %BC%E5%BF%B5%E7%9A%87%E7%94%AB%E6%B2%B3%E6%97%BA%E6 %95%99%E6%8E%88.

AUTHOR BIO

MIKE SHICHI LAN is Associate Professor of History at the National Chengchi University, Taiwan. His publications include "Trapped between Imperial Ruins: Internment and Repatriation of the Taiwanese in Postwar Asia-Pacific," in Barak Kushner and Sherzod Muminov, eds., *Overcoming Empire in Post-Imperial East Asia: Repatriation, Redress and Rebuilding* (2019).

NINE

THE COLD WAR, US INTERNATIONAL EDUCATIONAL EXCHANGE, AND THE DEVELOPMENT OF HONG KONG'S JOURNALISM AND COMMUNICATION EDUCATION

YANG ZHANG

INTRODUCTION

As is generally understood, the origin of Hong Kong's journalism and communication education in the modern sense dates back to the establishment of the Department of Journalism at the Chinese University of Hong Kong (CUHK) in 1965.[1] Essential to the department's establishment was assistance from the US government's cultural institutions, private funds, and educational support from individual American researchers. Shortly thereafter, Hong Kong Baptist College (now Hong Kong Baptist University) established its Department of Communication, and, around the same time, CUHK expanded its Journalism Department into a Department of Journalism and Communication. Since the establishment of the People's Republic of China (PRC), the US public and private sectors showed great interest in the circumstances of Hong Kong's journalism and communication education and provided funds, teachers, teaching materials, and equipment to support its development. The curricula, educational principles, and journalistic ethics underlying Hong Kong's journalism and communication education have therefore been strongly influenced by American academia, and Hong Kong has traditionally been viewed as an example of the successful export of American educational philosophies and values.

In fact, the attention that the US public and private sectors, including the Asia Foundation, directed toward Hong Kong's journalism and communication education, and the assistance they provided, were part of US efforts to export its knowledge in the early stages of the Cold War.[2] In the immediate postwar period, the US aimed to export knowledge, primarily through international education and cultural exchange, as a means of winning "hearts and minds." Introducing American models of knowledge, research interests and methods, and academic paradigms into and across target regions helped the US to strengthen its image, bolster its position in the struggle for global discourse power, and advance its political agendas and eventually its influence over the structure of international relations. In this context, because of its unique geographical location and historical background, Hong Kong was viewed by the US as an important target region for knowledge export.

The literature on the Cultural Cold War is now voluminous. It is well known that the superpowers of both the East and the West strove to win the hearts and minds of men in the fields of art, literature, music, sports, exhibitions, consumer culture, and so on.[3] Similarly, education and academics inevitably became entwined in the wider Cold War system, and there has been a growing body of research on US knowledge-dissemination efforts and their effects against the background of the Cold War.[4] Journalism and communication, in particular, is a discipline with distinctly American characteristics. However, as far as the author is aware, there have to date been very few studies on the dissemination and reception of communication studies in Hong Kong during the Cold War.

This chapter reviews US efforts in the establishment of the journalism and communication professions in Hong Kong's higher education system and examines its politically motivated knowledge-transfer activities and their impact. While recognizing the kinship between Hong Kong and US journalism and communication education practices, the chapter focuses on illustrating the capabilities of Hong Kong scholars during the Cold War period and the skills they demonstrated in applying what they learned.

One of the primary driving forces behind the establishment of Hong Kong's journalism and communication education was the urgent need of the Hong Kong intellectual elite for high-quality journalists with integrity in their journalistic standards. The elements that impelled Hong Kong scholars to willingly incorporate strong US influence into their journalism and communication education as academic diversity and to welcome cosmopolitanism lay not only in their keen awareness of the local need for more accountable journalists but also in their strong sense of identity. Thus, the influence of traditional Chinese culture remained strong in Hong Kong, resulting in the US efforts achieving only "invited influence"—that is, an inability to fully control the direction in which Hong Kong's journalism and communication education developed.

THE COLD WAR COMPETITION OVER "HEARTS AND MINDS" AND US ATTENTION TO THE MODERNIZATION OF HONG KONG'S EDUCATIONAL PROGRAMS

As is generally understood, US efforts to export its knowledge were initiated by individuals such as missionaries and private organizations with a strong sense of cultural and political consciousness. After the outbreak of the Cold War, the US transformed itself into a national security state and established a liberal internationalist policy of serving as leader of the "free world."[5] Accordingly, the US adjusted its foreign policy, and "winning hearts and minds" became a central geopolitical strategy in the global Cold War between the US and the Soviet Union. In the 1950 National Security Council Report 68/3 (NSC 68/3), the US government stated that "the degree to which other peoples and nations develop and maintain confidence in themselves and the free society of which they are—or hope to be—a part will depend in critical measure upon their confidence in the United States," and it emphasized that "circumstances and events have thrust upon the United States leadership in world affairs."[6] The new responsibility of serving as the world's leader and the ideological conflict of the early Cold War period united US citizens in a national consensus on the need for an immediate allocation of national resources.

Around the same time, private foundations also began increasing the importance they placed on exporting American knowledge. For instance, the Ford Foundation's Gaither Report, a document equivalent to the foundation's mission statement, expresses the following ideas: "As the tide of communism mounts in Asia and Europe, the position of the United States is crucial. We are striving at great cost to strengthen free peoples everywhere. The needs of such peoples, particularly in under-developed areas, are vast and seemingly endless, yet their eventual well-being may prove essential to our own security. To improve their living standards, they must import and use knowledge, guidance, and capital. The United States appears to be the only country able to provide even a part of the urgently needed assistance."[7]

Such reports are indicative of the contemporary view, shared by both the US public and private sectors, that the exportation of American knowledge was essential.

The Cold War competition over hearts and minds presented the US government with a rationale for the export of American knowledge, and the US Congress passed a series of legislation to support the legality of the practice. In 1946, the US Congress enacted the Fulbright Act (PL 584), which allowed the country to use foreign currency accrued in the sale of surplus war property abroad to provide international educational exchange programs. The Fulbright Act is generally not considered a direct product of the Cold War. However, as the US-Soviet Cold War progressed, the act also came to be used to export American knowledge through scholarly exchange projects. Furthermore, in 1948, to regulate the broadcasting of media produced for foreign audiences, the US Congress passed the Smith-Mundt Act (PL 402), under which President Harry S. Truman established the US Advisory Commission on Educational Exchange. This officially marked the beginning of US international educational exchange efforts to win the Cold War. The US Department of State at the time stated the aim of such efforts as follows: "Promoting free and democratic lifestyles worldwide through extensive exchange of technologies, culture, and knowledge with the aim of encouraging all nations, including the US, to abandon any peace-threatening prejudice we may hold between ourselves."[8] In other words, the original aim of the US educational exchange program was to promote mutual understanding and export their institutional and academic paradigms.

However, the 1957 Sputnik crisis cast doubt on US technological and educational superiority, on which its claim to leadership was based. In a sense, the Soviet satellite launch beat out the US in demonstrating the kind of social system that could maximize productivity and promote the greatest progress in science and technology. As Walt Rostow concluded, the 1957 Sputnik crisis brought to the forefront of history not only nuclear issues but also issues concerning the fate of developing regions (in Asia, the Middle East, Africa, and Latin America).[9] The US government's perspective on *undeveloped* nations in Asia was that while they possessed the natural resources and potential agricultural production capacity required for development, they lacked training opportunities and human resources such as professors and experts who could cultivate the specialized knowledge necessary for development.[10] While the citizens of Asian nations were struggling to conquer poverty, their leaders had little experience in modern state governance. Consequently, after the retreat of colonialism, separatism found its way back into such nations, and the youth came to reject the traditions and values of older generations. There was no immediate solution to these issues; resolving them required sound goals and intellectual approaches.[11] In other words, the Cold War competition over hearts and minds centered on securing opportunities to help Asian, African, and Latin American nations cultivate well-educated leaders and citizens, and, from the US perspective, the first step in doing that was to help them realize that fair and democratic governments could only be founded on freedom and accountability. This required providing developing nations with education designed to foster respectable citizens able to make informed decisions.[12]

The Sputnik crisis not only pushed the US Congress to pass the National Defense Education Act in 1958 but also convinced the US government of the need to develop and export knowledge as a national security measure. In 1960, the US government established Hawai'i's East-West Center with the mission to promote cross-cultural exchange to identify and share knowledge essential for economic and social advancement, authorized under the Mutual Security Act.[13] In 1961, the US Congress passed the Mutual Educational and Cultural Exchange Act, also known as the Fulbright-Hays Act. The act officially authorized US government agencies to spread American knowledge internationally through education, science, and culture development programs designed to aid participating nations in acquiring the knowledge and skills they needed, depending on their nation's developmental stage.[14] The Fulbright-Hays Act secured the legality of US international educational exchange efforts more firmly than all similar laws previously had and provided the US government with justification for investing in enhanced efforts to export American knowledge.

In the 1960s, the US government organized a greater number of international educational exchange events, labeling such exchanges as "international intellectual cooperation."[15] International educational exchange activities were held throughout Asia, not only because of increased US interest in Asia but also because intellectuals such as Rostow took official or advisory positions in the US government. According to some American intellectuals of the time, Asian universities lacked many professional disciplines required of modern society, including sociology, anthropology, geography, law, psychology, and geology, and had not been exposed to fields such as public management, international relations, business management, and mass communication. If such disciplines were to be incorporated into Asian universities, the direction of their development held relevance not only to their national development and their relationships with the US but also to the success of the "free world" anti-Communist strategy. For instance, international relations courses were expected to help cultivate students' potential to become national leaders equipped with the broad and deep expertise needed to identify and pursue national interests and thus their ability to successfully navigate their nations through complex real-world international relationships.[16] Moreover, the development of mass media and communication education was believed to help developing countries adopt effective large-scale measures to address issues relating to their nation's growth, stability, and social reform.[17] For these reasons, the US formulated policies to modernize education systems in Asia through measures tailored to each nation's unique circumstances.

Hong Kong found itself in the midst of the Cultural Cold War between the US and China. In August 1945, after regaining control over Hong Kong, Britain promoted the principle of freedom of the press, turning Hong Kong into a major battlefield for various political forces. In 1949, Hong Kong's geographical advantage began to attract media representatives from around the world, a trend that continued throughout the early Cold War period. These media representatives included newspaper, magazine, and other types of journalists from mainland China, who traveled to Hong Kong in large numbers on multiple occasions. Around this time, the local commercial media industry in Hong Kong had become relatively prosperous, although the number of US and Chinese political media organizations had also been growing since the outbreak of the Cold War. In addition, being the "free world" territory geographically closest to China, and thereby the most convenient location for gathering information about it, Hong Kong's news reports on China attracted worldwide attention. US diplomats in Hong Kong were quick to realize the importance of Hong Kong as an information and intelligence hub. According to the then Hong Kong representative of the Asia Foundation, "Hong Kong is an important Asian base for reporters from the US, the UK, and many other nations."[18] At the time, funded by the US Information Service (USIS) and the Asia Foundation, colleges and other educational institutions in Hong Kong undertook a large number of research projects looking into issues relating to China. The Union System, a nonprofit organization established with the purpose of providing information to the US, collected and sent to the US a considerable amount of research papers and news coverage on China through the Union Research Institute, the Union Press, and the Union Regional Centers.[19]

Another important feature of Hong Kong was that, as a Chinese cultural cluster within Greater China, it had great influence on overseas Chinese populations. Situated at the intersection of East and West, tradition and modernity, and Communism and liberal democracy, Hong Kong served as a bridge between cultures. As mentioned above, in the late 1950s and early 1960s, American political and social elites, motivated by development theories, were extremely determined to restructure developing countries as part of the fight against Communism. Modernizing education thus became a key aim of US international educational exchange efforts. George E. Taylor, renowned scholar of Chinese studies, submitted a report to the Asia Foundation in which he argued that scientific methodologies were one of the major weapons to ward off opponents in the ideological conflict between the East and the West; indeed, this was the overarching philosophy intended to keep democracy functioning. Gaining a scientific perspective was therefore a prerequisite to understanding Western traditions. Taylor proposed that the US should put more effort into aiding the development of various aspects of Southeast Asian education systems.[20] From the perspective of the Cultural Cold War, the US attached great importance to the education and modernization of Hong Kong, and Hong Kong received more help from the Asia Foundation than did any other Asian region. In Hong Kong, the US government, as well as private organizations, successively launched textbook programs to "promote modern educational principles," graduate exchange programs to "modernize conventional ways of thinking with inspiration and revitalization," and basic research programs of Chinese studies to "transform traditional Chinese culture."[21] Under these circumstances, those at the forefront of American cultural diplomacy gradually shifted their attention toward Hong Kong's journalism and communication education and decided to assist its development as part of the US political strategy to achieve its cultural aims in the Cold War.

MODERNIZATION OR AMERICANIZATION: THE US AND THE ESTABLISHMENT OF CUHK'S DEPARTMENT OF JOURNALISM

Establishment of a new discipline is influenced by many factors. Regarding journalism and communication education in Hong Kong, inherited knowledge and the cultural background of Hong Kong journalism, as well as the efforts of local scholars, were of course important. However, the large amount of financial and human resource investment from American public and private institutions was of equal importance. As mentioned above, the aims of the US in funding Hong Kong's higher education institutions during the Cultural Cold War were to promote mutual understanding, win support from Hong Kong's intellectuals, and export democracy and liberalism. In line with these aims, the US focus in the late 1950s shifted toward modernizing Hong Kong's education systems as a base for defeating Communism. Examination of the establishment and development of Hong Kong's journalism and communication education reveals that, through providing assistance to higher education institutions in the development of journalism and communication courses, the US also achieved considerable influence over the academic models, research interests, and academic principles of Hong Kong's journalism and communication education. In other words, US efforts that were initially aimed at modernizing Hong Kong's education systems in a sense shifted toward Americanizing them.[22]

262 PRACTICING KNOWLEDGE

*Earlier Attempts at Establishing Departments for Journalism
and Communication Education in Hong Kong*

In 1945, Hong Kong had only one officially recognized university—the University of Hong Kong. The university was, and remained for a considerable time, under the influence of British educational philosophy. As British academia had not traditionally invested in the journalism and communication fields, the University of Hong Kong also lacked faculties, departments, or programs related to journalism and communication education. After the Civil War and the establishment of the PRC, many intellectuals and students fled from mainland China to Hong Kong, and several Chinese Academies of Classical Learning and evening schools were founded. Although these institutions often struggled to survive, the refugee intellectuals nevertheless received great attention from the US public and private sectors. The USIS knew that Hong Kong's refugees from mainland China included many cultural or educational elites, as well as journalists with the potential to play significant roles in the US plan to spread anti-Communist propaganda.[23] The US State Department had long been planning to establish a "Chinese refugee university" in Hong Kong.[24] The State Department aimed to create, in the Far East, a favorable political atmosphere by influencing as many cultural institutions in Hong Kong as possible, including publishers, printers, media organizations, and schools.[25]

Around the time of the Communist revolution in mainland China, Hong Kong's media industry was developing rapidly, creating growing demand for journalists. In 1951, the British Hong Kong government began offering a three-year journalism course at the then recently founded Advanced Han Wen Evening Institute. However, the course was closed in 1956, after only four years. Another private school, Hong Kong United College, also launched a journalism course unsuccessfully. The journalism courses offered at these schools were vocational training programs to teach practical skills such as news gathering and editing. More importantly, all the instructors who were involved in these programs were prominent scholars originally from mainland China, including Tam Wai-hon, Tse Fu-ya, Fu Sheung-lam, and Chan Skek-yu, individuals whom it would be difficult to integrate into the political purposes of the US.[26]

At the time, the US public and private sectors had only recently begun offering cultural activities in Asia, and their only means of influence on Asian journalism and communication education programs were through training programs for reporters and teachers. A large number of American scholars, although exactly how many remains unknown, came to Hong Kong as researchers through the Fulbright Program. This group included Charles Clayton, who, among his cohort, came to greatly influence Hong Kong's journalism and communication education.[27] The US international information and educational exchange programs developed after the Smith-Mundt Act was enacted also included a project called Service to Foreign Journalists, which annually helped about five hundred participant reporters gather information on topics of their interest by introducing them to US leaders in charge of national projects, industrial and agricultural sectors, and other fields.[28] The US State Department's International Educational Exchange Service project, offered in the 1950s, provided international journalists with opportunities to visit American families to learn about life in the US through actual experience.[29] At the same time, the USIS Hong Kong began promoting pro–free world and anti-Communist magazines, books, movies, broadcast manuscripts, and other materials produced by Hong Kong's Chinese media elites, primarily targeted at overseas Chinese. Furthermore, the Asia Foundation established a Southeast Asian office in Hong Kong to help the USIS provide overseas Chinese with information and education programs.[30]

The Asia Foundation allocated a great quantity of human resources and funds to education in Asia, most heavily investing in journalism and communication. Yet the principal focus of the USIS and the Asia Foundation at the time was not on journalism or communication education specifically; they were rather focused more on helping a few refugee academies unite to form CUHK.[31] More importantly, the Asia Foundation lacked the know-how needed to help establish faculties of journalism and communication that met the ideal standards set by the US.

The quality of potential journalism education initiatives was also lacking. In early 1957, Chinese businessman Frank M. S. Shu announced that he would donate US$10,000 annually to an existing or new overseas Chinese academy that established a new faculty of journalism.[32] In September, L. Z. Yuan, then Hong Kong representative of the Asia Foundation, organized a number of educators, publishers, and Chinese journalists who had received education in the US and had them hold a debate contest to establish candidacy for the donations, which continued for an entire month. Unfortunately, the contest demonstrated that none of the three original constituent colleges of CUHK—Chung Chi College, New Asia College, or the United College of Hong Kong—met the conditions required to receive donations.

Chung Chi College had a solid English-language foundation, but its president, D. Y. Lin, had expressed clearly his disinterest in setting up a faculty of journalism, a view that likely represented the official position of the British Hong Kong government. Bishop Ronald O. Hall, former president of Chung

Chi College, also once clearly stated that establishing a faculty of journalism, as well as cultivating journalists, was unnecessary, as Britain had never done so.[33] As mentioned above, the United College of Hong Kong had once offered a journalism program, which had trained students for employment in Chinese media companies. According to L. Z. Yuan, however, the journalism course at the United College of Hong Kong had a serious problem: it did not offer such subjects as newspaper ethics, the philosophy behind a democratic press, and other requirements that would give the future newspapermen a broader outlook beyond the limited confines of Hongkong.[34] Mu Ch'ien, then president of New Asia College, was the only one of the three candidates who openly expressed a desire to establish a faculty of journalism for his college. However, according to L. Z. Yuan, as New Asia College specialized in Chinese studies, such as Chinese literature and history, and had only recently established an English-language department, it first needed to improve its students' English-language skills to the level required to qualify for funding, a process that was assumed to require at least a couple of years. The Asia Foundation had also previously discussed the possibility of collaboration with a school of journalism in the US—Medill School of Journalism at Northwestern University, through Charles L. Allen. Allen had a strong interest in promoting journalism education in Southeast Asia and desired to establish a faculty of journalism in Hong Kong to offer a personally designed curriculum to cultivate bilingual journalists.[35] However, for various reasons, including the above-mentioned lack of English-language ability, the final instruction from the Asia Foundation headquarters to L. Z. Yuan was to not take further action for the time being.[36] In other words, the Asia Foundation had absolutely no intention of funding traditional Chinese journalism education. As is evident from its emphasis on students' English-language skills, the US was interested only in helping Hong Kong develop Western-style journalism and communication education programs free of Chinese influence.

Nevertheless, having been stung by the Sputnik crisis, the US was extremely determined to invest in modernizing Asian education systems. At the time, the Asia Foundation was implementing "an exploratory science program, designed to establish close contact with Asian scientists and scientific organizations, and indirectly to influence them toward Western ideology."[37] The Asia Foundation placed particular importance on this science program because it introduced the principles essential to building true democracy, which the foundation considered a prerequisite for the mass media to properly function as Asia's primary means of overcoming political oppression.[38] The Asia Foundation set up a Journalism Training Project, with its resolution stating: "Because improved communication in the developing nations is an important factor in moving toward modern social and economic conditions, the Foundation helps advance sound training for journalists in Asia."[39] The project provided participants with an opportunity to receive training in the US, based on a systematic journalism and communication curriculum, which was more comprehensive than indicated by its title. In 1962, as a participant of the Asia Foundation's project, Timothy Yu, who was at that time teaching magazine editing at the University of Hong Kong's off-campus course department, studied at Stanford University's Institute for Communication Research under Wilbur Schramm, known in the US as the father of communication studies.[40]

Establishment of CUHK's Department of Journalism and the Transfer of Disciplinary Thought to Hong Kong

CUHK was established in 1963, presenting another opportunity for Hong Kong to develop journalism and communication education programs. At the time, C. M. Li, vice-chancellor of CUHK, was passionate in his desire to raise the quality of Hong Kong's journalism education from the vocational training level to the professional education level.[41] The university planned to establish a communication center, with the right to confer master's degrees, in the Institute of Social Studies and was also putting effort into establishing a journalism department to award bachelor's degrees. The Asia Foundation was the first to notice these efforts. In fact, records at the Hoover Institution Archives indicate that when the foundation discovered that CUHK was establishing a journalism department, it was delighted at the announcement because it had aimed at assisting Hong Kong's universities in establishing journalism departments that could offer bilingual education.[42] The Asia Foundation agreed to support the university financially with a visiting professor and a senior lecturer and launched a project devoted to helping CUHK manage its newly established Department of Journalism.[43]

The vital prerequisite for the transfer of disciplinary and academic thought is the cultivation of teachers and researchers. Records indicate that the pool of teachers who helped develop Hong Kong's journalism and communication education, including CUHK's Department of Communication, mostly comprised American scholars and Chinese scholars who had received education in the US. Also, according to records, the costs incurred in inviting teachers were primarily covered by either the US State Department's Fulbright Program or the Asia Foundation.[44] For example, until 1967, the Asia Foundation covered the costs incurred for employing Michael Wei, a former faculty member of CUHK's Department of Journalism.[45] In the 1970s, Hong Kong's local organizations also began to financially support its journalism and communication education; the purpose of these grants was to acquire educational concepts and academic thought from American academia to help develop Hong Kong's journalism and communication education programs, whether by inviting scholars from the US to give lectures in Hong Kong or by sending Hong Kong scholars to the US for training.

As a matter of fact, the US organizations, both public and private, screening educators for Hong Kong's journalism and communication education were almost entirely disinterested in the applicants' research achievements in the US or their stances on academic controversies between schools. Rather, they were chiefly interested in achieving US Cold War objectives and therefore in recruiting applicants who had close contact with governmental agencies and foundations or who could be reached through various interpersonal networks. Renowned American communication scholar Wilbur Schramm was an academic activist devoted to spreading the concept of communication education across regions outside the US. Schramm was also a so-called Cold War intellectual, working closely with cultural departments within the US administration and covert outfits such as the Asia Foundation, through which he greatly helped spread American communication education programs worldwide; he is credited as such in many documents on US international educational exchange efforts.

Initially, as part of its plan for helping CUHK establish a journalism department, the Asia Foundation considered recruiting Frederick T. C. Yu of Columbia University as a visiting scholar and Dr. Godwin Chu of Taiwan's National Chengchi University as a senior lecturer. Both scholars had ties to the Asia Foundation, and Frederick T. C. Yu was a good friend of Wilbur Schramm. However, at that time, neither Yu nor Chu could immediately leave their respective universities for the new position, and as a result, the university's plan to establish a communication center was almost postponed.[46] The Asia Foundation then reached out to Charles C. Clayton, a graduate of the University of Missouri's School of Journalism, who was then working at Southern Illinois University; Clayton immediately flew to Hong Kong under the Fulbright Program to join CUHK as a visiting scholar. Before assuming his position at the university, Clayton remarked, "This feat is some kind of record, for as of last August, all that existed was the idea and a grant from the Asia Foundation to underwrite the first two years of the school."[47] These anecdotes indicate the key role that the Asia Foundation played in the establishment of CUHK's Department of Journalism and Communication.

CUHK's New Asia College began offering a journalism course in 1965. The course's initial curriculum design is considered to have primarily been developed by Yu, who was still at Columbia University, and then taken over by Clayton, who came from Southern Illinois University.[48] Whether their curriculum designs were developed by Yu or Clayton, all journalism and communication courses at CUHK were clearly based on American course designs and academic paradigms from the very beginning.

In 1968, the Department of Communication was established at Hong Kong Baptist University, also heavily influenced by American disciplinary thought. The curriculum was developed by Timothy Yu, who had previously studied in the US under Wilbur Schramm with financial support from the Asia Foundation. In addition to key courses consisting of communication studies, such as International Communication, Psychology, and Communication Theory, the curriculum that Timothy Yu studied under at Stanford University also comprised courses clearly designed for students like himself, including Methods of Communication in Developing Countries and Case Studies of Communication in National Development.[49] After returning to Hong Kong, Timothy Yu shared with both Hong Kong Baptist University and CUHK what he had learned from US journalism and communication education programs. In addition to being a college instructor, Yu was an experienced translator and editor of American communication studies. Timothy Yu translated Wilbur Schramm's *Media, Information, and People: Introduction to Communication Studies*, which had long been the only comprehensive introduction available in Chinese on communication studies.[50] As stated by Timothy Yu himself, "This is the first book that systematically introduces in Chinese new trends in the field of behavioral science (i.e., communication studies)."[51] As a primary source of American academic thought, *Media, Information, and People* had a great impact on many early Chinese communication scholars.

In 1977, Wilbur Schramm was invited to the CUHK as an Aw Boon Haw professor to give lectures on communication education. By then, the university's Department of Journalism had been reorganized and had become the Department of Journalism and Communication. After arriving, Schramm further adjusted the curriculum of the new department and established the first master of philosophy in communication in Hong Kong. Almost the entire faculty of the Department around this time consisted of either visiting scholars from the US or Chinese scholars who had graduated from American universities, including Michael Wei, who had graduated from the University of Missouri, James C. Y. Shen of Boston University, Charles Allen of Northwestern University, Erwin Atwood of Southern Illinois University, Robert Bishop of the University of Michigan, Alex Edelstein of the University of Washington, and Godwin C. Chu of Hawai'i's East-West Center.[52] Judging from the development of journalism and communication in Hong Kong, the educational and cultural activities carried out by the US in Asia for the purpose of educational modernization had actually promoted the "Americanization" of journalism and communication in Hong Kong. On the one hand, American institutions, including the Asia Foundation, had accelerated the development of journalism and communication in Hong Kong; on the other hand, knowledge export motivated by Cold War strategy would inevitably foster dependence in the target groups, thus limiting diversified choices in journalism and communication education in Hong Kong.

LOCAL FACTORS THAT INFLUENCED THE DEVELOPMENT OF HONG KONG'S JOURNALISM AND COMMUNICATION EDUCATION PROGRAMS

Hong Kong's journalism and communication education was undeniably strongly influenced by American academia. CUHK's very first curriculum for the Department of Journalism was developed by Columbia University graduate Frederick T. C. Yu, and after he stepped aside, University of Missouri graduate Wei Da Gong took up the position of department head. These two figures determined the department's direction of development, as is stated on the official website of the university's School of Journalism and Communication: "Benefiting from the education traditions of Columbia University and the University of Missouri, and paving the way for the development of the journalism and communication at CUHK."[53] Subsequently, the curriculum of the university's communication courses continued to benefit directly from Schramm's guidance. In addition, as credited on Southern Illinois University's official website, the founder of the CUHK's Department of Journalism was Charles Clayton.[54] The preceding historical accounts indicate that Hong Kong's journalism and communication education programs were heavily influenced by American academic paradigms. However, while Americanization had a significant impact on Hong Kong's journalism and communication education, it was just one of the factors that determined its direction of development. Historical accounts clearly show that its establishment and subsequent direction of development were also influenced by many other factors.

First, the influence of Hong Kong's traditional Chinese culture was consistently strong: the arrival of intellectuals who had fled from mainland China, such as Mu Ch'ien, inspired a modern revival of Hong Kong's Chinese culture. Efforts put into the establishment of CUHK by Chinese refugee intellectuals played a large role in facilitating the coexistence of Hong Kong's colonial education and Chinese cultural education. Local intellectuals also voluntarily played an active role in the establishment of the university's Department of Journalism. In China, ever since the final days of the Qing dynasty, people have valued the proverb "Save the country with journalism; reward it with speech," and indeed, in Mu Ch'ien's proposal for establishing the Department of Journalism, he specifically used the word *reconstruction*.[55] For these Chinese intellectuals, the Department of Journalism adhered to the founding principle of CUHK—the protection and revival of Chinese culture.

Second, as journalism was a popular occupation in Hong Kong, the quality of work expected of journalists was consistently high, as was the demand for journalism education. The Aw family, Southeast Asia's media industry magnates, kept a close eye on journalism education. The Aw family had built a media empire, essentially dominating the newspaper industry. However, after the death of Aw Boon Haw, the family head, an internal conflict arose between the remaining family members. Eventually, Aw's daughter, Sally Aw Sian, inherited the family's newspaper empire in Hong Kong, which comprised the following: *Sing Tao Jih Pao* (Sing Tao daily), *Sing Tao Man Pao* (Sing Tao evening), *Sing Tao Zhou Kan* (Sing Tao weekly), and the *Standard*. Having control over Hong Kong's media empire, Sally Sian fully understood the development of its press industry. According to Sally Sian, Hong Kong's journalism education did not meet adequate standards and the majority of the journalists it produced were unable to use the Chinese language correctly; representatives from the Union Research Institute and the Asia Foundation shared this view.[56] In fact, it was the Asia Foundation's long-held concern that because of extremely poor journalistic standards, its westernized Chinese newspapers were unable to win the approval of local intellectuals and were thus allowing Communist newspapers to dominate the market.[57] Some scholars viewed the situation from a broader perspective—that Hong Kong had the potential to serve as Asia's base for journalism education and that it therefore needed to improve and maintain the quality of its journalism education at high levels. Stanway Cheng, then editorial manager at China News—a Taiwanese newspaper publisher—and Godwin C. Chu, who was then still working at Taiwan's National Chengchi University, shared that view.[58] In other words, from the perspective of scholars in Hong Kong, journalism education needed to develop if it was to meet local demand. At the time, Hong Kong's population was steadily increasing. Accordingly, newspaper publishers were seeing an increase in workload and also needed intellectual inspiration. According to local media reports on the views of Hong Kong intellectuals at the time, the newly established CUHK Department of Journalism was expected to "address the current shortage of newspaper practitioners in Hong Kong and . . . improve the quality of the journalists and promote the development of journalism."[59]

Third, the development of journalism and communication education directly stemmed from public need and was therefore not something that US financial clout could easily control. Traditionally, journalism education in Hong Kong had been offered as vocational education to meet this need. Li Chohming, then president of CUHK, was an ardent advocate of the development of journalism and communication education. However, he also understood that promoting education first required creating employment. At the time, the most popular career path was to become a newspaper journalist, and thus, while the press industry did want people who specialized in journalism, it had no need for scholars with college degrees.[60] This was the very reason that earlier attempts at developing communication studies had failed. However, after the mid-1960s, acceptance of the American paradigm, especially the theory of communication, in Hong Kong's education and academic circles grew, although this acceptance was largely related to the economic takeoff and consumption boom of Hong Kong society.[61] In other words, the influence that Hong Kong received from the US in establishing its journalism and communication education programs could be called "invited influence."[62]

On the other hand, as is evident from the establishment of the Aw Boon Haw Lecture Program and from the university's choice of Wilbur Schramm as its very first Aw Boon Haw professor, Hong Kong's "urgent local needs" provided the driving force behind the establishment of CUHK's Department of Journalism and Communication and the development of its curriculum. Thus, Hong Kong's journalism and communication education programs were deeply rooted in local traditions, including existing local programs. For example, faculties of journalism and communication at Hong Kong commonly place importance on providing students with practical training both on and off campus. This tradition has been collaboratively established by Hong Kong's media and education sectors and has existed since before the introduction of American educational models. Almost all faculties and departments of journalism and communication in Hong Kong publish their own newspapers and other periodicals and have also been well supplied with broadcasting and television production equipment. The practical skills and social influence of students at CUHK's School of Journalism and Communication rose to a level more than comparable with those of American students.[63] However, so did the political pressure on instructors and students at the school. For instance, 1967 bore witness to the sensational *Shatin News* incident, in which students at CUHK reported in their student newspaper that their efforts to find jobs were not producing the desired results. The student newspaper, *Shatin News*, attracted international attention, which led to the dismissal of four of the university's faculty and the suspension of the newspaper.[64] In addition, individuals and organizations in Hong Kong had always been aware of US political intentions behind offers of assistance and accordingly had been cautious about accepting them. During the aforementioned Aw family internal conflict over who would inherit the family newspaper business, Sally Sian considered collaborating with the US. However, when subsequently discussing conditions with the US through L. Z. Yuan, then representative of the Asia Foundation's Hong Kong branch, Sally Sian stated clearly that she would not tolerate her family's newspaper business being used for US propaganda purposes. This stance did not represent total ideological opposition—to the contrary, in response to the foundation's request, she also promised to put effort into functioning as Asia's largest independent non-Communist media organization.[65] In 1977, CUHK established its graduate program for communication studies, and when it did, the curriculum, designed by Wilbur Schramm and Timothy Yu, was also deeply rooted in local traditions. While the program devoted its entire first year to teaching communication theories and research methods, in the second year and thereafter, it offered various courses, including communication theory and its application, culture and communication, issues relating to communication, and traditional Chinese communication models.[66]

Finally, the British Hong Kong government and British academia also had significant influence on the development of Hong Kong's journalism and communication education. The degree of suspicion with which the US was viewed by Hong Kong in conducting its educational exchange activities may not have been as high as those in other countries. Nevertheless, two important groups maintained a distrust of the US. One, as already mentioned, was Hong Kong's overseas Chinese journalists and refugee intellectuals from mainland China, who suspected US political motives behind the help it offered. Another was the British Hong Kong government, which displayed an inconsistent attitude toward US intervention in Hong Kong. When one of Hong Kong's former directors of education, Peter Donohue, met with a local representative of the Asia Foundation, Donohue told the representative that the two organizations should stay in close contact so that they could avoid acting in conflict with each other's interests. However, in the early 1960s, when the British Hong Kong government was considering reforming Hong Kong's education system, it decided to take a practical perspective, rather than adopting an academic approach, and sought to place "greater stress on technical education as well as other important changes."[67] Officials like Nigel Watt, the British Hong Kong

272 PRACTICING KNOWLEDGE

government's director of information services at the time, who was interested in establishing a journalism department at CUHK, were inspired entirely by the need to secure more accountable journalists for Hong Kong, rather than by the American academic disciplines.[68] For this reason, it was only in 1999 that the University of Hong Kong, long guided by British educational philosophy, established its own Journalism and Media Studies Center.

CONCLUSION

US international educational exchange efforts during the Cold War promoted the rise of Hong Kong's modern journalism and communication education, and the aim of establishing the CUHK's Department of Journalism was to export American knowledge as part of US strategy to win the Cultural Cold War. US political and social elites constantly disagreed over whether their efforts should be aimed at modernizing or Americanizing the target region. John Fairbank once said, after the Second World War, that the US aimed to help China combine science with democracy in the context of traditional Chinese culture so that the large population of China could incorporate them into their daily lives.[69] In other words, Fairbank stated that the aim was not to Americanize China but to help promote its modernization. However, as the Cold War competition over hearts and minds intensified, the Charles River school, who maintained a modernization-equals-Americanization stance, developed a dominant influence over policymaking.[70] US efforts to promote journalism and communication education in Hong Kong could thus be considered a typical case of American Cold War operations for the purpose of Americanizing local knowledge. However, discipline construction is a highly complex issue. The social needs of the recipients, the motivations and academic consciousness of the target groups in acquiring knowledge, and the critical and reflective ability of local scholars should all be considered. The historical development of Hong Kong's journalism and communication education was, if at all, only superficially a case of the Americanization of local knowledge; fundamentally, it was a choice that the relevant nations or regions made themselves in pursuit of modernization.

NOTES

1. The establishment of the Department of Journalism at CUHK is generally regarded as a sign that journalism education in Hong Kong was "getting on the right track." In 1974, it was renamed the Department of Journalism and Communication. See Xu, *History of Journalism and Communication*, 511.

2. The Asia Foundation is a quasi-nongovernmental organization. Until 1967, the foundation received funding from the Central Intelligence Agency (CIA) and policy guidance from the Department of State, engaging in "activities that the government would like to achieve but cannot directly engage in." Asia Foundation, CIA CREST, DOC_0001088617.

3. There are several perspectives on American knowledge export: First is the perspective of the Cultural Cold War, a view through which covert institutions such as the Congress for Cultural Freedom and the Asia Foundation carried out knowledge export activities in Europe and Asia. See Frances Saunders, *The Cultural Cold War: The CIA and the World of Arts and Letters* (New York: New Press, 2000); Natalia Tsvetkova, *The Cold War in Universities: U.S. and Soviet Cultural Diplomacy, 1945–1990* (Leiden: Brill, 2021); Wolfe, *Freedom's Laboratory.* For a thorough discussion of this subject, see Gordon Johnston, "Revisiting the Cultural Cold War," *Social History* 35, no. 3 (August 2010): 290–307. Second is the perspective of imperial history: Some scholars have argued that knowledge mobilization as an aid to modern state power has become essential to worldwide imperial planning. American universities, large foundations, international organizations, and think tanks after World War II produced a cadre of highly trained agents whose fieldwork helped project imperial power abroad. See Axel Jansen, John Krige, and Jessica Wang, "Empires of Knowledge: Introduction," *History and Technology* 35, no. 3 (2019): 195–202; Chen Yun-Shiuan, *Modernization or Cultural Imperialism: A Critical Reading of Taiwan's National Scholarship Program for Overseas Study* (New York: Peter Lang Verlag, 2013); John Tomlinson, *Cultural Imperialism: A Critical Introduction* (Baltimore, MD: Johns Hopkins University Press, 1991). Third, on the perspective of transnational history, see Mark Solovey and Christian Daye, eds., *Cold War Social Science: Transnational Entanglements* (Cham: Palgrave Macmillan, 2021); John Krige, ed., *How Knowledge Moves: Writing the Transnational History of Science and Technology* (Chicago: University of Chicago Press, 2019). Fourth, on the postcolonial perspective, see Walter D. Mignolo, *Local Histories and Global Designs: Coloniality, Subaltern Knowledges, and Border Thinking* (Princeton, NJ: Princeton University Press, 2000); Catherine Hoppers, C. Odora Hoppers, and H. Richards, *Rethinking Thinking: Modernity's "Other" and the Transformation of the University* (Pretoria: University of South Africa, 2012); Simon Marginson, "Towards a Global University Hegemony," *Critique International* 39, no. 2 (2008): 87–107; Kathinka Sinha-Kerkhoff and Syed Farid Malas, *Academic Dependency in the Social Sciences: Structural Reality and Intellectual Challenges* (Daryaganj, New Delhi: Manohar, 2010).

4. Chou, "Cultural Education as Containment of Communism"; Shen, "Empire of Information"; Wolfe, *Freedom's Laboratory,* 5; Berghahn, *America and the Intellectual Cold Wars,* xii.

5. See Stuart, *Creating the National Security State*, introduction.

6. NSC 68/3, "United States Objectives and Programs for National Security," December 8, 1950, Annex 5, DNSA, ProQuest Information and Learning Company, PD00181, 4.

7. Gaither, *Report*, 26–27.

8. Department of State, "1949 Budget Estimates, General Justification," n.d., Bureau of Educational and Cultural Affairs Historical Collection (CU), box 35, folder: MC 468 Department of State, 1946 Budget Estimates (1 of 3), 35–2, Special Collections Division, University of Arkansas Libraries, 18.

9. Rostow, *Diffusion of Power*, 1, 21–22.

10. Project DTPILLAR, Request for Project Renewal, FY 1961, October 10, 1960, CIA FOIA, Collection: Nazi War Crimes Disclosure Act, DTPILLAR, vol. 3, no. 33.

11. Bureau of Educational and Cultural Affairs, *Annual Report to the Congress on the International Educational and Cultural Exchange Program*, FY 1965, Archives Unbound, SC5113137214, 45–46.

12. Representative Adam C. Powell, Statement on the Floor of the House of Representatives, Introducing a Bill to Provide 12,000 Scholarships for Students of Africa, Asia, and Latin America "To Become National Leaders," May 1, 1961, President John F. Kennedy's Office Files, 1961–1963, part 4: Subjects File, folder: 002250-006-0511, *ProQuest History Vault*, 4.

13. Bureau of Educational and Cultural Affairs, *Annual Report*, 80–81, 83.

14. Johnson, *Special Report*, 4.

15. Secretary of Health, Education, and Welfare to Honorable Walt Rostow, memorandum, May 9, 1966, Archives Unbound, SC5113137214; Bureau of Educational and Cultural Affairs, *Annual Report*, iii.

16. President to All Asia Foundation Representatives, Development Paper: "Education in World Affairs," May 10, 1966, box P-246, folder: US & Intl Program, General Development Papers, 7/62, Asia Foundation Records, Hoover Institution Archives, 2.

17. Haydn Williams, President, Monthly Report to the Board of Trustees, June 1965, box 590, Central Files, Asia Foundation Files, 1954–1969, Columbia University Archives.

18. L. Z. Yuan to the President of the Asia Foundation, "Journalism Training in Hong Kong," May 20, 1964, box P-266, folder: Hong Kong Program, Education Journalism Teacher Training 7/62, Asia Foundation Records, Hoover Institution Archives.

19. Social and Economic Groups: Cultural, Union Research Institute, n.d., box P-55, Hong Kong, Budget General 1954/55, Asia Foundation Records, Hoover Institution Archives.

20. Prof. George E. Taylor, Report on the Asia Foundation's Chinese Programs, Hong Kong, Octoner 31, 1955, box P-97, folder: General, Overseas Chinese Program, Asia Foundation Records, Hoover Institution Archives, 34.

21. Youth and Related Activities, box P-55, Hong Kong, Budget General 1954/55, Asia Foundation Records, Hoover Institution Archives; W. Mallory-Browne to Chien Mu, October 25, 1961, box P-171, Hong Kong Program, Education Schools & Univ, New Asia Research Institute Fellowship Program, Asia Foundation Records, Hoover Institution Archives.

22. There has been considerable research on US policy toward Hong Kong and its impact. Before the Second World War, the United States did not pay much attention to Hong Kong. Nevertheless, since the establishment of PRC, according to Nancy Tucker, the American consulate general in the British colony of Hong Kong quickly became the primary listening post in efforts to understand what was happening inside the PRC. See Nancy Bernkopf Tucker, ed., *China Confidential: American Diplomats and Sino-American Relations, 1945–1996* (New York: Columbia University Press, 2001), 101. In a recent study, Peter Hamilton argues that the relationship between the United States and Hong Kong grew closer during the Cold War. Hamilton believed that although Hong Kong remained under a British colonial flag, its residents increasingly pivoted away from British imperial systems and instead engaged with US international power structures through transpacific circulations. See Peter Hamilton, *Made in Hong Kong: Transpacific Networks and a New History of Globalization* (New York: Columbia University Press, 2021), 2. Hamilton also pointed out that against the background of the Cold War and decolonization, the United States was engaged in two "culture wars" in Asia: one was an ideological struggle with the Sino-Soviet bloc; the other was a competition for influence with traditional colonial powers such as Britain, with the ultimate aim to help establish and maintain a new regional order with the US as the "leader of the free world." See Zhang Yang, "Two Cultural Cold Wars: An Analysis of the Asia Foundation's Aid Program for Asian Universities," *Twenty-First Century* 193, no. 5 (October 2022): 105–19.

23. Assessment Report, "USIS Hong Kong, Objectives III," March 29, 1960, RG 306, box 3, Records of the Office of Research, Foreign Service Despatches, 1954–1965, National Archive at College Park.

24. Later, the Chinese University of Hong Kong. See Zhang, "Cultural Cold War," 148–69.

25. James L. Meader to Edward W. Barrett, December 14, 1951, DTPILLAR, vol. 1, no. 83, 2.

26. Leung, Chu, and Lee, "Journalism and Communication Education," 192–93.

27. Clayton to Head Journalism School in Hong Kong, CIA CREST, CIA-RDP73-00475R000402100001-0.

28. International Information and Educational Exchange Activities, box 35, folder: MC 468 EP Congressional Budget, 1950, 35–7, Special Collections Division, University of Arkansas Libraries, 323.

29. Participants in the Far Eastern Journalist Project, 1955, box P-39, folder: US & Intl. Individuals, General Tours Far Eastern Journalists, 1955, Asia Foundation Records, Hoover Institution Archives.

30. National Security Council, Paper regarding US Policy toward Hong Kong, n.d., Declassified Documents Reference System, CK3100473459.

31. Request for Renewal of Project DTPILLAR for FY 1957, December 18, 1956, DTPILLAR, vol. 2, no. 17.

32. Frank M. S. Shu owns Maurice May Inc. of New York City, Maurice May Ltd. of Singapore, Kung Shin Co. of Hong Kong, and many other companies.

33. L. Z. Yuan, Memo to the Record, "Journalism Education in Hong Kong," September 3, 1963, box P-266, folder: Hong Kong Program, Education Journalism Teacher Training 7/62, Asia Foundation Records, Hoover Institution Archives.

34. L. Z. Yuan to the President of the Asia Foundation, "Proposed Journalism School Grant," September 12, 1957, box P-57, folder: Hong Kong Program, MEDIA General, Asia Foundation Records, Hoover Institution Archives.

35. Yuan to President.

36. Jack E. James to L. Z. Yuan, "Proposed Journalism School Grant," October 2, 1957, box P-57, folder: Hong Kong Program, MEDIA General, Asia Foundation Records, Hoover Institution Archives.

37. Request for Renewal, FY 1959, December 1, 1958, DTPILLAR, vol. 2, no. 3.

38. Committee of Correspondence, "Seminar for Women of Press and Radio," August 10, 1960, Archives Unbound, Gale Document SC5105067430.

39. Seven Asian Journalists Study in US Programs, n.d., box P-266, folder: Hong Kong Program, Education Journalism Teacher Training 7/62, Asia Foundation Records, Hoover Institution Archives.

40. Seven Asian Journalists Study in US Programs.

41. W. Mallory-Browne to the President of the Asia Foundation, "Journalism Training Project in Hong Kong," November 3, 1964, box P-266, folder: Hong Kong Program, Education Journalism Teacher Training 7/62, Asia Foundation Records, Hoover Institution Archives.

42. Stephen Uhalley Jr., "Letter of Agreement: Mr. Timothy Yu," September 4, 1964, box P-266, folder: Hong Kong Program, Education Journalism Teacher Training 7/62, Asia Foundation Records, Hoover Institution Archives.

43. Edgar N. Pike, the Representative, Hong Kong, to the President of the Asia Foundation, February 9, 1965, box P-266, folder: Hong Kong Program, Education Journalism Teacher Training 7/62, Asia Foundation Records, Hoover Institution Archives.

44. Mallory-Browne to the President, "Journalism Training Project in Hong Kong."

COLD WAR AND US INTERNATIONAL EDUCATIONAL EXCHANGE 277

45. Edgar N. Pike, Memo to the Record, "Lunch Conversation with Dr. C. M. Li," June 2, 1967, box P-266, folder: Hong Kong AP-1022 I Program, Education School & Univ Chinese Univ Vice-Chancellor / Adviser on Chinese Studies, 7/62, Asia Foundation Records, Hoover Institution Archives.

46. Lawrence Eisenberg, "Timothy Yu and Mass Communication Center, Chinese University," letter, February 17, 1965, box P-266, folder: Hong Kong Program, Education Journalism Teacher Training 7/62, Asia Foundation Records, Hoover Institution Archives.

47. Clayton to Head Journalism School in Hong Kong, in CIA CREST, CIA-RDP73-00475R000402100001-0.

48. Leung, Chu, and Lee, "Journalism and Communication Education," 196.

49. Timothy Yu to Dr. Robert Schwantes, Head of the NE Asian Division, Asia Foundation, May 4, 1965, box P-266, folder: Hong Kong Program, Education Journalism Teacher Training 7/62, Asia Foundation Records, Hoover Institution Archives.

50. Wu, *Zhongmei chuanboxue zaoqi de jianzhishi yu fansi*, 140.

51. Yu to Schwantes, May 4, 1965.

52. Leung, Chu, and Lee, "Journalism and Communication Education," 196.

53. "A Brief History of 50 Years of Journalism and Communication Education at CUHK."

54. "Charles C. Clayton (1902–1988)."

55. Yuan to President, "Proposed Journalism School Grant."

56. Yuan, Memo to the Record.

57. L. Z. Yuan to the President, Asia Foundation, "Chinese Language Sunday Supplement," July 6, 1955, box P-57, folder: Hong Kong Program, General (Trip & Rpts-LZ Yuan) 1955, Asia Foundation Records, Hoover Institution Archives.

58. L. Z. Yuan to the Record, "Journalism Training: Conversation with Stanway Cheng and Godwin Chu," September 30, 1963, box P-266, folder: Hong Kong Program, Education Journalism Teacher Training 7/62, Asia Foundation Records, Hoover Institution Archives.

59. "Proposed Four-Year Journalism Department in Chinese University."

60. Mallory-Browne to the President, "Journalism Training Project in Hong Kong."

61. Leung, Chu, and Lee, "Journalism and Communication Education," 193.

62. Wheeler, *Role of American NGOs*, 2.

63. Xu, *History of Journalism and Communication*, 512; "A Brief History of 50 Years of Journalism and Communication Education at CUHK."

64. Feng, "Addendum to Old News: 'Sha Tin News' Event."

65. L. Z. Yuan to James L. Stewart, April 29, 1955, box P-57, folder: Hong Kong Program, General (Trip & Rpts-LZ Yuan) 1955, Asia Foundation Records, Hoover Institution Archives.

66. Zheng, *Dazhong chuanbo yu xiandaihua*, 280.

67. Memorandum to the Record, "Conversation with the Hon. Peter Donohue, Director of Education Department, Hong Kong," June 5, 1962, box P-171, folder: Hong Kong Program, Education General, Asia Foundation Records, Hoover Institution Archives.

68. Yuan to President, "Journalism Training in Hong Kong."

69. Fairbank, *Chinabound*, 304.

70. In the late 1950s and early 1960s, a group of economists, led by scholars from MIT and Harvard University, put forward new propositions on the economic growth of the Third World and the foreign aid policy of the United States from the perspective of social modernization, which was called the Charles River school. Leading figures included Walt Rostow, Max F. Millikan, and John Galbraith, among others.

REFERENCES

Primary Sources

Archives

Asia Foundation Records. Hoover Institution Archives, Stanford, CA.

Bureau of Educational and Cultural Affairs Historical Collection (CU). Special Collections Division, University of Arkansas Libraries, Fayetteville, AR.

Central Files, Asia Foundation Files, 1954–1969. Rare Book & Manuscript Library, Columbia University Archives, New York.

Records of the Office of Research. Foreign Service Despatches, 1954–1965. National Archive II, College Park, MD.

Databases

Archives Unbound, Gale Primary Sources.

CIA Freedom of Information Act Electronic Reading Room (CIA FOIA). Collection: Nazi War Crimes Disclosure Act, DTPILLAR records.

CIA Records Search Tool (CIA CREST).

Digital National Security Archive (DNSA). ProQuest Information and Learning Company.

History Vault: American Politics and Society from JFK to Watergate, 1960–1975. ProQuest.

Secondary Sources

Berghahn, Volker R. *America and the Intellectual Cold Wars in Europe: Shepard Stone between Philanthropy, Academy, and Diplomacy.* Princeton, NJ: Princeton University Press, 2002.

Chou, Grace Ai-Ling. "Cultural Education as Containment of Communism: The Ambivalent Position of American NGOs in Hong Kong in the 1950s." *Journal of Cold War Studies* 12, no. 2 (Spring 2010): 3–28.

Fairbank, John King. *Chinabound: A Fifty-Year Memoir.* New York: Harper and Row, 1982.

Gaither, H. Rowan, Jr. *Report of the Study for the Ford Foundation on Policy and Program.* Detroit, MI: Ford Foundation, 1949.

Johnson, Walter. *A Special Report on American Studies Abroad by United States Advisory Commission on International Educational and Cultural Affairs.* Washington, DC: US Government Printing Office, 1963.

Leung, Kenneth W. Y., Leonard Chu, and Paul S. N. Lee. "Journalism and Communication Education and Research in Hong Kong." In *Global Trends in Communication Education and Research,* edited by Kenneth W. Y. Leung, James Kenny, and Paul S. N. Lee. Cresskill, NJ: Hampton, 2006, 189–209.

Rostow, W. W. *The Diffusion of Power: An Essay in Recent History, 1957–1972.* New York: Macmillan, 1972.

Shen, Shuang. "Empire of Information: The Asia Foundation's Network and Chinese-Language Cultural Production in Hong Kong and Southeast Asia." *American Quarterly* 69, no. 3 (Fall 2017): 589–610.

Stuart, Douglas T. *Creating the National Security State: A History of the Law That Transformed America.* Princeton, NJ: Princeton University Press, 2008.

Wheeler, Norton. *The Role of American NGOs in China's Modernization: Invited Influence.* London: Routledge, 2013.

Wolfe, Audra J. *Freedom's Laboratory: The Cold War Struggle for the Soul of Science.* Baltimore: Johns Hopkins University Press, 2018.

Wu, Jing. *Zhongmei chuanboxue zaoqi de jianzhishi yu fansi* [A review of the early history of the institutionalization of communication study in China and USA]. Jinan: Shandong renmin chubanshe, 2011.

Xu, Peiting. *Zhongguo xinwen chuanbo Xueshuoshi* [History of journalism and communication in China, 1949–2005]. Chongqing: Chongqing Press, 2006.

Zhang, Yang. "Cultural Cold War: The American Role in Establishing the Chinese University of Hong Kong (CUHK)." In *The Power of Culture: Encounters between China and the United States,* edited by Priscilla Roberts, 148–69. Newcastle upon Tyne: Cambridge Scholars, 2016.

Zheng, Zhenming. *Dazhong chuanbo yu xiandaihua* [Mass communication and modernization]. Taipei: Times Cultural, 1981.

Newspapers

Feng, Dexiong. "Jiuwen buyi: 'shatian xinwen' Shijian" [Addendum to Old News: 'Sha Tin News' Event]. *Mingpao,* June 23, 2013.

"Zhongwen daxue ni kaishe sinianzhi xinwenxue xi" [Proposed Four-Year Journalism Department in Chinese University]. *Huaqiao ribao* [Overseas Chinese daily]. November 3, 1964.

Websites

School of Journalism and Communication, CUHK. "A Brief History of 50 Years of Journalism and Communication Education at CUHK." Accessed July 31, 2022. http://www.com.cuhk.edu.hk/zh-TW/about/school-history.

Southern Illinois University Special Collections Research Center. "Charles C. Clayton (1902–1988)." Accessed September 20, 2020. https://archives.lib.siu .edu/?p=creators/creator&id=233.

AUTHOR BIO

YANG ZHANG is Professor of History at Fudan University. She is author of *The Cold War and Academics: Chinese Studies in the United States, 1949–1972* (2019) and *Cultural Cold War: Youth Leadership Programs in the United States, 1947–1989* (2020).

TEN

US EDUCATIONAL EXCHANGE PROGRAMS FOR FOREIGN JOURNALISTS AND CHANGES IN SOUTH KOREAN JOURNALISM

JAE YOUNG CHA

INTRODUCTION

After the armistice of the Korean War in 1953, the US not only offered a vast amount of economic aid to South Korea for its reconstruction but also implemented various programs to promote a rapid American-style modernization of Korean society. Although the Rhee Syngman government was regarded as both very corrupt and authoritarian, the US was nevertheless compelled to action mainly because it recognized the special strategic value of South Korea in the Cold War. US leaders considered South Korea to be on the front line of a Cold War with North Korea. Therefore, the US provided a variety of support measures based on the strategic idea that South Korea should become a model nation representing liberal democracy in political, economic, and social sectors, among others. Of the US measures, it may be argued that the educational exchange program was the most important. The US Department of State invited Korean people working in various fields, including politics, public administration, law, education, arts, and journalism, to receive education and training at universities and other institutions in the US. At the same time, American specialists were sent to South Korea to disseminate advanced knowledge to university students and those working in relevant fields.[1]

The US placed great weight on journalism, among the various educational exchange programs for South Korea. Gregory Henderson, a cultural officer at the US Embassy in South Korea (1958–63), said that journalists accounted for the greatest proportion of specialist groups regarded as targets for the American educational exchange programs.[2] Considering that journalism is one of the most powerful means of mobilizing people's minds and hearts, many American officials shared the perception that it was imperative to nurture pro-US journalists. However, they also understood that, as South Korean newspapers were mostly aimed at the elite rather than the general public, they could not be expected, in their current state, to function effectively as mass media (and presumably thereby as an efficient propaganda tool).[3] Furthermore, South Korean journalism appears backward to the US, for it failed in distinguishing facts from opinions and, under the heavy influence of political factions, in observing the principle of verification, a state of affairs in stark contrast to American journalism, which had, since the 1830s, evolved from opinion-centered partisan reporting and developed a culture of fact-centered objective reporting.[4] It might, therefore, have been quite natural for US officials to consider that, to modernize journalism in South Korea, it would be necessary to Americanize the field.

Historically, since the appearance of printed newspapers such as *Hanseong Sunbo* and *Hanseong Jubo* (official newspapers) in the 1880s and the *Independent* (a private newspaper) in 1896, Korean journalism has tended to place more importance on the assertion of opinions than the reporting of facts. Until Korea was made a Japanese colony in 1910, Korean journalists made great efforts to enlighten the public with the introduction of Western modern knowledge and information and then to arouse nationalism by means of warning against and criticizing the imperial maneuvers targeted toward Korea, thereby trying to protect their sovereignty.[5]

In the Japanese colonial period, the *Sōtoku-fu* (Japanese Government-General in Korea) initially shuttered all Korean newspapers. After the nationwide nonviolent demonstrations for independence in 1919, the press policy was amended to allow three Korean newspapers, including the *Chosun Ilbo* and the *Dong-a Ilbo*, to begin publishing in 1920, albeit under strict censorship. Korean journalists sought to provide support to Nationalist movements both inside and outside the country, as well as to promote ethnic culture through press reports, before the people were placed under a wartime mobilization system because of the outbreak of the Sino-Japanese War in 1937.[6] After the Japanese occupation of Korea ended with the conclusion of the Second World War in 1945, South Korea was placed under interim US military governance for three years, during which time the people witnessed ideological confrontations between progressive and conservative newspapers. However, the intervention of the US military government caused progressive newspapers to gradually disappear, leading to the dominance of conservative newspapers in South Korea.[7]

After the Rhee Syngman government was established in 1948, and through the 1950s, most Korean newspapers were regarded as political papers, which were divided into three types: progovernment, antigovernment, and neutral.

Most journalists engaged in media activities in accordance with the political orientations of the companies to which they belonged.[8] In 1961, when the military junta seized power through a coup, all media came under the control of the government. Under this system, newspaper companies became more commercialized and sought to maximize profit instead of exerting political influence on the public, and they grew very quickly under the industrialization policies of the Park Chung-hee government. This tendency gradually intensified in the 1970s and 1980s, and most news media and their workers were criticized, both from within and outside the field of journalism, for capitulating to the authoritarian government and playing the role of its mouthpieces.[9] From the late 1980s, the process of democratization began in South Korea. However, its news media, and newspapers in particular, continued to be characterized as politically biased, and journalists were criticized for writing articles in which facts were conflated with opinions.[10]

To return to the postwar period, in the mid-1950s the US Department of State launched a program to invite large numbers of Korean journalists to the US for education and training. Simultaneously, American specialists in journalism were sent to Korea to educate local journalists and were tasked with reporting on the state of journalism in the country and suggesting measures to solve any issues that were identified.[11] The chief purposes of those programs were both to nurture pro-US journalists—journalists friendly to the US and willing to support its foreign policy—and to modernize South Korean journalism in the American tradition by disseminating the ideal of professionalism, or the American press system and culture, including objective reporting. "Professionalism" here meant a sort of professional ideology, on the basis of which people engaging in specific occupations, such as physicians and lawyers, seek to pursue specialized knowledge, ensure autonomy in the work process, and contribute to the public interest. In general, those engaging in professional work often establish norms for autonomy, such as codes of ethics, or establish self-governing organizations or education and research institutes to promote professionalism. In the US, the American Society of Newspaper Editors (ASNE) was established in 1923 and adopted a code of ethics known as the Canons of Journalism, which is considered to be the advent of professional journalism.[12]

After the end of the Second World War, the US government and press community made comprehensive efforts to disseminate the American-style press system and culture around the world. For example, the US Department of State cooperated with ASNE to spread such concepts as freedom of speech and professional journalism abroad.[13] As part of such efforts, the US government implemented educational exchange programs to educate and train foreign

284 PRACTICING KNOWLEDGE

journalists or provided financial support to establish and operate organizations designed to nurture or reeducate journalists in a number of countries and territories. In East Asia, the main targets were Japan, South Korea, Taiwan, and Hong Kong.

This chapter attempts, first, to analyze the contents and characteristics of the two programs launched for Korean journalists in the mid-1950s by the US Department of State—a program to invite Korean journalists to the US for education and training and a program to send American journalism specialists to Korea—and then to discuss the results of the two programs and their impact on Korean journalism. Moreover, comparisons will be made to two other cases of US support for journalism in East Asia: Taiwan and Hong Kong. These analyses and arguments are expected to help provide a deeper understanding of the changes Korean journalism underwent between the late 1950s and the early 1960s.

US EDUCATIONAL EXCHANGE PROGRAMS
FOR FOREIGN JOURNALISTS

This section provides an overview of the educational exchange programs for journalists launched in the early 1950s by the US Department of State. These programs were based on the Smith-Mundt Act, enacted in 1948. At the end of the Second World War, many American citizens came to express skepticism about the US government's continuing international information activities and enormous expenditure, putting pressure on the government to narrow the scope of those activities, including educational exchanges. However, with the escalation of the Cold War between the US and the Soviet Union, there was a turnaround in public opinion, allowing the US government to establish the new law necessary for expanding international information activities. Enactment of the Smith-Mundt Act enabled the Department of State to implement programs to invite leaders and specialists in various fields from abroad for education and training, as well as a program to dispatch American specialists to foreign countries.[14]

In 1953, the US Department of State notified diplomatic offices abroad of educational exchange programs launched under the Smith-Mundt Act, the most important objectives of which were to improve foreign peoples' knowledge of the US and to promote mutual understanding between American citizens and those in foreign countries. To accomplish these objectives, the Department of State prioritized educational exchange activities involving organizations that had exercised, or were expected to exercise, a powerful influence on the public.

Given this background, it was only natural for journalists to attract attention as a target of the State Department's educational exchange projects.[15]

There were three types of programs to invite foreign journalists to the US. One was a program for foreign leaders, which allowed newspaper or broadcasting company presidents and leading journalists to travel around the US, visit the newspaper or broadcasting companies and public organizations they desired to, and meet prominent figures. The other two programs were designed to foster advanced specialists. The first of these was the Jointly Sponsored Journalist Project, in which reporters were invited from a foreign country, for a set period of time, to gain work experience with newspaper or broadcasting companies around the nation. The other was the Multinational Foreign Journalist Project, in which journalists were invited from several foreign countries to learn the basic principles of American journalism and techniques necessary for reporting and editing at universities in the US, again for a specified time period, and then to gain work experience at newspaper or broadcasting companies for a few months, after which participants would be allowed to travel around the nation.[16]

Korean journalists were selected for all three educational exchange programs. The largest number of Korean journalists participated in the Multinational Foreign Journalist Project, followed by the Foreign Leader Program. Only a few Koreans were considered for participation in the Jointly Sponsored Journalist Project. This was likely because it was not easy to find Korean journalists equipped with both the English-language and occupational skills required to immediately begin work for newspaper or broadcasting companies in the US. Although participants in the Multinational Foreign Journalist Project were also required to have English-language skills sufficient to attend lectures at US universities, the Jointly Sponsored Journalist Project required participants with a much higher level of ability.[17]

On the other hand, for the programs to dispatch American experts to foreign countries, the US Department of State selected active journalists or professors in journalism. However, there might have been differences in the roles played by those two kinds of US journalism experts. Active journalists introduced American journalism not only to local journalists but also to labor union leaders, local community leaders, and government officials. The American journalists also provided explanations of issues facing the US, including labor, political, and racial issues, in which such leaders and officials showed interest. By contrast, the American professors provided foreign journalists with education on the principles of journalism and basic skills necessary for journalists. Moreover, they sometimes investigated the various issues with which local journalism was confronted and made suggestions for improvement.[18]

The early projects to dispatch American journalism experts to foreign countries were mostly evaluated as very successful by officials of the US Department of State. In 1953, Kenneth Olson, dean of the School of Journalism at Northwestern University, was sent to Greece to conduct seminars on the theme of the principles of American journalism and basic news-gathering and reporting techniques. His seminars attracted hundreds of local journalists each time, and presentations and discussions were lively.[19] The State Department publicized this success extensively, spurring a rush of requests for such seminars from diplomatic offices overseas, including from the US Embassy in Seoul. As a result, the US Department of State, in consultation with the US Embassy in Seoul, launched both a project to invite South Korean journalists to the US and a project to dispatch American specialists in journalism to South Korea.[20]

PROGRAM TO INVITE KOREAN JOURNALISTS TO THE US

In 1955, for the first time, the US Embassy selected eleven young journalists in South Korea and sent them to the School of Journalism at Northwestern University for education and training. All the journalists selected for this program were about thirty years old and had begun their careers as journalists after Korea's liberation from Japanese colonial rule. The US officials likely considered participants of this age and background to be more receptive to education and training than those who had played an active role as journalists in the colonial era. Under the same program, seven Korean journalists were invited to the School of Journalism at the University of Missouri in the first half of 1957, and eleven Korean journalists, together with journalists from other countries, received education and training at Northwestern University again in the second half of 1957. After that, the program was renamed the Multinational Foreign Journalist Project and was implemented in 1958 (seven Korean journalists) and 1959 (six Korean journalists), again at Northwestern University. The program continued until the 1970s, although in 1960 the venue shifted to Indiana University.[21]

The School of Journalism at Northwestern University was a mainstay for this project, possibly because on multiple occasions the school had had experience in supervising education programs for German journalists carried out by the Department of State under the policy of providing reeducation and reorientation to Germany from the early 1950s.[22] Moreover, Kenneth Olson, dean of the School of Journalism, who had great interest in the education of foreign journalists at an early stage, applied for the State Department's 1950 educational exchange program, together with other schools of the university, and was selected for the program.[23]

As mentioned above, the program to invite Korean journalists was intended to foster pro-US journalists in South Korea (as had been the case with the program implemented for German journalists), to nurture public opinion favorable to the US, and also to export the American liberal media system and culture to South Korea to modernize the country's journalism. A document sent to the Department of State by the US Embassy in Seoul clearly indicated the purpose of the project, stating that it hoped to continue sending young, talented journalists to the US for training in order to increase their influence on journalism in South Korea and improve the capabilities of Korean newspapers. The "influence" here may have referred to journalistic influence strong enough to foster pro-US public opinion, and "improving the capabilities of newspapers," to the ideal of transforming Korean newspapers by exporting American-style journalistic professionalism and objective journalism to South Korea, thereby hopefully modernizing the Korean newspapers.[24]

Officials at the US Embassy in Seoul surveyed comprehensively the reality of South Korean journalism and understood it well. With the cooperation of Korean journalists, the US Information Service (USIS) in Seoul prepared two kinds of reports regarding the current status of Korean journalism every year from 1954 and distributed copies to all US diplomatic offices in South Korea, private organizations, the military forces, and even several US organizations in Japan.[25] The general consensus was that, while the authoritarian South Korean government was strictly controlling the mass media, Korean newspapers—characterized as political papers taking different stances, whether progovernment, antigovernment, or neutral, and being willing to report in a sensational way—were disconnected from the masses.[26] Therefore, they concluded that journalism, in its present state, would not be able to play a functional role in the pursuit of US policy objectives to rapidly reconstruct and modernize South Korean society. To resolve this issue, the US decided to implement the program to modernize Korean journalism in the American tradition.

Participants for the program were selected through several stages and by consultation between the US Embassy in Seoul and the US Department of State. First, the US Embassy in Seoul narrowed down the list of candidates by giving an English-language test to journalists recommended by South Korean newspaper and broadcasting companies. Next, the number of candidates was further reduced through interviews conducted by a screening committee, which consisted of executives of major newspapers and officials from the Ministry of Foreign Affairs on the South Korean side, as well as officials responsible for journalism and cultural diplomacy from the US Embassy in Seoul. At this stage, a list of potential candidates, together with information about each individual, was submitted to the Department of State. After internal examination, the Department of State notified the US Embassy in Seoul of a short list of finalist candidates. In general, English-language skill was a critical factor in the selection of candidates, but sometimes consideration was given to the candidates' health condition and political factors.[27]

Korean journalists selected through this process embarked for the US, where they attended lectures at a university for two months, worked as interns for two local newspapers or broadcasting companies for another two months, and traveled around the nation for one more months. After completing this course, they attended seminars held in Washington, DC, or at Northwestern University, where they were asked to evaluate the program and make suggestions for improvement.[28]

The education program at Northwestern University consisted of three courses: American Journalism, Life and Culture in the US, and Comparative Journalism. Full-time professors of the School of Journalism were responsible for these courses, and special lectures were also given by professors of social sciences at Northwestern University and journalists working in Chicago as guest speakers. These courses were offered at the graduate school level and operated separately from the university's regular courses. In addition, the courses were designed to give participants the background knowledge and basic techniques necessary for internships at newspaper companies, a general understanding of social issues facing the US, and an opportunity to compare the US press system and culture with those of their home countries.[29]

It was reported that Korean journalists had a good impression of the education offered at Northwestern University. According to a report submitted by the US Embassy in Seoul, journalists who participated in the program held in 1957 rated their experience in the US positively, and responses indicated that the education offered by Northwestern University, in particular, was the most useful aspect of the program as a whole. Professor Floyd G. Arpan, responsible for the overall management of the program, also claimed that a majority of participants remarked that, although they felt the course offered at Northwestern University was too short, they nevertheless learned more from it than from the practical training at newspaper companies.[30]

The participants who completed the education course at Northwestern University, after consultation with Arpan, engaged in internships at two companies that they had chosen from among the newspaper or broadcasting companies recruited by the Department of State for the program. At the companies, they were able to choose between actively participating in news-gathering activities and writing news articles or simply observing the American journalists' activities.[31] After the practical work, the participants were given an opportunity to travel to areas they wished to visit. In some cases, in consideration of the travel expenses and daily allowances allotted equally to each individual by the Department of State, to reduce the financial burden, some participants adjusted their initial travel schedules in light of geographical logistics to facilitate easier visits to any destinations they desired en route to the newspaper companies for practical work.[32]

The Department of State recommended that program participants contribute articles to American newspapers or to newspapers in their home countries; participants could write for the newspapers while engaging in internships or during their travels. Of the few who did write articles, barring a handful of exceptions, their work contained friendly comments about American society and lifestyles. As contributing articles to a newspaper was not a requirement but simply a recommendation, only a few Korean participants actually did so. As a notable exception, Chung In-Ryang, a reporter from the *Segye Ilbo* who participated in the training program in the latter half of 1957, contributed about twenty articles to the newspaper company he belonged to. His articles included works dealing with the prominent American poet Carl Sandburg, the scenery of Christmas Eve and the days at the close of the year, NATO meetings, and a TV program hosted by the famous American journalist Edward Murrow.[33]

The US Embassy in Seoul sought to achieve the objectives of the educational exchange program by micromanaging the Korean journalists who returned home after completing the program in the US. The embassy's public affairs officer and relevant officials kept in touch with those journalists and encouraged them to engage in activities necessary for the modernization of Korean journalism. The embassy spared no effort in providing support for their activities. Then the public affairs officer, Henry Arnold, reported that a journalism study group, called the Kwanhoon Club, had been established mainly by young journalists who had returned from the State Department's program in the US; he also indicated that some behind-the-scenes support from the USIS had played a role in the formation of the Kwanhoon Club.[34] However, none of the journalists who formed and led the club mentioned any intervention of the US Embassy in their records or memoirs.[35] As an exception, in retrospect, Park Kwon-Sang said that the Kwanhoon Club received in-kind assistance of printing paper from the American Embassy when launching a new journal titled *Newspaper Studies* in 1959, and substantial financial support from the USIS in the publishing of the 1963 summer issue of the same journal.[36]

PROGRAM TO DISPATCH AMERICAN SPECIALISTS
IN JOURNALISM TO SOUTH KOREA

While the program to invite Korean journalists to the US for education and training was implemented every year, American specialists in journalism were sent to South Korea biannually. In 1955, Professor Roscoe Ellard of Columbia University was sent to South Korea, followed by Professor D. Wayne Rowland of Southern Illinois University in 1957 and Professor Arpan of Northwestern University in 1959.

The US Department of State conducted a thorough examination to select specialists in journalism for this program. In the screening process, applicants' worldviews underwent scrupulous inspection, as did their specialized knowledge and techniques; even candidates who had an excellent professional background or ability to perform required tasks could be rejected if their social activities or political philosophy conflicted with the US government's diplomatic policies or benefits. This might be reasonably attributed to the fact that Cold War tensions between the US and the Soviet Union were escalating during the period. Information on the screening process of the above-mentioned three professors is not readily available. However, it was found that when Curtis MacDougall, professor at the School of Journalism at Northwestern University, applied to a Fulbright Program to send lecturers to South Korea in 1963, his application was rejected for security reasons during the screening process, although he was well qualified in terms of his professional career and ability to perform duties. Related documents indicated that Professor MacDougall had raised questions about the US government's Cold War policies and, as a member of certain organizations, had been engaged in activities calling on the government to recognize the People's Republic of China (PRC) diplomatically. Thus, there was a major concern that if he were sent to South Korea, he might be utilized by political forces in opposition to the US and South Korean government.[37]

Those selected for the program visited the Department of State before their departure to receive a briefing on the present status of journalism and society in general in South Korea, as well as on their missions. After arriving in the country, they received further instruction from officials at the US Embassy in Seoul. This process enabled the specialists to better understand the circumstances of journalism in the country and to carry out their duties in accordance with such information.[38]

The detailed itinerary for each American specialist was finalized immediately after arrival in South Korea through consultation with US Embassy officials and the Korean members of the screening committee for the program to invite Korean journalists to the US. The roles and tasks of the American specialists were determined, with a focus on issues facing journalism in South Korea that required urgent solutions; their itinerary and activities are shown in table 10.1.[39]

Professor Roscoe Ellard, who was sent to South Korea in 1955, mostly stayed in Seoul, where he conducted two seminars for executive editors and two lectures for young newspaper reporters. In the seminars, he discussed the characteristics of Korean newspapers with editors and, on the basis of his experience in the US, suggested measures to address the issues facing Korean newspapers, receiving positive responses from participants. In the lectures to young reporters, he explained the basic principles of good journalism and good reporting—or perhaps techniques for American-style objective reporting—but the reaction of many of the young reporters was not positive, and the general accord was that there was nothing of value to learn from his lecture.[40] In those days, the Korean press was under the pressure of the authoritarian government, and thus, the young reporters might have considered American-style objective reporting, premised on the right to freedom of the press, as unfeasible in the South Korean context. US Embassy officials in Seoul were embarrassed by such a negative reaction from local journalists, because the officials had advised Ellard to give a lecture on basic news-gathering and reporting techniques to young Korean journalists who, they thought, had never received proper training.[41] Ellard also visited twelve newspaper companies and four news agencies in Seoul, at which he discussed current press issues with editors and interacted with other employees, including those involved in printing, to understand the situation of the Korean press system.

Upon completing his itinerary, Ellard concluded that Korean newspapers were no more than political papers, most biased in terms of reporting and editing. He also stated that there was no daily newspaper capable of providing accurate information to the public and that, in terms of production, the levels of technology and productivity were also extremely low. On the basis of these analyses, he proposed that to earn the trust of the public and enhance the popularity of newspapers, Korean journalists should adopt objective journalism and improve their newspapers' layout and fonts. In addition, he argued that Korean newspapers should reduce the use of Chinese characters, which were thought to constitute a major barrier for the common people.[42]

Professor D. Wayne Rowland, who was sent to South Korea in 1957, spent his first few weeks in Seoul, before traveling around large provincial cities for one month—about two-thirds of his stay in the country. He spent ten days each in

Table 10.1 Itinerary of American Specialists and Their Activities in South Korea

Name of specialist	University	Timing of visit	Areas visited	Media companies visited	Other activities
Roscoe Ellard	Columbia University	Sept. 22, 1955– Nov. 3, 1955	Seoul and its suburbs	12 newspaper companies 4 news agencies	Speeches at 6 universities
D. Wayne Rowland	Southern Illinois University	6 weeks from Sept. 18, 1957	Seoul (12 days) Daegu (10 days) Busan (10 days) Kwangju (10 days)	Several newspaper companies in each area	Several speeches in the Seoul area
Floyd G. Arpan	Northwestern University	Mar. 16, 1959– Apr. 25, 1959	Seoul (21 days)	12 newspaper companies 5 news agencies 4 publishing companies Korean broadcasting station	10 lectures 4 seminars 1 speech
			Kwangju (4 days) Mokpo (2 days) Jeonju (3 days)	3 newspaper companies 2 newspaper companies 2 newspaper companies	Speech for the public Lectures at Chonbuk National University
			Busan (3 days) Masan (2 days) Jinju (1 day)	4 newspaper companies 1 newspaper company 1 newspaper company	Lectures for journalists
			Daegu (4 days)	4 newspaper companies Daegu broadcast station	Speech for the public Lectures at Kyungpook National University, Daegu University, Chunggu University
			Gyeongju (1 day)		Sightseeing

Busan, Daegu, and Kwangju, where he discussed issues facing journalism with local journalists and suggested measures to solve those issues, again receiving positive responses.[43] After Rowland returned to the US, he contributed to an academic journal an article in which he overviewed the current status of Korean journalism and proposed a few measures for improvement.

In the article, Rowland stated that in South Korea, there were not many local newspapers, and of those that existed, all were suffering from financial hardship to the point of barely surviving. He added that even national papers produced in Seoul and distributed nationwide, bar a few exceptions, experienced similar difficulties. More specifically, he indicated that the Korean press system as a whole had been facing industrial challenges, including lack of paper, delayed mechanization of printing, low subscription rates, and poor development of advertising. In political terms, he recognized that as the Korean government loosened control, the newspapers and their journalists would gain more freedom.[44] In reality, however, this did not eventuate, as was clear from a 1958 amendment to the National Security Law that imposed further restraints on press freedom and from the government's order to cease the publication of the *Kyunghyang Sinmun*, the most overtly opposition daily newspaper, in 1959.[45]

Rowland also criticized local newspapers in South Korea for their policies of emphasizing national news and international news far more than local news and recommended that newspaper companies should make greater efforts to report community-based news. Moreover, he went on to say that in South Korea, he had urged journalists to advance professionalism by emphasizing the importance of the social and moral responsibility of journalists in a liberal democratic country, and he added that he had received a positive response from the Korean journalists. For the development of journalism in South Korea, he also proposed the establishment of an educational institution specialized in nurturing or reeducating professional journalists (i.e., a journalism school or college) and said that as part of such an effort, American professors in journalism should be sent to South Korea.[46]

Professor Arpan was sent to South Korea in 1959. He claimed to be familiar with the current status of journalism there because, as mentioned earlier, he supervised the State Department's program to educate and train Korean journalists at Northwestern University. To maximize the results of Arpan's visit, the American Embassy in Seoul made careful arrangements, preparing in advance a list of questions from Korean editors and announcing the details of his itinerary through Korean newspapers. During his visit, Arpan energetically engaged in various activities in Seoul and regional cities, visiting twenty-nine newspaper companies, five news agencies, four magazine publishers, and two broadcasting stations; giving lectures and seminars for journalists; and making speeches to the public.[47]

Unlike the other two professors, Arpan publicly criticized the South Korean government for its control over the mass media. Coincidentally, the International Press Institute also refused to accept South Korea as a member because of the aforementioned amendment to the National Security Law and the resulting lack of freedom of the press, and a dispute erupted among Korean journalists. A number of journalists asked Arpan his opinion on this issue, and he answered honestly, which caused friction with the South Korean government.[48] Further, he contributed to a South Korean newspaper an article critical of the Korean government's move to end publication of the *Kyunghyang Sinmun*, which had happened immediately after he left for Taiwan. In the article, he argued that this proved that the South Korean government had been suppressing journalism.[49]

Arpan also criticized the Korean press for its corruption, saying that monetary transactions influenced decisions to report certain stories and that, as a result, many intellectuals and citizens actually wished the government to control the press more strictly. To prevent such corruption, he emphasized education for self-regulation and ethical behavior. Like Rowland, Arpan proposed the creation of a school of journalism at a university to improve journalism in South Korea and suggested dispatching American specialists in journalism to the school.[50]

RESULTS OF THE US EDUCATIONAL EXCHANGE PROGRAM FOR SOUTH KOREAN JOURNALISM

This section examines the results of the educational exchange programs implemented in the 1950s by the US Department of State to modernize South Korean journalism and to nurture pro-US sentiment in Korean journalists. According to some previous research, the press in South Korea maintained a strong pro-American tendency until the country's democratization in the late 1980s, and, excepting a few progressive media companies, most appear to have maintained this tendency to the present day.[51] It can be inferred that the State Department's educational exchange programs for foreign journalists played a role—if not a crucial one—in fostering this tendency. However, the focus of this chapter is primarily on the other objective, the American-style modernization of South Korean journalism, and on the changes that were supposedly brought about by the programs in South Korean journalism.

As has been shown, the US Department of State and the American Embassy in Seoul devoted considerable effort to bringing about changes to South Korea's press system and culture, with American journalism as a model. The program to educate and train Korean journalists, implemented by the School of Journalism at Northwestern University under commission from the US Department of State, was designed for Korean journalists to study, through lectures, the history and philosophy of American journalism, as well as basic rules and techniques for news gathering and reporting. In addition, Korean journalists were provided with opportunities to compare the press systems and news-gathering and reporting styles of the US and South Korea and to engage in practical work at newspaper companies or broadcasting stations using the knowledge acquired through the lectures at Northwestern University.

Meanwhile, the American specialists in journalism dispatched to South Korea recognized that Korean newspapers, most of which were characterized as politically factional, dealt with news in a sensational way and were corrupt enough to engage in monetary transactions over decisions to publish or bury news articles, and they proposed measures to resolve these issues. The American specialists advised the South Korean journalists to adopt an objective reporting system to convey accurate news to the public. They also emphasized the importance of journalists' sense of social and moral responsibility in the pursuit of professionalism. Moreover, they proposed the creation of an organization for journalists, or the establishment of education or research institutes such as schools of journalism at universities.

What was the most significant result of the US State Department's educational exchange programs for South Korean journalism? Arguably, among the changes observed in the South Korean press system between the late 1950s and the early 1960s, it might be the emergence of new organizations and institutions, such as the formation of the Kwanhoon Club and the Korean Society of Newspaper Editors in 1957 and the establishment of the Korea Newspaper Research Institute in 1964. As mentioned earlier, the Kwanhoon Club was organized to promote research and friendship under the leadership of young journalists who had participated in the State Department's educational exchange program in 1955. The Korean Society of Newspaper Editors was a professional organization that was launched, allegedly, as a result of a proposal made by Kwanhoon Club members to senior journalists.[52] It can also be argued that the Korea Newspaper Research Institute was established under the influence of the advice of the American specialists sent to South Korea to create a school of journalism. The Korea Newspaper Research Institute has continuously provided education to journalists since it was founded in 1964 under the leadership of the Korean Society of Newspaper Editors—although its formation was delayed because of the military coup in 1961.[53]

296 PRACTICING KNOWLEDGE

However, the formation of these journalist organizations and education or research institutes did not bring about any dramatic changes to journalism itself in South Korea. It is commonly understood that media ethics and professionalism based on objective journalism did not take root in South Korea despite the various efforts of the above organizations. Such efforts included the creation of an ethics code at the time of the foundation of the Korean Society of Newspaper Editors in 1957, as well as guidelines for the practice of media ethics established in 1961 by the society, which incorporated the content of the US Canons of Journalism, including the separation of reporting and commentary, accuracy in reporting, journalistic integrity, and the protection of others' rights.[54] However, most South Korean journalists considered such codes and guidelines to be imposed by outsiders; difficult to comply with in real life, if perhaps correct in spirit; empty; and ineffectual.[55]

This attitude can be attributed, first of all, to the historical tradition of Korean journalism. From the establishment of modern newspapers in Korea, journalists tended to place importance on asserting opinion over conveying facts. Journalists viewed their duties as advocating for various national causes, such as the enlightenment of the people, defense and restoration of national sovereignty, nation building and reunification, economic development, and political democratization. The political environment of Korean journalism was also far removed from that of the US, where freedom of the press had been ensured from an early stage. In stark contrast, South Korean journalists were continuously placed under very strict control by the authoritarian governments, whether colonial, civilian, or military, until democratization in the late 1980s. Journalists were therefore forced to assume responsibility for the government in power rather than the public, as required by the norm of modern journalism, and thus did not pay much heed to media ethics or show interest in self-regulation. Meanwhile, South Korean media businesses grew very rapidly owing to great support under the industrialization policies of the military government from the 1960s. In fact, while the military government granted various kinds of economic favors to the subservient companies, critical or resistant outlets were sanctioned harshly. As a result, political parallelism or the factionalism of the news media was strengthened through connection to, or conflict with, the government in power. Thus, South Korean journalists typically came to produce news with only a veneer of objectivity, assuming a pretense of fairness, neutrality, or balanced reporting while generally disregarding the verification process as its core.[56] The pursuit of journalistic professionalism was mostly abandoned, although its importance was emphasized intermittently by a few concerned journalists and scholars and whenever serious misdeeds of the press were publicly revealed and severely criticized by the people.[57]

Consequently, it can be said that the US State Department's educational exchange programs for journalists, which aimed to modernize South Korean journalism in the American style, were successful to a certain degree at the institutional level but not at the cultural level.

CONCLUSION

As described in the introduction to this chapter, after the end of the Second World War, the US government and press cooperated in various projects, both officially and unofficially, to spread the American-style press system and culture throughout the world. In East Asia, the main targets of the programs included South Korea, Taiwan, and Hong Kong, among other nations and territories. These programs were developed on the assumption that the press can be one of the most effective weapons in ideological warfare—in other words, that the press can be utilized to increase public wariness or hostility toward Communism, to create favorable attitudes toward the US, and to foster pro-US public opinion. At the same time, the US expected that if East Asian countries could modernize their news media in the American style and thereby make them act as tools for persuasion, American-style modernization could be expanded more efficiently to other sectors in society.

It seems that the US provided support to the journalism field with different purposes and in different ways in each country and territory in East Asia. According to Mike Shichi Lan and Yang Zhang (see chapters 8 and 9 in this volume), US support, both officially and unofficially, was offered to Taiwan and Hong Kong for journalism education in undergraduate programs; this support included providing funding for the creation of journalism departments and sending professors necessary for these newly established departments.[58] In contrast, the US never offered direct financial support for establishing journalism departments or institutes in South Korea but rather invested in intensive educational exchange programs for working journalists. This contrast can be seen clearly in the participants of the Multinational Foreign Journalist Project, which was implemented by the School of Journalism at Northwestern University under commission from the US Department of State; a number of Korean journalists participated every year, whereas only a few journalists from Taiwan and Hong Kong were invited, and only intermittently.[59] Further, it seems that ideological factors were more heavily emphasized in the support for Hong Kong and Taiwan than for South Korea, because in the latter context, US officials were considerably less wary of Communist influence on local journalists, given that anti-Communism came to be a dominant ideology among the people after the end of the Korean War. In the case of Hong Kong, US support was offered in an attempt to block the influence of Communist China on its journalism sector. To Taiwan, it was provided for the purpose of dissuading Chinese students from Southeast Asia from seeking journalism education in Communist China.[60]

Zhang also argues that, in Hong Kong, the local intellectuals recognized the importance of journalism at an early stage, and their active participation, in addition to support from the US, served as an important factor in the process of creating journalism departments at universities.[61] Similarly, in South Korea, a number of educated elites also recognized at an early stage the need to establish an educational or research institute to improve the quality of journalism. Thus, when the Korean Newspaper Academy was established in 1947 as a private institution in South Korea under US occupation, chancellors of prominent universities and publishers and editors of major newspaper companies joined as board members and lecturers.[62] However, there is no record of any kind of support being provided by the US for the academy, although a US general did participate in its opening ceremony, where he gave a congratulatory speech. Later, in the mid-1950s, journalism departments were founded, for the first time in South Korea, at a couple of universities in Seoul—and, in contrast to Taiwan and Hong Kong, without support from the US.

Finally, Daniel Hallin and Paolo Mancini conducted a comparative analysis of Western nations' media systems and political regimes and found indications that journalism around the world had shown a tendency toward Americanization since the end of the Second World War. According to the analysis, however, the extant literature suggested that as yet relatively little research has been conducted on how Americanization "happens concretely—what kinds of changes in journalism education take place, what interactions there are among journalists from different countries, what consultants are brought in, and what seminars held, and so on."[63] In this respect, this chapter (as have others for other countries in this volume) has attempted to address this gap in the literature by exploring the attempt to Americanize South Korean media in the years after the armistice of the Korean War.

NOTES

1. Brazinsky, *Nation Building in South Korea*, 66–127; Heo, *Migugui hegemoniwa hanguk minjokjuui*, 13–31.

2. G. Henderson, "Hanmiganui munhwagwangye," 74.

3. USIS-Korea to USIA, "Semi-annual USIS Report," December 15, 1955, RG 469, Korea Subject Files, 1953–1959, box 36, National Archives at College Park (NACP).

4. Schudson, *Discovering the News*. Schudson argued that objectivity became an ideology in journalism after the First World War, ironically, because of the lost-cause status of factuality. By that time, both journalists and the people recognized that facts are not easy to grasp and can be easily distorted. Thus, it was suggested that objectivity be emphasized as a methodical guard against subjectivity in journalism. In the same vein, Tuchman argued that objectivity functions as a strategic ritual for journalists to "mitigate such continual pressures as deadlines, possible libel suits, and anticipated reprimands of superiors." Tuchman, "Objectivity as Strategic Ritual," 660. For more understanding of the continuing debate around the concept of objectivity in journalism, see McNair, "After Objectivity?"

5. Chung, *Hangukgeundaeeonronui jaejomyeong*, 14–30; Kang, *Hunmingwa gyemong*, 127–37.

6. C. S. Park, *Eonronundong*, 109–89.

7. M.-W. Kim, *Hangugeonronsa*, 323–404.

8. Kim, 415–18.

9. Y.-K. Park, *Hangugui eonronin jeongcheseongeul mutda*, 303–19.

10. J.-K. Lee, *Hangukhyeong jeoneollijeum model*, 72–88.

11. Heo, *Migugui hegemoniwa hanguk minjokjuui*, 235–38; Cha, "1950nyeondae migungmuseongui hanguk eonronin gyoyukgyoryu saeop yeongu," 219–45; Cha, "1950nyeondae migungmuseongui miguk eonron jeonmunga pagyeon saeop yeongu," 243–76.

12. Kang, *Hangug eonronjeonmunjigui sahoehak*, 221–27; Ward, *Invention of Journalism Ethics*.

13. Blanchard, *Exporting the First Amendment*, 1–4.

14. J. Henderson, *United States Information Agency*, 39–48.

15. "Educational Exchange Service-Foreign Leader Program," Foreign Service Information and Circular 6 from Department of State, May 28, 1953, RG 59, Bureau of Educational and Cultural Affairs Office, 1955–1959, Decimal File, box 1, NACP.

16. The State Department's educational exchange programs basically consisted of three elements: study, work, and travel. The three educational exchange programs for foreign journalists mentioned above were developed with various combinations of these three elements. The Foreign Leader Program allowed visitors to merely travel around the nation. The Jointly Sponsored Journalist Project consisted of two parts: work in the mass media and travel. The Multinational Foreign Journalist Project included all three elements of

study, work, and travel. See Dean Mahin, "History of International Visitor Program, 1948~1968," manuscript, 1968, J. William Fulbright Papers, Bureau of Educational and Cultural Affairs Historical Collection (hereafter CU), group IV, box 151, folder 32, University of Arkansas Libraries Special Collections.

17. According to the plan composed by the US Embassy in Seoul for the educational exchange program of the next fiscal year, only one Korean journalist was qualified for participation in the Jointly Sponsored Journalist Project. American Embassy, Seoul, to Department of State, "Educational Exchange: Prospectus Call 1955–56," June 25, 1954, RG 59, Decimal File, box 2541, NACP.

18. Grunwell, "Exchange of Journalists," 7–9, 15–16.

19. Grunwell, 9.

20. Department of State to American Embassy, Seoul, "Educational Exchange: Foreign Specialists, FY 1955-Group Project for Korean Journalist at Northwestern University, Evanston, Illinois," September 8, 1955; American Embassy, Seoul, to Department of State, "Educational Exchange: U.S. Specialist Roscoe Ellard-Visit to Korea," November 14, 1955, RG 59, 1955–1959 Decimal File, from 511/95B3/1-355 to 511.95B3/12-3156, box 2246, NACP.

21. Cha, "1950nyeondae migungmuseongui hanguk eonronin gyoyukgyoryu," 226–27.

22. This refers to the policy conducted by the Allied forces after the end of the Second World War, at least nominally, to turn education and culture tainted with totalitarianism toward democracy, with the aim of freeing the people of Germany, occupied by the Allied forces, from Nazism. Arguably, the ultimate purpose of the policy may have been to nurture pro-American attitudes among the Germans. Hurwitz, "Comparing American Reform Efforts in Germany," 321–50.

23. Kenneth E. Olson, "Education for Journalism: Watch Dog of Democracy," Address to the Northwestern University Trustees and Associates, February 24, 1949, Kenneth E. Olson Papers, Series 16/12, box 1, Library of Northwestern University, University Archives; US Department of State to American Diplomatic and Consular Officers, "Exchange-Visitor Program No. P-213," June 26, 1950, RG 59, Decimal File, box 2259, NACP.

24. American Embassy, Seoul, to Department of State, "Educational Exchange: Appraisal of Country Plan," March 15, 1956, RG 469, Korea Subject Files, 1953–59, box 53, NACP.

25. The reports were prepared under the titles of "Information and Press Policies of the ROK Government" (Confidential) and "Political and Professional Structures of the Korean Press" (Official use only). USIS, Seoul, to USIA, "Annual Analysis of the Korean Press," May 23, 1955, RG 469, Korea Subject Files, 1953–59, box 36, NACP.

26. USIS-Korea to USIA, "Semi-Annual USIS Report, January 1–June 30, 1954," September 9, 1954; USIS-Korea to USIA, "Semi-Annual USIS Report,

January 1–June 30, 1955," December 15, 1955, RG 469, Korea Subject Files, 1953–59, box 36, NACP.

27. American Embassy, Seoul, to Department of State, "Educational Exchange: FY58 Foreign Specialists Group Project in Journalism," March 10, 1958; Department of State to American Embassy, Seoul, "Educational Exchange: Foreign Specialists, FY 1955—Group Project for Korean Journalists at Northwestern University, Evanston, Illinois," September 8, 1955, RG 59, Decimal File, box 2246, NACP.

28. "Final Report of Program Coordinator for Foreign Journalist Program at Northwestern University, September 15, 1957, to February 1, 1958," CU, group IV, box 157, folder 17.

29. Professor Floyd G. Arpan, responsible for the overall management of this education program, said that the six-week course program was so short that it was not to be operated as a regular course for journalism and communication studies. "Final Report of Program Coordinator for Foreign Journalist Program at Northwestern University, September 15, 1957, to February 1, 1958," CU, group IV, box 157, folder 17.

30. American Embassy, Seoul, to Department of State, "Educational Exchange: FY58 Foreign Specialists Group Project in Journalism," March 10, 1958, RG 59, Decimal File, box 2246: "Final Report of Program Coordinator for Foreign Journalist Program at Northwestern University, September 15, 1957, to February 1, 1958," CU, group IV, box 157, folder 17, 12. The results of the evaluation made by Korean journalists can be attributed to the fact that although there must have been differences between individuals, most of them might not have had sufficient language skills or professional abilities to engage in actual news-gathering and reporting work at American newspaper companies.

31. Some major companies, such as the *New York Times*, declined the State Department's request for cooperation—despite many applications from Korean participants—because there were no mentors or guides, although a number of medium-sized companies, such as the *Boston Globe* and *San Francisco Chronicle*, agreed to cooperate, in the midst of escalating Cold War tensions and growing patriotism. Arpan, "Through Study, Travel, and Work," 30–32.

32. "Final Report of Program Coordinator for Foreign Journalist Program at Northwestern University, September 15, 1957, to February 1, 1958," CU, group IV, box 157, folder 17, 14. Young-Hee Lee, who participated in the program as a reporter for Korean Pacific Press in 1959, said in his memoir that his request to visit Cuba or Puerto Rico was rejected, possibly because of the political considerations. Lee, *Daehwa*, 222–24.

33. American Embassy, Seoul, to Department of State, "Educational Exchange: Evidence of Effectiveness," April 18, 1958, RG 59, Decimal File, box 2246, NACP.

34. USIS-Korea to USIA, "Annual Assessment Report, USIS-Korea, October 1, 1956, through September 30, 1957," October 25, 1957, RG 306, NND 51290, box 51, NACP.

35. K.-S. Park, "Gwanhunkeulleobiran mueosinga," 136–152; Cho, *Geuraedo sesangeun jeonjinhanda*.

36. Kwanhoon Club, *Kwanhoon keullop 30nyeonsa*, 132.

37. Ranard to Norred, "Subject: Suitability of Curtis MacDougall as Fulbright Lecturer in Korea," January 31, 1964; Norred to Ranard, "Subject: Views on Suitability of Curtis MacDougall as Fulbright Lecturer in Korea," February 3, 1964, RG 59, Bureau of Far Eastern Affairs, Office of East Asian Affairs, Central Files, 1947–1964, box 11, NACP.

38. Floyd Arpan to International Educational Exchange Service, State Department, "Report on Six Week[s] Assignment as Journalism Specialist in the Republic of Korea," n.d., RG 306, lot 66 D 87, box 11, 1.

39. American Embassy, Seoul, to Department of State, Foreign Service Despatch, November 14, 1955; American Embassy, Seoul, to Department of State, Foreign Service Despatch, April 30, 1957, RG 59, 1955–1959, Central Decimal File, box 2247, NACP.

40. American Embassy, Seoul, to Department of State, Foreign Service Despatch, November 14, 1955, NACP. Meanwhile, Young-Hee Lee showed a similar reaction in his memoir about the education program offered at Northwestern University, saying that there was nothing special to learn in terms of news-gathering or writing techniques. Lee, *Daehwa*, 221.

41. American Embassy to Secretary of State, August 19, 1955, RG 59, 1955–1959, Central Decimal File, box 2246, NACP.

42. "Dr. Roscoe Ellard's Report to John P. McKnight, Director, USIS-Korea," November 3, 1955, RG 59, 1955–1959, Decimal File, box 2246, NACP.

43. American Embassy, Seoul, to Department of State, "Educational Exchange Annual Report, Fiscal Year 1958," August 8, 1958, RG 59, 1955–1959, Decimal File, box 2247, NACP.

44. Rowland, "Press in the Korean Republic," 451

45. M.-W. Kim, *Hangugeonronsa*, 467–68.

46. Rowland, "Press in the Korean Republic," 453–54.

47. Floyd Arpan to International Educational Exchange Service, State Department, "Report on Six Week[s] Assignment as Journalism Specialist in the Republic of Korea," n.d., RG 306, lot 66 D 87, box 11; American Embassy, Seoul, to Department of State, "Educational Exchange: American Specialists Program—Professor Floyd G. Arpan," June 23, 1959, RG 59, Records of the Plans and Development Staff, Evaluation Branch, 1955–1960, box 31, NACP.

48. *Kyunghyang Sinmun*, April 16 and April 20, 1959. Interestingly, American Embassy officials in South Korea advised Arpan to criticize issues related to

Korean journalism in a fair and candid manner. In addition, USIS-Seoul stated that nobody from pro–Korean government newspaper companies participated in the farewell parties for Arpan, owing to the Korean government's dissatisfaction with his views and opinions. American Embassy, Seoul, to Department of State, "Educational Exchange: American Specialists Program-Professor Floyd G. Arpan," June 23, 1959, RG 59, Records of the Plans and Development Staff, Evaluation Branch, 1955–1960, box 31, NACP.

49. *Dong-a Ilbo*, May 19, 1959, 1.

50. USIS, Seoul, to USIA, Washington, "Subject: Professor Floyd Arpan's Observations on Korean Press," May 6, 1959, RG 469, 1948–61 Office of Far Eastern Operations, Korea Subject files, 1953–59, box 112, NACP.

51. Y.-J. Kim, "'Chinmi'wa 'banmi' saieseo," 258–61.

52. Kwanhoon Club, *Kwanhoon keulleop 50nyeonsa*, 70–74.

53. Three of the six members of the preparatory committee for the Korea Newspaper Research Institute were Jong-In Hong, vice president and chief editor of the *Chosun Ilbo* newspaper, who was actively involved from the beginning as a member of the screening committee for the educational exchange program, and Kwon-Sang Park and Se-Hyong Cho, both of whom were participants in the 1955 program. Korean Publishers Association, *Hanguksinmunyeongam*, 279.

54. Chung, *Gwanhunkeulleop 40nyeonsa*, 46.

55. Nam, "Jigeobideollogiroseoui hanguk eonronyunliui hyeongseonggwajeong," 73–75.

56. Nam, "Hanguk gaekgwanjuui gwanhaengui munhwajeok teukseong"; Yoo, "Gaekgwanjuui 100nyeonui hyeongsikhwa gwajeong," 112–21.

57. Y.-K. Park, *Hangugui eonronin jeongcheseongeul mutda*, 222–35, 324–33, 406–13. Schudson argued that professionalism in journalism was constructed by the American journalists in the early twentieth century to achieve occupational autonomy and social legitimacy. Schudson, *Sociology of News*, 81–84. Also see Nerone, "Historical Roots"; Waisbord, *Reinventing Professionalism*, 19–42.

58. Lan, "How the Cold War Shaped 'China'"; Zhang, "Cold War."

59. Floyd Arpan to US Department of State, "Address List Multinational Foreign Journalist Project, 1950~1972," 1973, CU, box 158, file 1. Of 285 journalists from sixty-seven countries, South Korean journalists constituted 67, the most in this program, whereas there were only five and three journalists from Taiwan and Hong Kong, respectively.

60. Zhang, "Cold War"; Lan, "How the Cold War Shaped 'China.'"

61. Zhang argued that the US merely exercised its "invited influence" on the development of journalism education in Hong Kong. However, it should be noted that this concept leaves much room for discussion in that the US provided support not because of requests from intellectuals and journalists in Hong Kong

but for its own purposes in blocking the PRC's impact on the news media in Hong Kong. Zhang, "Cold War."

62. Chung, *Joseonsinmunhagwonui gijayangseonggwa eonronhak yeongu*, 26–28. This academy made great efforts to foster journalists, but after the mid-1950s, it could not operate effectively, owing to financial struggles, and it was finally incorporated into Chungang University in 1969.

63. Hallin and Mancini, *Comparing Media Systems*, 303–4.

REFERENCES

Primary Sources

Fulbright, J. William. Papers. Bureau of Educational and Cultural Affairs Historical Collection. University of Arkansas Libraries Special Collections.

Olson, Kenneth E. Papers. Library of Northwestern University, University Archives.

RG 59, Bureau of Far Eastern Affairs, Office of East Asian Affairs, Central Files, 1947–1964. National Archives at College Park.

RG 59, General Records of the Department of State, Bureau of Educational and Cultural Affairs Office, 1955–1959, Decimal File. National Archives at College Park.

RG 59, Records of the Plans and Development Staff, Evaluation Branch, 1955–1960. National Archives at College Park.

RG 306, USIA, IAF, ITV General 1961–1962. National Archives at College Park.

RG 469, Records of US Foreign Assistance Agencies, Korea Subject Files, 1953–1959, National Archives at College Park.

Secondary Sources

Korean

Cha, Jae-Young. "1950nyeondae migungmuseongui hanguk eonronin gyoyukgyoryu saeop yeongu: hangugui eonron jeonmunjikjuui hyeongseonge michin yeonghyangeul jungsimeuro" [US State Department's educational exchange project for Korean journalists in the 1950s: Its impact on the rise of professionalism in Korean journalism]. *Hangugeonnonhakbo* 58, no. 2 (2014): 219–45.

———. "1950nyeondae migungmuseongui miguk eonron jeonmunga pagyeon saeop yeongu: hanguk eonrone michin yeonghyangeul jungsimeuro" [The US specialist program for Korean journalism in the 1950s: Its impact on Korean journalism]. *Hangugeonronjeongbohakbo*, no. 87 (2018): 243–76.

Cho, Se-Hyung. *Geuraedo sesangeun jeonjinhanda* [Anyhow, the world is moving forward]. Seoul: Hamkkeganeun sesang, 2010.

Chung, Jin-Suk. *Gwanhunkeulleop 40nyeonsa* [40 year history of Kwanhoon Club]. Seoul: Gwanhunkeulleop, 1997.

———. *Hangukgeundaeeonronui jaejomyeong* [Review of the Korean modern journalism]. Seoul: Mineumsa, 1996.

———. *Joseonsinmunhagwonui gijayangseonggwa eonronhak yeongu* [Education program and journalism studies of Chosun Journalism Academy]. Seoul: Seogangdae eonronmunhwayeonguso, 1995.

Dong-a Ilbo, "Bipaneonron hwangniptorok: Mi apaengyosu, hangukeonrone seongmyeong" [Toward the establishment of critical journalism: US Professor Arpan's statement on Korean journalism]. May 19, 1959.

Henderson, Gregory. "Hanmiganui munhwagwangye" [Korea-US cultural relationship]. *Gukjepyeongnon*, no. 2 (1959): 67–76.

Heo, Eun. *Migugui hegemoniwa hanguk minjokjuui* [American hegemony and Korean Nationalism]. Seoul: Goryeodaehakgyo minjokmunhwayeonguwon, 2018.

Institute of Communication and Information Studies, Seoul National University. *Seouldaehakgyo eonronjeongboyeonguso 50nyeonsa* [50 year history of Institute of Communication and Information Studies, Seoul National University]. Seoul: Keomyunikeisyeonbukseu, 2013.

Kang, Myung-Koo. *Hangug eonronjeonmunjigui sahoehak* [Sociology of Korean journalists]. Seoul: Nanam, 1993.

———. *Hunmingwa gyemong: hanguk hunmingongnonjangui yeoksajeok hyeongseong* [Education and enlightenment of people: Historical formation of Korean educative public sphere]. Seoul: Nanam, 2016.

Kim, Min-Whan. *Hangugeonronsa* [Korean history of journalism and media]. Seoul: Nanam, 2002.

Kim, Yung-Hee. *Eonronin bakgwonsanggwa hanguk hyeondaeeonron* [A journalist, Park Kwon-sang, and Korean modern journalism]. Seoul: Keomyunikeisyeonbukseu, 2019.

Kim, Yun-Jin. "'Chinmi'wa 'banmi' saieseo: Hanguk eonroneul tonghae bon migugui imijiwa migukhwa damron" [Between pro-America and anti-America: US image and the discourse on Americanization in the Korean media]. In *Amerikanaijeisyeon* [Americanization], 257–88. Seoul: Pureunyeoksa, 2008.

Korean Publishers Association. *Hanguksinmunyeongam* [Yearbook of Korean newspapers]. Seoul: Hanguksinmunhyeophoe, 1968.

Kwanhoon Club. *Kwanhoon keullop 30nyeonsa, 1957–1987* [30 year history of Kwanhoon Club, 1958–1987]. Seoul: Kwanhoon Club, 1987.

———. *Kwanhoon keulleop 50nyeonsa, 1957~2007* [50 year history of Kwanhoon Club, 1957–2007]. Seoul: Kwanhoon Club, 2007.

Kyunghang Sinmun, "'Chwijee jejae eopta': Mi apaengyosu, daegu jwadamhwoeseo eongeup" [No punishment on the news reporting: US professor Arpan claimed in a roundtable in Daegu]. April 16, 1959.

———, "'Eonronin jaje gangjohan geot': Gongbosilseo sinmun gamchuk bodoe haemyeong" ["Journalist's self-regulation was emphasized": Department of Public Information explained the news report on the reduction of newspaper companies]. April 20, 1959.

Lee, Jae-Kyoung. *Hangukhyeong jeoneollijeum model: hanguk jeoneollijeum seonjinhwareul wihan seongchal* [Korean journalism model: Review for development of Korean journalism]. Seoul: Ihwayeojadaehakgyochulpanbu, 2013.

Lee, Young-Hee. *Daehwa: han jisiginui samgwa sasang* [Dialogue: Life of an intellectual and his thought]. Seoul: Hangilsa, 2006.

Nam, Jae-Il. "Hanguk gaekgwanjuui gwanhaengui munhwajeok teukseong: gyeongchalgija chwijaegwanhaengui gujojeok seonggyeok" [Cultural uniqueness of objective journalism in Korea: Practice of news gathering by police beat reporter and its structural character]. *Eonrongwahagyeongu* 8, no. 3 (2008): 233–70.

———. "Jigeobideollogiroseoui hanguk eonronyunliui hyeongseonggwajeong" [The formation process of journalism ethics in Korea as a professional ideology]. *Hangugeonronjeongbohakbo*, no. 50 (2015): 73–93.

Park, Chan-Seung. *Eonronundong* [Journalism movement]. Cheonan: Dongnipginyeomgwan hangukdongnibundongsayeonguso, 2009.

Park, Kwon-Sang. "Gwanhunkeulleobiran mueosinga" [What is Kwanhoon Club?]. In *Bakgwonsangeonronhak: Hangugeonronhyeondaesa 50nyeon* [Park Kwon-Sang journalism studies: 50 year modern history of the Korean press], edited by Bakgwonsangginyeomhoe, 136–52. Seoul: Sangsangnamu, 2015.

Park, Yong-Kyu. *Hangugui eonronin jeongcheseongeul mutda* [Asking the identity of a Korean journalist]. Seoul: Nonhyeong, 2015.

Yoo, Sun-Yung. "Gaekgwanjuui 100nyeonui hyeongsikhwa gwajeong" [Formalization process of objectivism in 100 years]. *Eonrongwa sahoe*, no. 10 (1995): 86–128.

English

Arpan, Floyd G. "Through Study, Travel, and Work, Foreign Journalists View the United States." *International Educational and Cultural Exchange*, Spring 1972, 25–37.

Blanchard, Margaret A. *Exporting the First Amendment: The Press-Government Crusade, 1945–1952*. New York: Longman, 1986.

Brazinsky, Gregg A. *Nation Building in South Korea: Koreans, Americans, and the Making of a Democracy*. Chapel Hill: University of North Carolina Press, 2007.

Grunwell, Jane E. "Exchange of Journalists Helps Tell America's Story to the Free World." *Quill*, May 1954, 7–9, 15–16.

Hallin, Daniel C., and Paulo Mancini. *Comparing Media Systems: Three Models of Media and Politics*. Cambridge: Cambridge University Press, 2004.

Henderson, John W. *The United States Information Agency*. New York: Frederick A. Praeger, 1969.

Hurwitz, Harold. "Comparing American Reform Efforts in Germany: Mass Media and the School System." In *Americans as Proconsuls: United States Military Government in Germany and Japan, 1944–1952*, edited by Robert Wolfe, 321–50. Carbondale, IL: Southern Illinois University Press, 1984.

Lan, Mike Shichi. "How the Cold War Shaped 'China': U.S. Aid, Chinese Overseas Students in Taiwan, and Overseas Chinese Media." Paper presented at the Workshop on Public Diplomacy of Knowledge: Cold War in East Asia and the US, Kyoto University, January 11–12, 2020.

McNair, Brian. "After Objectivity? Schudson's Sociology of Journalism in the Era of Post-factuality." *Journalism Studies* 18, no. 10 (2017): 1318–33.

Nerone, John. "The Historical Roots of the Normative Model of Journalism." *Journalism* 14, no. 4 (2012): 446–58.

Rowland, Wayne D. "The Press in the Korean Republic: Its Status and Problems." *Journalism Quarterly*, no. 35 (Fall 1958): 450–54.

Schudson, Michael. *Discovering the News: A Social History of American Newspapers*. New York: Basic Books, 1978.

———. *The Sociology of News*. New York: W. W. Norton, 2003.

Tuchman, Gaye. "Objectivity as Strategic Ritual: An Explanation of Newsmen's Notion of Objectivity." *American Journal of Sociology* 77, no. 4 (1972): 660–79.

Waisbord, Silvio. *Reinventing Professionalism: Journalism and News in Global Perspective*. Cambridge: Polity, 2013.

Ward, Stephen J. A. *The Invention of Journalism Ethics: The Path to Objectivity and Beyond*. 2nd ed. Montreal: McGill-Queen's University Press, 2015.

Zhang, Yang. "The Cold War, American Overseas Educational Exchanges and the Development of Journalism and Communication Education in Hong Kong." Paper presented at the Workshop on Public Diplomacy of Knowledge: Cold War in East Asia and the US, Kyoto University, January 11–12, 2020.

AUTHOR BIO

JAE YOUNG CHA is Professor Emeritus of Communication Studies at Chungnam National University in Daejeon, Korea. He coauthored *The Liberation and the Construction of Korean Mass Media* (2006) and many other books and articles on media history.

ELEVEN

CIVIC ACTION AS COUNTERINSURGENCY IN SOUTH KOREA

Cold War at the Grassroots within and beyond the National Borders

EUN HEO

INTRODUCTION

The long-term Cold War that took place in so-called underdeveloped East Asian countries, in the borderland between the Communist bloc and the "free" nations, was a war over who would hold sway over the masses at the grassroots and how they would gain such influence. Capturing the "hearts and minds" of the people to gain their support became a burden that could no longer be borne solely by the on-site personnel of the US Department of State and the United States Information Agency (USIA). This was a major challenge that both US and local forces intervening in the East Asian region had to accomplish together.[1]

In the early 1960s, President John F. Kennedy and the US military command hoped that the armed forces of underdeveloped countries in the borderland of the Cold War in East Asia would actively participate in nation building and that they would effectively carry out counterinsurgency; thus, civic action became a major counterinsurgency strategy.[2] Army major general William B. Rosson, who had held prominent positions including commander in the US Military Assistance Command, Vietnam, said in 1963, just before the full intervention of the US military in the Vietnam War, that civic action was the core measure that could capture the "hearts and minds" of the people in the insurgency zones and that it could be considered the key to success or failure in counterinsurgency operations.[3]

The US and indigenous troops who conducted counterinsurgency operations in underdeveloped areas in East Asia had determined that the foundation of nation building could not be laid unless they won the Cold War in rural villages. Therefore, to secure victory in the Cold War and take control of the masses, they waged all-out war, mobilizing all available resources. In waging this war, while the military was deploying powerful operations to pacify the villages, it also had to provide physical and human resources for the reconstruction and restoration of those same villages, which would serve as the foundation of nation building. In this chapter, such wars—military or otherwise—waged in the villages to achieve the goal of nation building will be referred to as the "Cold War at the Grassroots."

The main objective of this chapter is twofold: first, to point out that the Cold Wars at the Grassroots in different geographical locations were linked to one another, and second, to show that it was the transmission of US knowledge and experience concerning the civic action—both within and across national borders—that linked the Cold Wars at the Grassroots in various different locations.

This chapter will focus specifically on the South Korean case, and especially on the South Korean military, because South Korea was regarded as a model precedent for developing a Cold War plan for grassroots nation building. The South Korean military also later consolidated the experiences and knowledge of other East Asian countries and practiced civic action as a method of counterinsurgency in the Vietnam War.

Although some of the existing scholarly works devote attention to the police alongside the military in their analyses of counterinsurgency promoted by the US government in East Asia during the Cold War, it is pertinent to give greater attention to the military in Korea, in terms of both counterinsurgency and civic action.[4] The Dwight Eisenhower administration supported the improvement of public safety and police modernization in newly independent and underdeveloped countries in the 1950s; South Korea also received such aid, although the amount was very small.[5] It was the Republic of Korea (ROK) Army—not the police—that had become the subject of carrying out civic action as the Cold War strategies beyond the national border. As the conflict in the Korean Peninsula and East Asia intensified in the 1960s, the ROK Army became the main body for sharing and implementing knowledge for the Cold War at the Grassroots at home and abroad. On the other hand, in the 1960s the ROK police had improved its ability to counter the infiltration of North Korea's armed agents, with the consequence of the diminution of police-public relations.[6] In fact, since the period of US military government and throughout the Cold War, the South Korean police never overcame the conception that they greatly depended on surveillance, control, and violence in counterinsurgency operations.[7]

ESTABLISHING A NEW ROLE OF THE
MILITARY FOR THE COLD WAR

A Shift in the US Cold War Strategy

Soon after the Soviet Union launched Sputnik in October 1957, the Lebanese Crisis occurred in July 1958, and the second Taiwan Strait Crisis ensued in the following month. These incidents served to make the US aware that it needed to prepare strategic assets commensurate with the Soviet retaliation capabilities. At the same time, the US recognized the continued existence of "another threat" that could not be blocked by mass retaliation strategies based on nuclear weapons: small-scale conflicts and insurgencies required agile military forces capable of quick intervention but not full-scale warfare and mass retaliation strategies. Those within the US military who focused on the dangers of "small wars" stressed the need to go beyond the conventional military operations and to devise more holistic countermeasures covering politics, economics, and society at large.[8]

President Eisenhower, whose military security strategy was based on mass retaliation strategies and the New Look policy, also sensed that military security strategy needed to change, and in late 1958, he ordered a full reexamination of foreign military assistance. As a result, the President's Committee to Study the United States Military Assistance Program, or the Draper Committee, was established. The committee submitted its final report to Eisenhower in August 1959.

One of the matters on which the Draper Committee deliberated deeply was the preparation of a countermeasure against the conflicts in the peripheral underdeveloped areas between the Communist and anti-Communist camps. In underdeveloped areas, security threats that could not be addressed by mass retaliation strategies with nuclear weapons could arise. The Foreign Policy Research Institute of the University of Pennsylvania, led by Professor Robert Strausz-Hupé, submitted a report to the Draper Committee, emphasizing the need for an integrated understanding of military security and "non-military domains," such as social and economic changes in underdeveloped countries.[9] The Foreign Policy Research Institute held a seminar in 1955 to review the methods of Communist aggression for the purposes of developing a new Cold War strategy. In the fall of 1956, researchers of the Foreign Policy Research Institute visited East Asian countries such as South Korea, Taiwan, Hong Kong, Cambodia, Vietnam, Thailand, and the Philippines, as well as India, Pakistan, and Israel.[10]

The Foreign Policy Research Institute saw that Soviet and Chinese initiatives were likely to increase their influence in underdeveloped countries by capitalizing on public aspirations for social and economic development and emphasized the importance of socioeconomic reforms to counter this possibility. At the same time, the institute asserted that the militaries of underdeveloped countries receiving US military aid must become the main "transmission belt[s]" to achieve socioeconomic reforms in an "orderly manner."[11]

In addition, the Foreign Policy Research Institute highlighted the importance of ensuring internal security to prepare against infiltrations, rebellions, coups d'état, subversion, and so on by the Communists. The institute pointed out that Communist nations had "swiftly returned" to traditional methods, such as guerrilla warfare and internal coups d'état, to counter US mass retaliation strategies. Moreover, the institute criticized the fact that despite this return, the US remained focused on military aid to prepare for traditional full-scale warfare, resulting in a weakened ability to deal with indirect invasions, guerrilla warfare, and rebellions in recipient countries.[12] Together with this criticism, the institute stressed that internal security capabilities must be increased. To this end, the military's tactical capabilities to cope with guerrilla tactics and other forms of irregular warfare had to be strengthened—in other words, civic action had to be conducted to reinforce public support, and measures had to be taken to improve the civilian-military relationship.[13]

Emphasis on the Role of a Dynamic Force

As Andrew J. Birtle pointed out, military personnel such as Robert H. Slover and Edward G. Lansdale joined the Draper Committee as members of the professional, technical, and research staff.[14] Slover, Lansdale, and others presented to the Draper Committee a report based on their experiences in South Korea and Southeast Asia, incorporating their view that the militaries of the aid-recipient countries should be actively utilized for social and economic development as well as for nation building.[15]

Slover, as a staff member under Eighth US Army commander Maxwell D. Taylor, promoted a civilian support program by the US Forces in South Korea in the 1950s.[16] He was also the one who emphasized the importance of civic action and its implementation as a counterinsurgency plan under the Kennedy administration. In 1963, Slover asserted that the military must support social and economic development for two reasons: first, the military had the skill and the expertise to contribute to various social and economic fields; and second, the military was a well-disciplined organization that could contribute to socioeconomic development and had efficient training capabilities.[17]

Lansdale was well known as a military adviser who had assisted Ramon Magsaysay and led the counterinsurgency operation in the Philippines.[18] On the basis of his experience in the Philippines, Lansdale emphasized that military interventions in social, economic, and political reforms had a profound effect on the success or failure of counterinsurgency, and, to reflect this view, he created the concept of civic action.[19] Thereafter, civic action and related policies spread to Southeast Asian countries where counterinsurgency operations took place in the 1950s. After observing the civic action carried out by the military in the Philippines, South Vietnamese civilian and military leaders developed the concept of civic action as "political military operations."[20] The concept further spread and was applied not only in Vietnam but also to the battlefields of Laos, Burma, and Indonesia.[21]

Lansdale openly criticized the Eisenhower administration's mass retaliation strategies and strongly urged the US military command to adopt a new strategy for Southeast Asia.[22] He also stressed that the most important determining factor of the outcome of the Cold War in Southeast Asia was the people, who were directly linked to the expansion of Communist forces. He explained that the Communist forces were strictly adhering to Mao Zedong's guerrilla warfare doctrine, which was to develop as close as possible a civilian-military relationship and to thereby foster a populace and a military force that even the US military could not easily withstand. Lansdale argued that in order to respond to this, the national militaries of the liberal camp must also become "Dynamic Forces." *Dynamic forces* here meant that the military should not only be a fighting force but also assume a proactive role in areas such as public labor, welfare, health, and education, to take control of the people. Lansdale pressed on, insisting that the "successful Cold War conflict doctrine," created by the "free" nations through fighting with the Communist enemy, was teaching military forces to expend all efforts not only in confronting the enemy but also in ensuring fraternity with the people.[23]

South Korea was noted as a viable place to set an example in creating the dynamic force for which Lansdale advocated; as mentioned above, the Draper Committee, in which Slover participated, highly evaluated the Armed Forces Assistance to Korea (AFAK) conducted by US Forces in South Korea and the civilian support plan by the Korean Civil Assistance Command (KCAC). In 1959, the Draper Committee recognized AFAK as a model case that had had a positive effect on community support projects without being detrimental to US military missions. In addition, the committee cited the KCAC activities as an example of successful utilization of military resources to support economic activities.[24]

The Draper Committee's evaluation of AFAK was inherited by the Kennedy administration. It was only natural that the Kennedy administration, which linked counterinsurgency with modernization theory and actively intervened in underdeveloped countries, gave high recognition to AFAK. In early 1962, the US secretary of the army, in a report summarizing the army's "Cold War activities" during 1961, evaluated AFAK as an exemplar case in which the US and the South Korean military successfully supported the development of the local communities and built a friendly civilian-military relationship.[25] Slover and Lansdale continued to emphasize AFAK as the most successful example of civic action under the Kennedy administration.[26]

Post–Korean War US Army Civil Assistance in South Korea

The civil assistance activities by the US military in South Korea were neither structured nor smooth at the outset. In the initial stage of the Korean War, civil assistance activities carried out by the US Department of State, aid agencies, the US military, and private agencies lacked both a commanding figure and a coordinated system. Given such disorder, activities could not be effectively carried out, which in turn confused the South Korean government. In 1952, those investigating the state of the US military's civil projects in South Korea criticized the military for repeating the mistakes made during the Second World War, when guidelines on civil affairs had not been properly prepared.[27] However, despite the operational turmoil in the early stages of the war, the United Nations Civil Assistance Command in Korea (UNCACK); its successor, KCAC; and the AFAK by the Eighth United States Army in Korea played a major role in expanding the influence of the US government and the US military on the people of local communities.

The UNCACK established branches in each province and every major city during the Korean War. They supported the administration, public security, health and hygiene, labor, and welfare activities of government agencies and oversaw the distribution of relief supplies. The United Nations Command established the purpose of the civil assistance program as preventing the war-related outbreaks of illnesses, famine, and riots among civilians. The primary concern of the UNCACK was providing relief for the massive number of displaced and otherwise war-affected persons. With the conclusion of the armistice agreement in July 1953, the UNCACK was reorganized into the KCAC. The KCAC inherited the former entity's duties, including the prevention of famine, illnesses, and riots, but its focus was on postwar rehabilitation rather than on immediate emergency relief as during the war. The KCAC branches set up in each province consisted of about twenty staff, including officers, civilian engineers, and US military personnel.[28] Although discussions of the need for integrated management of economic assistance plans had been raised in the second half of 1954, the KCAC ended its operations in November 1955.

Shortly after the UNCAC was reorganized in the KCAC, the Eighth Army commenced the AFAK plan in November 1953, after the conclusion of the armistice agreement. Realizing the value of the plan, Commander Maxwell D. Taylor of the Eighth Army requested assistance from the US Congress and received an allocation of US$15 million in aid for South Korea. The funds were invested in the construction and repair of schools, churches, orphanages, bridges, clinics, and major roads, among other things. By 1962, more than 4,600 AFAK plan projects had been implemented, the overwhelming majority of them being school constructions. This was likely due to both the South Korean government and the operators of local educational institutions actively requesting support.

The education sector incurred an enormous amount of damage during the war. According to a June 1952 UNCACK report, more than half of all school buildings had been destroyed in the war, and a further 15 percent had suffered sufficient damage to impair their use as education facilities. Even school buildings that had maintained sufficient integrity to provide education were often used instead as hospitals, shelters, or military buildings. Furthermore, 27 percent of school libraries and 81 percent of school materials were reported as having been destroyed.[29] It is thus unsurprising that after the armistice, the restoration of school facilities was the most pressing issue in the effort to normalize education.

In this endeavor, the US military provided the necessary skills and equipment as well as the core elements required for reconstruction, while the South Korean side provided personnel and supplies that could be locally procured. This meant that the US military's AFAK provided backup for South Koreans who were engaged in "self-help" efforts.[30]

The US military in Korea promoted AFAK as enhancing friendly relations with the masses at the "grassroots" level.[31] In 1955, the United States Information Service (USIS) Korea, in a special issue of *Free World* that dealt with the successful reconstruction of South Korea, portrayed the US military as having managed to form a close relationship with the local people through its civil assistance projects, and highly evaluated the result as the US military's first overseas accomplishment.[32]

Such an evaluation by USIS Korea cannot, of course, be said to have adequately captured the overall picture of how South Korean society perceived the US military. In actuality, the South Koreans were suffering from repeated violent assaults by the US military, and public criticism was on the rise; vocal

Table 11.1 AFAK Construction Programs, 1954–62*

Construction programs	Approval	Under consideration	Canceled	Not yet started	In progress	Completed	Nonconstruction (US$)†	Funding aid (US$)		Equipment & labor (US$)
								AFAK	Korea	
Schools	1,997	393	56	83	135	2,096		13,930,932	12,052,623	18,753,265
Churches	214	36	0	0	0	250		972,331	156,450	708,576
Orphanages	275	110	5	16	13	351		1,440,368	895,055	1,772,490
Bridges	105	8	2	0	0	111		471,962	59,116	629,900
Public welfare facilities	299	63	5	5	6	346		1,967,130	1,776,677	2,663,876
City halls	410	9	3	0	0	416		1,777,194	732,469	4,556,105
Public facilities	106	24	0	0	1	129		433,679	68,273	886,905
Land reclamation	44	9	0	0	0	53		134,272	17,258	476,935
Flood control	11	1	1	0	0	11		26,700	0	103,454
Highways	48	8	1	0	0	55		83,858	30,312	754,647
Pusan 103	813	0	0	0	0	813		1,097,018	27,817	3,616,364
Subtotal (number of programs)	4,302	661	73	104	155	4,631		22,335,444	15,816,050	34,922,517
Medical Facilities								1,797,417		3,415,434
Nonconstruction							3,083,476			
Grand total (number of programs)	4,302	661	73	104	155	4,631	3,083,476	24,132,861	15,816,050	38,337,951

Source: Headquarters, Eighth US Army, AFAK, Office of the Program Director, Subject: Consolidated Quarterly Report of Armed Forces Assistance to Korea Program—1st Quarter FY 1963, Incl #8 to AFAK Status Report, RG 84 Korea General Records, 1956–1963, box 17, National Archives.

*Years are fiscal years.

†The amount in "nonconstruction" is by contributions.

dissatisfaction toward the encroachment of sovereignty by the US and calls for the revision of the Korea-US administrative agreement were becoming louder.[33] Also, the perception that the US and the Soviet Union were ultimately the responsible parties in the Korean War and in the division of the Korean Peninsula was deeply entrenched in the thoughts of Koreans, including Korean military officers.

SHARING AND PRACTICING KNOWLEDGE OF COUNTERINSURGENCY

Introduction of Civic Action by the US Mission to South Korea

President Kennedy readily accepted the Cold War strategy in East Asia promoted by Lansdale. This is best reflected in the fact that at the end of 1961 Kennedy expressed concern that underdeveloped countries had not been able to devise plans to actively utilize the military for social and economic development and that, therefore, civic action must be implemented to the maximum extent in crisis areas facing subversion and other instabilities.[34] The Kennedy administration recognized civic action as a core means of strengthening economic foundations and connecting the military and the masses.

McGeorge Bundy, a special assistant to President Kennedy, communicated Kennedy's stance to the Department of State and the Pentagon. Bundy then encouraged them to focus on having the military engage in civic action initiatives in countries where the two departments were combating internal threats of subversion. To achieve this, he proposed the dispatch of US training teams to crisis areas to promote a swift and fundamental shift to push forward the civic action projects.[35]

The US training team described by Bundy is believed to have been a reference to both the Civic Action Mobile Training Team and the US Army Mobile Training Team. In 1961, the two mobile training teams were sent separately to South Vietnam, but in most East Asian countries, only the latter was dispatched. In Cambodia, the US Army Mobile Training Team was also responsible for the duties typically carried out by the Civic Action Mobile Training Team.[36]

In mid-1961, even before Kennedy's instructions, the US Army had already changed its Cold War policy in a direction that aligned with Kennedy's subsequent demands. At a security strategy seminar at the US Army War College in June 1961, George H. Decker, chief of staff of the US Army, prescribed the use of the militaries in underdeveloped countries as a medium that would directly connect the US to their governments and the masses. Decker disclosed his view that taking advantage of these strengths would be a major asset in preventing the "gradual invasion" of the Communists.

Decker created the "Cold War Task Forces," a new US military unit specializing in the Cold War. In addition, he made clear his policy that militaries in underdeveloped countries dealing with "low intensity Cold War" must be supported so that they could participate in nation building, acquire counterintelligence, and foster counterinsurgency capabilities, whereas areas facing "high intensity Cold War" required a focus on creating and training armed forces that could carry out counterinsurgency specifically.[37] The US Army became the department responsible for civic action in September 1961 and took steps toward concrete preparations for the promotion of overseas projects.

From March 1962, the "Country Team" led by Samuel D. Berger, US ambassador to South Korea, began full-scale deliberation on the implementation of civic action by the South Korean military.[38] The Country Team determined that civic action could form a friendly civil-military relationship and contribute to socioeconomic development, ensuring internal security.[39] In June of the same year, the team proposed to the South Korean military government the implementation of civic action, and Chairman Park Chung-hee of the Supreme Council for National Reconstruction readily agreed.[40] The coup d'état force had an urgent need to improve its image and expand its support base. For this reason, the proposal by the US Embassy in South Korea to carry out civic action was welcomed.

Civic Action Implementation and Changes in Policy

The US Embassy and the Country Team introduced civic action to the military government in detail, from its concept to concrete implementation policy. They added that civic action in South Korea would mean the use of military power in projects for the masses in areas such as education, public labor, agriculture, transportation, telecommunications, and health and hygiene. Regarding internal security, the US Embassy explained that civic action could "reduce the threat of subversion by Communist forces that utilize social dissatisfaction and lay a solid foundation for democratic development."[41]

The Country Team presented the principles with which the South Korean military must comply in the implementation of civic action projects. There were two demands: civic action projects must be promoted in a way that actualized the participation of residents of the local community without decreasing the fighting capabilities of the South Korean military; and the projects must not interfere with the major economic development plans on which the United

States Operations Mission (USOM) to Korea placed its focus.[42] The South Korean military was responsible for the implementation of individual projects.[43] The contents of the detailed plan were diverse, including education (support for new classroom construction), health and hygiene, road construction and maintenance, and construction support for irrigation facilities. Half of the support budget was allocated for "new construction and renovation/repair of classrooms."

It is worth noting that the civic action plan, as with AFAK, focused chiefly on the education sector, particularly on the construction of new classrooms. The reason for this similarity may be that the classroom shortage had not yet been resolved. In addition, it is necessary to pay attention to the implications of the "school support program" in areas where the Cold War at the Grassroots was intense. In connection with this, the view expressed by Lieutenant Colonel John T. Little, who led "A Mobile Training Team of Army Special Forces" in Laos and carried out civic action, is noteworthy. He stressed the need to send village children to school to show them the wider world and teach them that "the United States is a powerful friend" and that "Communist penetration is dangerous."[44]

US$2 million was budgeted for US civic action support during the military junta period (fiscal years 1962 and 1963) but was reduced significantly to US$400,000 from the 1964 fiscal year.[45] In late 1963, US ambassador Berger was concerned that the South Korean military's civic action projects would result in the South Korean government investing additional funds and labor into construction projects; he hoped rather that South Korea, which had limited funds and resources, would concentrate on economic development.[46]

Ambassador Berger endorsed downsizing civic action, likely because the situation had changed drastically in the period between early 1962 and late 1963. Early 1962 was shortly after Kennedy had urged the implementation of civic action. The US side was compelled to concentrate on supporting the South Korean military's civic action to repair civilian-military relations frayed by the military coup and remove "seeds of rebellion"—the masses directly intervening in politics and presenting lines that ran counter to the established Cold War system in South Korea.[47] On the other hand, in late 1963, as Park Chung-hee had won the presidential election in October and the coup d'état forces had succeeded in the transition to civilian rule, civic action in the context of counterinsurgency was no longer the priority.

However, despite Ambassador Berger's policy of downsizing civic action, the US military in Korea continued to implement the AFAK plan without interruption. The reason why the US military in South Korea continued AFAK,

Figure 11.1 Ribbon cutting at Bethany Orphanage, AFAK program, Pusan, South Korea, June 1965. National Library of Korea digital collection.

even though the South Korean government had achieved economic growth and was gradually establishing the ability to independently carry out construction plans, is that the US recognized the political value in continued contributions to establishing "community relations." Moreover, another major reason was probably the realization by the US Military Command in Korea that there was an affinity between AFAK and civic action—in that they both aimed at "establishing security through financial support" and "establishing friendly civilian-military relations."[48] Indeed, the South Korean community in the 1960s was not a place where the Cold War at the Grassroots was as intense as it was in the rural villages of, for example, South Vietnam, where authorities switched day and night. The fact that the US forces in South Korea continued to pursue AFAK nevertheless shows that they were not simply approaching their projects from a philanthropic standpoint.

The US military made sure to inform community residents of the AFAK plans. For ongoing projects, bulletin boards were erected to inform the locals of the joint construction between South Korea and the US.[49] Furthermore, all newly built buildings were marked with a nameplate engraved with the words

Figure 11.2 Sign reading "Armed Forces Assistance to Korea" for construction, Pusan, South Korea, January 1966. National Library of Korea digital collection.

"US military assistance." In the case of South Korea, there were US military bases in the major cities, and these bases continuously developed programs to form relationships with the residents. A system had been established so that even if the unit in charge of AFAK was replaced, the influence and image that the US military had built through its civil assistance activities would persist in the local community as long as the military base in the area remained.

Practicing of Civic Action by the ROK Army in the Vietnam War

Although support for civic action was fading from the interest of the US Congress, economic assistance organizations, and the US Embassy in South Korea, which prioritized economic development, the US and the South Korean militaries nevertheless continued to engage in civic action. In 1961, the US military dispatched mobile training teams to South Korea, South Vietnam, Cambodia, Taiwan, and so on to provide counterinsurgency training to the military of each country.

The six mobile training teams that visited Korea in 1961 consisted of four people at most and one at fewest, and the length of their stay varied from one month to three months. The training periods were varied: from January to February, May to June, July to August, and October to December. Those training teams were not in any way related to the military coup of May 1961. In 1962, one mobile training team for psychological warfare and special warfare was scheduled to visit Korea.[50]

As mentioned earlier, at the end of 1961, McGeorge Bundy stated his expectation for the US military training teams to act as a catalyst for spreading civic action. It was highly possible that there would be opportunities for the South Korean military to learn about civic action as a counterinsurgency strategy.

In 1963, the US Joint Chiefs of Staff revealed that civic action was the main strategy for "counterinsurgency."[51] In 1964, in expectation of the dispatch of combat soldiers to Vietnam, special warfare experts of the South Korean military also deemed civic action to be a core measure of counterinsurgency—the South Korean army was already prepared to jump into the battlefields of Vietnam, where the Cold War at the Grassroots was intense.

The Kennedy administration and the US military began to intervene in Vietnam through irregular warfare, combining anti-guerrilla warfare with the National Development Plan based on modernization theory. Influenced by the doctrine of the US military, the South Korean military began to view the promotion of the National Development Plan and the Community Development Plan as issues directly related to security. This doctrine presupposed that the internal hostile forces must be thoroughly eliminated for modernization—security and development were two sides of the same coin.[52]

The South Korean military intervened in the Vietnam War and constructed "new life hamlets" in the operation area under its tactical zone, actively engaged in civic action such as medical support and school construction, and even managed to inspire a spirit of self-help. The ROK forces implemented civic action in close cooperation with the Army of the Republic of Vietnam (ARVN) and the US military.[53]

The South Korean military in Vietnam adopted a method of controlling the tactical zone by constructing intensive support villages called sister hamlets, and as of 1968, the two divisions had more than 140 sister hamlets where the military focused on implementing civic action programs.[54] The South Korean military considered that such support for the people contributed to the development of the local community and to the promotion of welfare and fostered pro-Korean public opinion.[55] However, the Vietnamese in the ROK Army tactical zone had a different appraisal; they thought that "the ROK Army's civic action was oriented more toward intelligence acquisition and psychological operations than in helping Vietnamese hamlets."[56]

The South Korean military was highly evaluated for its outstanding ability in the sweeping operation against "Viet Cong"—US Army lieutenant general William R. Peers, who observed the South Korean military for two years from 1967 to 1968, remarked that he had never seen an army as specialized in "cordon and search" operations as the ROK Army.[57] The South Korean military, thoroughly aligning itself with the "free" world, intervened in the rural pacification of South Vietnam with the Cold War at the Grassroots policy, combining brutal military sweeping and civic action. Nevertheless, there remained insurmountable gaps between the Vietnamese people's considerations of decolonization and division and the ROK Army as not considering those issues.

CONCLUSION

Civic action was born from the accumulated US experiences of the Cold War at the Grassroots in underdeveloped countries situated in the borderlands of the Cold War in East Asia. Military personnel such as Lansdale and Slover, who had been deeply involved in the East Asian theater, evaluated AFAK as a model precedent that formed the basis of the civic action plan to win the hearts and minds of villagers. They also perceived such activities to be a necessary step for nation building from the ground up. They combined the US military's experiences in South Korea with those accumulated in the Philippines, Vietnam, Laos, and so on in the 1950s and created the US military's counterinsurgency concept of civic action.

In late 1961, President Kennedy, who had criticized the limitations of the Eisenhower administration's massive retaliation strategies and emphasized dealing with the Cold War at the Grassroots, stressed the need to conduct civic action in areas where internal security was unstable. Immediately following Kennedy's encouragement, representatives of the US delegation to South Korea, led by Ambassador Samuel D. Berger, promoted the introduction of civic action by the South Korean military.

The civic action during the military junta, led by Park Chung-hee, was a measure to ensure the stability of the military government. Upon taking power, the military junta suppressed the democratizing power of the April Revolution, which attempted to break away from the Cold War paradigm. The primary goal of civic action was to form amicable relations between the military and the masses of the recipient country with assistance from the US. Once the military coup group successfully transitioned to civilian rule and solidified its political foundation, the prevalent view within the US government was that South

Koreans should concentrate their efforts on economic growth. Thus, the US government's support for civic action was greatly reduced.

Unlike Ambassador Berger, the US and the South Korean militaries never lost interest in civic action as a strategic measure in the Cold War at the Grassroots. From 1961, the US military provided South Korean troops with psychological warfare training and special warfare training. Through such training, the South Korean military maintained an environment in which civic action was understood in the context of counterinsurgency and deepened this understanding even further. The South Korean military had already established civic action as a core measure of counterinsurgency by the time full intervention in the Vietnam War was imminent.

Once dispatched to South Vietnam, the South Korean military actively carried out civic action. However, Vietnam's battlefields were muddled by colonial rule and resistance, religious conflicts, and ideological conflicts. On such battlefields, the South Korean military's pacification plan to divide the anti-Communist and pro-Communist Vietnamese people and to gain Vietnamese support by simultaneously conducting military sweeping operations and civic action was perhaps doomed to be unsuccessful. This situation might have been foreseen, given that after the armistice of the Korean War, a majority of the South Korean society viewed the US as one party to blame for the war and partition, in spite of the continued efforts of the US Forces in South Korea in conducting civil assistance activities.

The experience and knowledge regarding counterinsurgency against the Cold War at the Grassroots shared by East Asian countries under the leadership of the United States had several blind spots in the issues of foreign intervention, nation building, and sovereignty in areas controlled by colonial empires. In this respect, there was a fundamental limit to capturing the "hearts and minds" of the grassroots and guiding modernization in East Asia.

NOTES

* This paper is the revision of chapters 4 and 5 of the author's book *Naengjŏn kwa saemaŭl: Tong Asia naengjŏn ŭi yŏnswae wa pundan kukka ch'eje* [The Cold War and the new community: Successive Cold Wars in East Asia and the system of divided nation] (Seoul: Changbi, 2022).

1. Since the US was deeply involved in the modernization of underdeveloped countries, "development" was inseparable from "security," in that it was a means to strengthen US external influence. In addition, the military domain was closely related to the social and economic domains because of the nature of the Cold

War in underdeveloped regions. For the US intervention in East Asia and the Third World, and for the development and military aspects of underdeveloped countries, see, for example, Brazinsky, *Winning the Third World*; Cullather, *Hungry World*; Latham, *Modernization as Ideology*; Latham, *Right Kind of Revolution*.

2. The concept of civic action (or military civic action) highlighted its significance as a set of measures to block the expansion of Communism's influence in irregular warfare. On the other hand, the concept of civil affairs meant measures to facilitate wartime military operations. Some argue that the concept of civil affairs is used only during periods of hostile acts and emergencies and that the concept of civic action covers all periods of peace, war, and occupation. See, for instance, Glick, *Peaceful Conflict*.

3. William B. Rosson, "Understanding Civic Action," *Army* 13–12, July 1963, 47. Rosson served in the Vietnam War from 1965 to 1967 as chief of staff of Westmoreland, commander of the US Military Assistance Command, and commander of the Twenty-Third Infantry Division. Subsequently, he served again as deputy commander of the US Military Assistance Command in South Vietnam from 1969 to 1970.

4. Rosenau, *US Internal Security Assistance to South Vietnam*; Kuzmarov, *Modernizing Repression*; Hyun, "Indigenizing the Cold War."

5. "History of Office of Public Safety, 1955 to Present," 1–2, RG 286, Subject files, 1956–1975, box 24, National Institute of Korean History Archive, http://archive.history.go.kr.

6. *Evaluation of the Public Safety Program USAID Korea*, June 28, 1971–July 18, 1971, 29–30, 55, IPS#2–3/PS and KNP/Evaluation Korea, Agency for International Development, RG 286, Office of Public Safety, Operations Division, East Asia Branch, National Library of Korea digital collection, https://nl.go.kr/NL/contents/N20401010000.do.

7. Regarding the Korean police from the period of the US military government, see Cumings, *Origins of the Korean War*, chap. 5; Kuzmarov, *Modernizing Repression*, chap. 4.

8. Birtle, *U.S. Army Counterinsurgency*, 158–59.

9. "Annex C, March 1959: A Study of United States Military Assistance Program in Underdeveloped Areas," *Supplement to Composite Report of the President's Committee to Study the United States Military Assistance Program*, vol. 2, August 1959, 51 (hereafter Annex C, vol. 2).

10. Strausz-Hupé et al., *Protracted Conflicted*, xii–xiii.

11. Annex C, 2:51–55; Birtle, *U.S. Army Counterinsurgency*, 159–60.

12. Annex C, 2:75.

13. Annex C, 2:57–58.

14. Birtle, *U.S. Army Counterinsurgency*, 160.

15. The report title submitted in June 1959 was "Annex D, 1959.6: Contributions of Military Resources to Economic and Social Progress" (hereafter Annex D, vol. 2).

16. Birtle, *U.S. Army Counterinsurgency*, 160.

17. Robert H. Slover, "This Is Military Civic Action," *Army* 13–12, July 1963, 48.

18. For the trajectory of Lansdale's activities in the Cold War in the United States, see Nashel, *Edward Lansdale's Cold War*.

19. Birtle, *U.S. Army Counterinsurgency*, 160; Walterhouse, *Time to Build*, 9.

20. For the case of South Vietnam, see Stewart, *Vietnam's Lost Revolution*.

21. Office of the Assistant Secretary of Defense (International Security Affairs), Report of Military Assistance Programming Conference Held in the Pentagon, Washington, DC, January 19–23, 1959, 218, Draper Committee Records, 1958–59, box 17, Category V—Central Files—(Military Assistance) January 1959 (1), National Institute of Korean History Archive, http://archive .history.go.kr.

22. Alfred H. Hausrath, *Civil Affairs in the Cold War* (Bethesda, MD: Operations Research Office, Johns Hopkins University, 1961), 51.

23. Office of the Assistant Secretary of Defense, *Report*, 215–16.

24. Annex D, 2:120, 133–34.

25. "Cold War Activities of the United States Army, 1 January 1961 to 26 January 1962," IV-4, John F. Kennedy Presidential Library and Museum Archive, https://www.jfklibrary.org/archives.

26. Rober H. Slover, "Action through Civic Action," *Army Information Digest*, October 1962, 8; Edward G. Lansdale, "Civic Action Helps Counter the Guerrilla Threat," *Army Information Digest*, June 1962, 53.

27. Stolzenbach and Kissinger, *Civil Affairs in Korea*, 4; Daugherty and Andrews, *Review of US Historical Experience*, 417–18.

28. Rodger Bradley, "The JOB of KCAC," *Pacific Stars & Stripes*, n.d. http:// www.koreanwar-educator.org/memoirs/bradley_roger/index.htm. (access date: 07/26/2024).

29. General Headquarters, UN Command, "United Nations Command Civil Assistant and Economic Aid—Korea, 1 October 1951–30 June 1952," RG 338, Records of HQ, US Army, Pacific Military Historian's Office Organizational History files, box 74, US National Archives, College Park, MD.

30. Daugherty and Andrews, *Review of US Historical Experience*, 427.

31. Headquarters, Eighth US Army, Subject: Effective until 13 December 1963, "Program-AFAK, JAN 1961," December 31, 1961, RG 286, Records of the Agency for International Development, National Library of Korea digital collection, https://nl.go.kr/NL/contents/N20401010000.do.

32. "Rebuilding Korea," special issue, *Free World*, 1955, 23.

33. Heo, *Miguk ŭi hegemoni wa Han'guk minjokchuŭi*, 400.

34. National Security Action Memorandum 119, Subject: Civic Action, December 18, 1961, 1, John F. Kennedy Presidential Library and Museum Archive, https://www.jfklibrary.org/archives.

35. National Security Action Memorandum 119.

36. "Cold War Activities of the United States Army, 1 January 1961 to 26 January 1962," III-11.

37. "Cold War Activities of the United States Army, 1 January 1961 to 26 January 1962," I-3.

38. American Embassy, Seoul, to Department of State, Subject: Civic Action Assessment, November 8, 1963, 1, "400 Civic Action, 1963," RG 84, Korea, Seoul Embassy, Classified General Records, 1952–63, National Library of Korea digital collection, https://nl.go.kr/NL/contents/N20401010000.do.

39. Telegram State-Defense Civic Action Team Preliminary Report, March 3, 1962, 1, "400 Civic Action, 1962," RG 84, Korea, Seoul Embassy, Classified General Records, 1952–63, National Library of Korea digital collection, https://nl.go.kr/NL/contents/N20401010000.do.

40. Park Chung-hee to Samuel D. Berger, "400, Civic Action, 1962," RG 84, Korea, Seoul Embassy, Classified General Records, 1952–63, National Library of Korea digital collection, https://nl.go.kr/NL/contents/N20401010000.do.

41. Civic Action Briefing for Ministry of National Defense, August 15, 1962, 2–3, "MAP 3 Civic Action," RG 286, Korea Subject Files, FY 61–63, National Library of Korea digital collection, https://nl.go.kr/NL/contents/N20401010000.do.

42. Telegram State-Defense Civic Action Team Preliminary Report, March 3, 1962, 2; Civic Action Briefing for Ministry of National Defense, August 15, 1962, 6; American Embassy, Seoul, to Department of State, Subject: Civic Action Assessment, November 8, 1963, 2–4.

43. American Embassy, Seoul, to Department of State, Subject: AFAK and US Support for ROK Forces Civic Action Program for FY 64, December 20, 1963, Enclosed 1, Proposed US Support of ROKF Civic Action Program for FY 64, 1–2, "400 Civic Action, 1963," RG 84, Korea, Seoul Embassy, Classified General Records, 1952–63, National Library of Korea digital collection, https://nl.go.kr/NL/contents/N20401010000.do.

44. John T. Little, "Counterinsurgency Campaign," *Army Information Digest*, July 1962.

45. American Embassy, Seoul, to Secretary of State, Joint Embassy / US Forces Korea / USOM Message, December 20, 1963, 2, RG 59, POL 23 S KOR, National Assembly Library, https://www.nanet.go.kr/.

46. National Security Action Memorandum 119, Subject: Civic Action Assessment, November 8, 1963, 2. Berger also judged the project (which was evaluated as a successful example of civic action carried out by the South Korean

military) skeptically, from the perspective of economic development. National Security Action Memorandum 119, 4.

47. At the National Security Council (NSC) held on April 28, 1960, shortly after President Rhee Syngman's resignation, top US government policymakers, including the president, were deeply concerned about the direct impact of Korean demonstrators on policy decisions. They regarded the Korean demonstrators as mobs. "Editorial Note, 1960.4.28," *Foreign Relations of United States (FRUS)*, 1958–1960, Japan; Korea, 18:651, https://history.state.gov/historicaldocuments/frus1958-60v18. Just before the May 16 military coup, US NSC member Robert Komer stressed that the discussion on reunification in South Korea should be limited to "the extent to which the interests of the free world are defended." "Memorandum from Robert W. Komer of the NSC Staff to the President's Deputy Special Assistant for NSC Affairs (Rostow) Washington, 1961.3.15," *FRUS*, 1961–1963, 22:426–27, https://history.state.gov/historicaldocuments/frus1961-63v22.

48. Headquarters, US Forces Korea, Civil Relations, Government Affairs Armed Forces Assistance to Korea Program, October 25, 1962, 2, "Program-AFAK, Jan 1962," RG 286 Korea Subject Files, FY 61–63, National Library of Korea digital collection, https://nl.go.kr/NL/contents/N20401010000.do.

49. Headquarters, United States Army TAGUE Base Command, 1968, Subject: AFAK Project Sign, "1505-100 AFAK Construction Project (FY 68–608), Kyongju Vocation Training Institute," RG 550 Records of United States Army, Pacific, National Library of Korea digital collection, https://nl.go.kr/NL/contents/N20401010000.do.

50. "Cold War Activities of the United States Army, 1 January 1961 to 26 January 1962," IV-3–IV-4.

51. Walterhouse, *Time to Build*, 73.

52. Heo, "Naengjŏnbundanshidae Taeyugyŏktaegukkaŭi Tŭngjang," 41–45.

53. In Phu Yen province, ROK forces, ARVN, and the US Army units met once each month in 1969. They established a working committee to coordinate further civic action projects conducted at the village and hamlet level. "1619-02/PROV, Chiefs Monthly Meetings," 1–10, RG 472, Advisory Team 28 (Phu Yen Province) Administrative and Operational Records: 1966–1972, box 291. See Hunt, *Pacification*.

54. Evaluations Branch Office of the Assistant Chief of Staff, Civil Operations and Revolutionary Development Support (CORDS). "Evaluation Report ROK Army Influence upon CORDS-Supported Pacification Programs II Corps Tactical Zone," October 13, 1968, RG 472, Records of the US Forces in Southeast Asia, 1950–1975, Office Files of Henry Lee Braddock 1968–1975, box 11, US National Archives, College Park, MD.

55. Headquarters of the Korean Army in Vietnam, *Wŏllamjŏn chonghap yŏn'gu (Vietnam War Integrated Research)*, 1974, 890–96. For the civic action

carried out by the Korean military in Vietnam, see Lee and Yim, "Military Civic Actions."

56. Evaluations Branch Office of the Assistant Chief of Staff, CORDS, "Evaluation Report," October 13, 1968, ii.

57. Subject: Senior Officer Debriefing Report: Lt. Gen. W. R. Peers, June 23, 1969, 8, "Historical Reference Collection 314.82 Debriefing, Burdett TO 314.82 Debriefing, Corcoran," Center of Military History, United States Army.

REFERENCES

Primary Sources

Draper Committee Records, 1958–59. National Institute of Korean History Archive. http://archive.history.go.kr.

National Security Action Memorandum. John F. Kennedy Presidential Library and Museum Archive. https://www.jfklibrary.org/archives.

RG 286, Office of Public Safety, Operations Division, East Asia Branch. National Library of Korea digital collection. https://nl.go.kr.

RG 286, Subject files, 1956–1975. National Institute of Korean History Archive. http://archive.history.go.kr.

Supplement to Composite Report of the President's Committee to Study the United States Military Assistance Program, vol. 2, August 1959.

Secondary Sources

Birtle, Andrew J. *U.S. Army Counterinsurgency and Contingency Operations Doctrine, 1942–1976*. Washington, DC: Center of Military History, US Army, 2006.

Boot, Max. *The Road Not Taken*. New York: W. W. Norton, 2018.

Brazinsky, Gregg A. *Winning the Third World*. Chapel Hill: University of North Carolina Press, 2017.

Cullather, Nick. *The Hungry World*. Cambridge, MA: Harvard University Press, 2010.

Cumings, Bruce. *The Origins of the Korean War: Liberation and the Emergence of Separate Regimes, 1945–1947*. Princeton, NJ: Princeton University Press, 1981.

Daugherty, William E., and Marshall Andrews. *A Review of US Historical Experience with Civil Affairs, 1776–1954*. Bethesda, MD: Operations Research Office, Johns Hopkins University, 1961.

Glick, Edward Bernard. *Peaceful Conflict: The Non-military Use of the Military*. Mechanicsburg, PA: Stackpole Books, 1967.

Heo, Eun. *Miguk ŭi hegemoni wa Han'guk minjokchuŭi: naengjŏn sidae (1945–1965) munhwajŏk kyŏnggye ŭi kuch'uk kwa kyunyŏl ŭi tongban* [American hegemony and Korean Nationalism]. Seoul: Research Institute of Korean Studies, Korea University, 2008.

———. "Naengjŏnbundanshidae Taeyugyŏktaegukkaŭi Tŭngjang" [The Emergence of the Counter-insurgent State in South Korea during the Cold War Era]." *Journal for the Studies of Korean History (Hanguksa Hakpo)* 65 (2016): 41–45.

———. *Naengjŏn kwa saemaŭl: Tong Asia naengjŏn ŭi yŏnswae wa pundan kukka ch'eje* [The Cold War and the new community: Successive Cold Wars in East Asia and the system of divided nation]. Seoul: Changbi, 2022.

Hunt, Richard A. *Pacification: The American Struggle for Vietnam's Hearts and Minds.* Boulder, CO: Westview, 1995.

Hyun, Sinae. "Indigenizing the Cold War: Nation-Building by the Border Patrol Police of Thailand, 1945–1980." PhD diss., University of Wisconsin–Madison, 2014.

Kuzmarov, Jeremy. *Modernizing Repression: Police Training and Nation-Building in the American Century.* Amherst: University of Massachusetts Press, 2012.

Latham, Michael E. *Modernization as Ideology: American Social Science and "Nation-Building" in the Kennedy Era.* Chapel Hill: University of North Carolina Press, 2000.

———. *The Right Kind of Revolution.* Ithaca, NY: Cornell University Press, 2011.

Nashel, Jonathan. *Edward Lansdale's Cold War.* Amherst: University of Massachusetts Press, 2005.

Lee, Eun Ho, and Young Soon Yim. "Military Civic Actions of South Korean and South Vietnamese Forces in the Vietnamese Conflict, 1955–1970." *Korea Observer* 13, no. 1 (Spring 1982): 3–35.

Rosenau, William. *US Internal Security Assistance to South Vietnam: Insurgency, Subversion and Public Order.* London: Routledge, 2005.

Stewart, Geoffrey C. *Vietnam's Lost Revolution: Ngô Đình Diệm's Failure to Build an Independent Nation, 1955–1963.* Cambridge: Cambridge University Press, 2017.

Stolzenbach, C. Darwin, and Henry A. Kissinger. *Civil Affairs in Korea, 1950–51.* Chevy Chase, MD: Operations Research Office, Johns Hopkins University, 1952.

Strausz-Hupé, Robert, William R. Kintner, James E. Dougherty, and Alvin J. Cottrell. *Protracted Conflicted.* New York: Harper Colophon Books, 1963.

Walterhouse, Harry F. *A Time to Build.* Columbia: University of South Carolina Press, 1964.

AUTHOR BIO

EUN HEO is Professor of Korean History at Korea University in Seoul. He is author of *American Hegemony and Korean Nationalism* (2008) and many other books and articles on modern Korean history.

INDEX

AAA (American Anthropological Association), 53–55

AAS (Association for Asian Studies), 25, 28, 35, 66, 81–82, 95

ACLS (American Council of Learned Societies), 66, 109, 116–17, 122–26

AEC (Atomic Energy Commission), 155, 168, 172–75, 177–78, 181–82, 185, 187–88

AFAK (Armed Forces Assistance to Korea), 312–15, 318–21, 322

AFOSR (US Air Force Office of Scientific Research), 213

AID (Agency for International Development, or USAID), 9, 168, 187, 192n41. *See also* ICA (International Cooperation Administration)

Americanization, 267–68, 272, 298; Americanize, 15, 282; Americanizing, 261

Argonne National Laboratory, 172, 180, 182–84, 187

Arnold, Henry, 289

Arpan, Floyd G., 288, 290, 292–94, 301n29, 303n48

Asia Foundation, 10, 22, 54–55, 170, 200, 202, 206, 213, 229, 255, 260–61, 263–69, 271

ASNE (American Society of Newspaper Editors), 283

Atoms for Peace, 168, 170–71, 199–200

Beardsley, Richard, 47, 55–56, 62–64

Benedict, Ruth, 8, 51

Bennett, John W., 59–62, 64–65

Berger, Samuel D., 317–18, 322–23, 326n46

BEW (Board for Economic Warfare), 114

Blum, Robert, 229, 246n22

Borton, Hugh, 49–50

Bowers, Faubion, 51

Bowles, Gordon, 50

Buechner, Helmut, 205–6

Bundy, McGeorge, 109, 316, 321

Bush, Vannevar, 142–43

Carnegie Endowment for Peace, 130

Chao, Chung Yao, 142, 144, 156, 159

Charles River school, 272, 278n70

Chiang, Kai-shek (Jiang, Jieshi), 3, 38n17, 41n37, 141, 145, 187, 228, 238

Chien, Ji-Peng, 180–81, 183–84, 186

China Foundation for the Promotion of Education and Culture (China Foundation), 30, 35, 161n10, 179

CIA (Central Intelligence Agency), 10, 15, 22, 56, 83, 187, 206, 213, 273n2

Civil Affairs Handbook, 8, 55

Cloak, F. Theodore, 114–15

COI (Coordinator of Information), 108, 112–14

Committee of One Million, 34, 41n45

331

INDEX

Conference on Modern Japan, 82–83, 98, 102n17

Congress of Orientalists, 27–28, 32–34

Coolidge, Harold Jefferson, 198, 201, 203–4, 206, 215n21, 216n29

CUHK (Chinese University of Hong Kong), 226, 232, 243, 255, 261, 263, 265–272

CULCON (US-Japan Conference on Cultural and Educational Interchange), 66

Cultural Cold War, 1–2, 34, 36–37, 206, 213, 217n44, 256, 260–61, 272, 273n3

Davis, W. Kenneth, 175

Decker, George H., 316–17

Department of State (State Department, US), 9, 40n35, 108–9, 114, 116–18, 129, 142–44, 150, 155, 161, 173–75, 201, 227, 243–44, 273n2, 281, 308, 313, 316; Chinese refugee university in Hong Kong, 262; Division of Japanese and Korean Economic Affairs, 117; Fulbright Program, 265; international educational exchange, 258, 263, 284; training of journalists, 283–90, 293–95, 297, 299n16, 301n31

Dickover, Erle R., 114

Dower, John, 81–82, 95–100

Draper Committee. See President's Committee to Study the United States Military Assistance Program

Eisenhower, Dwight D., 31, 168, 170–71, 174, 181, 200, 309–10, 312, 322

Ellard, Roscoe, 290–92

Embree, John F., 8, 51

Fahs, Charles Burton, 8, 109, 115–17, 118–26, 130

Fairbank, John K. (Fei, Zhengqing), 8, 23–31, 35–36, 38n16, 39n24, 40n30, 40n32, 41n36, 41n39, 115, 272

Farquhar, Florence Walne, 118–19

Ford Foundation, 9–10, 13–14, 21–31, 35–36, 38n11, 39n19, 39n24, 43n56, 206, 213; Gaither Report, 257; Hakone Conference, 82–83, 102n17; Korean Studies, 130; Overseas Training and Research Center, 38n16

Ford Motor Company, 168, 171; reactor, 177

Foreign Policy Research Institute (University of Pennsylvania), 310–11

Frank, Henry S., 176–77, 185

Fulbright Act (of 1946), 257–58; Foundation, 66; Fulbright-Hays Act (Mutual Educational and Cultural Exchange Act), 259; Program, 185, 262, 265–66, 290; scholarship, 182

Gaither Report, 257. See also Ford Foundation

Gale, Esson M., 8

Ge, Bao-Shu (Ko, Paoshu), 180–82

GE (General Electric Company), 180, 182–83, 186, 188

Gomberg, Henry J., 172–74, 176–77

Graves, Mortimer, 116–17, 122, 124–25

Gu, Yuxiu, 142–43

Hadley, Eleanor, 50

Hakone Conferences, 14, 68, 79–87, 89–100

Hall, John W., 8, 49, 62, 81–96, 99–100

Henderson, Gregory, 281

HRAF (Human Relations Area Files), 55–56

Hua, Luogeng, 141–42, 154, 161n5, 163n50

IAEA (International Atomic Energy Agency), 172, 176, 182, 186, 200

IBP (International Biological Program), 201–2, 204, 208–9

ICA (International Cooperation Administration), 9, 168–70, 173–75, 177–79, 183, 185–89, 191n21, 192n41, 193n58, 200. See also AID

International Military Tribunal for the Far East, 53, 70n26

Ishida, Eiichirō, 59–60, 64

Ishino, Iwao, 59, 62

ISNSE (International School for Nuclear Science and Engineering), 172, 175, 177, 180–83

IUCN (International Union for Conservation of Nature and Natural Resources), 201, 203, 212

Izumi, Seiichi, 54

INDEX

Jansen, Marius B., 47, 67, 81–83, 86, 89, 92, 95, 97, 100

Joliot-Curie, Frederic, 148, 152, 155, 160, 164n58

Jorden, Eleanor, 52

Kang, Young Sun, 200–202, 204, 207, 209–10

Kawashima, Takeyoshi, 83, 85–87, 89–93

KCAC (Korean Civil Assistance Command), 312–14

KCCN (Korean Commission for Conservation of Nature and Natural Resources), 201, 204, 210–11, 217n49

Keene, Donald, 9, 47

Kennedy, John F., 66, 229, 308, 311, 313, 316, 318, 321–22

Kerner, Robert Joseph, 116

Kerr, William, 174–79, 183–86

Kindaichi, Kyōsuke, 56

Kluckhohn, Clyde, 53

Kobayashi, Key, 51

Korean War, 3, 6, 7, 11; civil assistance, 313, 316, 323; impact on Chinese scientists, 139, 155; Korean journalism, 281, 298; Korean Studies, 129–31; science, 169, 197, 199–200, 203, 205, 212; Taiwan, 225

Kwanhoon Club, 289, 295

Lansdale, Edward G., 311–13, 316, 322

Li, Siguang, 144–45, 152, 155–57, 160

Li, Zhengdao (Lee, T. D.), 141, 154, 158

MacArthur, Douglas A., 48, 51, 61

MacDougall, Curtis, 290

Magsaysay, Ramon, 312

Maki, John, 50–51

Marshall, John, 116–17

Martin, Edwin, M., 117

Maruyama, Masao, 68, 79, 83, 85, 87–89

McCune, Evelyn B., 8, 14, 109–12, 120–26, 129–30

McCune, George M., 12, 14, 109–22, 124–26, 130

McCune, George S., 110

McCune, Shannon B., 110, 114

Mei, Yiqi, 141–42, 179–83, 185–86

Michigan Memorial Phoenix Project, 167–79, 181, 183, 185, 187–89

Minnesota Project, 200

Missouri model, 226–27

Mott, Frank Luther, 229

Murdock, George P., 55

Murrow, Edward, 289

Nagai, Michio, 62

National Academy of Sciences (US), 198, 200, 204; Pacific Science Board, 198

National Tsing Hua University (in Taiwan), 169, 171, 179–88. *See also* Tsing Hua University

Navy Japanese Language School (and Oriental Language School, US), 8–9, 116

NCCU (National Chengchi University), 15, 37n7, 225–29, 231–34, 236–44, 245n11, 266, 269

Norman, Egerton Herbert, 80–81, 94–96, 98

NSC (National Security Council), 171–72, 174, 257, 327n47

Odegaard, Charles E., 126

Oka, Masao, 53, 59–60

Olson, Kenneth, 286

Oppenheimer, J. Robert, 154, 156

OSRD (Office of Scientific Research and Development), 4

OSS (Office of Strategic Services), 4, 8, 50, 108–9, 111–15, 130, 215n21

overseas Chinese, 32, 34, 230, 232, 236–40, 242, 244, 260, 263, 271; journalists, 236, 239–40, 242, 271; scientists and engineers, 182, 194n90, 230; students (*qiaosheng*) 15, 32, 229–44, 242

OWI (Office of War Information), 8, 51, 59, 108, 112–13, 115

Pacific War, 5, 94–95, 99–101, 108–109, 111–112, 114–115, 117–118, 130. *See also* Second World War (World War II)

Park, Chung-hee, 283, 317–18, 322

Passin, Herbert, 8, 58–59, 61–62, 66

Pelzel, John C., 58–59

Pennington, Herbert W., 181–83, 185–86

PO&SR (Public Opinion and Sociological Research Division), 8, 58–62, 64–65. *See also* SCAP

President's Committee to Study the United States Military Assistance Program, 310–13

propaganda, 198, 227, 244; China, 242; Japan, 50–51, 53, 64; North Korea 205; Taiwan, 32, 34; US, 112, 170, 262, 271, 282

Qian, Sanqiang, 140, 148, 155–58
Qian, Xuesen, 144, 148

Raper, Arthur F., 61, 64
refugee intellectuals, 262, 268, 271
Reischauer, Edwin O., 49, 66, 79–81, 84, 94, 96, 99–100, 102n13, 110–11
Remer, Carl F., 113
Ripley, Sidney Dillon, 201, 215n21
Rockefeller Foundation, 8–10, 14, 23, 200, 227; Japanese Studies, 54–55; Korean Studies, 109, 112, 115–17, 119–26, 129–30
Roosevelt, Franklin D., 112–13
Rosson, William B., 308, 324n3
Rostow, Walt W., 80, 85, 258–59
Rowland, D. Wayne, 290–94

Sandburg, Carl, 289
Sawyer, Ralph A., 171–73, 175–77, 183–84
SCAP (Supreme Commander for the Allied Powers), 50–52, 54–60, 62, 64–65, 70n26
Schmid, Harry C., 185–86
Seaborg, Glenn, 187
Second World War (World War II), 3–4, 7–8, 11, 47–51, 54–55, 58, 80, 111, 130, 141, 168, 171, 179, 198, 225, 272, 273n3, 275, 282–84, 297–98, 300n22, 313. *See also* Pacific War
Seidensticker, Edward, 47, 68
Seok, Ju-myeong, 199, 213
Sino-Japanese War, 145, 159, 179, 282
Slover, Robert H., 311–13, 322
Smith-Mundt Act, 258, 263, 284
Smith, Robert J., 47, 52, 54, 63, 67
Smithsonian Institution, 15, 204–9, 213, 215n21
Social Science Research Council, 66
Sputnik, 258–59, 264, 310
strategic bulletins, 55

Strausz-Hupé, Robert, 310
structural power, 2–3
Sun, Benwang, 141, 149
Sun, Kuan-Han, 180–81, 183–86, 188–89
Sun, Yat-sen (Sun, Zhongshan), 238

Tai Power Company, 169, 180, 182, 184, 188
Takakura, Shin'ichirō, 56
Tang, Aoqing, 141, 149, 154
Taylor, George E., 8, 24, 34, 38n16, 260–61
Taylor, Maxwell D., 311, 314
Teng, Lee C. (Deng, Changli), 183–84, 187–88
Tsing Hua University (before 1949), 141–42, 159, 161, 161n5, 163n50. *See also* National Tsing Hua University (in Taiwan)
Tsuchiyama, Tamie, 59, 62
Tsurumi, Shunsuke, 68

UNCACK (United Nations Civil Assistance Command in Korea), 313–14
Union System, 260: Union Press 260; Union Regional Centers 260; Union Research Institute 22, 260, 269
University of Michigan, 9, 25, 27, 38n16, 52, 62, 66, 82–83, 143, 150, 167–77, 181, 183, 186, 188–89, 243, 267; Okayama Field Station, 62
USAID (US Agency for International Development). *See* AID
USIA (US Information Agency), 227, 308
USIS (US Information Service): East Malaysia-Brunei, 239; Hong Kong, 260, 262–63; Korea, 287, 289, 303n48, 314
USOM (US Operations Mission), 173–75, 191n21; Korea, 318; Taiwan, 182–83

Viet Cong, 322
Vietnam War, 7, 27, 81–82, 96–97, 308–9, 320–21, 323

Wang, Ruixin (Wang Jui Hsin), 141
Ward, Robert E., 9, 47, 63
Weng, Wenhao, 146, 154
Westinghouse Electric Corporation, 181, 183, 185–86, 188–89
Won, Pyong-Oh, 201, 205, 216n33

INDEX

Wu, Dayou, 141, 143, 152, 154
Wu, Youxun, 141–43, 146–147, 156, 159

Yanagita, Kunio, 59, 61
Yanaihara, Tadao, 64
Yang, Chen Ning (Yang, Zhenning), 154, 158–59
Yang, Yu-Dong (Yang, Rudy), 180–81, 183–84

Zeng, Zhaolun, 141, 153–54
Zheng, Zhen-Hua (Cheng, Victor), 180, 182–83, 186
Zhou, Enlai, 144, 146–47, 151, 153–55, 158–60
Zhou, Peiyuan, 144, 163n50
Zhu, Guangya, 141, 150, 154
Zhu, Kezhen, 142, 146–47, 155–56

For Indiana University Press

Sabrina Black, Editorial Assistant

Lesley Bolton, Project Manager/Editor

Tony Brewer, Artist and Book Designer

Dan Crissman, Editorial Director and Acquisitions Editor

Anna Francis, Assistant Acquisitions Editor

Anna Garnai, Production Coordinator

Samantha Heffner, Marketing and Publicity Manager

Katie Huggins, Production Manager

Dan Pyle, Online Publishing Manager

Jennifer Witzke, Senior Artist and Book Designer